HOOD CANAL
SPLENDOR AT RISK

Editor

Jeff Brody

Writers

Christopher Dunagan
and the Staff of The Sun

The Sun Newspaper, Bremerton, Washington
A John P. Scripps Newspaper
Division of Scripps Howard

Production: Merle Dowd & Associates
Design: Victoria Loe, Washington Sea Grant Program
Cover photograph: Steve Zugschwerdt
Graphics: John McCurdy and Theresa Aubin

Hood Canal: Splendor at Risk

The Sun Newspaper
PO Box 259
Bremerton, Washington 98310

Library of Congress Catalog Card Number: 91-66581

ISBN 0-9630365-0-5

Printed in the U.S.A. on recycled paper

CONTENTS

• • • • • • • • • •

Photo
Credits

Theresa Aubin: pages 37, 91, 94, 98, 107, 138, 175, 179, 193, 195, 197, 199

Amy Deputy: pages 229, 239

Ed Pieratt: pages 234, 235, 236

Larry Steagall: pages 64, 69, 79, 83, 85, 89, 126, 131, 134, 140-41, 142, 143, 145, 150, 202, 206, 209, 212, 216

Steve Zugschwerdt: pages 6, 8, 12, 17, 20, 23, 29, 41, 44, 49, 52, 103, 115, 120, 129, 137, 138, 139, 144, 155, 160, 165, 169, 181, 187, 190, 221, 252

Pope & Talbot Archives: page 59

Hood Canal has changed me. Even though I've worked for The Sun for 14 years, I am not the same writer I was a year ago. Even though I've lived in the Northwest for 21 years, I am not the same person.

It isn't so much the beauty of Hood Canal that has me enchanted. At some point, it's best to get beyond the pure splendor of the place.

Call it an appreciation that the wildness of nature still exists, one small life linked to another, all struggling to survive, humans included.

I shouldn't downplay the importance of natural beauty. As a child, I lived in Wichita, Kansas. I recall the annual vacation trek across dry, flat prairies toward the wonderland of the snow-covered Rocky Mountains in Colorado.

In our family, we all tried to be the first to spot the mountains, which first appeared as a razor-thin line of dark blue at the horizon, barely discernable from the sky.

I learned to camp and fish in a panorama of towering mountains and clear blue lakes. To a boy who spent most of his time in flatland, it always seemed as if someone had hung a grand painting on the sky.

When I came to Kitsap County in 1977, I was awestruck by the water, mountains and wide-open spaces. And I was pleased the county commissioners were trying to preserve the "rural character" of the county.

Fourteen years later, much of the urban area between Bremerton and Silverdale still has enough trees along the roadsides that it's easy to forget that it was designed for humans.

But most of the wildlife has been killed or driven away. Wetlands have been filled. Streams have been silted. The soft forest floor has been transformed into paved streets or grassy lawns in many places.

It was not a mistake, at least not the density part. The goal was to put as many new homes as possible around Bremerton and Silverdale, protecting the more rural areas from growth pressures.

But trees can be a facade, hiding the broken remnants of an ecosystem that no longer exists, just as sparkling waters can hide chemicals and human waste that drain down from the streams.

If we are to protect Hood Canal, we must begin with the upland areas — the watershed that drains down to the canal. We must understand the plant and animal communities that dwell there and try to keep them intact.

Streams and rivers are vital connections. They should get the highest level of protection by keeping logging and development far back from the water. Wetlands, which clean the surface waters and provide homes for an abundance of wildlife, are worthy of protection.

I'm convinced we can find room for human beings to live and work in the Hood Canal region, but I'm less eager to stake out my own chunk of Hood Canal as a homesite than I was a year ago.

I live in Bremerton, and I like what a city provides: fire, medical and police protection just minutes away. It's nice having grocery stores and shopping malls within easy reach.

I also like boating and swimming and hiking and camping. I enjoy picking oysters and digging clams. These things I can do now, though I encourage the government to provide more places to go.

I'm beginning to develop a personal ethic about Hood Canal and other unspoiled places: I like the idea of leaving them unspoiled even more than I like the idea of living there.

Like the boy from Kansas who experienced wonder and fascination without living in the mountains, I have learned a great deal about Hood Canal without building a driveway or cutting down a single tree.

Those who live in the Hood Canal area may well take the lead in protecting natural surroundings.

But the rest of us have a role, too, because Hood Canal is a national treasure.

It will require a huge vision to save Hood Canal as a whole, and it will require individual action to protect the smaller areas people discover: wetlands, nesting areas, migration routes.

I have yet to see strong leadership emerge, but the regional Hood Canal Coordinating Council provides the right forum for discussion.

I know people's hearts are in the right place, but individuals need to transform their desires into action. Get involved in watershed planning or join one of the Water Watchers classes.

I may not choose to move into the Hood Canal watershed, but I intend to keep an eye on its fragile ecosystem for the rest of my life. I hope that what we pass on to our children and their children is something more than just memories about the wildness of nature.

Christopher Dunagan

When we started to research the series of articles that became "Hood Canal: Splendor at Risk," we knew that people living on the canal would be interested. The challenge was to show others how Hood Canal was important to them.

Hood Canal is not well known outside the Puget Sound region. It's not the area the environmental groups write about saving when they mail out a flood of membership solicitations. But it is a waterway of national significance.

When an ecosystem is pristine, relatively easy steps can be taken to preserve it. When an ecosystem is destroyed, the task of bringing it back is often too complex and too costly to be attempted.

But the real challenge is to save an ecosystem that is teetering on the brink — one that's still basically sound but faces a threat.

That's when we learn about how to fit our human lifestyles into a natural system. What we learn is applicable not only in Western Washington, but also for other threatened ecosystems across the country and around the world.

And learning that lesson is the challenge of Hood Canal today.

After guiding this reporting project from initial planning to conclusion, a process that took more than 15 months, I am both better informed about Hood Canal and more concerned than ever about the myriad of seemingly conflicting interests that stand in the way of reaching a community consensus on how to save it.

It's not that the will isn't there — nearly everyone who lives along the canal, and in the watershed, would agree that the canal must be preserved. It's a question of finding a way that can unite rather than divide the canal's constituents.

Some of the most vocal defenders of canal waters are the property owners who are first to bulkhead their shoreline. Some of the most vocal critics of logging are among those willing to clear a view lot in the watershed to build a home.

Hood Canal is challenging us to rise above our special interests and to act in the general interest of the watershed. It was, all along, our hope that in telling this story we'd help our community face this challenge.

Like Andy Rogers, who talks extensively in the conclusion of this book about his memories of the canal, I wish I could see what the canal will be like in 50 years. And I would hope to see something that indicates those of us who are the canal's neighbors rose to the challenge when the canal was teetering on the brink, and helped pull it back into balance.

Jeff Brody
August, 1991

• • • • • • • • • •

PART

I

INTRODUCTION

A PLACE TOO WONDERFUL TO SPOIL

By Christopher Dunagan

Hood Canal

A great blue heron, its broad wings spread to the wind, dips out of an overcast sky and glides into the marsh. Extending its legs, the large bird lands gracefully among tall reeds near the water. The tweet-tweet-tweetering of songbirds creates an agreeable chorus, though each bird sings its own distinct song.

Untold numbers of wild birds share this place on Hood Canal, just outside of Belfair on the North Shore. River otter slink along the shore at sunset. Mink, beaver and muskrat mind their own ways, thanks to

what remains of this ancient swamp.

Human visitors may find themselves refreshed by the wildness here, as in other natural environs. Some people describe a warm feeling of enthrallment, a kind of mild hypnotic state.

It's as if the human heart yearns for a more primitive experience, away from the cluttered pattern of modern life, says Celia Parrot, caretaker of the property.

"The reason I go out two or three times a day is not just to walk the dogs," she said. "It's like a refueling. I go out to get another dose of that intimate feeling."

This moist land has seen the coming of

farmers, their cows raised on "sea oats" able to tolerate the brackish water of the marsh. Now, the cattle are gone and native plants slowly reclaim the land, under the protection of the Hood Canal Land Trust.

The land trust, formed in 1986 by Celia and her husband Gary Parrot, received the land as a precious gift from Elizabeth Klingel, who wanted to see this place protected. Theirs is just one effort to preserve the natural values so obvious in the Hood Canal region.

Other organizations protect Hood Canal by measuring pollution absorbed in the tissues of clams at Port Gamble or in oysters at Union, or by erecting fences to keep cows from tainting the clear streams flowing into Quilcene Bay, or by teaching boaters not to dump human waste overboard while cruising the open waters of the 61-mile-long canal.

The Legislature has recognized Hood Canal as a "shoreline of statewide significance." The list of preservation efforts is nearly as long as a list of places worthy of protection.

Hood Canal — actually a glacier-carved fjord — divides the Kitsap Peninsula, with its rolling hills and easy flowing streams, from the more rugged Olympic Peninsula, with its craggy peaks and rushing rivers.

Hood Canal has been loved by settlers and summer residents for more than 100 years. It has been home to salmon beyond abundance, to multitudes of clams, oysters and shrimp, and to a myriad of wildlife, from field mice to black bears.

As progress would have it, many of Hood Canal's natural areas have already been spoiled. Bulkheads have replaced wetlands; homesteads have replaced forests; and pollution has disrupted the web of life.

The canal has been exploited for its fish and shellfish resources, used and abused by homeowners and boaters, and imposed upon by logging interests.

In a sense, people have loved the canal just a little too much.

Yet, compared to many places touched by man, Hood Canal stands nearly unblemished, like a sparkling gemstone, its destiny yet to be determined.

Will today's press of human population destroy Hood Canal, the way advancing growth has spoiled waterways throughout the United States? Or will we somehow find room for people without disrupting the living forces that make Hood Canal a unique place?

Despite soaring real estate prices, people are swarming to buy the last vacant lands along the 242 miles of Hood Canal shoreline and to purchase upland view lots nearby.

A priceless recreation area, Hood Canal provides an outdoor showcase in which to enjoy the region's famous shrimp, salmon and oysters.

Some 94 percent of the state's prized "spot prawn" — known locally as "Hood Canal shrimp" — are collected from the canal. Once abundant, the average size of these giant prawns has declined, and the state has been forced to strictly regulate the harvest.

Salmon are slowly returning to local streams, but artificial growing efforts barely make up for the damage caused by new housing and commercial developments, biologists say. Sediments wash into streams, smothering eggs and ruining nesting gravel used by the mystical fish.

Commercial, Indian and sport fishermen report declines in nearly all species, while political and legal battles do nothing to increase the stocks.

For recreational oyster gatherers, Hood Canal is a godsend, offering practically the only inland waterway in the state where oysters can be found on public beaches. In an average year, about 56,000 pounds of oysters are hauled off state beaches, according to estimates by the Department of Fisheries.

Meanwhile, commercial oyster growers are especially proud of their sweet-tasting oysters, grown in crystal clear waters. "What makes Quilcene Bay famous is our mild-tasting oyster," said Gordon Hayes, general manager of Coast Oyster Co. of Quilcene.

Hayes credits the taste to the canal's gravelly bottom (as opposed to mud), along with a low concentration of algae, the main staple in the oyster's diet. The food shortage makes the oysters grow slower — and milder, said Hayes.

What makes Hood Canal so clear — the lack of algae and other plankton — results from a slow exchange of water washing in from the ocean. For Hood Canal

Hood Canal — actually a glacier-carved fjord — divides the Kitsap Peninsula, with its rolling hills and easyflowing streams, from the more rugged Olympic Peninsula, with its craggy peaks and rushing rivers.

as a whole, a year may pass before the waters are thoroughly "flushed." That's about twice as long as for Puget Sound.

The slow flushing action is the result of several underwater "sills" that block the circulation of deep waters. For example, while much of the main channel is more than 500 feet deep, the water is only 150 feet deep at one sill south of Hood Canal Bridge.

A number of Hood Canal bays flush themselves even slower than the main channel. High levels of human waste, primarily from septic tanks, have caused health officials to close portions of Lynch Cove to shellfish harvesting. Other closures include the tip of Quilcene Bay and areas near Union, Hoodsport and Seabeck.

At Belfair State Park, rangers once watched people gather their limits of succulent oysters. Two years ago, they were told to post signs, warning people about the dangers of eating polluted shellfish.

Likewise, Hayes said it is disturbing to see polluted oyster beds within two miles of his company's operation in Quilcene Bay.

"The oyster industry and the clam industry are the first affected by pollution," said Hayes. "We are the canary (in the coal mine). We mustn't let what happened in Chesapeake Bay happen here. That would be a travesty."

In the 1950s, on the north side of Baltimore, Md., a young David Peters used to walk through the woods. He hunted salamanders and snakes that would hide along the grassy banks of a stream.

"Today, that woods is gone," said Peters, who at age 39 lives in Poulsbo. "Now it's a housing development, and that stream was channeled — filled with concrete — so it would drain faster. Weed killers that people use on their lawns now flow through it."

The little stream — now a concrete culvert — still drains into Chesapeake Bay, a

Hood Canal Land Trust

Formed in 1986 by Celia and Gary Parrot, it represents one effort to preserve the fragile wetlands of Hood Canal.

body of water vast and beautiful, yet filled with toxic chemicals and other wastes of human endeavors, said Peters, who teaches ecology part-time at Olympic College.

"Where I grew up, we always had a boat of some sort," he said. "We'd go fishing, crabbing, you name it. You could catch your limit quickly."

But intervening years have brought housing developments, factories and pollution. Oysters became susceptible to a dangerous virus.

"Pollution weakened the oysters, and the virus pretty much decimated the population," said Peters. "Acid rain and phosphate runoff from farms have fertilized the bay to the point you have areas on the bottom that are basically anoxic (without oxygen)."

Pockets of anoxic areas grow and move, depending on tides and currents.

"Fishermen pull up crab pots, and they're all dead," he said.

Peters recently purchased five acres of view property near Hood Canal.

"The reason I'm here," he said, "is that (Hood Canal) is one of the prettiest places I've seen, and I'd like to keep it that way."

He says he is pleasantly surprised about the local attitudes.

"People seem to be concerned about the environment, and with the advent of the '90s, I think that attitude will increase," he said.

Hood Canal is not just any body of water, said Peters. The geology, the water quality, the beauty make it a special place.

"You have something that is probably unique in the world."

Squeezed next to the Naval Submarine Base at Bangor is a little waterfront community known as Bangor. An elbow of land, known as King's Spit, juts out into the water from the foot of the hill.

King's Spit, littered with oyster shells, is the southernmost landmark of what once was called "The Three Spits." The other two

"We have to get to know our forests and our marshes, so we know what we cannot do to them."
— Celia Parrot, Hood Canal Land Trust

spits were consumed by the massive naval base constructed during World War II.

"We're losing the point because people have put in bulkheads down the line," says Max Starcevich, who has lived on Hood Canal for years. His wife's family resided there since 1907.

An old wooden boat rots on the shore above the high tide mark, where it washed up in a storm years ago.

Streams meander down to the shore, bringing pollution from livestock waste, according to Starcevich. He worries about weed killers sprayed along the Bangor fence.

"This bay used to have a whole sea of eel grass," he said, shuffling along the shore at sunset and observing no signs of the saltwater plant so important to sealife.

As a sea breeze chilled him, Starcevich pulled his sweater tighter. He thought back to days when fish, birds and wildlife were more abundant.

"We saw migrations of brant and even

Max Starcevich, a leading supporter of environmental protections for Hood Canal, died in August 1990, just two months after he was featured in the opening story of The Sun's series, "Hood Canal: Splendor at Risk."

The following December, Max and his wife Ester, were recognized for their longtime efforts by the Hood Canal Coordinating Council.

"Max was often a public spokesman for environmental and water quality issues, while Ester provided support and organization," said Lois Sherwood as she announced the award for the coordinating council.

Hood Canal Coordinating Council is a cooperative forum for managing policy issues related to Hood Canal. Voting members are representatives from Kitsap, Mason and Jefferson counties plus the Skokomish and S'Klallam tribes.

Starcevich and his wife lived at the old community of Bangor in Kitsap County, not far from the tall fence that encloses the giant Navy submarine base, which adopted the same name.

A longtime member of the Hood Canal Environmental Council, Starcevich was an early opponent of the Bangor base as well as numerous smaller projects he felt would damage the Hood Canal ecosystem. He also was active in Kitsap Audubon.

Max's wife Ester and son Al Starcevich continue the family tradition of environmental activism, remaining major players in groups such as Olympic View Environmental Review Council (OVER-C), which has assumed a citizen-based role in overseeing the cleanup of hazardous waste sites at the Navy base.

Max Starcevich also won another posthumous honor in 1990. The former All-American for the University of Washington's football team was inducted into the National Football Foundation's College Hall of Fame.

By Christopher Dunagan

Max Starcevich

geese," he said. "Now, I can't remember the last time I saw any. The fishing was good until they opened it up to commercial boats. The purse seiners take everything, including lingcod."

While some areas of Hood Canal are on a downward path, others mount a recovery. The future is by no means certain. But nearly everywhere there's a growing fear that this fragile body of water is paying a price as man taxes the biological limits of the ecosystem.

"We have to get to know our forests and our marshes, so we know what we cannot do to them," says Celia Parrot, walking slowly through the moist grass at the Klingel wetlands.

A flock of ducks takes wing, soaring low over the water, as if the birds were tied together with string. A red-wing blackbird lands in the twisted branches of an aging snag. Parrot smiles, relishing its distinctive song.

Bill Hunt, now serving as president of the Hood Canal Land Trust, has lived in the area 30 years.

"That's a lovely thing," Hunt says of the bird's song.

As he talks, a pair of mallard ducks waddle through the grass at shore's edge. The proud, colorful male stands guard facing the human visitors, his body erect. The female scuttles over to a grassy mound and settles on her nest.

"He doesn't want us to get any closer," Hunt said. "He'll probably fuss at us if we get any closer. We're not encouraging a lot of visiting here, such as building walking trails and what have you."

Not far away lies another marshy area, managed under a different philosophy. Under ownership of the Mary E. Theler Community Center in Belfair, these marshy lands were to be filled by a bulldozer with new ballfields taking their place.

But experts pointed out the importance of these fragile lands, and now the grassy swamp is the centerpiece of a future nature center, complete with carefully constructed trails and boardwalks into the marsh.

Because so much of Hood Canal is rocky, especially in the main channel, saltwater marshes are precious islands of habitat between long stretches of pebbly shore.

"Many people think that if you disturb these areas the wildlife will just go someplace else," said Linda Kunze, a botanist with the state's Natural Heritage Program. "It's just not true. In most cases, if something happens, the wildlife just die."

Kunze splits her time between the human world at her Olympia office, where politics and economics rule, and the natural world in which she immerses herself into her work.

"When I'm out in the field, I feel like a visitor," she said. "I need to put my values and understanding aside so I can learn from the environment. Being out in the field is a time of learning and a time of refreshment. It helps me to realize that the human-centered world is not all there is."

"As we build more and more cities, we need to keep a natural connection, to see the changing of the seasons and weather patterns," Celia Parrot said. "You can live in an apartment and no matter what happens outside, you can be comfortable. That's why I see a danger as more and more of us live in cities."

Places throughout the country — Chesapeake Bay, the Great Lakes, Hudson River, the Everglades and even Puget Sound — have suffered greatly before human caretakers decided to change their ways. Hood Canal challenges us to find a better way while there's still time.

Bangor

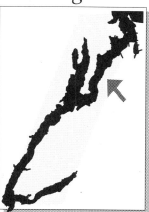

Nestled between the shores of Hood Canal and the boundary of the Naval Submarine Base, Bangor is a small community of older homes.

• • • • • • • • •
In a sense, people have loved the canal just a little too much. Yet, compared to many places touched by man, Hood Canal stands nearly unblemished, like a sparkling gemstone, its destiny yet to be determined.

CHAPTER 2

TAKING A LOOK AROUND

· · · · · · · · · ·

Alderbrook Inn is the canal's most developed resort.

SECTION 1

GIVE YOURSELF A TOUR

By Deborah Woolston

Steady there, big fella. Park your compass and Lewis-and-Clark fantasy because we're not going off the map on our circle-tour of Hood Canal. We'll settle for the basic West Puget Sound survival package on this one-day circuit: Park and road maps so we don't get lost, sweaters in case of cold, walking shoes for exploring beach and trail, and rain gear just in case.

Great picnic places probably outnumber the restaurants, which are confined to the few commercial crossroads. There's even a winery equipped with a tasting room in Hoodsport. So let's wing food and drink.

The only good thing about this Silverdale traffic snarl is that you appreciate the instant countryside on the west side. Are you ready for your first scenic hit around the next bend of Anderson Hill Road? The world doesn't often serve up a mountain-water combo like this, the jagged Olympic Mountains towering above the deep, shining canal.

This four-star scenery lasts until

Seabeck, which gives a good sneak preview of territory we'll cover today. Timber used to be the main game in this little waterfront village now populated by tourists and a growing number of permanent locals.

First, a stop at Scenic Beach State Park, where we can stretch our legs along the beach and the wide-open lawns. This is a prime spot for watching sunsets all year and rhododendrons in season.

From here we need a map to navigate the road maze between Seabeck and Tahuya, our next waterfront stop. At the bottom of Elfendahl Pass Road, we'll hit the canal again.

Bingo. Surprised at all wall-to-wall houses along North Shore Road? They peter out to the west, but the road does too in a northern jungle of massive trees carpeted with moss and ferns. It's beautiful and privately owned.

So we'll turn east and drive along the canal's most populated section — both sides of the arm that juts into Mason County from Union to Belfair. The water sparkles behind the almost unbroken row of waterfront houses, but it's off-limits to the public except for two popular state parks. Unlike most of Washington's saltwater, this still, shallow stretch is warm enough to swim without getting frostbite.

On summer weekends, Belfair State Park and Twanoh State Park on the north and south sides respectively are packed with families.

"This is my favorite campground in the whole wide world because you can do so much with the kids," explains Carol Ward about Twanoh. "And I've gotten to the stage where I want a little luxury with my camping," confesses the Pierce County woman who likes the campground showers as much as the waterfront.

The park is so busy in the summer, says resident ranger Larry Otto, that the campground fills up by Wednesday for the weekend. Most campers are families, and they come from everywhere.

Maybe we should have packed lunch. For all the people living and traveling down this busy stretch of Highway 106, there are few feeding stations. But nobody could miss Alderbrook Inn.

Hang on. We're in for culture shock at the resort. Big-screen TV beside the big-window view in the lounge, covered walk-ways everywhere, and a glassed-in heated pool. Those two yuppies wearing pressed blue jeans and sipping beer sure aren't loggers.

This is the civilized side of canal life down to the espresso coffee, quiche, fancy candles sold at restaurant/gift shop next door. This commercial patch stretches for 10 miles through Union, Hoodsport, and Potlatch, which are the canal's southern supply stops. Here's where to pause for gas, beer, food, bait, souvenirs, and information.

A popular stop is Hunter Farm, which has been on the delta of Skokomish River since 1843. The merchandise mix — fresh produce, hay, top soil, calf and pig feed, geranium flats, seeds, potpourri packets, cards and cookbooks — give a good idea who the customers are.

"It's pretty desolate in the winter," said Steve Hunter, the fifth generation of Hood Canal Hunters. But all summer and most fall and spring weekends, business is humming.

And traffic will pick up just down the road when we hook up with U.S. 101. It funnels the north-south I-5 traffic and the east-west U.S. 12 traffic into the skinny corridor between the mountains and the water.

Hoodsport's short main street is almost the last chance to spend money for miles — on ice cream, T-shirts, antiques, scuba equipment, or Hoodsport Winery wines.

From here the wilderness stretches north and west for miles across forests and mountains.

But it's silly to plunge into the woods without a good guide. The Hoodsport Ranger Station is a supermarket of free information.

Joanne Conrad, crisp in her uniform, is fielding the questions from the steady stream of visitors. What about wildlife? Bald eagles, kingfishers, and blue herons in the bird family and deer, marmots, mountain goats, elk and backcountry black bear in the mammal division.

Are you ready to tackle the wild side of the canal? The Lena Lake Trail up a paved road north of Eldon off the Hamma Hamma River sounds perfect for a mini-hike — easy, pretty, and accessible. As Conrad said, it's no a secret. There must be 20 cars parked at the trailhead.

"It was lovely but pouring down rain," says Muriel Bewick of Bainbridge Island as

The nine-mile stretch from Holly to Dewatto is the least populated part of the fjord.

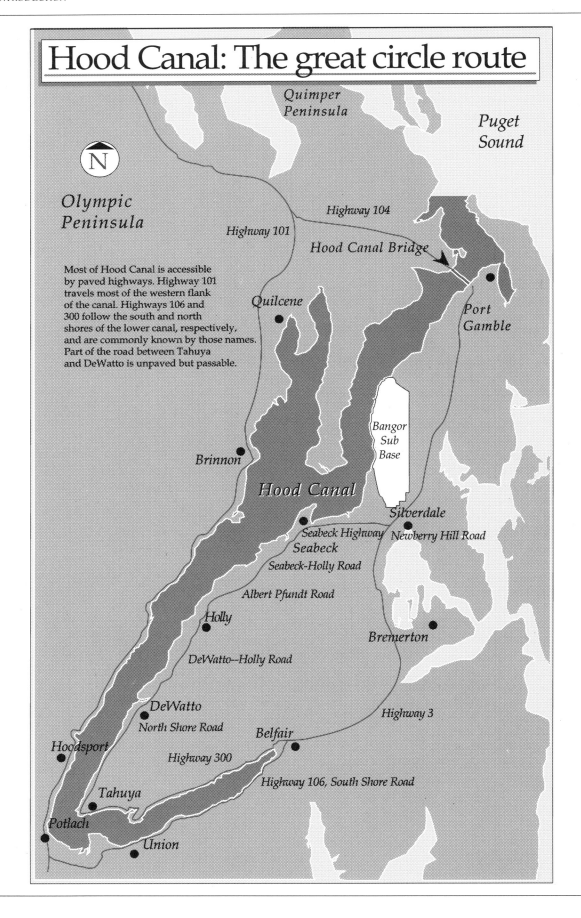

Hood Canal: The great circle route

Quimper
Peninsula

Puget
Sound

N

Olympic
Peninsula

Highway 104

Highway 101

Hood Canal Bridge

Most of Hood Canal is accessible
by paved highways. Highway 101
travels most of the western flank
of the canal. Highways 106 and
300 follow the south and north
shores of the lower canal, respectively,
and are commonly known by those names.
Part of the road between Tahuya
and DeWatto is unpaved but passable.

Quilcene

Port
Gamble

Bangor
Sub
Base

Brinnon

Hood Canal

Silverdale

Seabeck Highway   Newberry Hill Road
Seabeck
Seabeck-Holly Road

Albert Pfundt Road

Holly

Bremerton

DeWatto–Holly Road

DeWatto
North Shore Road

Highway 3

Belfair

Hoodsport

Highway 300

Highway 106, South Shore Road

Tahuya

Potlach

Union

she unlaces her muddy boots. "By the time we came back, the sun was coming out."

Along the trail is a fragrant mix of fern and cedar and rain. And all those shades of green — velvety chartreuse moss on the rocks, deep green cedar branches, and pale little maple leaves glowing in the gloom.

Back on the road, running north along the canal, the scenery is gorgeous. There's another oyster farm — the baby oysters attach themselves to those big bundles of shells hanging in the water. There's Dosewallips State Park just in time for a pit stop, and a stretch. If you look over the marsh grass and tangle of wild roses, you'll see Seabeck and Scenic Beach, only five miles away as the crow flies.

Up ahead in Brinnon is the Whitney Rhododendron Farms, which attracts hundreds of visitors during the spring blooming season. Also Seal Rock, where packs of harbor seals are supposed to hang out, Mount Walker, a drive-up lookout with a 360-degree view from Seattle to the Strait of Juan de Fuca to the Olympic glaciers.

For more information on north end attractions, the Quilcene Ranger Station is the best bet.

Clearcuts are ugly, but they've opened up a stupendous view on the Toandos Peninsula, which juts 15 miles south into the canal. Down below are water-access-only public areas for a completely different view of the canal.

Driving north to Highway 104, a right turn leads to the Hood Canal Bridge — hope a sub isn't going through on the way to or from Naval Submarine Base Bangor.

There's time to pop north to Port Gamble, the historic lumber village modeled after a Maine town, where there's a popular general store, seashell museum, and logging museum.

Now let's wrap up the exploration by watching the sunset from Kitsap Memorial Park. The popular waterfront park has front row seats on the canal all year.

And you can put the map down. We're almost home.

Off the Beaten Path

You don't need a boat to find the quiet parts of Hood Canal, but it certainly helps. While most of the traffic and most of the people can be found along the south and west shores of the canal, you'll find most of the solitude and least of the traffic along the north and east shores. Boaters will find beaches available only to them on these quiet shores.

If you've only got an auto, you still might find places to get away from most of the canal crowds.

Take a drive out to Holly, for example. Follow the Seabeck Highway past Crosby to Hintzville, and follow the Albert Pfundt Road to Holly.

It's private property out here, where the Olympic Mountains across the canal seem to lean out over the fjord to see their reflections. The people are friendly, to be sure, mostly because the visitors who stop along the road respect private property.

There are state Department of Natural Resources public tidelands just north of Holly and south of Tekiu Point. They are accessible only by boat, although both the Tekiu Road and a road west from Nellita Road drop all the way to the canal.

The Tekiu Road ends just north of Tekiu Point; the road west from Nellita Road drops down to Frenchman's Cove.

One of the most delightful drives on the canal is following the Dewatto Bay Road from Anderson Cove, just north of Holly, to Tahuya. This is the wildest, quietest part of the canal.

In the summer, cars traverse the road on bluffs 200 feet above the fjord once every 15 minutes or so during the day. In the winter, one car every hour is more likely.

Stop on any one of the high bluffs overlooking the canal from Dewatto south to Tahuya, and all you will be able to hear are the waves lapping the shore, and the whisper of traffic on Highway 101 across the canal.

From Holly to Dewatto, the road crosses the lonely country above the canal, cutting through private forest land where only a few gated logging roads lead west to the canal. This nine-mile stretch is the least populated part of the fjord.

The few waterfront houses barged to this section of the canal are without electricity.

Dewatto Bay is a quiet estuary and wetland. Cabins huddle along the southern shore, along with commercial oyster shacks.

There's a public beach at the southerly end of the drive to Tahuya, just south of Rendsland Creek at Musqueti Point. Here the visitor can look south across the water to the busy side of the canal, or west, to the Olympics. For the remainder of the quiet spots along the canal, try a boat. There are three Department of Natural Resources beaches between Dewatto and Chinom Point and — on the Toandos Peninsula — DNR and state park beaches at Fisherman Harbor, Tabook Point and Brown Point.

By Seabury Blair Jr.

Union Marina on the South Shore of Hood Canal.

● ● ● ● ● ● ● ● ● ●

SECTION 2

A
MYSTERIOUS
WATERWAY

*By Christopher
Dunagan*

A scuba diver visiting southern Hood Canal in the fall may enter the water only to find that he can barely see his hand in front of his face.

The view can change rather dramatically, however, as the diver goes deeper. Suddenly, without warning, he finds himself within a layer of crystal clear water. What had been 2 feet of visibility in one moment can become, all at once, a sight range of 50 feet.

It can be heart-stopping, according to those who have experienced it.

The phenomenon is caused by a layer of silty water from the Skokomish River overlaying a layer of denser sea water, said Barry Moore, a diving instructor at Washington State University who uses lower Hood Canal for field trips.

In addition to the layers of fresh and salt water, other layers may contain a mixture of each.

"It's almost like an atmospheric weather system," he said, "and it's something a lot of people don't expect, almost like going through cloud layers."

Layered waters — accompanied by abrupt changes in temperature — are among the odd and curious things about Hood Canal, both above and below the surface.

Other mysteries include missing hordes of gold, long lost shipwrecks and even sea creatures worth searching for.

About 3 miles north of Hoodsport lie the famous "octopus holes," which are located within an underwater cliff that drops into the depths of Hood Canal, according to Shirley Smith, who runs Mike's Dive Shop with her husband, Mike Smith.

A portion of the vertical wall contains a ledge some 3-4 feet wide. In that area, one may find octopus, ranging from small ones you can hold in one hand to some that are 60-70 pounds. Tentacles can stretch 6 feet or more, said Mrs. Smith.

"Octopus are very shy, very intelligent," she said. "Divers have pretty well protected them in that area. It is an unwritten rule that you don't touch."

In that same rocky area, one may also come upon dangerous-looking wolf eels with nasty, sharp teeth. The eels may dart out of their holes if threatened, though they rarely bite, she said.

Hood Canal offers a variety of underwater experiences, but surface dwellers may be happy to settle for watching the playful harbor seals that inhabit most of Hood Canal. One can spot their gray or black heads bobbing on the water's surface just about anywhere in the canal.

If you're extremely lucky, you may spot a pod of killer whales. The large black-and-white mammals venture into Hood Canal on occasion, usually in the late fall, according to local residents.

One of the great Hood Canal mysteries is a low humming noise, so faint that only Navy officials know when it comes and goes.

The Navy uses highly sophisticated listening equipment along the bottom of Dabob Bay to track torpedoes along its torpedo testing range. The acoustic equipment has picked up an intermittent droning noise, which was traced to Quilcene Boat Haven.

Marjorie Belt, whose husband is harbormaster there, got to listen through a set of headphones several years ago.

"It sounded like a World War II movie with a bunch of bombers going overhead," she noted. "I was told it would get louder at night, then die out toward morning."

There has been much speculation about the cause, and the Navy even had the high-voltage power lines de-energized one time, but the noise was still there.

John Curtis, spokesman for the Naval Undersea Warfare Engineering Station at Keyport, said the noise hasn't been noticed lately, and some Navy officials suspect it may be associated with a breed of frogs. Anyway, it is so faint it causes no problem, he said.

On the opposite side of Hood Canal, near Seabeck, lies the sunken wreck of the Panama, a ship that had sailed around Cape Horn, serving first in the passenger trade and later running cargo in the Puget Sound area, according to local historian Fredi Perry.

The Panama was the sister ship to the Oregon, the first steamship to scurry from New York to the West Coast at the start of the California Gold Rush.

Anyway, the Panama had been purchased by owners of the Seabeck mill to carry finished lumber to California, but the ship collided with a German ship in the Strait of Juan de Fuca. Its cargo was off-loaded in Port Townsend, and the damaged ship was towed back to Seabeck, where it sank.

"At the turn of the century, the masts could still be seen at low tide," said Mrs. Perry, who owns a copper nail from the wreck. The nail was picked up by a diver exploring the rotting remains, now sunken into the mud.

Another Seabeck mystery also dates back to the time of the mill. The story is that of Ah Fong, a Chinese cook who worked for the mill company. He must have saved up plenty of money, for if a ship didn't arrive from San Francisco to pay the mill workers, Ah Fong was ready with a loan.

Observers would see Ah Fong disappear into the woods and come back with the needed number of $20 gold pieces. During one of these trips, however, he failed to return.

Was he killed by a wild animal? Did he fall into a hole? Or was he killed by someone who wanted his money? Nobody knows, but more than a few people have hiked the woods around Seabeck searching for the treasure.

• • • • • • • • • •

About 3 miles north of Hoodsport lie the famous "octopus holes," in an underwater cliff that drops into the depths of Hood Canal.

By Seabury Blair Jr.

Visitors to Olympic National Park find a vantage point over the cascading Dosewallips River.

Mount Anderson cups the infant Hood Canal between her West and main peaks like a lumpy nursemaid, 7,300 feet above sea level.

Up here, Olympic ravens coast above ragged ridges of rock. The black bird-gods of the Indians wheel east and, without a single wingbeat, glide 22 miles to the mother fjord.

Up here, you can walk on the surface of Hood Canal. Up here, the canal is not deep green water, but the 100-foot-thick blue ice of the Eel Glacier, fed by 140 inches of precipitation every year.

Even in June, it is winter on the Eel Glacier.

The glacier crawls two miles north, where Silt Creek tumbles from it and rips a rugged mile-long gash in the mountain.

The Dosewallips River gouges gorges sharp and steep. It slams the round river rocks together so hard that at night, in your tent far above the river, you hear them clucking together.

Then 6,300-foot Olympic Mountain peaks turn the racing water to the northeast.

Here are high mountain meadows where Olympic marmots whistle and shriek, and cannot move across the snowfields without waving their tails like starting flags. These marmots are unique to the Olympics.

Silt Creek rages through the springtime meadows. It chatters down an untrailed canyon into the virgin forest of Olympic National Park, past trees born before Columbus. It plows four miles and packs the power of an express train.

Here the hiss and rush of Silt Creek is shouted silent by the rumble and roar of the Dosewallips River. Now the milky glacial soup of Silk Creek sullies the crystal snowmelt of the Dosewallips at their junction, six miles and 3,800 feet below the glacier.

Now away from the awesome canyon, deep in the forest, you'll hear the single note of a thrush, as clear as the dawn it greets. Columbia blacktail deer rustle through the salal of the dry east-facing slopes above the river.

They make a different sound than the occasional black bear that wanders these woods. Bears slap salal with their forepaws as they walk. It sounds as if someone were shuffling cards. Deer daintily lift their feet and stamp a snare-drum cadence.

Now the Dosewallips gouges gorges to the east, sharp and steep. It slams the round river rocks together so hard that at night, in your tent far above the river, you hear them clucking together.

They call the noise "river voices."

Here is a mineral spring, just above the spot where the river crashes into the West Fork of the Dosewallips, where the smell of sulphur wrinkles your nose. Elk — Roosevelt Elk so plentiful in these mountains they are more commonly referred to as "Olympic Elk" — come here to lick the rock. Their trails scribe the forest floor like intricate scrollwork.

Olympic Elk and deer graze around the mineral lick so heavily that, even in the

Eel Glacier

Glacial melt from the east flank of the Olympics is the source of the Dosewallips River, 26 miles from Hood Canal.

summer, the absence of greenery is noticeable. It was not always so; this spot was once a likely hunting ground for the Olympic wolf and cougar, which held the elk population in check.

But the watershed of the Hood Canal has not heard the howl of a wild wolf since 1934.

The Dose, as locals call it, never slows. It races to the canal, plunging an average of 218 feet every one of its 26 miles. That drop is enough that water of the Dosewallips becomes a jackhammer that rips at the pillow lava of Mount Constance as it cascades towards the sunrise.

Mountain goats play 4,000 feet above the river on the same lava, frozen by an ancient sea. They stray from the national park to the national forest, and the migration may well save them from park efforts to control their population.

The Dosewallips — a Twana name for the legendary man who was transformed into Mount Anderson — is not the wildest river to feed the canal. That record belongs to the Hamma Hamma River, which drops an average of 339 feet in each of its 18 miles.

Unlike other rivers in the 550-square-mile Hood Canal watershed, however, the Dosewallips carries fine glacial flour from the Eel. It adds unique water to a unique body of water.

Other snowfields dump millions of gallons of water into the canal every day. Massive permanent snowfields and dead glaciers feed the headwaters of the Skokomish, Duckabush, Hamma Hamma and Big Quilcene Rivers. But the Dose is the only Hood Canal river born of a living, grinding glacier.

More than 200 watercourses feed the canal. About 48 are named. They range from the longest river — the Skokomish at about 34 miles — to the tiny, quarter-mile creeks of the Bolton Peninsula or the bluffs south of Holly.

The fresh water pours itself into a nine-foot-deep blanket over the fjord. Because tidal mixing is slow in Hood Canal, this layer remains relatively free of salt.

It floats on a body of dense saltwater like a giant foam hot tub cover, and it accounts in part for the reason you and your children can swim in the canal during the summer. The layer of less salty water warms more quickly, so could be as warm as 69 degrees Fahrenheit at Twanoh State Park.

Two-hundred feet below, however, the dense salty water could be close to freezing. Salt water of the deeps can actually drop below freezing temperature without turning to ice, due to salt content and pressure.

Since it rides on top of the saltier water, this blanket flushes from the canal faster than the water underneath. The layer could provide critical clues into understanding the ecology of Hood Canal.

The rivers and creeks are lazier on the Kitsap side of Hood Canal and along the North and South shores. Even major tributaries such as the Union River, Twanoh Creek, Dewatto River, Mission Creek, Tahuya River and Big Beef Creek gurgle and coo.

They don't haul big loads of earth to dump into Hood Canal, like their tortured brothers to the west.

Wildlife on this side is as quiet as the waters. Wrens softly sing songs six times their size as summer dawns near. Deer and bear wander the woods, although they are not seen so often as their Olympic Peninsula counterparts.

Smaller animals fill the woods on both sides of Hood Canal. Here you will find spotted and striped skunk, coyote, fox, bobcat, beaver, muskrat.

One of the shyest creatures throughout the mother fjord's watershed is the sewellel,

or mountain beaver. This nocturnal rodent, as large as a house cat, can live for years in dens dug along road embankments or under tree roots without being seen.

One of the boldest of the watershed's wildlife is the raccoon, which residents sometimes foolishly mistake as being domesticated. These wild animals raid garbage cans and chicken coops regularly. Besides being nuisances, they pose real danger to pets and small children.

In its last eight miles, the Dosewallips slithers through country populated — albeit sparsely — by man. As they do along most of the watercourses that drain into the canal, loggers clearcut hillsides above the rumbling river. Cattle graze unchecked along the Dose's banks.

As the river reaches sea level at Brinnon, it flows deep and fast through summer home tracts, a state park and finally, into the canal.

Besides the glacier's flour, the Dosewallips is filled with much the same micro- and macroscopic flotsam and jetsam all watercourses bring to the canal.

There is the silt scraped from the sides of mountains and washed into the river from clearcuts. There are phosphates, nutrients and bacteria from cattle and fertilizer, organic matter and minerals ripped from the earth by the water's passage.

Yet standing on the bridge where Highway 101 crosses the Dosewallips at Brinnon, the visitor can look down to watch trout and sea-run cutthroat play during the summer. They often comment upon how clean the water looks.

Brinnon

By the time it reaches Brinnon on Hood Canal, the Dosewallips has slowed to a meandering stream.

• • • • • • • • • •

The watershed of Hood Canal has not heard the howl of a wild wolf since 1934.

The Great Bend of Hood Canal, seen from the peak of Mount Ellinor in the Olympics.

CARVED FROM THE ROCK

By Travis Baker

The geologic forces that make Hood Canal what it is today — one of only two fjordlike bodies of water in the continental U.S., its water flow limited by a shallow sill near its mouth —are only partially understood.

Much of what we know is only theory, and some of that theory is in dispute. But it appears Hood Canal is the work of rivers and a series of glaciers that exploited a weakness along the edge of the Olympic Mountains, a weakness probably created by a geologic faultline.

For millions of years, the subterranean ocean plates have moved under North America in the never-ending reshaping of the earth.

Two or three yards at a time every 1,000 years or so, volcanic rock created on the Pacific ocean floor migrated to what has become the west coast of America. Some was thrust upward, building the Olympics. But most moved under the continental plate until it reach depths where temperatures melted it.

That molten rock sought escape in a series of volcanoes that created the Cascades.

In between were the Puget Lowlands, and what would become Hood Canal, which stretches 63 miles from its mouth to the tip of Lynch Cove at Belfair.

One might be mystified by the geologic force that could turn a glacier more than 90 degrees, as at the elbow of the canal where the Skokomish River enters. In fact, there is no such force.

Tom Walker, geology instructor at Olympic College, says what seems to be an abrupt turn in the canal was the result of east-west stream erosion meeting the north-south scouring done by at least four vast glaciers that entered the Puget Lowlands in the most recent Ice Age.

Though the basic contour of the lowlands was established by the growth of the Olympics to the west and the creation of the Cascades to the east, the often mysterious interplay between glaciers, the immense lakes that sometimes formed ahead of them and the rivers that drained those lakes account for much of the smaller-scale topography in the region.

Walker says the common conception of

Hood Canal topography

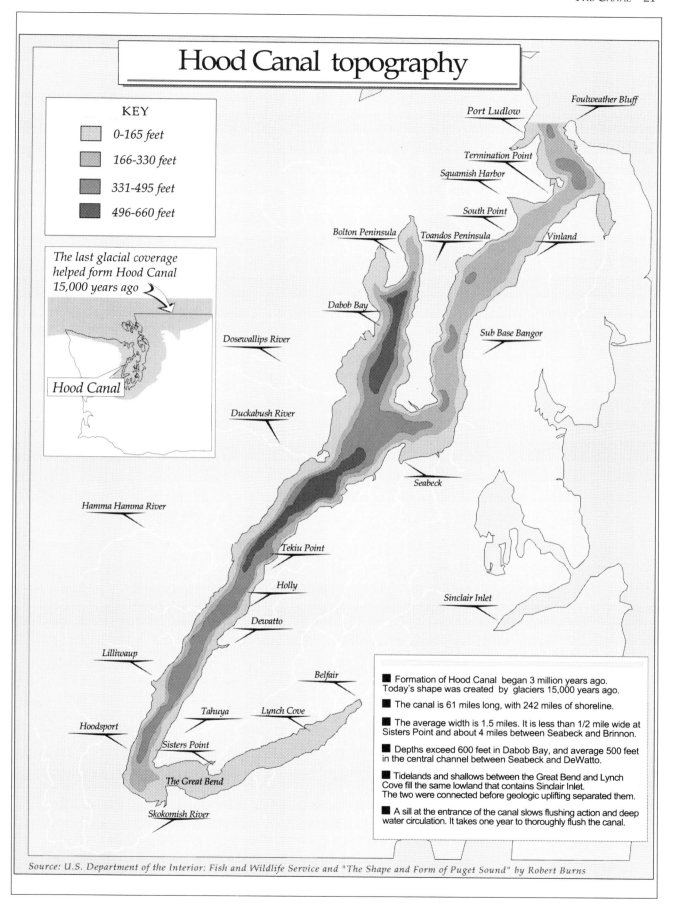

KEY

- 0-165 feet
- 166-330 feet
- 331-495 feet
- 496-660 feet

The last glacial coverage helped form Hood Canal 15,000 years ago

Hood Canal

Foulweather Bluff

Port Ludlow

Termination Point

Squamish Harbor

South Point

Bolton Peninsula

Toandos Peninsula

Vinland

Dabob Bay

Sub Base Bangor

Dosewallips River

Duckabush River

Seabeck

Hamma Hamma River

Tekiu Point

Holly

Dewatto

Sinclair Inlet

Lilliwaup

Belfair

Tahuya

Lynch Cove

Hoodsport

Sisters Point

The Great Bend

Skokomish River

■ Formation of Hood Canal began 3 million years ago. Today's shape was created by glaciers 15,000 years ago.

■ The canal is 61 miles long, with 242 miles of shoreline.

■ The average width is 1.5 miles. It is less than 1/2 mile wide at Sisters Point and about 4 miles between Seabeck and Brinnon.

■ Depths exceed 600 feet in Dabob Bay, and average 500 feet in the central channel between Seabeck and DeWatto.

■ Tidelands and shallows between the Great Bend and Lynch Cove fill the same lowland that contains Sinclair Inlet. The two were connected before geologic uplifting separated them.

■ A sill at the entrance of the canal slows flushing action and deep water circulation. It takes one year to thoroughly flush the canal.

Source: U.S. Department of the Interior: Fish and Wildlife Service and "The Shape and Form of Puget Sound" by Robert Burns

a frozen landscape as glaciers advanced into this area is erroneous.

For much of the advance, the ice sheet was "melting furiously" but advancing nonetheless, propelled by the huge accumulations of ice farther north. The melt water at one point created what's called, in retrospect, Lake Russell, which filled the lowlands in front of the glacier to a depth 120 feet above today's Puget Sound, until the lake spilled out to the southwest along the course of today's Chehalis River.

> • • • • • • • • • • •
>
> *At least four times the ice sheet came and went from the Puget Lowlands. Boulders trapped beneath its tremendous weight exploited weaknesses in the land surface to gouge out valleys.*

At least four times the ice sheet came and went from the Puget Lowlands. Boulders trapped beneath its tremendous weight exploited weaknesses in the land surface to gouge out valleys. Many, including Hood Canal, filled with sea water when the ice receded and sea level rose from the melt.

Stands of trees fell before the advancing ice and can be found buried in the landscape to this day, said geologist Bob Carson of Whitman College in Walla Walla. They usually don't have their bark, but they're still wood. "You can put them in your fireplace," he said.

Between glaciers, tens of thousands of years of stream erosion created other valleys, one of which linked what is now the bottom arm of Hood Canal to Sinclair Inlet via the approximate route of the railroad tracks leading from Belfair to Bremerton.

Why a portion of that channel is now Kitsap and Mason county uplands while another part of it is now the floor of the canal remains a geologic mystery.

So are the sills left by the last glacier that are now covered by the waters of Hood Canal.

The sill, at the opening of the canal, acts almost like the lip of a sink, impeding the natural flushing action of the canal and placing its water quality in a fragile balance.

"We're lucky we don't have as much industry along Hood Canal as along Puget Sound," said Carson. "We hope for not too many fish pens, that the Navy will be a good neighbor and we get good sewage treatment from the towns."

The sill is not bedrock, too hard to have been wiped away by the most recent glacier. Rather it's made of "unconsolidated sediments" that accumulated over the past few million years.

Why those sediments collected just a few miles northeast of Dabob Bay, where the Canal floor plunges to depths of 600 feet or more, is among the unanswered questions.

But Hood Canal isn't a freak in that regard. Many fjords have a sill, said Carson, who has studied the canal for years from a summer residence between Holly and Dewatto. Between glaciers, nature works to fill valleys.

The Skokomish River has made a good start, depositing sediments at the bend. Given another 10,000 years with no interference from man, Carson said, the river would seal off the tip of the canal, which would gradually be desalinated by fresh water runoff and rain.

Green and Gold mountains in Kitsap County are the only formations of upthrust bedrock between the Olympics and Cascades. They were shaped but not eradicated by the ice mass that covered this area to a depth of more than 3,000 feet, almost twice the height of the two promontories. The rest of Kitsap County was created by the leavings of the retreating glaciers.

There was animal life in the path of the ice, though apparently not human life. Birds and land animals, including mammoths and mastodons, simply moved south, but saltwater fish, trapped in the desalinated and increasingly icy glacial lakes flooding their homes, ceased to exist over the thousands of years.

Ann Sleight, anthropology instructor at OC, said no one is sure whether the paleo-Indians that populated the Hood Canal area came through the ice-free corridor or down the coast, but it's generally agreed they arrived via the "land bridge" that linked North America to Asia when ice sheets consumed much of the earth's water and dropped the sea level.

The first arrivals, 10,000 years ago, more or less, were hunters and gatherers with no special affinity to Hood Canal, she said. The marine Indian culture developed along local shorelines between 5,000 and 3,000 years ago.

It was their descendants noted by Capt. George Vancouver and his crew when, in 1792, he explored Puget Sound on a mission to learn whether the Strait of Juan de Fuca might reach all the way to Hudson Bay. He gave many of the features names by which they are known today, including Puget Sound, named after one of his lieutenants, Peter Puget, and Hood Canal, for the British Lord Hood.

CHAPTER

4

• • • • • • • •

WATER
RESOURCES

SECTION 1

A PRECIOUS
COMMODITY

*By Christopher
Dunagan*

*Large pipes carry
rushing water from the
impounded Skokomish
River to the powerhouse
below Cushman Dam.*

T he North Fork of the Skokomish
River begins its journey from a
massive snowfield on the slopes
of Mount Skokomish in Olympic
National Park. As surrounding
forests surrender their store of
rain water — creek by creek, stream by
stream — the North Fork becomes a surging
river, a force to be reckoned with.

At Staircase Rapids, reached by hikers
along a picturesque trail above Lake
Cushman, the river rushes swiftly down a
hillside of boulders.

In late May, the roaring waters are so
fresh and clear that it is difficult to perceive
the swiftness of their flow. A ripple sparkles
in the noonday sun, but is quickly gone,
rushing downstream in the blink of an eye,
following the water's course toward Hood
Canal.

Experts measuring the flow in the
North Fork say 7,000 gallons pass this point

in a single second. That's enough water to flush every toilet in Bremerton, then do so again and again every 30 seconds.

Water is so plentiful in this green land surrounding Hood Canal that it seems impossible to ever run out. The wild and free-flowing rivers provide what seems like an endless bounty of water as they flow out of the snow-capped Olympic Mountains.

Duckabush, Hamma Hamma and Skokomish. Their Indian names suggest an ancient history of never-ending flows. Dosewallips and Quilcene, Dewatto and Tahuya.

You might think there would be plenty of water for all uses — for drinking and for flushing toilets, for generating electricity and for diluting industrial pollution. And there ought to be water left over for fish, birds and all sorts of wildlife we treasure.

But as Will Rogers might say of water, as he once said of land: "They ain't makin' any more of it."

In Bremerton and Port Townsend, when somebody turns on a water faucet, he expects to get clean drinking water. A Gig Harbor resident expects that his lights will go on when he flips a switch.

These people who live miles from Hood Canal can be thankful for its mighty rivers.

Bremerton water customers can thank the Union River.

Port Townsend residents and employees at the town's paper mill can thank the Quilcene.

Gig Harbor residents can thank the North Fork of the Skokomish (as well as a power swap among electric utilities).

The roaring rivers are never heard in the city, which makes it easy for people to ignore subtle ways that humans can tilt the balance of nature.

Even families on private wells cannot escape the water equation. They, too, are dependent on rainfall to replenish the groundwater supply. Hydrologists sometimes worry that this hidden store of water is more vulnerable to depletion because people cannot observe it.

Water is the common denominator among all living things, but it is easily taken for granted — especially in the wetter years when people joke about growing webbed feet.

Despite heavy precipitation, despite ever-flowing streams, the amount of water is indeed limited. And people who understand this indisputable fact have already begun to engage in a tug-of-war over its future use.

Downstream from Staircase Rapids, a shaft of sunlight breaks through a heavy growth of fir and cedars. The sunbeam illuminates a deep pool of cold water, which glows like a giant green emerald.

Nearby, in the shallows, water glides smoothly over shaded gravel, an ideal nesting spot for salmon and trout.

Somewhere in these waters, a unique population of juvenile salmon has begun an instinctive journey downstream. These young chinook salmon are the descendants of an ancient race of salmon that grew to ponderous size in the ocean.

But these juvenile fish will never see the ocean. They remain trapped forever, like their parents, by Cushman Dam, a massive concrete structure that has blocked the normal flow of the North Forth since 1926.

"I've always been intrigued by those fish," said Frank Haw, a former Department of Fisheries expert and now a private consultant.

Haw first became aware of the land-locked salmon more than a quarter-century ago when he saw the silhouette of a big salmon painted on a board, which was hanging in a bar near Cushman. Someone told him the imprint was from a king salmon taken out of the lake.

"In 1967, I caught one, a 12-pounder," said Haw. "That was the first one I'd actually seen in there."

Haw was fascinated by the realization that these salmon are being born in the stream above Lake Cushman, but they live most of their lives in the lake, never able to get past the man-made structure.

Since then, fall chinook have been planted in Roosevelt Lake behind Grand Coulee Dam as well as in Lake Chelan, both in Eastern Washington.

"But the interesting thing about Cushman," said Haw, "is that it appears to have gotten going without anybody's help."

The numbers of Cushman chinook are never very high, and these fish grow more slowly than they would in the ocean. Lakes are not the most suitable habitat for salmon. But the mere survival of these fish, says Haw, is a tribute to their adaptability.

While the unique land-locked chinook are at least a curiosity, another issue at Cushman is brewing into a multimillion-dollar controversy.

The Cushman Project, built by the city

The roaring rivers are never heard in the city, which makes it easy for people to ignore subtle ways that humans can tilt the balance of nature.

of Tacoma, consists of two dams and power-generating facilities, producing a total of 124 megawatts of electricity, enough to power 20,000 average homes.

The project, which is due for a new federal license, is being examined by Tacoma officials, the Skokomish Tribe and various resource agencies for its continuing impacts on the environment.

The dam not only blocked migration of salmon into the upper reaches of the North Fork, but it essentially dried up four miles of prime fish habitat downstream from the dam.

Water from the North Fork flows into Lake Cushman, then through a power plant before returning to the stream channel. A mile downstream, the water enters a second manmade lake, known as Lake Ko-kanee, a fraction of the size of Lake Cushman.

Tacoma City Light operates the two dams in concert to produce far more power than a single dam could alone.

As it leaves Lake Kokanee, the water takes a controversial left-hand turn. Instead of returning to the stream channel, the flow is diverted through three 10-foot-tall pipes, which slope down the side of a hill overlooking Hood Canal.

From a technical viewpoint, the project is marvelous. The falling water produces maximum output from a second power plant constructed at the bottom of the hill next to Highway 101.

The water gives up its energy to a whining turbine, which spins a generator, sending electric current down a high-voltage power line toward Tacoma. Its hydro-potential expended, the water is then dumped directly into Hood Canal.

Somehow forgotten in the design of this power project was the original stream channel of the North Fork. Eight miles of the river suffered massive depletion of water; at least four of those miles became unsuitable for spawning, a major blow to the salmon resource.

Today, the only flow in the North Fork below the two dams is that which Tacoma

Lake Cushman

The 4,000-acre lake feeds a Tacoma City Light hydroelectric power plant capable of powering 20,000 typical homes.

officials agree to release, about 225 gallons per second. Original flows in that stretch of river ranged from 1,500 to 12,000 gallons per second.

To compensate for lost fish habitat, Tacoma built a fish hatchery on Purdy Creek, a tributary to the Skokomish River. The George Adams Hatchery, now run by the state, produces substantial numbers of coho and chinook. But fishery experts say it has contributed to the depletion of wild salmon runs in the Skokomish River system.

The Skokomish Tribe, which traditionally depended on the Skokomish and its tributaries, plans to seek increased streamflows in the North Fork as well as additional compensation as Tacoma City Light seeks its new operating license.

A similar licensing program on the Elwha River near Port Angeles has led to a well-considered proposal to remove a pair of dams and attempt to restore one of the most productive salmon runs in the history of the Olympic Peninsula.

Nobody proposes tearing out the Cushman dams, but Tacoma City Light acknowledges its responsibility to care for the environment if the city is to continue enjoying power from the North Fork.

A new way of thinking about water is evident today, argues David Fluharty of the Institute for Marine Studies at the University of Washington.

"Before, we thought only about how water could be put to beneficial use," he said, "but now we realize that even in areas of abundance, water is already allocated to something."

State law is based on the notion that the first person to remove the water and "use" it has first rights to own it, said Fluharty. But that way of thinking could change.

Under a pact signed at Lake Chelan in November 1990, every group interested in the future of water resources agreed to a

7,000 gallons of water pass a point on the North Fork of the Skokomish River every second. That's enough water to flush every toilet in Bremerton, then do so again and again every 30 seconds.

step-by-step process that could alter state water law in new and interesting ways.

The first-use rule may have worked in the Wild West, said Fluharty, but today people are asking whether it serves the best interest of society as a whole. A new proposition is taking hold: That the ecosystem itself has water rights.

Meanwhile, small and large hydro projects have been proposed on all the major rivers of Hood Canal. In addition, Bremerton, Port Townsend and the Kitsap County Public Utility District have asked for the right to remove drinking water from the Hamma Hamma, Dosewallips and Duckabush rivers.

If any of these projects are pushed forward, they are likely to face opposition from people who believe the water is more valuable left alone in the rivers.

Garth Jackson, a Tacoma official in charge of winning a new license for Cushman, stood outside a concrete building and listened to a high-pitched whine coming from within: the sound of spinning turbines at Cushman's upper power plant.

The amount of power you get from a dam is governed by the volume of water as well as the "head," or vertical distance the water drops through a pipe and into a turbine, Jackson explained.

"That dam generates more power," he said, glancing in the direction of the lower dam. "This one gives more regulation."

Lake Cushman covers 4,000 acres and can hold 150 billion gallons of water. The dam controls flooding in the valley below, and virtually all of the water can be sent through both power plants to generate electricity.

The big lake provides recreation for boaters and fishermen, a state park for camping, not to mention 23 miles of shoreline property, now dotted with vacation homes.

Nobody argues that fish and wildlife habitat were destroyed when the dam was built, says Jackson, but the benefits of the dam have stood the test of time. The project continues to produce clean, non-polluting power when the alternatives are coal or nuclear generation.

"We are bringing a 1920s-vintage project into the current world," he said. "The process for relicensing is recognizing what our responsibilities will be for the next 30 years. We have significant proposals for fish, wildlife habitat and wetlands."

One of Tacoma's proposals is to purchase 3,000-4,000 acres to be protected as wildlife habitat, said Jackson. State agencies have suggested that 15,000 acres would be more appropriate.

The Federal Energy Regulatory Commission is supposed to balance all the interests in considering the license application.

Whatever costs are expended to mitigate damage from the dams will be passed along to power customers as a rate increase, Jackson noted, as he stood outside the upper power plant and watched a series of small whirlpools created by the turbulence of water rushing out of the turbines. He pondered the future of Cushman and how much might be expected in the name of the environment.

• • • • • • • • • •

The Cushman Project, built by the city of Tacoma, consists of two dams and power-generating facilities, producing a total of 124 megawatts of electricity, enough to power 20,000 average homes.

Rivers of Hood Canal

The major rivers of Hood Canal still bear their Indian names:
• **Dewatto** (De-WAH-toh): From du-a-to, meaning "home of evil spirits who make men crazy."
• **Dosewallips** (dohs-ee-WAH-lips): From Twana Dos-wailopsh, a legendary man who was turned into a mountain, which is the river's source.
•**Hamma Hamma** (HAM-uh HAM-uh): A phonetic corruption of Hab'hab, the name of a Twana village at the mouth of Hood Canal.

• **Quilcene** (KWIL-seen): From quil-ceed-o-bish, meaning "salt water people." It was the name of a band of Twana Indians who lived around Dabob Bay.
• **Skokomish**: From Skokomish s'kaw, meaning "fresh water," and mish, meaning "people."
• **Tahuya**: From Twana ta and ho-i, meaning "that done" in reference to some notable occurrence long ago.

— *Source: James Phillips, Washington State Place Names*

Negotiating Water Rights

Tacoma's Cushman Project is about to be thrust into a process that could either settle a number of environmental issues in southwest Hood Canal — or else lead to a major court battle.

By fall of 1991, Tacoma officials will sit down with lawyers for the Skokomish Tribe to work out a mitigation plan for relicensing the two Cushman dams.

How much water should flow in the North Fork of the Skokomish River? Should a fish passage be built over the dams? What lands will Tacoma purchase for wildlife? Will the North Fork be restored? What can be done about cultural and archaeological values lost when the dam was built 65 years ago?

Ultimately, the Federal Energy Regulatory Commission (FERC) will issue the license, but the tribe is an acknowledged player in the decision.

Today, the city and tribe seem miles apart on the issues — but that's just the nature of negotiations, says Russ Busch, chief negotiator for the tribe.

"People always look far apart at the beginning," said Busch, a lawyer with Evergreen Legal Services in Seattle. "Sometimes there is unrealistic thinking at that point, but eventually you have reality checks and say, 'We can get this, but we can't get this.' "

One of the major differences is what is called the "baseline issue."

"Our position," said Busch, "is that Tacoma must provide mitigation and compensation as if it didn't have the dams there."

Under that theory, all the lost resources — fish, wildlife, etc. — would be measured and replaced in areas away from the dam site.

But even Busch acknowledges that FERC has taken a dim view of that approach. The agency believes instead that relicensing provides an opportunity to improve environmental conditions where appropriate.

What people don't realize, said Busch, is what the tribe gave up when the dam was built.

"The North Fork was the productive portion of the Skokomish system, much more than the South Fork or the main stem," he said.

Furthermore, the 4,000 acres now occupied by Lake Cushman contained vast populations of elk that were hunted by the tribe. There were waterfalls with religious significance that now lie underwater.

"It is just a vestige of what it once was," he said.

Non-Indians may not understand the cultural significance of hunting and fishing sites, of particular types of salmon, of special plants, of so many things, said Busch.

"The European analysis has it all broken down into fish, wildlife, etc.," he said. "But when you ask about it, you realize it is just as complex as a city."

The difficult thing will be to articulate the Indian values, Busch said.

"We know by talking to the tribes that a lot was lost by them," he said. "We don't want to miss something because we don't know how to put it in the right language for some judge in San Francisco."

According to Busch, the tribe is seeking to increase production of salmon in what remains of the North Fork. That means increasing flows from the dam and restoring some segments of stream suitable for spawning.

The dam currently is releasing 30 cubic feet (about 225 gallons) per second. "They have agreed to up to 70," said Busch, though the tribe is asking for more.

Restoring the stream may mean adding logs and other large woody debris to catch gravel to provide spawning areas and to create habitat for insects, which are eaten by the fish.

The tribe also wants to explore archaeological sites that may lie under water, he said.

"We have filed a motion to draw the reservoir down and investigate what is down there," he said. "The tribe isn't willing to say, 'That's progress and we don't want to bother anybody.' "

In the 1920s, land owned by individual Indians was condemned to build portions of the dam project, which

"We know by talking to the tribes that a lot was lost by them. We don't want to miss something because we don't know how to put it in the right language for some judge in San Francisco."
—Russ Busch, chief negotiator for the Skokomish tribe

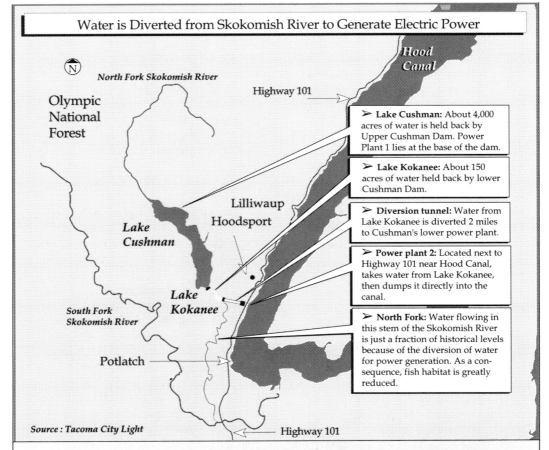

Water is Diverted from Skokomish River to Generate Electric Power

Hood Canal

North Fork Skokomish River

Highway 101

Olympic National Forest

Lilliwaup
Hoodsport

Lake Cushman

South Fork Skokomish River

Lake Kokanee

Potlatch

Highway 101

Lake Cushman: About 4,000 acres of water is held back by Upper Cushman Dam. Power Plant 1 lies at the base of the dam.

Lake Kokanee: About 150 acres of water held back by lower Cushman Dam.

Diversion tunnel: Water from Lake Kokanee is diverted 2 miles to Cushman's lower power plant.

Power plant 2: Located next to Highway 101 near Hood Canal, takes water from Lake Kokanee, then dumps it directly into the canal.

North Fork: Water flowing in this stem of the Skokomish River is just a fraction of historical levels because of the diversion of water for power generation. As a consequence, fish habitat is greatly reduced.

Source : Tacoma City Light

reduced the size of tribal lands, according to Busch.

"From my point of view the tribe has been subsidizing nice, inexpensive power for the city of Tacoma," he said.

Garth Jackson, who is handling the relicensing issue for Tacoma, says the tribe's perspective may be different from that of other interests involved in the relicensing issue, including state agencies.

Several projects, including a fish hatchery, boat ramps and parks, have been constructed by Tacoma, he noted.

"We recognize our current obligations as stewards of the resource," he said.

Similar negotiations between Seattle City Light and resource groups on the Skagit River resulted in a settlement announced just last week.

The agreement is expected to cost Seattle's utility $55 million-$60 million on measures to protect the environment, including the purchase of 4,000 acres of land to protect wildlife. In addition, the utility will forego $40 million-$45 million in lost power revenues to increase stream flows to benefit fish.

Recreation projects, an education center, landscaping and cultural protections are part of the settlement.

Cushman is a much smaller power project, but officials say key issues are much the same.

By Christopher Dunagan

• • • • • • • • • • •

SECTION 2

JOCKEYING
FOR THE
RESOURCE

*By Christopher
Dunagan*

*A Quilcene National
Fish Hatchery worker
pushes young salmon
out of a rearing pen and
into the Big Quilcene
River.*

At the Quilcene National Fish Hatchery, Larry Telles opened the gates of the fish raceway and said goodbye to 350,000 little coho salmon.

The fingerlings, hatched here 18 months ago, splashed vigorously as they were pushed unceremoniously toward the next stage of their lives, a dangerous journey to the wide open ocean. How many will survive is anybody's guess.

"They look like fancy herring to bigger fish," noted Telles, as the little fish disappeared into the Big Quilcene River.

Success of the hatchery operation is largely dependent on the amount of water flowing in the Big Quilcene River and nearby Penny Creek. In a dry year, for example, more fish at the hatchery will share the same water as it passes through the hatchery, said Telles. The risk of disease becomes greater.

In a sense, these fish also share water

with the residents of Port Townsend. The city operates a dam on the Big Quilcene and controls the amount of water that flows downstream to the hatchery.

Usually, there is plenty of water for both hatchery fish and Port Townsend residents. But habitat for Quilcene's wild salmon has been reduced, both by blockage of Penny Creek and by adjustments to the Big Quilcene flows.

In nature, all things are connected, and nothing connects everything more closely than water. In fact, water is so vital to all living creatures that controlling the flow of water often means controlling life itself.

People have been jockeying for a piece of the water resource since before the turn of the century. (The Quilcene Hatchery was built in 1911.)

So far, only an abundance of water in Western Washington has prevented a political explosion, the likes of which could make the spotted owl debate seem like a neighborhood squabble. But a day of reckoning lies ahead.

In 1984, Washington residents were given a hint of things to come when political forces tore apart a plan for managing water flows in rivers and streams on the western side of Hood Canal between the Skokomish and Dosewallips rivers.

All at once, water took on a new significance in Western Washington. The Hood Canal issue revealed various political powers lining up to do battle, and it eventually forced them to negotiate a common path out of the political minefield.

At the time, Donna Simmons of Hoodsport had just been appointed to the Washington State Ecological Commission by Gov. John Spellman. Simmons, a former president of Hood Canal Environmental Council, began asking some uncomfortable questions about the water resource plan.

"Nobody was bringing up any problems," she said, "but I was looking at it and something wasn't quite right."

Simmons, a soft-spoken woman not used to making loud assertions, found herself reviewing a plan that would have established minimum flows for the most pristine rivers in Hood Canal. It was all part of the Department of Ecology's effort to establish legal water rights for fish and wildlife — before all the water was taken for man's purposes.

Similar plans already had been adopted for the Kitsap Peninsula, Lower Hood Canal and several other areas throughout the state.

But in talking to state and tribal fisheries experts, Simmons quickly learned of serious concerns about the amount of water being reserved for fish.

"They did not feel the water levels would be sufficient to support fish habitat," said Simmons.

Her questions continued. Environmental groups began raising objections to the plan. When it came time for a vote, members of the Ecological Commission rejected it unanimously.

Meanwhile, behind the scenes, water utilities and other user groups were lobbying the new governor, Booth Gardner, and other state officials about their concerns.

As proposed, the plan would have prevented the largest rivers — Dosewallips, Duckabush and Hamma Hamma — from being used as a source of drinking water.

All the while, Bremerton, Port Townsend and Kitsap County had their eyes on those rivers for future water supplies.

"Water supply systems," said Ed Dee, a member of the legislative staff, "... felt the level of protection advocated for fisheries resources was too great a price to pay."

The Ecology plan suffered a quick death, but the dispute imprinted an image of possible battles yet to come. If interest groups could not establish minimum flows while water supplies are abundant, what will happen when population growth intensifies the demand for additional water?

Even today, the danger remains that minimum flows will not be established for those important Hood Canal rivers.

"There were times when I despaired over what I had done," said Simmons. "But we really needed to go back and look at the whole water resource issue. I've always felt I did the right thing."

Washington State has struggled with complicated water laws since 1917. As with most Western states, the concept of prior appropriation ("first in time, first in right") has been the governing principal.

In 1967, the state entered the environmental era. Needs of fish and wildlife were recognized, and the Legislature granted the

Despite heavy precipitation, despite ever-flowing streams, the amount of water is indeed limited. And people who understand this indisputable fact have already begun to engage in a tug-of-war over its future use.

Department of Water Resources (now Department of Ecology) the authority to set minimum stream flows.

But, if anything, the Legislature has added confusion to a difficult subject. In 1971, lawmakers passed the Water Resources Act, which offered two guiding principals: Water should be used to promote the state's economy, and water should be used to preserve natural systems.

Steve Shupe, an expert in water law, was hired in 1988 by a legislative committee to sort through Washington's various laws and to outline major issues for new legislation.

State laws clearly recognize a balance between water use and preservation, Shupe concluded. "They apparently fail, however, to provide sufficient guidance for implementation of this policy."

Indian tribes have also become major players in water issues. In 1982, Federal District Judge William Orrick ruled that treaties not only guaranteed tribes the right to take fish but also to see that fish habitat is not continuously destroyed.

"Were this (destructive) trend to continue, the right to take fish would eventually be reduced to the right to dip one's net into the water ... and bring it out empty," Orrick said.

Faced with growing conflicts over who controls water resources, the Legislature last year called for a cooperative planning process involving water users, local governments, tribes and interest groups.

In late 1990, more than 200 officials met at Lake Chelan and agreed to a process designed to settle differences over water uses in Washington state.

"It was a sight to behold," declared Terry Williams, commissioner to the Northwest Indian Fisheries Commission. "More than 200 people were there. Legislators, mayors, tribal chairmen, fishermen, recreationists, environmentalists, farmers, ranchers and business executives...

"These were people who have vastly different uses for water. But by coming together in forging the Chelan Agreement, they have recognized that we must work together to protect our precious water resource and all the living things that depend on it."

The Chelan agreement calls for two pilot projects, one in Eastern Washington and one in Western Washington. The projects will bring various groups together to plan the future of specific rivers.

For a time, it looked as if the Hood Canal rivers that had so troubled Simmons when she first joined the Ecological Commission were about to be selected for review under the program. Planners would have faced controversial questions about future water supplies for Kitsap and Jefferson counties.

In the end, however, the focus came back to the region containing the Big Quilcene River, the Quilcene Fish Hatchery and Port Townsend's existing water supply system.

Jefferson County Commissioner Richard Wojt says he looks forward to the pilot project. What is becoming the fundamental question — whether water should be used by people or saved for fish — will generate a good deal of discussion, he predicted.

Port Townsend's complex water supply system no doubt will be examined over the next two years. Unlike Bremerton, which operates a single dam on the Union River in Kitsap County, Port Townsend operates interconnected dams on both the Big Quilcene and Little Quilcene rivers. In addition, a major portion of the water goes to Port Townsend Paper Mill, which helps operate the system.

The city has a legal right to 215 gallons per second out of the Big Quilcene. But during a period of drought, there is some question whether that much water would be available, said Bob Wheeler, director of public works.

"Our water right is senior to any streamflow rights," said Wheeler, "but if we had a drought, would it be realistic to take all the water?"

The Quilcene Fish Hatchery has rights to nearly as much flow as Port Townsend, but the water is not always available. In fact, there are times when flows past the hatchery drop below a critical level of 38 gallons per second.

When the rivers gets that dry, hatchery officials ask the city to release water out of its reservoir, Telles said.

"We're real dependent on rain as to what the river will do," he said.

A hatchery is considered a "nonconsumptive" use because the water is

"Before, we thought only about how water could be put to beneficial use, but now we realize that even in areas of abundance, water is already allocated to something."
—David Fluharty, Institute for Marine Studies at the University of Washington

put back in the river. Nevertheless, the river's flow is decreased for about a quarter mile as it goes past the hatchery.

The Quilcene River is not known for its natural salmon production because it falls so steeply out of the mountains. But water withdrawals have only made the problem worse for migrating salmon, which require extra flows to bypass boulders and other obstacles in the river.

Tradeoffs of one kind or another seem to surround every water issue.

"What you see here is the classic struggle in water use," said Telles. "One answer would be to divert less water to Port Townsend."

The Big Quilcene River and Penny Creek might have produced giant-sized salmon before the hatchery was built, but that was a long time ago, Telles said.

"Hatcheries themselves are not evil things," he said. "We raise probably what the stream would raise in seven miles of perfect spawning habitat — which never existed here."

But biologists worry that hatchery production, paired with an intense rate of commercial and sport fishing, have depleted natural runs of wild salmon.

Native coho from Hood Canal have declined to levels so low that biologists are worried that genetically distinct populations (stocks) may not survive.

"Stocks are the basic building blocks," said Jim Lichatowich, a biologist with the Lower Elwha Klallam Tribe and a nationally recognized expert on salmon populations. "Whether management of our salmon resource succeeds or fails depends on how well these building blocks are maintained."

Lichatowich is a member of the American Fishery Society's Endangered Species Committee. A recent report by the committee raised alarms about several distinct Hood Canal stocks.

Spring chinook from the Skokomish and Dosewallips rivers may already be extinct, according to the report, and fall chinook from the Dosewallips and Duckabush are at "high risk" of extinction.

The report, based on available information, does not mention Hood Canal coho, mainly because so little information is available on individual coho stocks, said Lichatowich.

Hood Canal salmon are managed as one unit, which means coho from the rushing rivers of the Olympic Peninsula are lumped together with those from the meandering rivers of the Kitsap Peninsula, even though the fish are adapted to different stream environments.

A number of Hood Canal's wild populations could be in danger without anyone realizing it, said Lichatowich.

Mike Reed, a biologist for the Port Gamble S'Klallam Tribe, says wild stocks are uniquely suited to swim up a specific stream while resisting diseases and eating insects of that particular stream. Alterations in the water flow, temperatures and even insect production can affect the salmon run.

People must be cautious about how they affect the water flow, said Reed. That goes beyond the issue of dams to logging and even to development.

"Hatcheries play a role, but they cannot replace the natural systems," said Reed.

Reed says he can see powerful political forces at work, both at the state and local levels. But whether streams and rivers ultimately survive depends on whether people care enough to speak out about resource planning.

"So far," said Reed, "what we have been saying to future generations is that we don't value our natural resources enough to pass them on in any condition that we can be proud of."

• • • • • • • • • •

"So far, what we have been saying to future generations is that we don't value our natural resources enough to pass them on in any condition that we can be proud of."
—Mike Reed, a biologist for the Port Gamble S'Klallam Tribe

Plans to generate electrical power from two Hood Canal rivers — the Dosewallips and the Hamma Hamma — may have gained new life following completion in 1991 of a management plan for Olympic National Forest.

Both proposals are for "run-of-the-river" projects, built with an inflatable dam, or weir, which diverts water through a power plant only when the river is running high. During low flows, the weir is deflated and has much less impact on the river.

The changing power supply situation in the Northwest is beginning to make small hydro projects more attractive, said Katherine Leone of Tacoma City Light.

"Right now the region is in a load-resource balance," she said. "What we generate equates to just about what we use."

Even though the need for more power may make the Dosewallips and Hamma Hamma projects more feasible, environmentalists promise that neither will be constructed without a fight.

The Dosewallips project, known as Elkhorn Hydroelectric Project, was proposed in 1982 by Tacoma City Light and Jefferson County Public Utility District 1.

The Hamma Hamma Hydroelectric Project is a joint effort of Mason County PUD 1 and PUD 3. It was proposed in 1986 after PUD 1 abandoned plans for a much larger dam on the river.

The projects were both given a boost by the final plan for Olympic National Forest, which suggests special protections for the Duckabush River under the Wild and Scenic Rivers Act. The Duckabush is the only Hood Canal river proposed for nomination under the act.

Although many people argued that both the Dosewallips and Hamma Hamma would qualify for wild-and-scenic status, both would remain available for water diversion and power production under the forest plan.

For the Elkhorn project, said Charles Black, another Tacoma City Light employee, "the punch line is the Forest Service plan would now designate the Dosewallips as being compatible with this type of power project."

Studies to determine the environmental consequences of building the Dosewallips project began in late 1991.

Meanwhile, Mason County PUD 1 and PUD 3 were getting ready to decide whether to move ahead with the Hamma Hamma project, said Pat McGary of the PUD 3 staff.

"It all depends on some decisions to take place in the next month or two to

Hydroelectric proposals

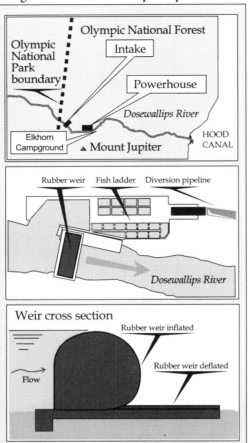

Source: Jefferson Co. PUD., Tacoma City Light

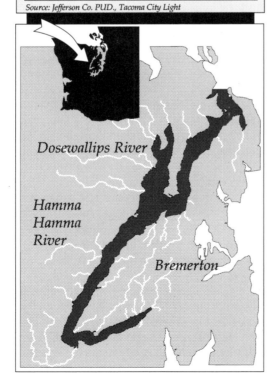

• • • • • • • • • •

The Elkhorn Hydroelectric Project and the Hamma Hamma Hydroelectric Project were given a boost by an Olympic National Forest plan that seeks wild and scenic protections only for the Duckabush River.

determine how much we will spend (on the project) next year," he said.

A steering committee will be set up to discuss the alternatives before the issue comes up in a public meeting, he added.

Both run-of-the-river projects would work basically the same way. By using an inflatable weir, the dams can be operated during late winter and early spring when river flows are high. During other parts of the year, the weirs would be deflated, allowing the natural movement of river gravel downstream.

Proponents of run-of-the-river projects argue the environmental problems for fish and wildlife are minimal because the dams are small and used only at particular times of the year.

Construction would begin with a concrete foundation poured in the river bed, from one side to the other. A rubber weir, something like an inflatable sausage, is attached tightly to the foundation.

When the weir is inflated, it impounds water behind the dam. At one end of the dam, an intake structure directs the impounded water through a "trash screen" and into a diversion pipe.

The power plant is placed at the opposite end of the pipe, as far downstream as feasible. The greater the drop in elevation, the greater the generating capacity.

Environmentalists generally concede that run-of-the-river projects are much better than traditional impoundment dams that trap the entire flow of a river. But they can still create problems, especially for fish.

"A hydropower facility — on any river — should be constructed only if a real need for such power exists," said Carol Volk of Olympic Rivers Council. "We are a spoiled, consumptive society. We must first look to methods that conserve the tremendous power resources we already have."

Several state and federal agencies have already recommended against the Dosewallips project, largely because it would destroy fish habitat and increase sediment problems, which can kill fish eggs in the streambed.

"The project would adversely impact the existing steelhead trout stock and would limit the potential for successful rebuilding of the spring chinook salmon run," wrote Einar Wold of the National Marine Fisheries Service in a letter commenting on the plan.

But Tacoma City Light officials argue

that they located the project above a series of waterfalls, which forms a natural barrier to fish. In a fish population survey, only two steelhead reached the site one year.

In a separate letter regarding the Hamma Hamma project, Wold said the river supports important runs of chinook, coho, pink and chum salmon, as well as summer and winter steelhead and rainbow trout.

He noted that two alternatives have been proposed for the Hamma Hamma.

"However," he added, "we should state at the outset that NMFS would not support a license ... under either configuration because of the project's potential adverse impacts to anadromous fish resources."

John Kuntz, owner of Olympic Kayak in Poulsbo, is the only outfitter licensed to run the Dosewallips River. While the proposed hydro project would not affect his river-rafting operation, which is downstream from the proposed dam site, he says it would be a crime to put any type of manmade structure on the Dosewallips.

The dam would be built in a deep canyon, one of the most remote and pristine spots along the beautiful river, he said.

"I don't see the reasons they want to put this structure up there and change the habitat and environment for the small amount of energy they will get," he said.

"If we allow this dam to go in there, there will be nothing to keep from putting one on the Hamma Hamma."

• • • • • • • • • •

"A hydro-power facility — on any river — should be constructed only if a real need for such power exists. We must first look to methods that conserve the tremendous power resources we already have."
—Carol Volk, Olympic Rivers Council

Wild and Scenic Designation

To preserve a river forever, to keep it flowing in its natural state for generations to come, involves a momentous decision reserved for the U.S. Congress or state Legislature.

In Hood Canal, the Forest Service studied the Olympic Peninsula rivers for inclusion in the National Wild and Scenic Rivers System. The agency declared that four rivers — Dosewallips, Duckabush, Hamma Hamma and South Fork of the Skokomish — all have unique qualities that would make them suitable for special designation.

But, in the Forest Service view, only the Duckabush has enough "outstandingly remarkable" values to be named a wild and scenic river.

The Dosewallips came in nearly as high in the Forest Service analysis. And it might have been nominated had the agency chosen to name more than one Hood Canal river.

Shawn Cantrell of the Northwest Rivers Council says all four rivers should have been proposed to Congress, as well as the upper portion of the Big Quilcene River. (The Forest Service found the Big Quilcene to have generally "average" conditions not even suitable for consideration.)

The first four rivers should certainly be set aside for protection, said Cantrell.

"You look at what the Wild and Scenic Act specifies, and those are all excellent candidates and truly deserving," he said. "From scenery to wildlife to geology to recreation, all those rivers are truly extraordinary."

Cantrell says his group is preparing a petition for congressional consideration later this summer that would protect a number of Olympic Rivers in their natural state.

Among Washington's delegation to Congress, Reps. John Miller, R-Seattle, and Jim McDermott, D-Seattle, seem particularly interested in pushing special rivers legislation, according to Cantrell.

"The imperiled status of many of the major fish runs has helped focus attention on the need for river protections," he added.

For every river attaining Wild and Scenic status, federal agencies must develop a management plan outlining what changes will be allowed and what will be precluded in and along the river.

Jean Phillips of the Wild Rivers Conservancy, a group generally opposed to designating wild and scenic rivers, says she sees no need for special status since two-thirds of most Olympic rivers pass through federal land. Congress should not cut off its future options, she added.

"Personally, I think we're going to need electricity," she said. "I am not in favor of nuclear power, and coal produces dust and dirt in the air. The one thing the Northwest has is plenty of water, especially in the winter."

As she talked, Phillips led the way outside her house, which lies a quarter-mile uphill from the Duckabush River. Her colorful garden, which offers a high-level view of Hood Canal, contains non-native azaleas and rhododendrons.

Phillips worries that Wild and Scenic River legislation would force her to grow only plants that are native to the region.

Cantrell argues that Phillips' fears, and those of other private property owners, are groundless. The legislation would affect private property only if the federal government wishes to purchase a conservation easement from property owners, he said.

"They can continue to use the land as it has been used in the past," he said, "and they can pass the property on to their children or sell it."

Dosewallips

The Dosewallips River, which begins high in the Olympics and flows into Hood Canal, has been declared suitable for "wild and scenic" designation.

Vern and Ida Bailey have lived along the Dosewallips River for 50 years. In 1941, at the age of 19, the Baileys bought 80 acres of river bottomland for a mere $700, and later increased their holdings to 250 acres. Until a few years ago, they raised 50 head of cattle.

Bailey, with his long white sideburns and black-framed glasses, talks softly and with an obvious knowledge of conservation techniques. Though he appears to be a good caretaker of his waterfront property, Bailey has serious concerns about federal protection for the Dosewallips.

"When we first heard it was being considered," he said, "we were really thrilled because we thought it would stop development. But when you get the law and read the fine print — having worked for the government, I know about fine print — they could take a half mile on either side and it would wipe us out."

Every home built in the Hood Canal watershed places a new burden on the region's water supply.

"We're in stuff now that's silt-bound!" shouted Joel Purdy over the deafening pulsation of metal slamming against metal. Inch by inch, the 12-inch pipe slipped slowly into the ground under the rhythmic pounding of the drilling rig. Just a week earlier, the same well casing had slid down easily, like a hot knife through butter.

"Clang...clang...clang..." The noise echoed in the hills overlooking Hood Canal near Seabeck as operator Todd Michelsen of Charon Drilling gripped the controls.

Purdy, a hydrogeologist for the firm Robinson & Noble, stood nearby observing. Numerous times over the past month of drilling, Purdy had halted the operation and gathered soil samples brought up out of the deepening hole. Now, at 370 feet, progress was slow.

This exploratory well was commissioned by Kitsap County Public Utility District. The district has been searching for new pockets of groundwater in hopes of easing the county's coming water shortage, perhaps 30 years away.

Over the past 40 years, surface water diverted from the Hood Canal region has supplied a major portion of Kitsap County's population. Even today, about a third of the

● ● ● ● ● ● ● ● ●

SECTION 4

GROWTH
MAKES NEW
DEMANDS

*By Christopher
Dunagan*

residents get their water from Bremerton's Casad Dam on the Union River, which feeds the southern tip of Hood Canal.

But the shift to groundwater supplies has been rapid over the past decade or so as rural Kitsap's growth has exploded. Now, experts hope to discover a vast, but still uncertain, water source that may lie hidden underground along Hood Canal's shores.

"With what we've gone through so far, it looks promising," said Purdy of the new well, already deeper than a water-bearing zone discovered 318 feet below ground. At that point, driving the well casing became easy for 33 feet before it struck a more solid formation — a dense mixture of silt, sand and gravel.

Underground pockets of clean, loose gravel, unencumbered by clay or silt, may not seem like much of anything. But to Purdy and his boss Cliff Hanson, these gravel formations raise expectations of finding fresh, clear water.

"Sand and gravel are like a big sponge," said Purdy. "Precipitation is soaked right up."

Most of Kitsap County's soils were laid down by glaciers during Puget Sound's ice age more than 14,000 years ago.

"You may think of glaciers as being pristine," said Hanson, "but actually they're awfully dirty animals. They carry an abundance of sand and all kinds of materials."

As the glaciers melted into water, they dropped their loads of silt, sand and gravel onto the Kitsap Peninsula. Sometimes the mixed stuff was packed so tightly together — siltbound — that it could never absorb much water. Drill bits and well casings make little progress through such material.

But in other places the melt water picked up speed and washed away the silt, leaving a glacial deposit in which water can flow easily through the spaces between sand and gravel particles.

After burial by successive glaciers, the formation became an underground stream to be tapped by advanced technology.

For well drillers today, finding a water-bearing zone in all this mess is a big gamble, said Hanson. "That's the joy and consternation of working in glacial terrains."

A basic choice for the Hood Canal region is whether to build new homes close to water supplies or to pipe water to population centers, wherever they may be.

Cities generally pipe their water. In its early years, for example, Bremerton chose to transport water from Gorst, 3 miles away; then later from Twin Lakes, 2.5 miles farther out; then later still from McKenna Falls and Casad Dam, another 2 miles beyond.

Port Townsend gets its water from the Quilcene River, about 28 miles away.

David Fluharty of the Institute for Marine Studies at the University of Washington says the old way may still be the best.

"It makes sense from a growth-management standpoint to keep people in a central area, where it is easier to provide needed services, than to disperse the people and build multiple small water systems," he said.

Concentrating populations also decreases the "footprint of development," said Fluharty.

Under state law, all three Hood Canal counties are planning for future growth. But due to its large population, its rapid growth as well as its limited surface supply, Kitsap County may run dry before either Mason or Jefferson.

Before Kitsap as a whole suffers a water shortage, regional shortages are likely to develop, according to David Siburg, manager of Kitsap County Public Utility District. Island Lake in Central Kitsap and parts of Bainbridge Island have been identified already as potential problem areas.

Siburg speaks fluently the language of growth management, but a number of water issues seem to trouble him. Urban centers, as defined by Kitsap County, may not have adequate water supplies for their projected populations, he said.

"We have to make some tough choices as a county," said Siburg. "Water may have to be captured from areas where it is available and brought to areas of development."

This idea, certainly not new, might mean a massive public works project, such as piping water from the Olympic Peninsula. As an alternative, it might mean developing a series of public wells in undeveloped forest lands, such as those near Hood Canal in the southwest part of Kitsap County.

Either alternative would not be without its effects on the natural environment.

Determining how much water is actually out there in underground formations is the reason Purdy and Michelsen

Surface water diverted from the Hood Canal region has supplied a major portion of Kitsap County's population. About a third of the residents get their water from Bremerton's Casad Dam on the Union River, which feeds the southern tip of Hood Canal.

Where the rains fall: How the canal fits in

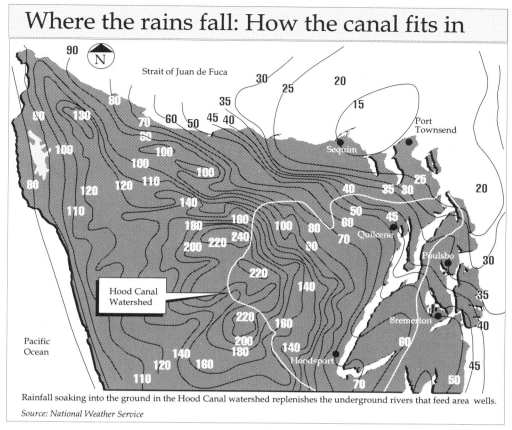

Rainfall soaking into the ground in the Hood Canal watershed replenishes the underground rivers that feed area wells.

Source: National Weather Service

• • • • • • • • • •

A basic choice for the Hood Canal region is whether to build new homes close to water supplies or to pipe water to population centers, wherever they may be.

have been drilling near Seabeck. The newest well is the second to be drilled in that area by the PUD.

A large well nearby, developed by the University of Washington for its Big Beef Research Station, proved to be a big producer, said Purdy. That suggests a major water-bearing formation underground.

The water-bearing formation has been given the name "Big Beef Aquifer." It is just one of several possible sources of groundwater in that region, said Siburg.

"Estimates are, on gross magnitude, there may be enough water in Kitsap County to support growth until the year 2020," he said. "The trick comes in being able to capture that water — groundwater — without affecting streams or other wells."

Hydraulic continuity — the hottest word in the parlance of water management — describes the much-misunderstood relationship between surface water and groundwater.

When surface water flows into the ground, which it does continuously, it is known as aquifer recharge. When groundwater escapes in a spring at the surface, it's discharge. The geology can be incredibly complex, but wells can and do affect streams, and vice versa.

The state Department of Ecology is beginning to pay attention to this complex issue, said Siburg. In fact, in Clark County, the department refused to approve a well that might have reduced the flow of a nearby stream by just half of 1 percent, he said.

As Kitsap, Mason and Jefferson counties develop growth management strategies, they will be required to identify and protect important aquifer recharge areas, to maintain adequate groundwater supplies and to maintain a natural balance in the system.

Development of roads and houses tilts the water balance toward surface flow by covering up bare land, which can recharge the underground streams. Furthermore, hard surfaces — roofs and driveways — speed up the surface water flow, pushing the water off the face of the land and into sea water.

In addition to growth management, Kitsap County has been studying groundwater management for several years under the direction of Siburg and the PUD.

Conservation is one way of increasing water supplies, said Siburg, and it will no doubt become increasingly important in the Hood Canal region.

If people can learn to be careful about

watering their lawns and use low-flow fixtures, it can extend the life of water systems for years. Water systems themselves can save water by repairing leaks in their transmission lines.

But with so little agricultural irrigation in the area, huge water savings may be out of reach, said Siburg.

The Kitsap County Groundwater Management Plan, which will outline the future options, should be completed in about six months, he said.

"Some people would say 'stop everything; close the door until we understand all of this,' " said Siburg. "But we can't stand still. We are charged by law with the responsibility to get the water to the people."

One of his biggest fears is that the Hood Canal region in southwest Kitsap County will be developed before anybody knows the value of the groundwater resource, he said.

"That may be a tremendous recharge area," he said. "It would be nice to define the resource before we make substantial changes to that area. You don't want to close the barn door after the horses get out."

Water is the lifeblood of the Hood Canal region and Puget Sound as a whole. The management of this priceless resource — both above ground and below — will determine the survival of fish and wildlife, as well as the quality of human lifestyles, for years to come.

• • • • • • • • • •

SECTION 5

PRESERVING
WATER
QUALITY

*By Christopher
Dunagan*

*Despite the seemingly
endless supply of water
in the Pacific Northwest,
population pressures
and pollution are
causing new concerns
about quality drinking
water.*

W hile most water systems in the Hood Canal region face questions about future water supplies, many also are dealing with immediate concerns related to federal drinking water standards.

Port Townsend, for example, is considering the prospect of building a $10 million filtration plant to make sure its surface supply from the Big Quilcene and Little Quilcene rivers remains of high quality.

To avoid filtration, surface waters must

meet stringent federal standards, including extremely low levels of bacteria, turbidity and chemicals, as measured by a host of expensive tests.

"Frankly, in Port Townsend's case, we have some real concerns about whether we can meet all the criteria," said Public Works Director Bob Wheeler.

Rivers flowing out of the Olympic Mountains are among the purest in the state, but logging in the upper reaches and development in the lower areas may suspend dirt particles in a stream.

Most of the Quilcene watershed is on undeveloped land managed by the U.S. Forest Service, which has been attempting to maintain the lowest impact to water quality, officials say. But the federal standards are tough.

It might be best to move ahead with the expensive filtration plant instead of gambling that the water supply won't be shut down on short notice, said Wheeler.

Of the 15 million gallons of water coming out of Port Townsend's reservoirs, 80-90 percent goes to the Port Townsend Paper Mill, which doesn't need filtered water for its industrial operations.

The city's options include building a new water main from the Quilcene watershed or else locating the filtration plant closer to town to get by with a shorter pipeline.

Bremerton also faces the prospect of filtration, but has the advantage of owning almost all the Union River watershed above McKenna Falls. City officials intend to buy the remaining 160 acres to keep the entire area natural and free from human activities. (The watershed contains an elaborate alarm system to help keep out trespassers.)

Bill Duffy, director of Bremerton utilities, hopes that these actions, plus a continuing battery of water tests, will prevent the city from being forced to build a $10-$15 million filtration plant.

The city has altered its management of Casad Dam on the Union River to keep

> **"So far, what we're saying to future generations is that we don't value our natural resources enough to pass them on in any condition that we can be proud of."**
> — Mike Reed, Port Gamble S'Klallam tribe

Quilcene River

Waters of the Quilcene River system have been dammed to provide water supply for the City of Port Townsend, 28 miles to the north.

turbidity to a minimum. Duffy plans to hire special staff to keep their eyes on water quality issues.

Casad Dam supplies more than half of the 8 million-10 million gallons a day used by the city and outlying areas. Of that amount, about a third goes to Navy operations at Puget Sound Naval Shipyard.

Just 20 years ago, Casad Dam — along with an older facility in Gorst — was able to supply virtually all of the city's water. The dam can hold 1.35 billion gallons.

The Gorst facility was taken off-line due to water quality problems. But Duffy said the facility may be activated again, possibly for irrigating Bremerton's Gold Mountain Golf Course, which uses 50 million gallons of water a year. Eventually, a small filtration plant at Gorst would bring 3 million gallons a day back into the city's water system.

"We feel pretty comfortable that over the next 10 years we will be OK in terms of water supply," said Duffy. "It's a resource we took for granted in the last decade, and it will be a much bigger issue in the next decade."

The city intends to hire a consultant to update its comprehensive water plan over the next six months under a $160,000 contract.

Big systems have their unique problems, but federal requirements are costing small water systems more and more money, too, said Jerry Deeter, water quality specialist with the Bremerton-Kitsap County Health Department.

Some of the smaller systems, operated by part-time managers, are having trouble with maintenance and operations, which sometimes leads to health concerns, he said. Some managers fail to do all the testing required by the new regulations.

"As more and more testing comes on, cost for the testing is going to get really high," said Deeter. "Systems with more than 15 customers have to do monthly bacteriological testing."

A wide spectrum of chemical tests is

also required, depending on the size of the system.

The county is attempting to coordinate small water systems by requiring uniform design standards for expansions. Systems may be eventually tied together to help transport water from areas of plentiful supply to areas of short supply.

It would be beneficial to expand medium and large systems, as opposed to increasing the number of small systems, said Deeter. But the opposite may be happening.

Large- and medium-sized systems must obtain water rights in advance, a process that now takes up to three years, he noted. The Department of Ecology, which processes the applications, simply can't keep up with the growth.

"We haven't seen a lot of the larger systems going in," said Deeter.

On the other hand, small systems with six or fewer customers can avoid the delay through assumed water rights. Some developers have chosen to create two or more small systems, as opposed to putting in a larger system, said Deeter.

"Since April 4 of last year, we've done approximately 91 new public supplies," he said. "Normally in a full year we do an average of about 50."

In 1991, nearly 1,000 water systems now exist in Kitsap County, compared to 450 in 1978.

The number of small, individual systems may set up a competition for existing water and create problems in who owns the rights to the water.

"I think groundwater is going to become a real important issue," said Deeter. "More people are concerned about it than ever before because of the growth we are experiencing."

One challenge will be to coordinate all the big and little systems as groundwater in the county grows scarce.

• • • • • • • • • •

SECTION 1

FOOD STORE
FOR THE
WEB OF LIFE

*By Christopher
Dunagan*

*Protecting the Theler wetlands,
bequeathed to the community of Belfair,
is one of the most significant wetlands
projects in the state of Washington.*

At the edge of the Theler Wetlands, a grove of skinny alder trees stood dripping in the cold January rain. The soft sounds of a million raindrops muffled other noises, such as the slosh of footsteps through an inch of standing water.

In the distance, out beyond acres of brown, dormant marsh grass, stood Hood Canal, shrouded in the misty rain. Its stony gray color matched the monochrome sky, making it impossible to distinguish one from the other.

Within these shallows — somewhere between the skinny alders and Lynch Cove — lies the innermost point of Hood Canal, some 63 miles from the entrance.

Hundreds of species, from ants to otters, from wild rose to willows, make their home in and around this place where freshwater flows into saltwater, forming the most productive type of ecosystem known to the planet.

"When I first came down here, all I saw was brown grass," said Jerry Walker, sloshing quickly away from the alder grove. "It didn't mean a thing to me."

Walker, a volunteer for Theler Community Center, wanted to find some use for the apparent wasteland. He sought the help of biologists and wetlands experts.

"As I saw it through the eyes of other people," said Walker, "I gained further insight. It wasn't long before I realized we had a real treasure."

Like other wetlands in Hood Canal, Belfair's wetlands might have been filled and used for other purposes. Not far from town, waterfront housing developments displaced saltwater marshes adjacent to Big Mission Creek and Little Mission Creek, says local historian Irene Davis. Even Belfair State Park was built largely on fill, she said.

Elsewhere in Puget Sound and throughout the nation, wetlands have been filled, drained and polluted as long as man has been on the scene, said Brian Lynn of the state Department of Ecology. People simply believed they had no value in their natural state.

A century ago, the director of the American Health Association proposed eliminating all wetlands everywhere. He claimed they were a source of disease.

Until the 1970s, federal policy encouraged filling wetlands for farming and other economic development.

It's no wonder that more than half the nation's wetlands and more than a third of the state's wetlands no longer exist, according to estimates by the U.S. Fish and Wildlife Service.

Hood Canal may have fared somewhat better, experts say, though nobody has estimated the exact loss.

From his vantage point in the marsh, Walker pointed toward the sky.

"Those are brant geese flying there," he said. "They are making their home in the little slough (on the property)."

Walker learned to observe wildlife from individuals he has brought to the marsh. One day, a professor and a graduate student gave him a tip on bird watching.

"I had seen maybe three birds," said Walker, "and I asked them how many they had seen. One had seen 19 and the other 17. I said, 'How do you do that?' and they said you have to stand still and let the birds come to you."

Theler Wetlands

The North Mason School District has made environmental study in the Theler Wetlands, deeded to the Belfair community in the 1960s by Samuel Theler, an integral part of its curriculum.

Naturalists coming to Lynch Cove have listed nearly 100 species of birds in and around the marsh.

Walker's own time has focused on attracting attention to this place, a place that goes unnoticed by hundreds of people driving through Belfair every day. The few irregular trails are too fragile for unlimited visitors, but Walker intends to change that. Under his leadership, the community has received a series of state grants that may establish the community-owned site as one of the Northwest's premier wetland nature centers.

Plans call for combining the community's 72 acres of wetlands with 63 acres of state land along the Union River. Together, the nature preserve will represent three of the five major wetland types. It's as if Nisqually Delta and Padilla Bay, two of Washington's best known nature preserves, were concentrated in one small spot, says Walker.

In terms of wetland values, Hood Canal is no longer pristine, but it has fared better than many places. Wetlands at the mouth of Seattle's Duwamish River and along Tacoma's Puyallup River are close to 100 percent destroyed, mainly due to industrial development.

Early settlers often diked and drained estuaries to provide flat, fertile ground for farming. The Nisqually River near Olympia lost about 28 percent of its function that way. In Hood Canal, about 33 percent of the Skokomish River wetlands were converted for farming.

Major deltas on the western shore of Hood Canal — the Dosewallips, Quilcene

• • • • • • • • • •

Experts say a salt marsh can produce more biomass (plant material) per acre than a tropical rain forest, twice as much as an upland forest.

and Duckabush rivers, for example — were diked and drained to varying degrees.

The Lynch Cove estuary also was diked about 1890, but the longest dike was not maintained, and saltwater has returned to much of the original estuarine wetland.

According to Walker, ongoing farms provide clues to the colorful history of the region and he's not particularly eager to see the existing dikes removed.

An operating farm next door to the community's wetlands makes a pretty good neighbor, said Walker. Some birds, such as Canada geese, even prefer the open fields to the more natural wetlands.

For visitors, "the farm gives a contrast

> *Estuarine wetlands are the most often impacted by development, but the least often replaced.*
> — Michael Rylko, EPA

Lynch Cove Wetlands to be Preserved

Belfair's soggy back yard, once considered a worthless piece of real estate, is helping the community forge a new identity around an environmental ethic.

"This has become the key wetlands project for the state," says Jerry Walker, with no hint of overstatement. "Virtually all the natural resource agencies have gotten involved."

Walker is director of the Hood Canal Wetlands Project, an environmental education program that promises to turn the Lynch Cove wetlands into a new nature center, complete with a trail system and classroom complex.

But the wetlands have taken on an even greater meaning as they become a symbol for environmental awareness in the community, said Marie Pickel, superintendent of the North Mason School District.

In 1990, the district was invited to become part of an exclusive project known as Schools for the 21st Century. A state grant of $600,000 will help the little district design a new curriculum that will prepare students to live in the next century.

When North Mason first applied for the grant in 1988, proposing some innovative ideas for incorporation into the district curriculum, application was denied. The second time around, the wetlands were brought into the picture. The district proposed incorporating the wetlands into studies at every grade level.

"The environmental issue was the trigger that has gotten us going," said Pickel. "The other things we already knew and were incorporating them bit by bit."

The $600,000 grant gives the district six years to design and test its new approach to education, but nearly every student already has visited the wetlands at least once, said Pickel.

Gary Seelig, a third-grade teacher at Belfair Elementary, says his students focus on the subject of salmon, among other things. Science will teach them about the biology and ecology of fish, he said. "But we're also writing about them in English and learning about them in social studies."

This integration of a topic through all the subjects taught is a key concept in North Mason's new curriculum.

Belfair Elementary is privileged to have a stream running through its schoolyard, a stream that eventually spills out into the wetlands. Seelig hopes one of his future classes can restore a salmon run in the stream.

Meanwhile, North Mason's Sand Hill Elementary School already is raising chum salmon and was to begin releases into the Union River in 1991.

At North Mason High School, students are advanced enough to do basic research on plant and animal life in the wetlands, said biology teacher Karen Lippy.

In addition to producing an inventory of the plants and animals in the marsh — an important contribution to the future nature center — some students are doing "four-season" studies of small areas they picked out themselves, areas that may change dramatically when spring arrives, said Lippy.

Thanks to a grant from the Puget Sound Water Quality Authority, the high school students have been working in the marsh alongside students from The Evergreen State College, who are conto show that's the way we used to do it," he noted.

Ecologists say wetlands are a critical link in the food chain for many fish and wildlife. State officials list more than 175 important wildlife species that use wetlands for primary feeding habitat and more than 140 species that use wetlands for primary breeding habitat.

Waterfowl are dependent on wetlands for nesting, food and cover. Many species of fish spawn in freshwater wetlands. Juvenile marine fish avoid predators by hiding in shallow saltwater marshes.

Experts say a salt marsh can produce more biomass (plant material) per acre than

ducting formal inventories.

"It is really unusual that a school district can own a piece of property so valuable and so close," said Lippy.

North Mason School District has agreed to share the use of its wetlands with school districts in Kitsap and Jefferson counties. About 52,000 students are within a 40-minute bus ride of the wetlands.

Walker, who moved to Hood Canal in his retirement, got involved in the wetlands project in 1988 when an opening was announced for the board of directors at Theler Community Center, which oversees the wetlands. He soon found himself involved in discussions about what to do about the property deeded to the community by Samuel Theler some 20 years before.

In the late 1970s, the board had proposed filling the wetlands to create ballfields, but state and federal officials were beginning to restrict wetland fill. But Walker had a grander vision for what could be done, based on nature centers such as the Nisqually Delta near Olympia. Since 1988, he has worked steadily and without pay to develop that vision into reality. The success that Walker and his fellow volunteers have experienced is nothing short of amazing.

The group commissioned development of a master plan with a grant from the Department of Ecology. The plan calls for a series of trails throughout the wetlands. In more fragile areas, boardwalks and bridges will be used to avoid impacts to the fragile wetland. An education center with exhibit areas, classrooms and offices is also proposed.

The sudden recognition by numerous state officials has Walker, school personnel and many North Mason residents riding a wave of enthusiasm as they realize their wetlands are not wastelands at all, but rather wonderlands of nature.

"There's a feeling of satisfaction, as well as surprise," said Walker, "that so much attention has been drawn to this."

By Christopher Dunagan

Theler Wetland Master Plan

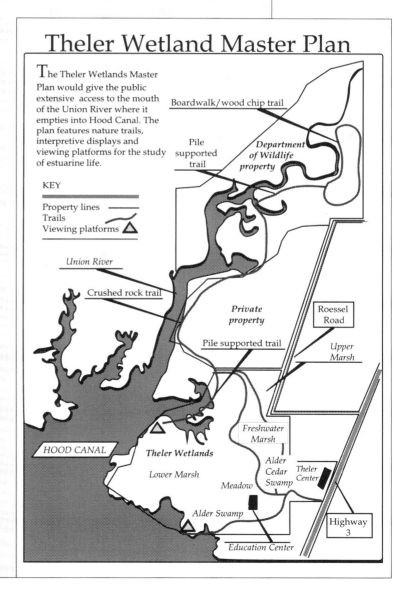

The Theler Wetlands Master Plan would give the public extensive access to the mouth of the Union River where it empties into Hood Canal. The plan features nature trails, interpretive displays and viewing platforms for the study of estuarine life.

KEY

Property lines ———
Trails
Viewing platforms △

Boardwalk/wood chip trail

Pile supported trail

Department of Wildlife property

Union River

Crushed rock trail

Private property

Pile supported trail

Roessel Road

Upper Marsh

Freshwater Marsh

Theler Wetlands

Lower Marsh

Meadow

Alder Cedar Swamp

Theler Center

HOOD CANAL

Alder Swamp

Education Center

Highway 3

a tropical rain forest, twice as much as an upland forest.

More than 150 kinds of plants have been identified at the Theler wetlands next to Belfair. Dozens of insect species feed on the plants and each other. The insects, in turn, become food for larger creatures.

"Some people say the plants in a salt marsh are far more valuable after they are dead," said Lynn of Ecology.

Bacteria and fungi go to work on the dead plants, turning them into material that is consumed by worms, which are eaten by birds and fish, for example. Decaying plants also provide nutrients for plankton, which are consumed by fish, shrimp and oysters.

"If you dig into the mud, you will find worms, shrimp, crabs...," said Lynn. "The value of a salt marsh is buried in the stinky mud flats, and that is one reason nobody ever thought much of them."

In addition to wildlife values, wetlands maintain water quality by trapping sediments and filtering out pollutants. Wide river deltas that have not been channeled for agriculture, as well as many upland marshes, can hold an incredible amount of stormwater, thus reducing the level of flooding.

Wetlands can reduce erosion from waves, wind and river currents. Studies have shown that coastal wetlands, such as those around Hood Canal, absorb the energy of storms and protect upland areas. Property owners who insist on replacing their wetland beaches with concrete or wooden bulkheads tend to transfer this violent energy to neighboring properties.

"The bottom line in ecosystems is that nothing is isolated," says Linda Kunze, a wetlands specialist with the state Department of Natural Resources. "We human beings tend to think of ourselves as separate from the ecosystem. But what we do affects the entire ecosystem — including ourselves.

"It seems to me," she added, "that the people who live around Hood Canal are starting to think that way, and I'm very encouraged and excited by that."

Some wetlands around Hood Canal remain largely untouched. An estuary at Foulweather Bluff near Hansville has been protected by the Nature Conservancy as well as private property owners. Some areas have simply escaped development until recent years when government began to play a stronger role in protecting wetlands.

On the North Shore of Hood Canal, not far from Belfair, the Hood Canal Land Trust is protecting other valuable wetlands under a philosophy of preservation, as opposed to the goal of encouraging visitors.

Walker's footsteps squished over damp leaves as he entered a flat, grassy meadow.

"Some people tell us there was once a farm here," he said. No remnants of any buildings remain, but the site has been proposed for a future interpretive center, including offices and classrooms.

• • • • • • • • • •

SECTION 2

NATURE'S
PURIFICATION
SYSTEM

*By Christopher
Dunagan*

*Freshwater wetlands,
like this beaver pond
near Lilliwaup, perform
important water
purification, stream flow
regulation and wildlife
sanctuary roles.*

S piky, wooden poles poke up
through the shiny ice at Lilliwaup
wetlands as if planted by some
crazed power company employee in
the middle of a pond in the middle
of a marsh, miles from civilization.
This is not the work of a person at all,
but of another creature known for its
engineering ability. A huge mound of sticks
nearby marked the home of *Castor canadensis*,
the beaver.

On this frosty morning in January, no
beavers were in sight. But Jerry Gorsline, a
biologist with Washington Environmental

Council, stood upon their stout dam and explained how beavers, like man, alter their habitat to suit their own needs.

Gorsline's words were accented by a "hack, hack, hack..." sound coming out of the woods. A downy woodpecker's hammering echoed in the hills as the bird searched for bugs in a dead tree.

Time and evolution have made the beaver an integral part of the wetland ecosystem, creating habitat not only for itself but for birds, fish and other wildlife, said Gorsline.

The beaver had dammed this tiny stream, a tributary to Lilliwaup Creek on the eastern side of Hood Canal. Water behind the mud-packed beaver pond had drowned the roots of the alders, but now some birds and animals were finding the trees more valuable dead than alive.

"People say that's terrible, beavers killing trees," said Gorsline. "Beavers have traditionally been regarded as enemies, but that attitude is turning around."

Beaver ponds provide wintering areas for salmon and trout. In fact, more than half of all fish sold commercially in the Puget Sound region rely on wetlands for some portion of their life cycle.

The frozen beaver pond is one of several such ponds around Saddle Mountain, north of Lake Cushman. But it's not just the beavers that make this place valuable.

Gorsline and his associate, Carol Bernthal, have documented dozens of unique plant and animal communities spread out over 6,000 acres around Saddle Mountain. They are doing their best to convince the state to protect the area as a natural preserve.

The area is home to migratory and resident elk herds, numerous waterfowl and several sensitive plant and animal species, they say.

"If you wander off," said Gorsline, "you will find yourself in a vast mosaic of wetlands and forests, thousands of acres."

Gorsline and Bernthal have petitioned the Department of Natural Resources, which manages the land, to avoid harvesting timber in the wetlands and connecting forests and to limit logging activities in other parts of the 6,000-acre area.

"This type of wetland ecosystem is really, really rare," said Bernthal. "There is not much left like this in the Puget Sound lowlands."

Before the arrival of civilization, an unlimited mosaic of wetlands was spread throughout the Hood Canal watershed. Where the topography and soils were right, fresh water formed ponds naturally. In other places beaver dams helped slow the movement of freshwater back to the ocean.

But that was another time, almost forgotten now.

To early trappers, beaver pelts were more valuable than beavers. To early loggers, free-flowing streams were more valuable than beaver dams. To early farmers, dry land was more valuable than wildlife habitat.

What remains of the wetland mosaic today can be found in undeveloped regions, such as the Tahuya-Dewatto river drainages in Southwest Kitsap County. But the land is fragmented by multiple ownerships, and each owner has plans for his own particular piece of land. Freshwater wetlands still exist throughout the Hood Canal area, but it's as if pieces of the puzzle are missing.

That's why it is so important to preserve the largest areas still remaining, such as the proposed Lilliwaup Wetland/ Wildlife Area, argue Gorsline and Bernthal.

Arden Olson, division manager for DNR's Land and Water Conservation Division, said his agency is considering the Washington Environmental Council's nomination, submitted by the two biologists.

Some or all of the area could be taken out of timber status and listed as a "natural resource conservation area," he said. Since the land belongs to the state's school trust fund, the schools would have to be compensated with other land or money, he said. Some funding sources exist, but they are very limited.

"We have a real interest in not impacting the wetlands in that area," said Olson. But how much of the area might be preserved has not yet been determined.

In addition to unusual swamps, bogs and near-pristine lakes, the Lilliwaup area contains a few scientific oddities.

"This area," said Gorsline, standing next to a frozen, shallow pond, "is incredibly dry throughout most of the year."

In fact, he added, the area is so dry that few plants will grow, except Columbia sedge, a prairie-type plant rarely seen on the west side of the Cascade Mountains.

At the water's edge, long strings of lichen hang from a tree like green spider

• • • • • • • • • •

Beaver dams are one of nature's ways of creating a wetland. It is illegal to destroy a beaver dam without a permit from the state Department of Wildlife.

webs mussed by the wind. Mounds of crusty earth push up through the ice, probably as they did a million years ago. To form this wetland/prairie requires just the right soil and groundwater conditions, according to Gorsline.

"A forester who doesn't relate to visual clues such as this would take one look at this place and say it isn't a wetland at all because it is so dry throughout much of the year," he said.

Clarence Martin of Port Orchard, a member of Kitsap Audubon, spent much of last summer in the Lilliwaup wetland area. He and his wife, Dorothy, recorded hundreds of species to assist with the nomination.

"She (Dorothy) recorded everything, plants, insects, animals, birds," said Martin. "We lived in the back of a truck and moved around a lot. A neighbor loaned us a brand new canoe and we explored all over. It's a beautiful area."

Price Lake, five acres in size, is the largest lake in the 6,000-acres of state land. Ducks fly into the lake all winter.

At Melbourne Lake, several golden eyes — saltwater ducks — were swimming in an unfrozen part of the lake.

"They will breed and nest here," explained Gorsline.

At Osborne Lake, something triggered Gorsline's enthusiasm. He pointed first to one plant, a dryland species called kinnikinnick, and then to a sedge at the lake's edge.

"This is the only place I can think of where you have such a range of plant diversity in a 10-foot distance," he said.

Nelsa Buckingham, a leading expert on Olympic Peninsula plantlife, says the Lilliwaup area includes an array of "unusual habitats," including some rare plants, but it is typical of wetlands before the arrival of white man.

The area contains many plants native

Lilliwaup Wetlands

The extensive freshwater wetlands that remain in the Lilliwaup River basin contain unusual bogs and pristine lakes, and is home for animals ranging from wintering ducks to the endangered fisher.

to Western Washington as well as some that have been imported from other continents. Even an untrained eye notices that native plants seem to speak in softer, milder tones, as if an artist had painted the landscape with no dominant elements.

If people are careful — if they wash the bottom of their boats and keep their cars back from the water's edge — this area may avoid an invasion of loud, harsh, obtrusive plants such as scotchbroom, which can out-compete the natives for space, said Gorsline.

"We should think about directing recreational uses so as not to introduce exotic plants," he said.

A dozen years ago, when the Lilliwaup property was owned by Simpson Timber Co., several dilapidated cabins were still standing near Price Lake. But those cabins were removed after the state traded forest lands for the property, said Bernthal.

Still, lots of people come to the area to camp in the summer. In the winter months, the gates are locked to protect elk herds that must conserve their energy to survive the colder weather.

Non-migrating elk are dependent on the area both winter and summer. Migratory elk move to the higher alpine areas in the summer.

"Forage and cover are the primary factors that limit deer and elk populations, and the health of the herd is dependent on the availability and quality of both," said Bernthal.

Other animals known to use the Lilliwaup area are bear, cougar, bobcat and numerous small mammals as well as amphibians and reptiles — the same animals that occupy other unpopulated regions of Hood Canal.

Red legged frogs, beavers and musk-rats are dependent on wetlands during all phases of their life cycle. Rough skinned newt and many aquatic birds spend most of their lives in lakes or ponds but nest in the

In addition to unusual swamps, bogs and near-pristine lakes, the Lilliwaup area contains a few scientific oddities. One is an area so dry that few plants will grow, except Columbia sedge, a prairie-type plant rarely seen on the west side of the Cascade Mountains.

cavities of trees, such as those created by woodpeckers.

Lilliwaup is the last known location on the Olympic Peninsula for the endangered fisher, a little weasel-like creature now believed to be extinct throughout much of its original territory. According to Martin, wildlife experts have talked about reintroducing the fisher to the area by taking animals from British Columbia, where they are more common.

The greatest concern Gorsline and Bernthal have is that the area will be logged off to bring income to the state. The trees are now 60-70 years old, the ideal time for harvest. DNR has invested money in fertilizing and thinning the trees, said Gorsline.

"They (DNR officials) are pretty much driven by the need to produce income for the trust," said Gorsline. "It's just outrageous the lack of protection these wetland areas have."

It appears unlikely that DNR will allow logging to the edge of a lake or wetland, "but if that's all you have, you are leaving out major components of the ecosystem," said Bernthal.

She would prefer protecting the entire area from one ridgetop to the next, but she realizes that isn't realistic. Her proposal to preserve 6,000 acres would permit carefully planned logging uphill from the low-lying wetlands.

But without state money to offset the loss of timber potential, Olson said, the future of the property remains unclear.

• • • • • • • • • •

SECTION 3

TRYING TO
SAVE A
VALUABLE
ECOSYSTEM

By Christopher
Dunagan

*Celia Parrot keeps watch over a wetland
area owned by the Hood Canal Land
Trust near Lynch Cove.*

T he turnaround in governmental attitude toward wetlands is truly amazing, says Bob Wiltermood, a private wetlands consultant and conservation chairman for Kitsap Audubon.

Folks like Wiltermood have always understood the importance of wetlands, but it has only been recently that government — federal, state and local — has begun to insist that property owners preserve the wet portions of their land.

Today, sensitive developers hire Wiltermood and other biologists to prevent destruction of fragile wetlands. At the same time, state and local officials are growing ever more vigilant in their role of protecting natural resources.

"Two years ago," said Wiltermood, "we were slamming the county for what was happening to the wetlands in Silverdale. Now, I think the county is doing a damn good job — and without even a wetlands ordinance."

Wiltermood offered his opinion during an unofficial visit to one of Kitsap County's most prized wetlands, the Foulweather Bluff Wildlife Preserve near Hansville. He was joined at the saltwater estuary by Ron Fox, a habitat biologist for the state Department of Wildlife.

"This is a fantastic place," said Wiltermood, looking through his binoculars at a widgeon, one of many types of ducks found at the wetland.

The estuary has been preserved, thanks

In terms of wetland values, Hood Canal is no longer pristine, but it has fared better than many places. About 33 percent of the Skokomish River wetlands were converted for farming.

to efforts of the Nature Conservancy and private property owners in the area.

Fox explained that hundreds of small wetlands have been destroyed because landowners were able to convince government officials that their little wetland was unimportant in the overall scheme of things.

" 'Small, isolated wetlands.' You hear that term over and over," said Fox. "Well, they may be small and isolated, but that creates diversity of habitat. In ecology, everything is connected."

"You can even ask," injected Wiltermood, "whether there is such a thing as an isolated wetland."

Wetlands once were strung like pearls through the creeks, streams and rivers of Hood Canal. Now, the strings are broken and fragmented by development. But they remain important islands of habitat — food and shelter for a large number of species, said Wiltermood.

The losses make the remaining wetlands even more valuable because the houses, roads and shopping centers being developed cause more and faster runoff, says Joy Michaud in her book "At Home with Wetlands."

With development, she said, "we not only create the need for more of the environmental functions of wetlands, we also destroy or damage the resources that provide those functions."

In addition to wildlife habitat, wetlands offer water filtration and purification, flood protection, shoreline stabilization and groundwater recharge.

But state wetlands specialist Brian Lynn warns that "not all wetlands perform all those functions equally well. Some may be great for flood storage without providing a lot of habitat. It's important to look at each one individually."

Just 20 years ago, the Department of Agriculture encouraged farmers to fill their wetlands and grow crops to feed the world. Today, as a result of the state's new Growth Management Act, many of Washington's counties are rapidly coming to grips with their role in protecting natural resources.

Washington's fastest growing counties are now required to identify their resources and approve protection standards, including protections for wetlands.

Of the three Hood Canal counties — Kitsap, Mason and Jefferson — Mason County could have opted out of the state's program. But the county commissioners

actively entered the struggle to manage growth, especially in the North Mason area where homes are rapidly going up near Hood Canal.

Mason County, which had practically no controls on development in 1989, has implemented a grading ordinance, strengthened shoreline regulations and tackled long-range planning, said Erik Fairchild, the county's planning coordinator.

"The North Mason Water Quality Protection Plan has been adopted as part of the comprehensive plan," he noted, adding that wetlands still don't have the protection they deserve. But the county is attempting to deal with the problem through the new growth management effort.

None of the three Hood Canal counties had a wetlands ordinance in 1991, such as one proposed by the state Department of Ecology. The model ordinance defines categories of wetlands and establishes non-development buffer zones, depending on local conditions. When impacts to wetlands cannot be avoided, the ordinance provides for mitigation, such as creating or enhancing an area larger than the wetlands being damaged. All three counties have received state funding to develop their own wetlands ordinance along similar lines.

"The problem we have," said Craig Ward, wetlands specialist for Jefferson County, "is that we have no way of defining whether something is a wetland. We have no consistent procedure for dealing with them."

Jefferson officials review maps developed by the Fish and Wildlife Service from aerial photos, said Ward. They try to identify and protect wetlands on a case-by-case basis, but the maps are not always accurate. "We acknowledge that what we have is inadequate," he said, adding that the county should have a stronger program ready before long.

Kitsap County follows a similar process, but may have more staff to examine proposed development sites.

"I think Kitsap County has been real aggressive on wetlands over the last couple of years," said Larry Ward, a Poulsbo homebuilder who works on growth issues for the Building Industry Association of Washington. "I think they have been fairly effective. They have thwarted a number of developments that would have degraded wetlands."

Developers want predictable regulations but also must face the fact that every new rule puts the price of a new home out of reach for a few more people, said Ward, who is not related to Craig Ward.

"Wetlands are absolutely vital to Hood Canal," he said. "I want to keep it as pristine as it was when I got here, and I will stand with everyone else when the canal is threatened."

A few developers intentionally destroy wetlands to avoid tangling with the regulations, he acknowledged, "and I think that government can and should come down hard against them."

But that's easier said than done.

It's up to counties to enforce Gov. Booth Gardner's policy calling for "no net loss of wetlands," but there are only general laws not specifically designed to protect the function of wetlands.

The federal Clean Water Act and state Shorelines Management Act, for example, have numerous exemptions for small, inland wetlands. Only about 10 percent of the 2,000 acres of wetlands lost every year in Washington state are subject to federal regulations, according to Michael Rylko of the Environmental Protection Agency.

And state shoreline rules don't apply to most smaller streams. Clear Creek, which is associated with wetlands in Silverdale's urban area, is too small to fall under shorelines jurisdiction, said Renee Beam, Kitsap County's shorelines manager. A shorelines permit is required for developments within

Wetlands of Hood Canal

Unspoiled Wetlands Are A Key Component In The Survival Of Hood Canal

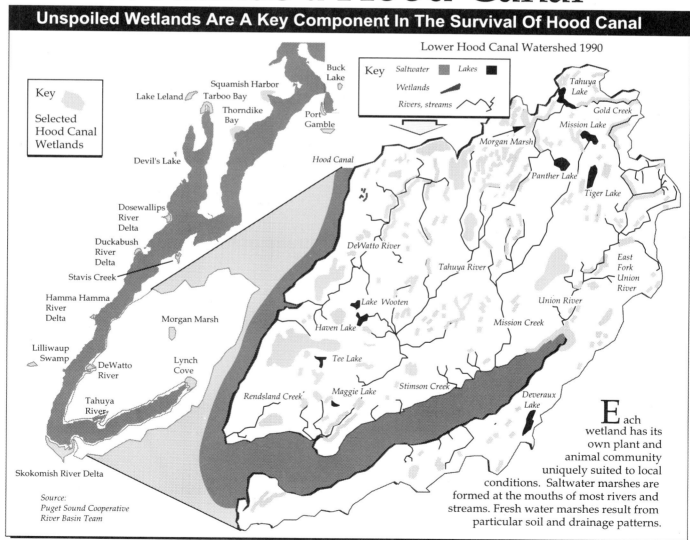

Key

Selected Hood Canal Wetlands

Lower Hood Canal Watershed 1990

Key — Saltwater — Lakes — Wetlands — Rivers, streams

Buck Lake
Squamish Harbor
Lake Leland — Tarboo Bay
Thorndike Bay
Port Gamble
Devil's Lake
Hood Canal
Tahuya Lake
Gold Creek
Mission Lake
Morgan Marsh
Panther Lake
Tiger Lake
Dosewallips River Delta
Duckabush River Delta
Stavis Creek
DeWatto River
Tahuya River
East Fork Union River
Hamma Hamma River Delta
Morgan Marsh
Lake Wooten
Union River
Haven Lake
Mission Creek
Lilliwaup Swamp
DeWatto River
Lynch Cove
Tee Lake
Tahuya River
Rendsland Creek
Maggie Lake
Stimson Creek
Deveraux Lake
Skokomish River Delta

Source:
Puget Sound Cooperative River Basin Team

Each wetland has its own plant and animal community uniquely suited to local conditions. Saltwater marshes are formed at the mouths of most rivers and streams. Fresh water marshes result from particular soil and drainage patterns.

250 feet of Hood Canal's major rivers, but not generally the creeks and streams, she said.

State fisheries and wildlife experts can help the counties identify wetlands that weren't noticed before, but their role is strictly to protect fish.

"We don't really stop anything," said Fox, who is in charge of the permits for the Wildlife Department. "We just try to mitigate damage and prevent loss of fish habitat."

So it falls to the counties to impose restrictions on specific developments, something not always easy to do, despite the no-net-loss mandate.

The situation should become more predictable when the counties classify their most important wetlands and adopt new protection rules, said Larry Ward.

The state also recognizes the importance of purchasing wetlands. Money has been approved for purchasing and preserving valuable wetlands, and various tax incentives are available for individuals willing to protect privately owned wetlands.

"One of the worst things we face," said Fox, "is when you're called out to a site and the place is stripped bare. Then someone says, 'Oh, we have a wetlands?' That is most depressing."

• • • • • • • • • • •

P<small>ART</small>

III

U<small>SING THE</small>
R<small>ESOURCE</small>

Huge logs from the shores of Hood Canal once kept workers scrambling at the Pope & Talbot sawmill at Port Gamble.

Majestic evergreens, towering 250 feet into the sky, must have provided an awe-inspiring greeting to early explorers who entered Hood Canal in their sailing ships. Some men dared to dream of houses and villages, but years would pass before the hand of civilization would disfigure the natural wonderland. Something captured Capt. George Vancouver's imagination in May of 1792 as he sailed past rugged, snow-capped peaks and approached the long, narrow channel he named Hood's Canal.

The English explorer had been sent here to solidify his country's claim on the lonely wilderness, known to contain vast riches in furs, timber and marine life. Spanish explorers had sailed inland, but not this far. Only a very young nation — the United States — maintained a defendable claim to the region.

After sailing for more than a year — with stops in Tahiti and Hawaii —

SECTION 1

RISING FROM
TOPPLED
TREES

*By Christopher
Dunagan*

Vancouver was not disappointed with the sights and sounds of this untamed land. Yet on the morning of May 12, 1792, the world seemed to hold its breath as Vancouver's ship followed the western shore of Hood Canal.

"Animated nature," Vancouver wrote, "seemed nearly exhausted, and her awful silence was only now and then interrupted by the croaking of a raven, the breathing of a seal or the scream of an eagle."

Vancouver sailed southward into Hood Canal and met with a friendly band of Indians near the Skokomish River, which he described as "the finest stream of fresh water we had yet seen."

"Early on Sunday morning, May 13, 1792, we again embarked," Vancouver wrote, "directing our route down the inlet, which, after the Right Honorable Lord Hood, I called Hood's Channel."

There is some confusion about the name, variously Hood's "channel" and "canal." As Edmond S. Meany explains in his book *Vancouver's Discovery of Puget Sound*, "It is a curious fact that Vancouver named many places 'channels' in his journal, but wrote them down as 'canal' on his excellent charts. This was the case with Hood's Canal."

The name, formalized by the U.S. government, will forever remain linked to one Samuel Hood, an admiral in the British Navy who became famous for his victories against the United States during the Revolutionary War.

Fifty years after Vancouver named Hood Canal, the United States had strengthened its claim to the area. Still, only a handful of white settlers could be counted. Trappers and traders in sparse numbers may have visited the shores of the canal, yet it remained largely the domain of Indians.

To encourage settlement, the United States in 1844 began offering homesteads of up to 640 acres. Homesteading had barely begun by 1848, when gold was discovered in California.

Gold mines would need heavy timbers, and homes would need lumber. Ships would be needed to maintain the flow of commerce. Gold dust would power the Northwest economy for years.

Some folks came to Hood Canal country just for the timber, homesteading long enough to claim the giant trees, noted Eva Luella Buchanan in her *Economic History of Kitsap County*. "The timber was so close to the water's edge that nearly anyone with a team of oxen could get out a boom of logs in a short time."

Skippers would pay 8 cents a lineal foot for the huge logs, delivered alongside their vessels. They would sell them to mills in San Francisco for $1 a foot, said Mrs. Buchanan.

It didn't take long for wealthy lumbermen to realize the potential of sawmills closer to the woods. Andrew Jackson Pope and Frederic Talbot were sons of timber and shipbuilding families. Together with Capt. J.P. Keller and shipbuilder Charles Foster, they started Puget Mill Company at Port Gamble on Hood Canal, the heart of Indian country.

In September 1853, the Port Gamble mill — one of the first steam-powered mills in Washington territory — came on line.

Three years later, Marshall Blinn and William J. Adams financed a new mill at Seabeck, a picturesque town on Hood Canal that outgrew Seattle for a time.

By 1857, the Port Gamble mill was the greatest lumber manufacturing plant on Puget Sound, and two or three schooners might be seen in port at one time, their lumber bound for San Francisco and the Orient.

That same year, when Kitsap first became a county, four major sawmills were operating in the area. Settlements were springing up, and Kitsap County had the highest assessed valuation of any county in the territory.

In addition to mills at Port Gamble and Seabeck, there were two on Bainbridge Island. The world seemed hungry for timber, and the industry found new and faster ways of cutting trees and making lumber.

A new "circular mill," installed at Port Gamble in 1858, was the biggest in the West. It could handle logs 9 feet thick and turn out planks up to 60 feet long.

Big axes, used by early loggers, gave way to felling saws, first used in the redwood forests of California. Oxen gave way to steam donkeys and railroads.

There seemed to be no end to the demand for lumber. Dozens of logging camps in the Hood Canal area sprang up to supply the big mills, which grew and added shipbuilding operations. Small, independent mill owners also carved out a niche among the trees.

"The timber was so close to the water's edge that nearly anyone with a team of oxen could get out a boom of logs in a short time."
—Eva Luella Buchanan, *Economic History of Kitsap County.*

Timber was king, and every community had ties to the forests, while agriculture and fishing helped feed the hungry loggers and maintain the local economy.

Seabeck and Port Gamble grew into bustling mill towns. In 1876, Seabeck, population 400, had a store, two hotels and four saloons. One newspaper account called it the "liveliest" place of its size on Puget Sound.

Mill towns were the most obvious stops for early steamships carrying passengers, supplies and mail. With few roads, the growing "mosquito fleet" of boats became the principal link between the communities of Port Gamble, Bangor, Seabeck, Brinnon, Quilcene, Duckabush, Nellita, Holly, Dewatto, Hoodsport, Potlatch and Union City.

"Union City," wrote Murray Morgan in *The Last Wilderness*, was the "Venice of the Pacific, on the narrow stretch of land connecting the Olympic and Kitsap peninsulas..."

The town, which began as a trading post on the south shore of Hood Canal in 1857, was platted in 1890 amid a flourish of land sales. Rumors were wild that the town would become a crossroads of several railroads. For a time, land speculators were paying the whopping price of $1,000 for a single building lot.

Meanwhile, Quilcene, a single homestead in 1860, was even more blessed. Port Townsend was booming with international trade, and local entrepreneurs were convinced that the world would beat a path to their door if only they could obtain a rail connection to Portland, Ore.

With a local donation of $100,000, the Oregon Improvement Company (a subsidiary of Union Pacific) agreed to begin the long track. Some 1,500 workers laid the rails from Port Townsend to Quilcene, but that's as far as they got.

The country's economic panic of 1893 dashed the hopes of Quilcene and other towns along the western shore of Hood Canal. The folks of Union City quickly dropped the "City."

Down toward the very tip of Hood Canal, the town of Clifton was growing. One of the early roads in Kitsap County linked Seabeck to the head of Hood Canal along Lynch Cove.

Later, Clifton would become a crossroads when a new road to Sidney (now Port Orchard) was built. The route is still referred to as the Old Clifton Road. In 1925, the name "Clifton" was changed to "Belfair." Belfair has had but moderate growth over the years, but today it stands as one of the fastest growing communities around Hood Canal.

Demand for Northwest lumber continued to increase as the 20th century drew to a close, and Washington's mills were expanding. The billion board feet of production in 1888 had doubled to 2 billion by 1895 and tripled to 3 billion by 1902. By 1905, with 3.5 billion board feet a year coming from its mills, Washington produced more lumber than any other state in the nation.

Unlike many sawmill companies, however, the owners of the Port Gamble mill bought their own land and saved it for the future. While others exhausted their timber supplies, the Puget Mill bought raw logs from other people's land. Eventually, the dwindling supply forced Pope and Talbot to cut its own magnificent trees around Hood Canal.

Today, Pope Resources, a spinoff of the company, remains the largest private timberland owner in Kitsap County and has found success in developing lands for housing.

Conservationists had been arguing about protecting a portion of the ancient Olympic Peninsula forests ever since naturalist John Muir first visited the area in 1889.

President Grover Cleveland, as one of

Seabeck

There's not much left today, beyond a plaque, to indicate that the tiny community of Seabeck once was home to a bustling lumber mill, one of the first in the Puget Sound region.

• • • • • • • • • •

Seabeck and Port Gamble grew into bustling mill towns. In 1867, Seabeck, population 400, had a store, two hotels and four saloons. One newspaper account called it the "liveliest" place of its size on Puget Sound.

his last official acts, created the 2.2-million-acre Olympic Forest Reserve in 1897. But that only intensified the debate. U.S. presidents would push and pull public acreage in and out of protected status throughout this entire century. The question is always the same: how much acreage should be saved for "natural values" and how much acreage should be used for "human values."

On June 29, 1938, President Franklin Roosevelt signed a bill setting aside Olympic National Park for future generations.

Today, as a century ago, Hood Canal receives much of its water from high in the Olympic Mountains, now protected for eternity. Streams flow through wilderness areas, logged-off lands and even places where timber refuses to grow. They flow through National Forest lands that timber companies have come to depend on for raw materials. But those forest lands are now being set aside to protect the northern spotted owl, a species that depends on healthy old-growth ecosystems for its survival.

And the tug of war between use of the resource and preservation continues; the clash of values, whether trees are worth more standing or cut, remains unresolved.

"As long as the great trees remain in the park," proclaims Murray Morgan, "there will be men willing to cut them down, saw them up and ship them away to all parts of the country. And there will be others — I suspect a majority — who would rather come to see them than have them sent."

• • • • • • • • •

Unlike many sawmill companies at the turn of the century, Pope & Talbot bought their own land and saved it for the future. Today, Pope Resources, a spinoff of the company, remains the largest private timberland owner in Kitsap County.

A Company Town Grows Around a Sawmill

More than a century ago, when the S'Klallams plied the waters of Hood Canal in canoes and dense forests hugged its shores, great lumbermen staked their claim at a spot called Teekalet. Mills sprouted along the canal like mushrooms but none quite so fine as the Puget Mill Company, founded in the mid-1800s by Andrew Pope and Frederic Talbot in the deep-water port later known as Port Gamble.

Over the years hundreds of workers flocked to the fledgling community, challenged by Douglas firs so mighty they dwarfed husky lumberjacks eager to earn a living.

Among them was the father of Ida Faler and Chuck Hirschi of Poulsbo, who came from Canada searching for work to feed his family.

He tried Skid Road in Seattle, but was told his best bet was the mill at Port Gamble.

"He didn't know where Port Gamble was," Hirschi said, "but he boarded a little boat and went there. While he was gone, our house burned and we lost everything. He had to work awhile before he had enough money to send for us."

It was 1917 when Ida, 7, and Chuck, 9, stepped off the boat in Port Gamble with their mother, four siblings and all their worldly possessions. Little did they realize this tiny community would provide the framework for their adult lives.

Pope & Talbot, perhaps a bit homesick for their native East Machias, Maine, built a mill town that reflected New England tastes and rented the homes to workers and their families.

"We paid $15 a month for the house in those days, including the electricity for lights," Hirschi said.

"We loved it," Faler said. "My mother thought it was wonderful. It wasn't too modern, but it was more modern than what we had before."

The family settled in a house

behind the community's steepled church. They lived 42 years in the same house, which still stands today.

Photos of the town's early years show muddy streets, wooden sidewalks and bleak, severe houses. There were vegetable gardens in abundance as thrifty housewives raised produce for their tables, augmenting the groceries purchased at the company store.

But there wasn't much time for flower gardens or fancy landscaping, a hallmark of the carefully restored town today. The pigs running loose in the community probably would have rooted in the flowerbeds.

"Well, it was tough at first, not speaking English, you know," Hirschi said, "but we got along and made friends. It became our home." Their first language had been Swiss.

There were probably 600 people living in the town during those years, Hirschi said, all of them working for the mill. Workers poured into the logging camps, and there were times when the whiskey got the better of them. But, for the most part, Port Gamble was a family town.

"I went to work at the mill when I was 16 because we needed money," Hirschi said. "Two years later my father died of cancer and I helped support the family. I worked for 35 cents an hour, 10-hour days, sometimes even longer. Sometimes those days stretched to 12 hours. But I was glad to have the work. I started by tying lumber bundles then kept changing jobs. Most of my life I graded lumber."

The social life was simple, but busy.

"The Thompsons ran the little theater there, and there were matinees for those who worked the night shift," Faler said. "There were dances and an outdoor pavilion outside the post office. At Christmas there was a big party and every child in town received a present from the mill owners."

"People knew everyone in town, and there was a lot of visiting," Hirschi said.

In those days travel was difficult. Seattle was some distance by boat, and Poulsbo, which was the nearest thing to a big city, was too far if you didn't have a car.

Hirschi, now 83, worked for the mill 50 years before retiring in 1973, the only Pope & Talbot employee to work 50 years in the same location. Brother Fred also spent 50 years with the company, although he relocated to the Oak Ridge, Ore., plant.

Faler retired in 1971 after 42 years. "It was a wonderful place to work," she recalled. "I have never regretted it."

Many of the homes now are gone. The once-proud Puget Hotel fell victim to the Columbus Day storm of 1962, and the old schoolhouse was demolished after David Wolfle School was built. The hospital, where generations of Port Gamble babies were born, also is a memory.

But Port Gamble remains a company town. The 137-year-old sawmill, the oldest continuously operating one in North America, has undergone many renovations. It continues to operate, but has been buffeted by national recession and the uncertainties caused by the spotted owl.

The once-bleak buildings have been lovingly restored by the descendants of the original founders, and when the 4 o'clock whistle blows, many workers are just a few steps away from home. The company store (next to the office) recently has been updated, but folks still stop by for bread and milk between trips to Poulsbo, now just minutes away by car.

Down the road a piece, near the picturesque church, sits the Thompson house, the oldest continuously occupied home in the state of Washington. James Thompson came to Port Gamble on the schooner Towana and his descendants lived in the house more than 99 years. And on the hill, carefully tended and enclosed with a fence, is the quiet graveyard where generations of families are buried.

These were the men and women who toiled in the mills and helped build a lumber empire that left an indelible mark on Hood Canal.

By JoAnne Marez

• • • • • • • • • •

In 1857 the Port Gamble mill was the greatest lumber manufacturing plant on Puget Sound, and two or three schooners might be seen in port at one time, their lumber bound for San Francisco and ports in the Orient.

• • • • • • • • • •

SECTION 2

A LOG'S LONG JOURNEY

By Christopher Dunagan

Logger Chuck Stewart fells a 75-year-old tree that was to become part of log lot CU-25.

Sept. 24, 1990: Deep in the woods near the tip of the Toandos Peninsula, a logging crew has been felling timber since daybreak. Damp winds have erased the warm days of summer in forested lands east of Dabob Bay. Although clouds threaten to turn the dry soil to mud, only a few drops have fallen so far this day.

10:11 a.m.: Chuck Stewart Jr. , a skilled timber cutter, sizes up one of the larger Douglas firs on this 45-acre tract of state timberland. Observing more limbs on one side of the trunk, Stewart quickly calculates the face cut he'll need to make the tree fall cleanly to the ground.

He revs up his chain saw, a 36-inch Husqvarna, and guides it carefully toward the tree. The surging teeth slash through bark and into the sapwood of this 75-year-old tree.

Stewart, who lives near Hadlock, and

hundreds of others who work the woods around Hood Canal are members of an ancient and proud profession. It was their predecessors who opened Hood Canal to civilization even before the first mill was built at Port Gamble in 1853.

Today's powerful saws complete the work faster and with fewer workers than ever before. As they did 100 years ago, logging tools help transform trees into houses, bridges, ships, docks — even the book you're reading.

Despite improvements in safety, logging remains the most dangerous job in the state, according to the Department of Labor and Industries. More than a few loggers have been surprised by snapping tree trunks, falling limbs and whipping saplings. Next to a towering fir tree, a human being looks fragile.

The danger, says Stewart, is part of the excitement: "You have to stay on your toes."

10:12 a.m.: Stewart completes the first of two cuts that will form a notch. The notch is critical in aiming the tree. A miscalculation could leave the tree hung up in others or broken, with little value.

The logger begins his second cut below the first, angling the blade upwards. After the notch falls out, Stewart visualizes how the tree will fall, then uses his saw to slice a little more wood from one edge of the notch.

The saw still roaring, Stewart begins his "back cut." Sawdust flies, and seconds later the wood begins to crackle loudly. The massive tree leans, as if on a hinge. It falls, faster and faster. Then, with a thundering crunch, the tree crushes limbs and under-brush as it strikes the ground, dead on target.

Stewart quickly shears the limbs from the tree. Knowing the requirements of Pope & Talbot, he uses a steel tape measure to mark the fallen tree and bucks it into logs. One 36-foot log is 40 inches across at one end — the largest diameter that can go through the mill.

11:03 a.m.: Erick "Pete" Peterson steers his John Deere skidder toward the hefty log cut by Stewart. The machine grabs the log and hoists one end off the ground. With a loud roar, the skidder rushes off, dragging the log uphill and leaving a cloud of dust.

In days gone by, the primary concern was to cut the logs and get them out of the woods as cheaply as possible. Teams of horses were used. Then came logging

railroads. When possible, rivers were used to move logs to open water.

It didn't much matter whether streams were filled with dirt, smothering salmon spawning areas, or if baby birds were left to die on the bare ground.

Personal accounts of those days are filled with the romantic side of logging life — and death. Discussions about "the environment" were left for future years.

Today, more care is required to protect the natural elements, even on private land. A growing awareness of natural systems has brought changes in logging practices and land management — and the change is far from over.

11:20 a.m.: Gary Hintz, 31, the owner of this logging company, pushes and pulls at controls that maneuver the powerful loader under him. The machine picks up logs brought to the landing by skidders, then spins around, loading the trimmed trees onto logging trucks.

Individual logs sometimes sit at the landing for hours or even days, but today the automatic de-limber, a relatively new machine that strips the limbs from smaller logs, is out of service. The log that Stewart cut and bucked earlier is picked up right away.

Hintz, a Seabeck resident, learned the logging business from his father, Carl. Starting at age 15, Gary worked every job in the woods before taking over the company seven years ago.

His son Brandon, 7, sometimes sits at the controls, moving the heavy machine as Hintz watches closely. Brandon wants to be a logger, too, said Hintz.

"I tell him 'no, no — think banker, football player, anything ...' But moments later, while talking about this piece of state land and how it will be replanted with seedlings, Hintz comments, "By the time Brandon grows up, he will thin this."

11:29 a.m.: Truck driver Bif Corey of Poulsbo keeps his eye on the truck's weight scale (just inside the driver's door) as the logs are loaded. When the digital numbers tick off 80,100 pounds, he calls for Hintz to stop loading.

The load is 26 $^3/_4$ tons of raw timber. Corey grabs a hammer and climbs within reach of the logs. He strikes the butt end of each one, leaving the brand "CU-25." Now, anyone can figure out where these logs came from.

• • • • • • • • • •

With modern technology, it takes a little less than five minutes to fell a 75-year-old Douglas fir with a trunk 40 inches across.

It takes one 100-foot-tall tree to provide the wood and paper products used annually by the average American.

Corey throws one end of a steel cable (a "wrapper") over the pile of logs and brings it up tight. For a load this size, state law requires three wrappers.

11:32 a.m.: Corey shifts his truck into gear and pulls out of the landing area. He heads downhill toward Port Ludlow, 15 miles away.

12:14 p.m.: The truck pulls up next to a long wooden dock at the scaling station in Port Ludlow. Scaler Tom Kegley, 58, of Poulsbo measures the width of each log and figures the length from marks on the dock. He keeps track of the volume of timber with a handheld computer. Then he marks the bundle with a yellow tag bearing the number 9395.

12:23 p.m.: The truck arrives at Pope & Talbot's log dump at Port Ludlow, where the load will become part of a log raft destined for Port Gamble. Mel Morgenson, 39, and Don Tuson, 62, are in charge here. The two replace the cable wrappers with steel "bands," designed to hold the logs together throughout their voyage. Five minutes later, a huge "log stacker" — larger than the logging truck itself — grabs the entire bundle of logs off the truck and heads toward the water. At the controls is Morgenson, who has worked for Pope & Talbot 15 years.

This is a heavy load, weighing 40 percent more than most. At water's edge, Morgenson drops the bundle into the water. Unexpectedly, the bands snap, probably due to the weight and angle of fall. These logs will have to float free in the log raft, formed by 60 truckloads of timber transported out of the woods.

Oct. 4, about 3 p.m.: The log Stewart cut in the woods more than a week earlier is still waiting to be towed to the Pope & Talbot sawmill. Resident manager Jerry Clark stands before his mill crew in Port Gamble. He has some particularly bad news. The mill will shut down for 30 days.

Toandos Peninsula

With national forest land being restricted to logging more and more, timber cutters are being forced to depend on second growth trees on state and private lands in the Hood Canal watershed.

The housing market in Southern California — where most of Pope & Talbot's "green" (not kiln-dried) lumber is sold — won't support the mill's output of 13 million board feet of lumber each month.

Forty-eight employees will remain in various positions at the mill, while 125 workers will have to do without a paycheck for at least a month. Saw motors are switched off, one by one.

Oct. 10, 2 p.m.: No logs have moved from Port Ludlow. The mill at Port Gamble stands quiet except for a low hum coming from a sawdust blower at the planing building. There, 15 members of the planing crew are still on the job, smoothing the rough boards produced before the mill closed down. Usually 25 people work in that building.

Plant manager Brad Fountain stands near the "head rig," looking out upon the water. In normal times, he would see workers push floating logs toward the sawmill. And, normally, his voice couldn't be heard above the noise of that first big saw.

"It's an eerie silence, almost a silence of suffering," says Fountain. "This is one of the finest mills on the West Coast and to see it sitting idle is pretty devastating."

The lumber industry is familiar with economic cycles tied to housing construction, interest rates and the national economy. This mill was last shut down during the recession of 1982. But there's a different feeling this time. People are thinking about issues such as the northern spotted owl, which has been declared threatened under the Endangered Species Act. A shortage of timber on federal lands, competition from overseas markets and increasing environmental regulations could put a severe squeeze on mills like Pope & Talbot.

"We can't expect to have the kind of industry we've had for the past decade," says Fountain.

Oct. 25, 2:45 p.m.: Bruce Bell, a 39-year-old saw filer, removes a load of clothes from the washing machine at his home in Port Gamble. Bell has been out of work since the mill shut down three weeks ago.

Normally, he'd be at the mill, operating equipment that sharpens the huge band saws, which now lie quietly on the wooden floor of the filing room.

Since he has been out of work, Bell has repaired his pickup truck and looked for other jobs. He doesn't see much future in his career.

"I enjoy it, but I don't see how it will keep going," he explained.

Congress recently approved, and the president signed, a bill that would limit exports of raw logs from state lands. The action was designed to preserve Northwest sawmill jobs as the timber supply grows tighter.

Competition may drive mills out of business, but Clark hopes the waterfront location of the Pope & Talbot mill will provide a competitive edge in transportation costs.

Oct. 29, 7:03 a.m.: David Olson reaches

* * * * * * * * * *

The average new single-family home uses about 13,000 board feet of softwood lumber and 9,500 square feet of wood panels.

Pope Resources a Major Canal Player

The largest owner of private timberland around Hood Canal didn't exist five years ago.

Pope Resources in Poulsbo was created in December of 1985 to own and manage the extensive land holdings of Pope & Talbot in western Puget Sound. It bought the 80,000-plus acres under Pope & Talbot's control, most of it in the Hood Canal watershed.

Management of the 65,000 acres of timberland hasn't much changed from when Pope & Talbot owned them, says George Folquet, Pope Resources president. Pope Resources has stepped up the pace of development of properties close enough to major population areas to become housing.

It has sold all but one small portion of the Bucklin Hill ridgetop overlooking Silverdale. It's winning awards for its New Port Ludlow development in Jefferson County, and hoping to create a major housing development around a new golf course it plans to build near Kingston.

The logging of acreage near Gig Harbor is being done selectively, leaving those trees that will add value to the land as housing. And a land trade with Bremerton may enable Pope Resources to create the largest housing development in the city's history in the Sinclair Heights area.

But little of the development has been in the Hood Canal basin. Pope Resources acreage along Paradise Bay Road from the Hood Canal Floating Bridge north has been sold in large lots.

And the company is trying to satisfy state and county requirements to convert 185 acres near Seabeck (a relatively small parcel by Pope Resources standards) to housing.

In 1985, the board of directors of Pope & Talbot was nervous about corporate raiders. So the company reorganized, creating a limited partnership it called Pope Resources. In addition to making a hostile takeover more difficult, said Folquet, it enabled the company to claim full value of its land holdings. And it avoided the double taxation that corporations and their stockholders then faced — once when the corporation makes the profit, and again when it distributes dividends.

Pope Resources has become a profitable operation, but the realignment had its costs, said Folquet. Because Pope Resources bought the land from Pope & Talbot, it paid a substantial real estate transactions tax.

"It was always presumed that a mill needed its own land and timber base," Folquet said. "But I think it's quite the contrary, the mill (at Port Gamble) has operated very satisfactorily."

Sawmill manger Jerry Clark said of the reorganization, "We had to become a lot smarter about how we purchased logs on the open market. From that standpoint, it has been a difficult transition, but I think we have the people here who are capable of doing the job."

By Travis Baker

over the stern of tugboat P&T Pioneer and shackles the boat to 11.2 million pounds of floating cellulose — an estimated 8,400 individual Douglas fir logs.

Among these logs is broken bundle 9395, which contains the tree cut by Stewart more than a month earlier.

At the wheel of the 60-foot Pioneer stands Doug Vondersmith, 57, an employee of Pope & Talbot for 22 years. The boat edges forward, playing out 1,000 feet of tow cable. That's enough distance to reduce drag from the wash of the tug's propeller.

The boat emits a low, grumbling noise. The cable grows taut. The giant wooden rectangle begins to move.

Today's tow is four complete log rafts, 840 feet long and 140 feet wide. That's nearly the length of three football fields, though not quite the width of one.

11:55 a.m.: The log tow passes the main dock at the Port Gamble mill and proceeds toward the storage area beyond the mill.

Here it will stay until the saws are spinning again.

Nov. 1: Just three weeks before Thanksgiving, mill manager Jerry Clark has good news and bad news for his crews. The mill will reopen Nov. 12, but with one shift instead of two. Sixty-eight hourly employees will not come back. In addition, 15 supervisors will be removed from the payroll.

"I thought I had the toughest job of my life when I faced those guys a month ago," said Clark. "Now I have to do it over again, and there's some permanency this time."

A feeling of uncertainty has seeped into the souls of the men and women who depend on trees for a living.

Times are changing. Nobody wants the Hood Canal region to stop growing trees, but the issue is complicated. The region is no longer dominated by a single-minded industry. In Hood Canal, the days of endless timber are coming to an end.

Steep grades in the watershed make clearcutting the most economical method for commercial timber harvesting.

ike Handly nudges the control knob gently with his right hand and 500 board feet of prime Douglas fir nestles into place on the back of the logging truck below him. Suddenly the big diesel engine powering his loader begins to chortle and cough, then chugs to a halt.

Cussing a blue streak, Handly swings out of the big loader.

"Ran out of (expletive deleted) fuel," he yells to the truck driver, asking him to pull his rig forward. Then Handly sprints up the road to a battered pickup carrying a tank of diesel fuel. Another vehicle is blocking the road. Handly swears some more and sprints

off to find the driver and his keys.

"This is the way logging is," he yells over his shoulder. "It's a full-bore-type occupation!"

The break in routine is rare for Handly and his crew. They get no breaks. No lunch break, no potty break, no coffee break. From dawn to dusk, they don't stop unless something forces them.

Handly has been a logger all of his life. So has his dad, Pat Handly, who also lives in Quilcene.

"I've been doing this since I was big enough to go out and set chokers," he laughs in a deep whiskey baritone. He was 12 at the time. At age 25, he got together enough equipment and a crew to go into business for

• • • • • • • • • •

SECTION
3

THE
ECONOMICS
OF A
CLEAR CUT

By Jack Swanson

himself. That was in 1983.

Handly is a barrel-chested 6-footer with a grizzled beard. Two centuries ago, he would have been a pirate. A century ago, a trapper, miner — or logger, probably right here on the frontier. He is single. Logging doesn't leave a lot of time for long-term relationships, he says.

Handly and his men are just finishing a 90-acre clearcut high above Hood Canal. The land is steep hillside overlooking the Dosewallips River about 2,000 feet above sea level.

Because the land is so steep, clearcutting is the only practical way to log. That was decided by the property owner, not Handly. If the land had been more level, it could have been logged selectively, using a tractor or other equipment to skid the logs out to where they could be loaded onto trucks.

But in this case, Handly has to use a device called a "yarder," a tall pole attached to a truck bed, fastened to the ground with heavy cables. Atop the pole is a 2,000-foot-long loop of steel cable that stretches down the hill and is attached to a pulley hooked to a tree.

One of Handly's crewmen operates the yarder from a cab at the base of the pole. Four 20-foot-long cables called "chokers" dangle from the middle of the long wire. Half a mile down the hillside where freshly cut logs lie like matchsticks, three chokermen wait for the dangling cables.

Tim Love, Handly's rigging slinger, presses a button on a radio-control device attached to his belt, which sets off a series of blasts on an air horn atop the yarder. That's the signal for the cable operator to send the chokers downhill to the men. They grab the chokers and wrap them round the butt end of the logs, then Love signals again and the yarder engineer winches them up the hill, depositing them in a pile beside Handly's loader.

Another chokerman working next to the loader releases the cables, then dances nimbly along the logs, cutting them to proper length with a chainsaw.

Handly and his crew of seven have spent the last four months logging this piece of land. They have a couple more weeks to finish pulling the logs out and getting the land ready for replanting.

Then he will move his equipment out, repair the roads and culverts behind him and move on to the next job — if there is one.

Handly has no job to move on to. The bottom has dropped out of the lumber market because of the nationwide slowdown in home construction. Mills are closing. Hundreds of independent loggers like Handly are out of work, and the used equipment market is flooded with loaders, tractors and other rigs.

It's not the spotted owl that's causing problems for Handly. It's not the debate over cutting old-growth forests. It's the economy. People aren't buying houses anymore.

During a brief break, Handly chats with two young hikers who ask how to get to a hiking trail above where his crew is working. He explains they can't get past his rig on the road right now and that he informed the Forest Service he would be working in the area.

The hikers aren't very nice about it, and one of them makes a snide remark about how many spotted owls Mike and his crew killed that day. Handly scowls but keeps his cool, remarking that this isn't a very good spot to pick a fight with a bunch of loggers.

He asks them what they do for a living and they say they work at Puget Sound Naval Shipyard on nuclear weapon systems. After the hikers drive off in search of another trail, he makes it clear how he feels about people who work on nuclear weapons then climbs back into his rig.

Any visitor to the area Handly is clearcutting would be struck by the beauty of it. The hills, covered by the patchwork of other clearcuts, drop down to Hood Canal in the distance, and on a clear day you can see Seattle's skyscrapers. The air is clean and carries the pungent aroma of diesel exhaust and crushed fir needles.

The visitor has time to take in the scenery. Handly's crew seems oblivious to it all. They're too busy keeping alive.

Handly and his crew are typical. They don't have time to stop and debate the wisdom of clearcuts or spotted owl habitat. That's something the land owner has to worry about.

Handly has other things he has to worry about: keeping his equipment running, moving out 15 to 20 loads of logs a day, seeing that none of his men gets hurt and making sure everybody gets paid.

When Handly is finished, the 90 acres of 90-year-old trees will have provided 13

Handly and his crew don't have time to stop and debate the wisdom of clearcuts or spotted owl habitat. That's something the land owner has to worry about.

people with jobs for between two and four months, depending on the work they were doing. That crew consisted of two sawyers, four chokermen, a yarder engineer, five truck drivers and Handly, who operates the log loader.

Only five of the men actually work directly for Handly on the site. The sawyers are independent contractors whose work is done when the last tree hits the dirt. The truck drivers work for the truck owners, who rent their rigs out to Handly by the load or by the day.

Each working day Handly and his men fill those five trucks three or four times with between 50,000 and 75,000 pounds of wood — 20 to 25 logs containing about 5,000 board feet of raw lumber.

In all, Handly expects the 90 acres to yield up about 3.7 million board feet of timber. At a market price of between $450 and $500 a thousand board feet, that timber is probably worth in the neighborhood of $1.5 million. Handly ends up only with a small percentage of the total.

The world of logging economics is pretty complex. According to John Walter, timber lands vice president of Pope Resources, Pope bought the property several years ago as part of a 1,200-acre purchase. It had previously been Crown Zellerbach land.

The parcel had been logged around the turn of the century but was not replanted. The natural regrowth was extremely dense and full of debris that needed to be cleaned out, Walter said. About two years ago, Pope sold the "stumpage" or the right to cut the trees, to ITT-Rayonier.

Under the contract, Pope continued to own the logs until they were cut. After cutting ITT had to pay Pope a certain fixed price for the timber. If the market price is higher now than the price Pope sold it for, ITT makes money. If it's lower than the fixed price, Pope makes more than it would have if it had harvested the trees itself.

"That's why, at times, timber sales like these can be a very advantageous tool," Walter said. "If the market is low, people are willing to speculate that the market will go up later on. On the other hand, the market can work against you."

The contract specifies that the trees had to be cut by March 1991 or ownership would return to Pope. ITT sold the Douglas fir logs to Pope & Talbot (P&T and Pope used to be one company) and decided to keep the hemlock taken from the property. ITT sold the pulpwood to a Port Angeles firm. Handly was hired by ITT to do the logging.

When the trucks leave the mountain, Handly never sees the logs again. They are measured at a scaling yard, where a computer estimates the board feet contained in each log. It spits out a ticket that shows the credits that are added to ITT's account. The trucker takes the logs to Pope & Talbot's holding pond near Port Ludlow, where they are dumped into the water and stored for later processing.

Handly gets roughly one-third of the proceeds from each load. Figure a truck holds 5,000 board feet at $450 per thousand, that's $2,250 per load. He has five trucks and each makes three trips a day, so that's $33,750 and his one-third comes to $11,250 per day.

But he has to pay the truck owner $130 per load in rent and each of his men around $120 per day plus benefits. And his fuel bill comes to around $3,500 per day.

"I figure I've gotta have at least $2,300 a day after expenses to pay for all of the men and the state industrial insurance," Handly said. "And diesel fuel just went up another 30 cents a gallon. So that doesn't leave much."

Out of what's left over, Handly has to pay for the equipment, repairs and maintenance. He figures he has more than $100,000 invested in equipment. Add everything up and Handly figures his company will show a gross income of more than $100,000 this year, but he personally will end up with about the same amount his men make.

"It all depends on how good a logger you are," he says. "It's a matter of production. You gotta get the wood out."

There's one big difference, however, between Mike and his men. When they get laid off, they can apply for unemployment compensation. If Handly can't come up with another logging contract, he will have to go to work for somebody else — if he can find someone who is hiring. If he couldn't log, what would he do?

"What I really want to do is all I've ever done," he said. "I wish we could keep logging. If I can't do that, I guess I'd want to work with equipment of some kind. But I just don't know what else I would do."

Handly has to worry about keeping his equipment running, moving out 15 to 20 loads of logs a day, seeing that none of his men gets hurt and making sure everybody gets paid.

Each working day Handly and his men fill five trucks three or four times with 20 to 25 logs containing about 5,000 board feet of raw lumber.

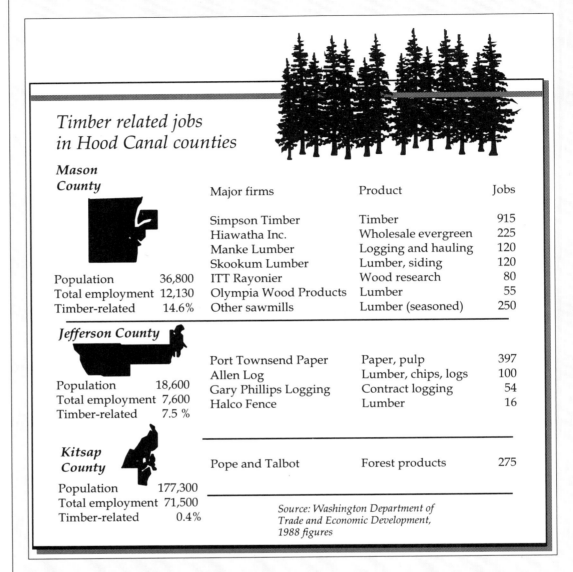

Timber related jobs in Hood Canal counties

Mason County

Population 36,800
Total employment 12,130
Timber-related 14.6%

Major firms	Product	Jobs
Simpson Timber	Timber	915
Hiawatha Inc.	Wholesale evergreen	225
Manke Lumber	Logging and hauling	120
Skookum Lumber	Lumber, siding	120
ITT Rayonier	Wood research	80
Olympia Wood Products	Lumber	55
Other sawmills	Lumber (seasoned)	250

Jefferson County

Population 18,600
Total employment 7,600
Timber-related 7.5 %

Port Townsend Paper	Paper, pulp	397
Allen Log	Lumber, chips, logs	100
Gary Phillips Logging	Contract logging	54
Halco Fence	Lumber	16

Kitsap County

Population 177,300
Total employment 71,500
Timber-related 0.4%

Pope and Talbot	Forest products	275

Source: Washington Department of Trade and Economic Development, 1988 figures

Logging Is Region's Bread and Butter

As a region, the area west of Hood Canal produces more timber than any other similar-sized area in the state except for Lewis and Cowlitz counties to the south.

Mason and Jefferson counties rank sixth and eighth, respectively, among the 19 counties west of the Cascades in amount of timber harvested in 1989. Jefferson County produced more timber from state-owned land last year than any other county in the state.

Kitsap County, which forms the canal's eastern border, is at the bottom of the list in timber production, however. It ranks 17th and produced less than 1 percent of Western Washington's 1989 harvest.

Nevertheless, it is home to one of Hood Canal's oldest and most productive mills, Pope & Talbot in Port Gamble at the head of the canal.

Pope Resources, a timber and land development company with headquarters in Poulsbo, is one of the major land owners on the canal.

Looking at the three-county area as a whole, officials say one of every four persons owes his livelihood to the timber industry. Dependence on timber is heaviest in Mason County where timber-related firms are seven of the top 10 employers and provide more than 1,700 jobs. Nearly 15 percent of those who hold jobs in Mason County work for timber-related firms.

In Jefferson County, nearly 8 percent of the work force is employed in timber production or processing.

No one tracks timber and jobs just for the Hood Canal watershed, but officials say they believe the dependence on timber-related jobs is somewhat higher in the small towns that ring the canal than overall county figures suggest.

Towns like Hoodsport and Quilcene have dozens — perhaps even hundreds — of small, independent "gypo" loggers. Many families subsist on the income of a single logging truck or bulldozer. Countless others work sporadically as choker setters and sawyers for independent loggers.

As a result, officials say the number of persons around Hood Canal who depend on the timber industry for jobs could be as high as 50 percent.

For the Olympic Peninsula as a whole, more than 11,000 persons received more than $305 million in direct wages from the timber industry and more than 46,000 persons benefitted indirectly. Total direct and indirect benefits to the region's economy amounted to more than $1.3 billion, according to a recent study conducted by industry and state agencies.

By Jack Swanson

• • • • • • • • • •

"It all depends on how good a logger you are. It's a matter of production. You gotta get the wood out."
—Mike Handly, Quilcene

• • • • • • • • • •

SECTION 4

WHO OWNS THE CANAL WATERSHED

By Travis Baker

Timber is a game played with thousand-acre chips, and in the Hood Canal basin, Pope Resources is the private operator with the biggest stack.

Its stack still is smaller than that held by the federal government. But among private owners, no one rivals Pope's approximately 60,000 acres in the watershed.

That private ownership has been in flux in Jefferson and Kitsap County, but relatively stable in Mason, where Simpson Timber Co. is king. While only 8,000 of Simpson's 170,000 acres in Mason County are on the slopes draining into the canal, Simpson is still the second largest private timberland owner in the watershed.

Current Hood Canal timberland ownership includes three companies with experience in residential and commercial development, plus a major insurance company. But there appear to be no active plans to convert any substantial amount of canal forestland to any other use.

Only one company, Christmas tree grower G.R. Kirk in Mason County, sees a short-range likelihood of conversion from timberland.

Jefferson County has seen the most active trading in timberland.

Pope is the big player there, but others include a real estate arm of Traveler's Insurance, with 4,600 acres in the watershed, and about 12,000 total in eastern Jefferson; Pacific Funding Corp. of Lynnwood with about 3,000 acres; and ANE Forests of Puget Sound, owned by a Dane, Sorn Nymark, and holder of 4,600 canal acres. Manke & Sons of Tacoma has only 660 acres in Jefferson, but more in Kitsap and Mason, and Trillium Corp. of Bellingham has recently acquired 630 acres of canal timberland.

Pope Resources, Pacific Funding and Trillium are the three who have ties to development. Pope has thousands of acres converted to housing or about to be, but almost none of it is in the canal watershed. Pacific Funding is owned by some of the same people who own First Western Development, which builds and owns shopping centers. Mile Hill Plaza, Target Plaza and Winslow Village in Kitsap County are First Western projects. Trillium is part owner of the Semiahmoo Resort in Whatcom County, and Belles Faire Mall in Bellingham is on land it put together.

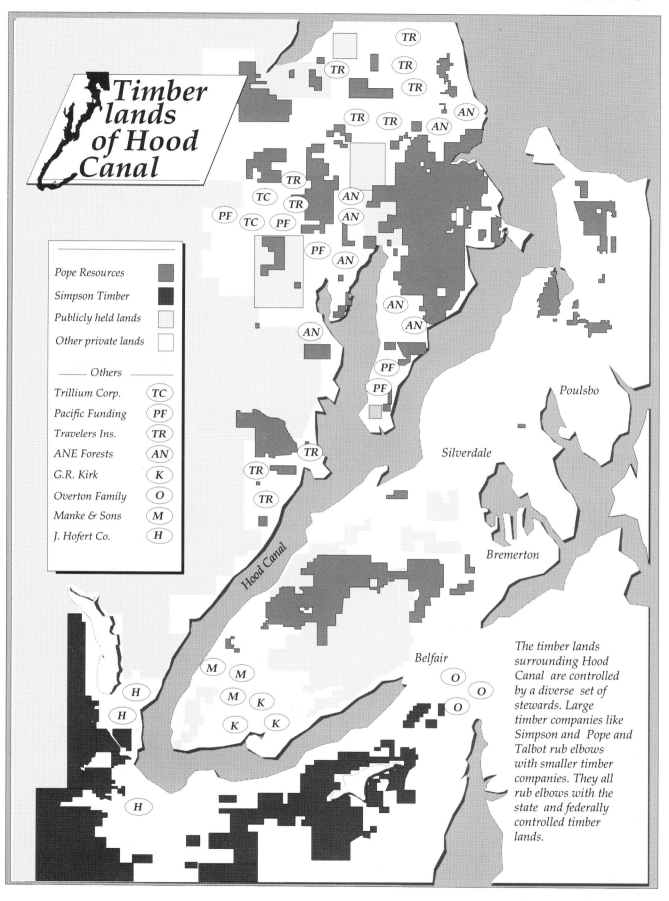

Timber lands of Hood Canal

Pope Resources
Simpson Timber
Publicly held lands
Other private lands

— Others —

Trillium Corp. TC
Pacific Funding PF
Travelers Ins. TR
ANE Forests AN
G.R. Kirk K
Overton Family O
Manke & Sons M
J. Hofert Co. H

Poulsbo

Silverdale

Bremerton

Belfair

Hood Canal

The timber lands surrounding Hood Canal are controlled by a diverse set of stewards. Large timber companies like Simpson and Pope and Talbot rub elbows with smaller timber companies. They all rub elbows with the state and federally controlled timber lands.

The corporate raid of Crown Zellerbach by Britisher Sir James Goldsmith led to liquidation by his company, Cavenham, of its Jefferson County timberland, which has been bought by various new owners.

John Calhoun, the Olympic Region manager for the state Department of Natural Resources, called the buy-log-and-sell practices of Cavenham "despicable forestry." But DNR was unable to require any more of Cavenham than that it replant the logged acreage as demanded by state law. Though it took longer than DNR would have liked, it's now all replanted, said Calhoun.

Travelers, ANE and Pope Resources are among those who own some of the land now.

Pacific Funding traded some of its land with Pope Resources and acquired most of the rest from a Taiwanese owner called Golden Springs. Like Cavenham, Golden Springs was slow to replant after logging and paid little attention to the long-term welfare of the land, said Calhoun.

John Walter, vice president for timberlands at Pope Resources, says up to 45 percent of the young trees on a parcel it acquired from Golden Springs will have to be replaced. The replanting was done too long after logging, he said.

Trillium picked up its Jefferson County land from Georgia Pacific.

In Mason County, the major canal owners other than Simpson are Los Angeles-based J. Hofert Co. and G.R. Kirk Co. of Tacoma. Both are Christmas tree growers who have been in the county for decades. Scott Scott, a Hofert vice president, estimates it has 2,000 acres in the canal watershed. Rick Kirk of the Tacoma firm said 3,500 acres on the Tahuya Peninsula are the bulk of its holdings.

Pope far exceeds any other owner in timberland in Kitsap County. There are few other large blocks of ownership in the canal watershed. Manke & Sons of Tacoma appears to be the only one with more than a thousand acres. The Overton family of Olympia owns a lot of land west of Bremerton National Airport, but only a few hundred acres drain toward Hood Canal, said Peter Overton.

Policies on management of the land and its harvesting vary among the companies. Since Pope and Simpson have the most land, their policies have the most to say about the future of the canal.

Both log annually, aiming for what is essentially an industry standard of harvesting 1 1/2 - 2 percent of their lands each year. That allows a 50-to-60-year cycle in which part of their timber is reaching maturity all the time. But both emphasize that market fluctuations increase and decrease any year's harvest as they try to get the best price for the timber.

Both Pope and Simpson are trying to "block up" their holdings, consolidating them in a few areas through trades with other owners so they can avoid trying to manage widely spread parcels. Pope surrendered 6,000 acres south of Hood Canal in Mason County in a three-way trade under which it acquired timber on state land, Simpson blocked up its Mason County holdings and the state got some Simpson land.

Aside from that trade, said George Folquet, president of Pope Resources, his company is seeking to increase its land base.

All timberland owners who log use clearcutting in mature stands. Nearly all also do commercial thinning, in which selected trees are taken. That makes room for the remaining trees to grow while generating revenue from sale of the trees taken.

Some are logging very little. Buyers of Cavenham and Golden Springs land weren't left much to log. ANE Forests, for example, logged three of its Jefferson County acres in 1990, Pacific Funding an estimated 50 acres, Trillium none and Travelers almost none. All have larger holdings in other parts of the state or nation they will log while waiting for their Jefferson trees to grow, they say.

Only Kirk foresees subdivision of its productive land in the near future. President Rick Kirk said the trend in Christmas trees is toward sheared trees grown on fertile land such as the company owns in Thurston County. That is making its 3,500 acres in Mason County more and more marginal. Its rural location, however, would dictate subdivision into only large lots if that is what the company decides to do with it in the future.

As poor as it is, the Tahuya Peninsula land produced 120,000 cut trees last Christmas, about 10 percent of Kirk's production, he said.

Tax Structure Seeks Commitment to the Land

Taxation of timberland in Washington state has followed a basic premise for nearly two decades. The premise is that the owner, government and public benefit when timber is taxed at cutting rather than annually as it grows.

Prior to 1971, timberland was taxed as any other real property — each year, based on the county assessor's estimate of its value with the timber included, said Bill Derkland, forest property tax program manager for the state Department of Revenue.

Annual taxation created an incentive to cut the timber, eliminating forestland, said Derkland. By harvesting, the land owner reduced his property taxes and took the revenue represented by the trees.

In 1971, the Legislature moved to reduce that incentive. The biggest tax bite, it decided, should come when the trees are cut.

Annual property taxes were greatly reduced. The state Department of Revenue established a 29-category ranking of timber land, based on its productivity and the ease of logging it.

Each year since, the state has established a value per acre for each of the 29 categories.

Those values are much lower than under the "highest and best use" standard that county assessors apply to other land. Kitsap County Assessor Carol Belas estimates them to be only 3 percent of normal value, on average. On an 885-acre parcel on Bainbridge Island, it was closer to 1 percent.

And no annual tax is paid on the timber on the land.

Statewide, the designated values of timberland range from $1 to $135 per acre this year. Most timberland in Mason, Kitsap and Jefferson counties is in a medium category valued by the state at between $70 and $100 per acre.

In return for the minimal valuations, the state collects a 5 percent excise tax on the timber when it's cut.

And, if the owner removes land from the forestry classification, the state charges a rollback tax that is greater than the owner would have paid over 10 years had the land not been designated for forestry.

Four-fifths of the 5 percent tax from logging on private land goes to the counties. All 5 percent from logging on government land goes to the state.

The payments are made to the state quarterly. Much like federal income tax, payments are on the honor system, with penalties of up to 50 percent, plus interest, for inaccurate reporting, when it is caught.

A 10-year rollback of taxes on land being withdrawn from timber classification can be a windfall for counties and other local governments if the land is in an area with escalating property values, said Derkland.

When land is withdrawn from forestry taxation, the county assessor calculates its current value, subtracts its forest land value, and the county then applies the current tax rate to that value. The result is multiplied times 10, and the land owner must pay that amount.

If land values in that area have, say, doubled in those 10 years, the rollback amount paid for each of the 10 years could be as much as double what the company actually would have paid had the land not been taxed as timberland.

There have been no recent conversions of timberland in Kitsap's portion of the Hood Canal basin, Belas said.

By Travis Baker

• • • • • • • • • •

Both Pope and Simpson log annually, havesting 1 1/2 - 2 percent of their lands each year. That allows a 50-to-60-year growth cycle.

• • • • • • • • • •

SECTION 5

LOGGING
AND THE OWL:
THREE
PERSPECTIVES

Cut Out of the Future?

Quilcene logger Dick Pederson has his share of bumps, bruises, cuts, and stitches to show for a steady 21 years of work in the woods.

"I cut it right down to the bone; the only thing that stopped the blade was my knuckle," Pederson says, pointing to a scar on his hand. "And the time I had 37 stitches in my neck when I fell down and the sharp teeth of the saw ripped into me."

Pederson's experiences would not dispute Department of Labor and Industries statistics that say logging is the most dangerous occupation in the state. A total of 163 loggers lost their lives in the woods between 1980 and 1990.

It is a measure of the people who do the work that they continue despite these statistics, and despite an increasing crunch on the number of logging jobs available in Washington generally, and in the Hood Canal watershed in particular.

It's not that there aren't rewards.

Pederson earns between $150 and $200 a day cutting trees, and wonders where else a 42-year-old with no high school diploma can get a job with that kind of pay.

Logging is what he knows, what he feels comfortable with. He can't picture himself in an office job. But he sees that there's little future in logging and he hopes he'll be able to stick with it for another five years, long enough to pay for his new truck.

"If there is a normal job that someone would train me for, ... I'll take it," he says.

After his current job, a clearcut on Forest Service land in the Dungeness watershed, there isn't another one in the foreseeable future. The job is supposed to keep him busy for eight months, but there are no more timber sales pending. And there is always the threat that the Forest Service might revoke the cutting permit if spotted owls are located in the area.

"I won't take my kids out in the woods," Pederson says as he sights the lean of a second-growth Douglas fir he prepares to fell near Slab Camp south of Sequim. He doesn't want them to get hooked on it like he did as a kid. "There's not much of a future left in this business," he sighs.

The stocky Pederson is a proud man who moved to Quilcene when he was 3. He began working in the woods as a teenager, joining with his father, Harold, who had been logging for 37 years.

Pederson began first by running the heavy equipment cat, then moved up to the skidders, and on to cutting standing timber.

While he takes pride in his work, his wife Celine hesitates to mention in public what her husband does for a living. Some people have confronted them and called him a tree killer, Pederson says.

His typical day begins at 5 a.m. He dresses in a worn plaid shirt and ankle-length logging jeans that are held up by typical red suspenders. After grabbing a quick breakfast, he carpools with two fellow loggers to the logging site.

"It's dark when I leave in the morning and dark when I get home," he says. Twelve-hour days are not unusual for a logger.

As a light rain falls at the logging site, the three men part to go to their respective jobs. Pederson heads to the woods, while Ken Akerman from Quilcene jumps into the skidder, and Bud Smith of Brinnon starts bucking fallen timber.

Pederson moves from tree to tree.

In each case, he first decides which way he wants it to fall. He then yanks the starter pull on his chainsaw and begins to fashion the notch that directs the tree's descent.

With the wood from the notch removed, Pederson cuts from the opposite side of the tree along the plane set by the top cut of the notch. Using a bright orange axe, he hammers in a plastic wedge that keeps the weight of the tree from binding the saw bar.

Before the backcut reaches the notch, the tree begins to creak. The fall begins slowly as the wood fibers that still hold the trunk upright begin to crack, but then accelerates quickly as the weight of the tree pulls it off the stump.

The cut continues as the tree begins its descent, one last opportunity to alter the direction of the fall.

As soon as it's down, Pederson jumps up on the tree in his cork boots, measures and marks the tree for log lengths.

The process is repeated 39 times in Pederson's typical day in the woods.

Celine, Dick's wife of one year, is busy in the kitchen of their home on the bend of the Little Quilcene River just outside of

Dick Pederson

town. She knows her husband will be hungry when he walks in the back door.

About 5 p.m., Akerman drops Pederson at the house. Dick ambushes Celine with a kiss, then goes straight to the shower to wash off the accumulation of dirt, grease, sawdust, and sweat.

Cleaned, and in fresh clothes, he comes to the dinner table with Celine, son Justin, 12, and a friend of Justin's.

After dinner Pederson has but a short time to play with his son before it's bed time. The two go out into the living room to shoot ducks on the Nintendo game.

Celine Pederson tries not to think too much about the possibility that Dick will lose his job. An estimated 28,000 timber industry jobs in Washington, Oregon and northern California are expected to disappear in the next decade because of the proposals to set old stands of timber aside for owl habitat.

But many more jobs have been lost in recent years as the industry has automated. These days, only seven loggers are employed in a crew that clearcuts 90 acres.

Celine instantly fell in love with Quilcene when she moved from Tenino in 1988. Where else can you leave your doors unlocked, plus hunt, fish, collect oysters, or go crabbing right outside your door?

The Pedersons wish they could live there forever.

But in a small timber town, there aren't many other kinds of jobs available and growth is slow. They admit they may have to leave, but Pederson says he would go crazy in a big town.

By Larry Steagall

Nest Egg Soured by an Owl

About 50 years ago, Jim Goodpaster Sr. had a good idea. He was helping to log a nice stand of timber above Lake Cushman when it occurred to him that the land might be worth something someday.

It certainly wasn't then. After the logging was done, the land was practically worthless. It would take another 50 to 90 years for a new crop to grow.

Goodpaster bought the 80 acres for $240 — $30 an acre. Oh, well. It was, he decided, a good investment for his old age.

He was wrong.

In July of 1990, Goodpaster, 84 and dying, needed the return on that investment. Unable to care for himself, he was bed-ridden in a Shelton nursing home that was costing his family $75 a day. The timber on that 80 acres up near Lake Cushman was now worth nearly half a million dollars.

The only thing standing in the way was a spotted owl two miles away on federal land.

The Goodpaster family's predicament provides a prime example of the legal tangles private timber owners can find themselves in as a result of efforts to save the threatened spotted owl.

Nationally, the controversy over the owl has revolved around setting aside old-growth timber stands in national forests in Washington, Oregon and California. Those regulations say nothing about protecting them on private or state land.

But in Washington, the state Department of Natural Resources has set up guidelines to protect the owls by prohibiting cutting trees on state and private land within as little as two miles and as much as four miles from where an owl is seen or known to be nesting.

There was never a suggestion that owls might live on Goodpaster's land. It was second-growth forest, after all, and it is well known that spotted owls live in old-growth or virgin timber where decayed trees provide lots of homesites for the owl's favorite food — flying squirrels.

But when Jim Goodpaster Jr. went to the DNR to obtain a cutting permit for his father's land, he was told he couldn't get one until someone from the state Department of Wildlife did an owl survey. The DNR told him a spotted owl had been seen on national forest land within 2 1/2 miles of the Goodpaster property.

DNR officials are quick to point out that it was the timing more than anything else that caused the delays on Goodpaster's application.

"Our agency was scrambling to figure out how to administer the new federal regulations," said Ben Cleveland, regional resource protection specialist in DNR's Enumclaw office, which oversees the Hoodsport area. "There was confusion over implementation of the new regulations and the effect on our regulations."

Jim Jr. was furious. "Here we have private land that has been logged before and we can't get permits to log our own land. That's not right," he said. "Our security was that land."

Jim Jr. is a huge, friendly bear of a man who operates heavy equipment for a living and lives in Hoodsport. He is one of three children in the Goodpaster family. His mother also resides in Hoodsport.

He readily agreed to give us a tour of the property, talking a mile a minute and driving two. When Goodpaster drives a logging road, you don't take notes. You brace your feet, grit your teeth and hang on.

Not only was the family having a problem with Goodpaster Sr.'s medical bills, he explained, time was against them for getting the land logged at all this year. Because the land is part of the Lake Cushman drainage, logging would be

"If there is a normal job that someone would train me for, ... I'll take it. I won't take my kids out in the woods. There's not much of a future left in this business."
— Dick Pederson

impossible after the fall rains began. Goodpaster Jr. would have to wait until next spring — "and who knows what regulations will be in effect then?" he said.

Another major concern was what the timber market might do in the next several months. The housing market already was cooling off nationally and prices were getting soft. Jim Jr. figured the property has about 1.6 million board feet of timber on it that would have sold in June 1990 for between $400,000 and $500,000.

"That's gross," he growled, shoving harder on the gas pedal of his four-wheel-drive pickup, sending dust flying on the narrow road. "By the time we pay 30 percent logging cost, a 5 percent timber tax, 1.3 percent real estate tax, B&O tax, corporation tax and personal income tax, there's not going to be a lot left. We'll be damned lucky if we end up with a few thousand. Meanwhile, the property has been raped and then we're looking at another 50 years before it can be logged again."

It isn't just the 80-acre piece the family worries about. Goodpaster Sr., who spent 28 years as a Mason County school superintendent, collected about 650 acres of land in small parcels around the county. Several years ago, he underwent surgery to remove a brain tumor, and afterward his health began to decline. The family set up a trust to pay Jim Sr.'s medical expenses, and the money from the timber sale was supposed to go into that.

His son worries about whether the family will have the same problems logging the other parcels as they have with the 80-acre piece near Lake Cushman.

August went by, then September. Goodpaster Sr.'s condition grew worse. Jim Jr. finally was able to get someone to come in and look for owls. He smirks at the scientific methodology used for the survey.

"You call this owl lady," he said. "She comes and looks at the land. If she sees an owl, she is supposed to give it a dead mouse. If the owl jumps up into a tree and eats the mouse, it's just a transient owl that lives someplace else.

"But if it flies off with the mouse to a nest nearby, you're in trouble."

In September, the DNR told the Goodpasters their land was clear of owls and

Jim Goodpaster Jr.

wasn't considered suitable owl habitat. The first week of October, Jim Jr. got the cutting permit.

On Oct. 8, 1990, Jim Sr. died.

Suddenly, the whole equation changed.

"Dad's death has eased things," Jim Goodpaster Jr. said in November 1990. "Logging is no longer a necessity. It's now a matter of if we get the opportunity, should we? Because if we don't do it now, we may not get another one."

The rainy season has begun. The bottom has dropped out of the timber market. Although the price for Douglas fir remains fairly high, the price of alder and other timber on the property has declined at least by half.

If the Goodpasters go ahead and cut this fall, they probably will end up with half what they would have gotten last summer. What is the post-election climate going to be like? What kind of regulations will be in effect next year? Will prices go up or down?

Goodpaster brings the pickup to a bouncing halt on the edge of his property and climbs heavily out of the cab. He points out the tracks of dirt bikers who have trespassed on the land, chewing up the muddy trail.

"Simpson has quit buying altogether and is talking about shutting down. Pope & Talbot shut down," he said. "Everything is up in the air right now. A lot of owners are converting their property to 5-acre tracts for recreational homesites."

But Goodpaster's property is land-locked with no access to the Forest Service road a couple of miles away. He leans an elbow on the lip of the pickup bed and scans the forest around him. "Eventually, we'll be like Europe," he said. "We'll be picking up sticks in the forest and the government will be telling everybody what they can and can't cut."

By Jack Swanson

> "Here we have private land that has been logged before and we can't get permits to log. That's not right. Our security was that land."
>
> — Jim Goodpaster Jr.

In Search of an Elusive Owl

The air is chilly and the Seven Sisters are so bright in the sky overhead they almost hurt your eyes. The small pickup with government license plates pulls to the side of the narrow dirt road and stops.

When the door opens, the dome light silhouettes the face of a young, pretty, dark-haired woman.

It is 4 a.m., and she is 20 miles from the nearest civilization. Alone.

She doesn't waste time thinking about the surroundings. After locking the door, she opens the rear canopy door and dons heavy hiking boots. She stuffs a plastic box full of mice and a walkie-talkie into the back of a combination rucksack-vest. Flashlight in one hand and surfing rod in the other, she trudges into the thick forest, picking her way carefully through boulders and rotting logs. There is no trail.

Deep inside the forest, she pauses, listens. Minutes go by.

"Oooh!" she cups her hands around her mouth and the sound comes out more like a sharp bark than a hoot. "Oooh! Oooh! OoooHhh!"

The final note is louder and trails off more slowly. She waits a minute and repeats the series. Then she moves on through the forest another quarter of a mile and begins calling again.

Finally, in the distance, her call is answered. After a week of nights like this, the caller has found what she was looking for: a spotted owl. During the next few minutes, if all goes well, the owl lady will coax the owl from his tree to a spot where she can slip the nylon loop at the end of her fishing pole around its neck and place a plastic band around its leg. Feathers and dignity slightly mussed, the owl will get a nice fat mouse for its trouble and will fly away, hopefully to a nest nearby.

And for her trouble, the owl lady will get to draw a circle on a map marking the home of another spotted owl. At the end of the month, she will get a check for $9.68 for each hour she spent out in the forest hooting in the dark.

Ivy Otto, 31, grew up in Newark, N.J. She is compact, sturdy and can walk the legs off just about anybody. She wears red and gray tennis shoes, well worn, baggy black Levis, a formless black sweatshirt with brown logging shirt underneath and a blue nylon vest. Lots of layers for warmth.

She has been an owl lady since 1987.

"It goes back a long ways," she says, explaining how she took up her unusual profession. "My interest in biology goes back to when I was a kid. I started working for the Forest Service on the Hood Canal Ranger District, worked in fire suppression, fire guard, ended up going on a lot of forest fires for two summer seasons. In 1987, they merged the ranger districts and started surveying for spotted owls."

She got the job and later transferred to the Forest Service's research laboratory in Olympia.

"The lab is trying to find out exactly how many owls there are in the forest and trying to learn more about the mortality, population changes and fluctuations. It's research-oriented, where the district is management-oriented. The district's task is to look at the effects of their management on wildlife."

But with recent new federal regulations

designed to protect the spotted owl as an endangered species, Otto's job has taken on new significance. The research she and dozens of others like her do not only will help determine whether spotted owls survive but how the entire forest industry conducts its business.

Thousands of jobs are at stake, not just among loggers who have depended on federal timber land for work.

Next March when the state Department of Natural Resources places its new regulations into effect, the existence of one pair of nesting spotted owls near state or private land can prevent harvest of timber within a 4-mile circle of their nest.

Because the stakes are so high, it is easy to understand why the government has hired people like Otto. They search the forests alone, counting and banding the owls, checking what they eat, measuring the size of the territory they claim for themselves.

In all of the Olympic Peninsula, there are only six owl counters like Otto. As of 1990, they have found 23 adult owls and 10 babies.

In the forests surrounding Hood Canal, surveyors have found nine pairs of owls. Their presence will have a major impact on the amount of logging that will be done around the canal. There will be less logging in the area than probably any time since logging began more than a century ago.

On a recent fall morning, Otto left her Olympia home at 2 a.m. and drove to Hood Canal to talk about her work and try to woo a spotted owl close enough for a photographer to take its picture.

Hormones and the time of the year doomed the venture to failure, however. A morning of hooting brought Otto only a sore throat and the faint, distant bleats of a pygmy owl in response. Spotted owls generally only answer intruders in their territory during spring mating season, she explained.

Do they actually expect to find every owl on the Olympic Peninsula?

"Our goal is to find them all," she said. "It's my understanding there's an intensive study area on the peninsula. They think they're pretty close to having almost all the pair sites down."

When they are found, the owls get

Ivy Otto

brightly colored leg bands on either or both legs so trackers can tell them apart.

"When you go back to the site the next year, you don't have to catch the bird and read the band again," Otto said. "You can just look at the color of the bands. You can usually get close enough or sometimes they will come down to you or will preen themselves and lift their leg up. And if you don't see it you keep going back until you do, until you're sure they're either banded or they're not. And if they're not, then you band them."

The job looks a lot easier on the printed page than in practice. What it means in reality is that Otto sometimes has to spend night after cold, lonely night out in trackless wilderness. Owls, after all, are nocturnal. They hunt and feed at night.

Does she ever worry about getting lost? She thinks about it a minute. Nope. Breaking a leg? Getting hurt? Sometimes. That's why she always carries water, food and her two-way radio.

She doesn't even mind working in a "temporary" position without benefits.

"I really enjoy my job," she said. "It's a lot of fun and I would probably keep doing this for a long time, but just recently my husband started graduate school in molecular biology at the University of Wisconsin in Madison and it makes it difficult to be apart. I'll probably do this for at least one more breeding season but I'm going to try to get into graduate school myself."

Otto earned an undergraduate degree from The Evergreen State College, studying natural history, ornithology, agriculture and ecology.

With that kind of background, Otto said it was only natural for her to become interested in more than just counting owls. Lately, she has been collecting and analyzing the lump of debris owls cough up after feeding. It usually contains the skulls and other bones of the animals they eat.

Spotted owls are so important because they are what scientists call an "indicator species," a group of animals that shows the overall health of an ecosystem's inhabitants.

Compared to most birds and other animals, spotted owls are relatively delicate. They generally have only one or two babies each season, and the babies often do not survive.

Spotted owls thrive only in old-growth forests where there are lots of dead or decayed trees that provide secure nesting places for themselves and their main food source — flying squirrels. Young trees don't have decay pockets. Young forests don't have thick shade canopies that keep animals cool on hot summer days. Flying squirrels like to eat the fungi that grows on rotting logs. That doesn't grow in clearcuts or new second-growth stands either. No food, no owl.

But for Otto, the spotted owl is more than just an indicator species.

> "I'm not against logging. My personal feeling is that the old-growth forest is a resource to our society and our country in other ways than just for wood products. We're losing it before we know anything about it in detail."
>
> — Ivy Otto

"To me, the owl is valuable aesthetically," she said. "It's beautiful. It's an animal that is interesting. It's neat to learn something about their behavior and I think that's every reason in the world to protect it."

Ask her opinion about the ruckus the spotted owl has created among lumbermen and she is careful to say that her opinions are hers and in no way that of the U.S. Forest Service.

"I think we have to decide as a society what we value. I don't think it's necessarily an owls vs. jobs issue. My personal opinion is that if jobs were the issue there would be more effort by industry to retrain the loggers. All of the money that's put into maintaining logging roads and building logging roads and replanting harvested units and setting up units, which is paid for by the federal government when their land is logged by private industry, should be channeled into helping these folks adjust to some changes that are inevitable down the road, even if there were no spotted owls and it weren't an issue.

"To industry I think that's just a tool to stir people's emotions. They have a lot to lose. A lot of money."

The biologist is gone. In her place stands a natural philosopher in the mould of Henry Thoreau or Edward Abbey.

"I'm not against logging. My personal feeling is that the old-growth forest is a resource to our society and our country in other ways than just for wood products," she said. "I think that it's diminishing rapidly. If we look at the time scale since people first settled in this area, we're losing it before we know anything about it in detail.

"For example, people are looking at the yew tree as a possible cure for cancer. In the past, we cut them all down and didn't think twice about it. There's all kinds of plants out there that grow in the forest that we don't know anything about. Most of our medicines come from these plants. There are so many things to learn, and it would be a real tragedy if the forest was cut down and gone forever and we couldn't learn anything from it."

By Jack Swanson

• • • • • • • • • •

SECTION 6

FOR TIMBER
OR FOR THE
ENVIRON-
MENT?

*By Christopher
Dunagan*

*Policymakers will
eventually have to
decide whether the
harvest of forest lands
in the Hood Canal
watershed will proceed
in a way that's
environmentally
benign.*

F rom an airplane, the forests of
Hood Canal seem to clothe the
bare earth with quilted fabric.
Green patches vary in texture,
revealing different ages of trees.
Brown patches demarcate recent
clearcuts.

Toward the west, jagged mountain
peaks thrust upward to the sky. Below, a
swath of blue water shines in the sunlight.

This is the Hood Canal watershed, a
fragile and interconnected ecosystem.

How people feel about this region —
and the decisions they make — will determine what natural features remain for future
generations. In the intense debate over

forests, no two people see the value of trees
in quite the same way.

To Gary Phillips, a logger from
Quilcene, a tree represents a way of life
passed down from his father and grandfather. Cutting a tree means feeding his family
and providing raw material for someone's
house.

To Aargon Steel, Adopt-A-Forest
coordinator for Washington Audubon, the
trees offer food and shelter for animals
ranging from cougars to elk, from eagles to
salmon, not to mention the tiniest organisms
at the beginning of nature's food chain.

Still others see trees as part of the
landscape, an important element in the

beauty that defines Hood Canal today.

Both Phillips and Steel have strong feelings about trees and wildlife, but they realize the issues are far too complex to resort to convenient slogans, such as "Save a tree; eat an owl."

Donna Simmons of Hoodsport, a member of the state Ecological Commission, has worked intensively on timber issues. Needed more than anything, she says, are bridges of understanding.

"The reason the timber industry is in a crisis today is not just because of crazy environmentalists trying to lock up every stick of timber," she says. "There are issues of export, automation — we can log 10 times faster with 10 times fewer people — as well as the over-harvesting of the past."

It is well understood that many species of wildlife would disappear without trees. But if uncontrolled logging threatens the natural system, total preservation threatens the human system.

Already, the impacts are being felt in the timber market as the federal government protects timber for wildlife habitat, said Jerry Clark, resident manager of the Pope & Talbot sawmill at Port Gamble.

"We're going to price a lot of people out of the housing market," said Clark. "We, as the public, have to make some tough decisions about how we want to approach our lifestyle."

Despite their successes, environmentalists are not celebrating. Logging has been halted in many critical areas of Olympic National Forest, but the northern spotted owl alone seems to be taking the heat.

Protecting the owl under the Endangered Species Act has disrupted old-growth logging, mobilized special owl biologists and forced officials to look for other places to cut timber.

But while everyone has his eye on the spotted owl, it has been too easy to forget other animals also struggling to survive. These include the marbled murrelet, a seabird that nests in very old trees; the fisher and pine marten, weasel-like animals that live in hollow logs; and the Roosevelt elk, a majestic beast whose numbers have declined drastically in some areas around Hood Canal.

Some environmentalists talk about hitting the federal government with a

massive petition, asking that a host of other forest species be considered for the endangered list.

"What we really need," says Bob Crowley of Olympic Environmental Council, "is an endangered ecosystem act."

"Old-growth" is one type of forest ecosystem targeted for protection as a result of spotted owl studies. Protection measures may well save other species in the process.

But Crowley worries that the spotted owl issue has failed to force federal officials to consider the biological limits of human activities. The issue has simply shifted attention to trees that can be marketed without affecting the spotted owl itself.

"They are under a lot of pressure to get the (timber) volume out again, but with a much-reduced land base," said Crowley.

But some gains have been made. Crowley, a Port Townsend resident, is participating in a unique Forest Service experiment in the Mount Walker area near Quilcene. The concept is to evaluate the area's resources — timber, wildlife, plants, dead material, etc. — and decide how many trees can be harvested (and by what method) without destroying the ecological health of the area. No targets for timber were identified in advance, as would normally be the case.

"We give up some of our advocacy role in going into this kind of process," said Crowley. "We have to recognize there are valid concerns on the part of industry and that some level of harvest is acceptable."

If successful, the program may encourage other efforts of its kind.

Related issues are boiling up on state and private lands. A critical winter range for Roosevelt elk along the Dosewallips River is on land owned by Pope Resources. The company had proposed logging about 2,000 acres needed by the elk.

That logging could have destroyed the last of the Dosewallips herd, according to Greg Schirato, regional biologist for the state Department of Wildlife.

Elk are an important part of the Hood Canal ecosystem, said Schirato. They spend their summers in Olympic National Park, then wander down though the national forest and onto private lands as snows chase them out of the high country.

The national park was first formed in

"The most economically distressed counties in the Northwest are those that depend on logging for their livelihood. The most prosperous are those that have unchained themselves from their mills."

— Tim Egan,
The Good Rain

1909 as Mount Olympus National Monument, primarily to protect the elk herds that had been decimated by settlers. Today, elk in the Hood Canal area may again be in danger.

Schirato guesses the combined Dosewallips and Duckabush herds may be down to 80 animals from a 1984 estimate of 127.

Elk populations have been squeezed by declining habitat as well as increased hunting, said Schirato. Elk need a combination of open range for grazing and protective trees for hiding and shelter. Clearcuts already in the Dosewallips area have limited forest habitat.

And, last year, 37 animals were killed, mostly by members of area Indian tribes. (Tribes establish their own hunting seasons in "usual and accustomed" areas.)

"That herd," said Schirato, "couldn't sustain another four or five years of that kind of harvest."

Hunting by both state residents and tribal members has been limited to three-point bulls or larger this year to help the herd recover, he said.

Pope Resources has been required to develop a long-range strategy for protecting the elk before the state will allow any logging on its private lands. How the issue will be resolved is uncertain, said John Walter, vice president for timberland management.

"We are in this business as timberland owners to operate on a profit level," said Walter. "We're going to have to find a balance: what management is required for timber, and what management is required for wildlife?"

Some private landowners don't acknowledge their responsibility to wildlife or to the public. Landowners do have rights, but some hold to a frontier ethic that says they should be able to use their land as they wish.

Walter doesn't go that far. His company — the largest private timber owner in the Hood Canal region — was among the first to buy timberland with the idea of keeping it forever. But Walter does worry that the public expects too much.

"There seems to be a tendency to want to make the timber companies pay the price," he said. "My fear, as a professional in this business, is that regulations are going to get so strict that it will discourage timber

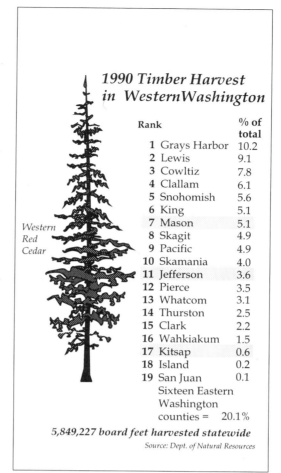

1990 Timber Harvest in WesternWashington

Rank		% of total
1	Grays Harbor	10.2
2	Lewis	9.1
3	Cowltiz	7.8
4	Clallam	6.1
5	Snohomish	5.6
6	King	5.1
7	Mason	5.1
8	Skagit	4.9
9	Pacific	4.9
10	Skamania	4.0
11	Jefferson	3.6
12	Pierce	3.5
13	Whatcom	3.1
14	Thurston	2.5
15	Clark	2.2
16	Wahkiakum	1.5
17	Kitsap	0.6
18	Island	0.2
19	San Juan	0.1
	Sixteen Eastern Washington counties =	20.1%

Western Red Cedar

5,849,227 board feet harvested statewide

Source: Dept. of Natural Resources

"Forestry needs to expand its focus beyond wood production to the perpetuation of diverse forest ecosystems."
— Jerry Franklin

companies from holding onto their land.

"Then," he said, "you will have a lot of short-term investors buying the land who don't have much concern about stewardship."

Schirato says he recognizes Pope's financial commitment, and he's trying to work out a plan that would allow some logging over time.

Out in the woods, it is not always easy to see the impacts of logging. But a growing cadre of foresters, biologists and hydrologists are studying old logging methods and coming up with new approaches.

One afternoon in 1990, Robin Sanders, a technician with Olympic National Forest, slipped on a pair of hip boots and stepped into the Big Quilcene River. Loose rocks littered the bottom of the swift stream. She made her way quickly, but carefully, from one side to the other, stopping several times to take water samples.

Erosion from logging activities can be measured in the stream by testing the water

"It took more than 3,000 years to make some of the trees in the western woods. God has cared for these trees, saved them from drought, disease, avalanches and a thousand straining, leveling tempests and floods; but he cannot save them from fools."
— John Muir

for suspended sediment. Some sediment occurs naturally, but history has proven that logging can unleash huge quantities of silt — enough to destroy salmon runs.

Sanders, who works out of the Quilcene Ranger District, has been searching for sources of erosion all summer and fall. Today, the water remains clean, but pressures to preserve older forests may increase logging in this area.

Kathy Snow, district ranger at Quilcene, says erosion in new areas being logged is not the problem it was even 10 years ago, though past problems still plague the Hood Canal watershed.

Roads cause the greatest problem because they concentrate and accelerate water movement. Years ago, road banks were routinely "cut and filled" as they snaked along the edge of a mountain. Often material cut from the cliff was used to fill valleys crossed by the road. In time, water falling on the road would wash into the valleys with enough energy to erode the filled material.

New roads must avoid fill altogether if there is a high danger of erosion.

Still, large portions of the Quilcene and Hood Canal ranger districts look like a tangle of rope when viewed on a map. Closing some roads — and possibly restoring the ground — have become major issues.

The Forest Service also is experimenting with new techniques of logging, including combining traditional clearcutting with thinning.

Under a national program called "New Perspectives in Forestry," timber sale managers are attempting to preserve fish and wildlife habitat as well as scenic qualities, while reducing water and air pollution. Every timber sale gets attention.

Along Townsend Creek (a tributary to the Big Quilcene), loggers were directed to leave woody debris on the ground and not to disturb the forest floor, according to Steve Ricketts, a forester in the Quilcene District. In years past, the entire area might have been burned down to bare soil.

Rotting debris becomes the first habitat in the next forest. Bacteria and insects initiate the food chain, encouraging birds and larger animals to move back over time.

When possible, standing snags or dying trees are left as homes for woodpeckers and other critters that live within hollowed-out areas of the decaying wood, said Ricketts.

Every snowflake is different, they say, because of the many ways ice crystals can form. The same might be said of forests.

A 300-year-old tree growing in good soil near Hood Canal would stand taller than the same tree grown in poor soils in the high wilderness country. One ancient forest is not the same as the next.

It's no wonder that there's confusion over what forests are needed to protect the spotted owl or that different groups have their own definition of "old growth."

Just as important, nobody is keeping track of the overall Hood Canal ecosystem. Private lands blend into state lands, which blend into federal lands.

"The problem I have seen is that there is not a lot of cooperative long-range planning," said Simmons of the Ecological Commission. "I don't think anyone knows how much of the whole Hood Canal drainage can be harvested and converted to other uses. If we continue to chop it up into little pieces and convert it to roads and houses, it is gone."

"The reason we have to protect so heavily on federal lands," added Snow, "is because the private lands were cut over so many years ago. Most forest lands have been lost to urbanization."

Vital links among plant and animal species are beginning to unravel in the Hood Canal area. It's up to humans to decide — in their cumbersome political way — how far the damage will go.

"It's like we've been on a feeding frenzy and now the bill comes due," said Steel of Washington Audubon. "I don't think we have to throw everybody out of the woods ... but we have to wake up and realize it's not morning in America anymore. It's late afternoon."

Critics question whether clearcutting whole hillsides can be considered environmentally sound.

I f the natural wonders of Hood Canal are to survive, logging activities in privately owned forests may be even more important than on state and federal lands, observers say.

Some of the most important fish and wildlife habitat can be found among the trees on private land, according to Marcy Golde of the Washington Environmental Council.

"It's important that we start to look at things as one forest," she said. "I think there's a growing understanding that you protect wildlife by protecting the habitat."

The state's Timber, Fish and Wildlife (TFW) agreement, which has been in effect three years, allowed scientists for the first time to scrutinize logging proposals on private land.

Biologists for the state Department of Fisheries and Department of Wildlife, as well as for the Washington Environmental Council and Indian tribes, are routinely making recommendations to protect natural systems.

"TFW has put a microscope on the whole process of resource protection," said Mike Reed, who reviews proposals for the S'Klallam Tribe. "What we are seeing is not a pretty picture."

The Department of Natural Resources, which has the final say on logging applications, does not always follow the recommendations. And biologists for every agency are overburdened by the sheer number of applications.

"We're in decline for a large number of wildlife populations," said Reed. "Our policies ... are not meeting the true functional needs for fish and wildlife populations. We must allow the landscape to be left in an unmanaged state or walk lightly across it without disrupting the movements of wildlife species."

In many places around Puget Sound, it is too late to preserve intact ecosystems, but there may be hope for Hood Canal.

Kitsap, Mason and Jefferson county governments must take an active role to protect forest lands from urban sprawl, according to Reed. Once a forested area is

• • • • • • • • • •

SECTION 7

TOWARD
KEEPING
TIMBERLANDS
INTACT

By Christopher Dunagan

developed with houses, it is lost as wildlife habitat.

On the other hand, logging activities need not destroy fish and wildlife habitat if done carefully, with an eye to resource protection, he added.

How to balance resource protection with the financial interests of timber owners was the goal of the Sustainable Forestry Roundtable, which brought together landowners, state agencies, counties, environmental groups and Indian tribes.

Roundtable discussions continued for a year before a settlement was proposed in 1990. It would have, among other things, limited timber harvesting in a watershed and required major landowners to retain 10 percent of their holdings as "late successional" (eventual old-growth) habitat.

"For the first time," said Golde, in talking about the proposal, "we have a portion of private land devoted to the protection of wildlife."

For timberland owners, the 10-year agreement offered stability as the winds of change continue to blow, said Bob Gustavson, negotiator for the Washington Forest Practices Association.

"SFR (Sustainable Forestry Roundtable) is part of a continuing reflection of both knowledge of the resources we're dealing with and the changing values of society," he noted.

The proposal introduced concepts that biologists have long desired. One is "thresholds," which trigger more and more scrutiny as the environment becomes more severely damaged.

For example, one threshold focuses on streams. Proposed logging in an area would be subject to restrictions if silt levels in a nearby stream exceed 10 percent of the bottom gravel (as measured by established methods.) A 25 percent silt-to-gravel ratio would trigger even stronger measures, such as halting all logging in the watershed.

A few streams in the Hood Canal area already exceed 10 percent, said Reed, who sees the threshold provisions as a major concession by landowners.

Other thresholds would be established for different types of wildlife.

Another new concept is that of "perimeter." The idea is to retain good-sized trees around any new clearcuts. Logging would not be allowed unless 90 percent of the perimeter (surrounding forests) contained trees at least five years old, or 60 percent were at least 15 years old, or 30 percent were at least 30 years old.

Furthermore, a team of scientists would review the impacts, and possibly prevent logging, when a landowner proposes to harvest 500 acres or 4 percent of his holdings (whichever is larger) in a watershed in one year.

Altogether, the proposal provided a framework for long-term timber management while protecting habitat, said Gustavson.

"You don't just paint the landscape to look different overnight," he said. "When you fly in an airplane, the pattern you see is what was happening 10, 20, 30, 40, 50 years ago."

But the Sustainable Forestry Roundtable agreement broke down in 1991 when environmental groups refused to endorse the proposal their representatives helped negotiate. The groups complained that too many concessions had been made to win agreement from the timber owners. They were particularly concerned about the 10-year term of the agreement, worried that much could be lost in 10 years if the agreement contained unforeseen loopholes.

State lands commissioner Brian Boyle tried to take the proposal to the state Legislature anyway, submitting it without the endorsement of the environmental groups. The proposal died for lack of support from both the environmental lobby and the timber growers. Boyle intends to try again to win approval of the landmark proposal.

But the Sustainable Forestry Roundtable experience offers graphic evidence of just how difficult it is to forge an agreement that bridges the differing views of a resource such as timber. Is it more valuable as lumber or as a forest?

• • • • • • • • • •

"The problem is that there is not a lot of cooperatiave long-range planning. I don't think anyone knows how much of the whole Hood Canal drainage can be harvested and converted to other uses."

— Donna Simmons, state Ecological Commission

*Bernard Tom patrols the waters of
Hood Canal as an enforcement
officer for the S'Klallam Tribe.*

F iltered sunlight painted the water a deep, dark green as Bernard Tom guided his patrol craft between the concrete piers of Hood Canal Bridge.

A cool breeze kicked up a slight chop on the surface, producing what sounded like a drumbeat as the hull contacted each approaching wave.

It was the last Wednesday in August, and the earliest tinges of autumn were in the air.

Tom gazed out upon the water, searching for fishermen with nets in the water or any boater signaling for help. Hood Canal looked especially empty this day and not much in need of a fishery patrol officer. Northern Hood Canal would remain quiet until the arrival of the coho and chum later in the year.

Tom, who grew up on the Little Boston Reservation at Port Gamble, wore the uniform identifying him as an enforcement officer for the S'Klallam Tribe, a job he has held for 13 years.

Fifteen years ago, his job didn't exist. The state Department of Fisheries wrote the rules and carried out the enforcement.

Fifteen years have brought dramatic changes to Hood Canal and, in fact, all of Puget Sound. Today, the local Indian tribes — Skokomish and S'Klallams — play an equal role in managing the complex fishery.

Scientists have learned much about salmon in the past 15 years. They have a better understanding of their migration, feeding patterns and habitat needs.

Harvest managers balance issues of wild salmon versus hatchery stocks, of one salmon species versus another, and of sport fishing versus commercial fishing.

Habitat managers face the potential extinction of wild salmon runs due to logging practices and commercial development — activities never given much consideration in the past.

Managing the resource means using computers to keep track of five species of migratory salmon traveling in mysterious pathways through state, national and international waters.

In the mid-'70s, everyone seemed to be talking about salmon. Commercial fishermen had been catching the powerful fish from the Pacific Ocean to the inland waters, while Indian fishermen waited at the end of the line for a declining number. Their catch: just 5-10 percent of the Puget Sound total.

The prized salmon, revered by the ancient Indians, were pushed and pulled through court battles and legislative scuffles. Even on quiet Hood Canal, gunshots could be heard in the turmoil that followed a federal court ruling by an audacious judge named George Boldt.

Boldt. The name still stirs strong feelings among fishermen. His controversial decision, later upheld by the U.S. Supreme Court, assured Indians an equal role — no more, no less than the white man's — in determining the future of the salmon resource.

Even more controversial at the time was Boldt's division of the resource. With the judiciousness of King Solomon, Boldt ruled that century-old treaties ensured tribal fishermen an equal share of the allowable salmon harvest.

Overnight, non-Indian fishermen were faced with a 40 percent reduction in their supply of salmon.

The transition that followed Boldt's dramatic decision has been less than smooth. In the emotionally charged atmosphere of the time, both Indian and non-Indian fishermen complained that the other side had fired shots at them.

In one incident, a non-Indian gillnetter was critically wounded by a Fisheries officer patroling at the entrance to Hood Canal. The officer claimed his boat was about to be rammed, though no charges were issued. Facing a $4 million lawsuit, the state agreed to pay the paralyzed fisherman $250,000 in damages.

Many fishermen still can't swallow Boldt's ruling, but after years of negotiations, state and Indian authorities have reached a working accommodation. Joint management of the resource and coordinated enforcement of the fishing industry are evident on Hood Canal.

State and Indian fisheries experts use a complex system of calculating returning salmon. They account for the Pacific Ocean catch as well as fish taken from the Strait of Juan de Fuca. They provide for "escape-

ment" — the number of fish necessary to sustain the natural runs. Then they divide what is left.

"We set up a fishing schedule to deal with our share of the fish," said Dennis Austin of the Department of Fisheries. "The tribes do the same, but they have to deal with each other."

At first, Boldt's decision triggered disagreements between the tribes and state. Parties relied on the courts to settle disputes over the allocation of specific runs.

"We don't seek third-party resolution as often as we used to," said Austin. "We realize we can cut the baby in half as well as Solomon if that's what it comes down to."

Nick Lampsakis, senior biologist for the Point No Point Treaty Area, worked in fisheries research at the University of Washington and with the National Marine Fisheries Service before coming to Hood Canal.

"A lot of professionals were hoping things would end up as they have," he said. "The acrimony and the fighting have ended and the professionalism has increased."

Prior to Boldt, the Department of Fisheries had been a "closed book," said Lampsakis. Now, estimates of salmon runs — as well as the computer calculations on which they're based — are all subject to negotiation.

"A feeling of goodwill kind of just came along," said Lampsakis, "because people on both sides realized that they could sue each other forever or sit down and work things out."

The two sides don't always agree with each other's numbers, officials say, but everything is open to discussion.

Boldt's ruling overturned the state law that kept commercial fishermen out of southern Puget Sound and eliminated what had been known as a "salmon preserve" on Hood Canal. Boldt's reasoning was that allocations among tribes should be based on traditional fishing areas, so managers must deal with the returns to streams and rivers where salmon originate. That couldn't be done if the fish were caught before reaching Hood Canal.

Nevertheless, the Hood Canal Salmon Management Plan (a negotiated agreement approved by the courts) discusses the canal as a single management area.

Some folks, like state Sen. Brad Owen, D-Shelton, would like to reserve the non-

■ ■ ■ ■ ■ ■ ■ ■ ■ ■

"The right of taking fish, at all the usual and accustomed grounds and stations, is further secured to said Indians in common with the citizens of the territory."
—Point No Point Treaty

Indian share of Hood Canal salmon primarily for sport fishermen. He has pushed that proposal in the Legislature since 1988.

The Boldt ruling was like a declaration of independence for Hood Canal tribes. It not only boosted the struggling economies of the reservations, it also united tribal members behind a single issue.

"People used to leave the reservation," said Lampsakis. "I have been around a number of years and have seen families moving back."

The tribal harvest isn't making anybody rich, he said, "but it gives people something to call their own."

Today, more than 300 fishermen are registered with the Skokomish and Port Gamble S'Klallam tribes alone. At the time of the Boldt decision, the numbers of Indian fishermen could be counted on one hand.

Fishing meant money to buy equipment as well, and today about 40 Indian gillnet boats operate in the Hood Canal region. (Local tribes do not allow purse seine operations.)

Hood Canal fish hatcheries — operated separately by federal, state and tribal governments — have greatly expanded the commercial salmon harvest in the canal since the mid-70s, yet sport fishermen have noticed a severe decline in their catch.

State officials blame the problem on the type of fish being reared in the hatcheries, among other things, and they've negotiated a partial solution.

Hatchery production has been shifted to increase the catch of coho and chinook salmon by non-Indian sport fishermen without reducing the tribal harvest; the salmon were then held in net pens on the canal over the winter to encourage them to stay in the canal. The first releases of the salmon came in the spring of 1991. So far, the results of the effort are inconclusive.

In the meantime, Bernard Tom, other Indian enforcement officers and their counterparts in the state department continue to patrol the canal, and work with increasing harmony.

"Our working relationship seems to be getting better all the time," said Tom. "If state officers see tribal members who are violating (fishing regulations), they can turn them over to us. We do the same for them. We weren't always confident with that type of relationship.

"When I first came on, I noticed a lot of poaching activities, but it mellowed out," he said. "I'm not saying it stopped ..."

The controversial Boldt decision allowed Skokomish tribal member Bill Smith to make Hood Canal waters his office.

• • • • • • • • •

SECTION 2

RECLAIMING
THE SALMON
CULTURE

*By Julie
McCormick*

Bill Smith makes his first set of the night off Dewatto, eyes the seal waiting to bite the belly out of his livelihood and jokes about the money he's losing.

"He's saying, 'Here's Bill, it must be dinner time'," cracks the 45-year-old ex-college quarterback. Smith also is an ex-college administrator, the former chairman of the Skokomish Tribe, founder and first director of the Northwest Indian Fisheries Commission and sometime househusband — in the off-season — with a 17-month-old baby girl.

It costs $25 to fuel the twin 350s that power Smith's 32-foot gillnetter between its moorage at Union and the open fishing area of the canal.

He is still making payments on the sleek, $60,000 Cougar, trimmed in the gray-and-maroon of Washington State University and named for his alma mater.

Between the July 8 opening and this mid-August evening in 1990, the 200 tribal members who fish the canal or the river running through the reservation for which their tribe is named have caught 400 of the year's 10,000 king (chinook) allocation. The tribe's actual king catch was 2,000 fish in 1990.

Smith fears the Skokomish may not even have reason to bother going out for the next run of 1990, the silvers (coho) are that scarce. He blames it mostly on ocean factory draggers. Their 30-mile-long death nets snag everything from sea birds to dolphins along with many of the millions of salmon heading back to spawning grounds in North America.

The real living from fishing in the canal depends on chum, a late salmon that sportsmen cannot attract in the saltwater canal.

The tribal half of the 1990 late fall run was about 200,000.

"If you can't get 200 a day, you're just not trying," Smith says. He "picks" the second water haul of the night for his 1,800-foot net. Slippery, orange jellyfish "marmalade" collects instep-deep on the Cougar's pointy deck, and Smith sloshes around carefully in high rubber boots.

It's dark now and all hope for a catch at the light change is gone. Bill Smith radios his brother Dave, whose smaller gillnetter lies off a point just south of Cougar. Light changes and point locations seem to promise more fish — sometimes.

Dave has caught two 10-pound kings, and Bill decides to take up residence off another point across the canal. He cranks the net out at an angle. Phosphorous lights it like a star chart in the dark water.

"The best thing that ever happened to Northwest fisheries was Boldt," he says of the 1974 court decision that put his people in the fishing business beyond subsistence for the first time in 150 years.

Early whites noted the rotund figures common among West Coast tribes. Salmon, their main food source, was so abundant that they turned to farming only when the white man's government forced it upon them.

Their hunting and gathering culture was unique in its sophistication — rich in art, religion and organization. Their potlatches particularly galled whites, who were repulsed by and soon outlawed the achievement of social status through dispersal of wealth, rather than the hoarding of it.

Boldt was good because the resource was declining and there were too many licenses, Smith says of the pre-Boldt period. Fish greed drove the badly regulated, non-Indian commercial fleet to double between 1965 and 1974.

Pre-Boldt, the Skokomish had no gillnetters. They still have no purse seiners, a decision most tribes have made to spread the resource more evenly among tribal members, Smith says. A giant seiner or two could take the entire Skokomish allocation in a season.

Smith believes all tribes should do what the Skokomish have done from the beginning — spread their allocation equally among tribal members, not allow those who are economically better off to take the lion's share of the catch.

Tribal members once set nets across their river — now known as a "termination point" — and operated traps and weirs. Many still do, including younger brother Jake Smith, who's operating nets exactly where his grandfather's were.

Unlike many other coast tribes, whose "usual and accustomed" fishing grounds extended into the sound or the straits, where the Fraser River sockeye run at the same time as king, Skokomish tribal members are restricted to their river and Hood Canal.

Bill Smith was moving up the administrative career ladder as financial aid director for The Evergreen State College in 1974. He also was tribal chairman and sitting in on the fishing rights trial.

When Judge Boldt surprised most of the state, including the tribes, by granting them half the salmon and steelhead catch, Smith quit his job, started the Northwest Indian Fisheries Commission and plunked down his first payment on a $30,000 boat.

"Everybody was so afraid the red horde was going to take all the fish," he recalls.

Instead, the Point No Point Treaty Council spends about $200,000 in federal money annually on salmon enhancement for the canal.

Smith considers his decision to buy a boat "one of the pivotal points" in his life. The way he tells it, he believed in the decision, believed in the tribal right, and was a workaholic for Indians at the time. Someone needed to get the ball rolling, take the financial risk and learn how to fish commercially.

"It was just by guess and by golly. See, we didn't have any experience, we fished in the river."

Smith organized the Skokomish, the Port Gamble S'Klallams, and the Lower Elwha and Jamestown Klallams into a new version of the old 1855 Point No Point Treaty Council. The Chimacums had died off long ago, of smallpox, historians say.

His attempts to reestablish the regional councils that had bargained in 1855 and 1856 with Washington Territorial Governor Isaac Stevens failed beyond his own area.

Indian tribes differ as much between themselves as nations do, he said, but to white society "an Indian is an Indian is an Indian."

Bill Smith's fishing earns about $20,000 a year to support himself, his youngest daughter and wife, who recently left her

> *"The best thing that ever happened to Northwest fisheries was Boldt."*
> —Bill Smith

school administrator's job to stay home with their child. The couple decided to stick with it as long as they can, despite the fact they could probably increase their income by returning to the rat race.

"I'm not an idiot, I've been blessed," Smith says. "Most of the people I know fish not for the money but for the lifestyle ... A school teacher or a nurse makes more than I do. But how can you measure that where I work, people spend thousands of dollars to come and vacation — right outside my office window."

The Boldt Decision

More than 100 years of history weighed upon Judge George Boldt as he sat down to write the federal court order that changed salmon management throughout Puget Sound.

"This should have been brought 50 years ago," the judge said in court, as an assistant attorney general took down his words in longhand. "There has been much damage, both physically and spiritually, for want of adjudication in a court of law.

"Hopefully," said the judge, "we have reached a turning point, and this decision will improve the situation between Indians and non-Indians, who should be acting like brothers."

Boldt was in his final years as he made his historical decision, not only dividing up the salmon resource in a numerical way but helping the Indians continue their culture.

Some say it cost him physically and emotionally. How did he feel about the angry fishermen who defied his order or the bumper stickers that said, "Save Our Salmon — Can Judge Boldt"?

While non-Indian fishermen were immediate losers in his decision, many biologists argue that Boldt's interference helped prevent the further demise of the resource.

But it was history, not protecting the salmon, that shaped his opinion.

When white men first arrived in Hood Canal, salmon were abundant. Hundreds of miles of streams on the Kitsap and Olympic peninsulas provided spawning habitat for chinook, chum, coho and pink salmon, as well as steelhead.

To the Indians, salmon were more than just food. They embodied spiritual connections. Since return of the mystical fish must be voluntarily, Indians approached the relationship with care, even honoring the first salmon to be caught each year.

In the 1850s, it must have seemed impossible to deplete the salmon runs. In a peaceful acquisition of millions of acres of land, Isaac Stevens, the first governor of

Washington Territory, assured Puget Sound tribes they would have the right to fish forever.

During the signing of the Point No Point Treaty, which governs the Hood Canal area, Stevens said, "This paper secures your fish."

The treaty included this language: "The right of taking fish, at all usual and accustomed grounds and stations, is further secured to said Indians in common with the citizens of the territory..."

This troublesome language, at the very core of the Boldt decision, was maintained as federal law — but without legal interpretation — for more than 100 years.

Meanwhile, white settlers proceeded to burn the candle at both ends. While disrupting salmon runs and destroying stream habitat with logging operations, non-Indians also caught increasing numbers of salmon on their way to remaining spawning areas.

"Traditionally, the Indians stopped fishing and removed their gear from the streams when they had caught their winter's supply," said Anthony Netboy in his book *Salmon: the World's Most Harassed Fish*. "In contrast, the white men ... fished as long as the runs continued unless restrained by law (which they often defied)."

In 1921, the Department of Fisheries was created to halt the uncontrolled exploitation. In 1934, the state passed Initiative 77, which banned fixed fishing gear. It also moved net fishermen out of Hood Canal and southern Puget Sound. But the number of fishermen continued to increase, and fishing efforts moved farther and farther away from salmon streams.

It became a matter of too many fishermen chasing too few fish, according to economists studying the Puget Sound fishing industry. As the fish disappeared, they were chased ever more vigorously by modern equipment.

To the state, the treaty language "taking fish ... in common with" meant that all regulations applied equally to

Indians and non-Indians. But Indians, who traditionally fished at the entrance to streams, found the runs depleted by the time the salmon reached them. Some began to fish in defiance of state regulations.

After a violent confrontation in 1970 between Indians fishing on the Puyallup River and state game wardens, U.S. Attorney Stan Pitkin challenged the state's authority on behalf of seven tribes. Other tribes later joined the suit.

Judge Boldt decided the harvestable salmon should be split 50-50 between Indian and non-Indian fishermen.

It wasn't an arbitrary division. As early as 1899, the U.S. Supreme Court ruled that a treaty should be construed "not according to the technical meaning of its words to learned lawyers, but in the sense in which they would naturally be understood by the Indians."

Boldt studied the language in which the treaties were presented to the tribes in the 1850s. He faced the fact that nobody had anticipated the future of the salmon resource. And he decided that Indians and non-Indians, as two distinct groups, should be "sharing equally the opportunity to take fish."

Steelhead, which are strictly a game fish in Washington state, were not considered any different from salmon at the time of the treaties, so Boldt ruled they also should be split 50-50.

Boldt determined that tribes should be allowed to regulate their own fishermen, in keeping with the desires of Congress to increase tribal self-government. But first, he said, they must establish well-organized governments, set up enforcement units, maintain accurate membership rolls and be able to collect information about salmon harvest.

Boldt retained jurisdiction in the case, and the federal court was soon called upon to approve a number of early management plans. Issues still before the court include whether tribes can insist that salmon be protected from man-caused damage to habitat in the streams.

By Christopher Dunagan

• • • • • • • • • •

"Most of the people I know fish not for the money but for the lifestyle. ... People spend thousands of dollars to come and vacation — right outside my office window."
—Bill Smith

Nick Jerkovich wonders whether another generation of his family can make a living catching fish.

• • • • • • • • • •

Section 3

Making a Livng from the Water

By Jeff Brody

Nick Jerkovich of Gig Harbor is the third generation in his family to make his living hauling fish from the sea, but he may be the last. Not yet 40, Jerkovich believes he will see in his lifetime a ban on commercial fishing in Washington waters.

The Gig Harbor native is a successful purse seine fisherman. He takes his 58-foot boat yearly to the herring fishery off San Francisco and to Alaska for salmon, before returning in the fall to fish for salmon in Puget Sound.

Like most purse seiners with license to fish in Puget Sound, Jerkovich spends a few days each year fishing in Hood Canal.

He sees the political battle between sport and commercial fishermen in Hood Canal specifically, and Washington state more generally, as one that commercials eventually will lose.

"I can sympathize with the loggers on the Olympic Peninsula," he said. "I know how they feel. I don't think the fishery can support the number of fishermen who are out there."

Larry Charrier, a commercial fisherman for 20 years, chooses to be more opti-

mistic than Jerkovich.

"It goes against common sense and good management for there not to be a commercial fishery," said Charrier, who resists the suggestion that politics will dictate a closure. "I don't want to give people the excuse to just phase out the commercial fishery. There's no reason it can't be a viable industry in Hood Canal and Puget Sound."

Jerkovich opened his boat last fall to observers from sport fishing groups interested in closing Hood Canal to commercial fishing. He had what he considered a typical day on the canal, catching about 800 chum salmon.

The observers saw none of the violations that sport fishermen suspect of the commercials. Jerkovich thought they gained an understanding that the commercial effort doesn't interfere with sport fishing opportunities, but was disappointed to hear later that some of the people he had hosted were still speaking out strongly to keep commercials out of the fishery.

"I have a hard time fathoming why people would be against commercial seiners in Hood Canal," Jerkovich said.

The vast majority of the commercial catch is chum salmon, not generally considered a sport fish because chum resist taking bait. Chinook and coho, which are targets of sport fishermen, are caught by commercial fishermen in the canal, but not in great numbers.

And Jerkovich is willing to let the sportsmen have the coho.

"The silvers (coho) are so small, we don't need to be there. It's not worth the kind of hard feelings that are generated just so we can go after 4,000 fish," he said.

Charrier believes there is more opposition from waterfront and view property owners than from sport fishermen.

"A lot of pressure is coming from property owners along the canal," he said. "They resent commercial fishermen on the water. They have the perception that what we're doing is something that should be done where they can't see it."

When Jerkovich started fishing Hood Canal more than 10 years ago, fewer than 100 purse seiners would participate in the fall Hood Canal chum run. The run was smaller, and there were better fishing opportunities elsewhere.

But now, due to pressures in other fisheries and more limited U.S. access to the Fraser River sockeye salmon run through the Strait of Juan de Fuca, commercials are "forced to fish all over," Jerkovich said.

"I wouldn't be surprised if there are 200 seiners out on the canal on peak fishing days," he said.

In the same 10 years, enhancement efforts have boosted the number of chum in the canal considerably.

Robert Zuanich, executive director of the Purse Seine Vessel Owners Association, says there are about 350 state purse seine licenses to fish the Puget Sound region, which includes Hood Canal. About 230 of those licenses are active, he said, and nearly every active Puget Sound license holder will fish in Hood Canal during at least part of the chum run.

A purse seiner after chum salmon needs to catch between 2,500 and 3,000 fish in the six days it is likely to be on Hood Canal to make the effort worthwhile. That catch, worth about $30,000 at market, is about a quarter of what the boat will earn fishing all Washington waters.

Most purse seiners also fish in Alaska and off Oregon, and the canal hosts fishermen from Alaska and Oregon on the dozen-or-so days it's open, Zuanich said.

Purse seiners take about 80 percent of the commercial salmon catch on Hood Canal. Gillnetters like Charrier are more numerous — 1,110 licenses and about 600 active boats but take only about 20 percent of the Hood Canal catch.

Purse seiners, larger boats with much more expensive gear, catch fish in a net that closes at the bottom. Fish swim into the holes in a gillnet's mesh and can't back out to escape. Fish so caught are subject to predators, and Charrier says seals in Hood Canal "patrol" his net and often get to his catch before he does.

Most of the Hood Canal catch is chum. The value of the non-Indian Hood Canal commercial chum fishery has ranged in the last decade from a low of about $483,000 in 1983 to a high of almost $5 million in 1987.

In comparison, the canal has a very small commercial fishery for bottom fish. Only $4,900 worth of bottom fish were taken in 1988, according to state Department of Fisheries records. The Legislature banned the use of bottom trawling rigs on the canal in 1989 because of the damage caused by the drag nets.

As a result, dogfish, a type of shark, is the only bottom fish now being taken commercially from the canal in any numbers, according to Greg Bargmann of the Department of Fisheries.

"It's insignificant as a commercial fishery from a bottom fish perspective," Bargmann said of the canal.

There is a small commercial fishery for surf perch in the late winter and early spring, and a more significant fishery for herring, mostly north of the Hood Canal Bridge, in the summer.

Commercial fishing boomed in Puget Sound in the early decades of the 20th Century, and the resource started to decline. Despite increasing attempts to regulate the catch, commercial fishing continued to grow and salmon stocks continued to decline.

In the wake of the Boldt decision in 1974, which guaranteed tribes the right to half the salmon in Washington waters, the state and the tribes began salmon enhancement efforts designed to offset the increased catch of the tribal fishermen.

Fish hatcheries in the canal watershed boosted production, especially of chum.

"Boldt caused a lot of money to be devoted to enhancement," said Zuanich, "and a lot of money went into hatchery

Hood Canal is the third best commercial salmon fishery in Puget Sound, trailing the Fraser River sockeye run in the San Juans and the coho and chum runs in the southern part of the sound.

Hood Canal commercial fish catch

Non-Indian commercial salmon catch, in pounds

	'76	'78	'80	'82	'84	'86	'88
Chinook	8	24,792	3,670	9,159	15,355	38,573	20,580
Coho	0	54,217	1,837	142,227	121,347	267,423	15,497
Chum	188,366	2,161,068	130,174	789,500	1,618,295	1,990,961	2,188,439
Total value	$108,151	$2,687,063	$582,100	$615,996	$1,339,485	$1,206,802	$781,024

Indian salmon catch, in pounds

	'76	'78	'80	'82	'84	'86	'88
Chinook	269,105	141,772	71,227	76,311	97,854	172,288	193,282
Coho	465,042	264,127	774,384	352,493	126,688	237,108	34,488
Chum	136,206	2,222,671	753,347	1,041,899	1,679,443	1,816,456	1,946,614
Total value	$768,292	$2,327,975	$1,398,977	$880,756	$1,068,443	$932,111	$1,904,725

Commercial bottomfish catches, by pounds

	'76	'78	'80	'82	'84	'86	'88
Flatfish	51,969	67,305	33,874	43,889	4,170	33,182	607
Dogfish	2,149,963	425,078	571,284	75,305	123,072	11,476	15,666
Rockfish	6,943	11,910	4,213	1,860	0	977	11
Pacific Cod	75,075	64,301	19,796	279	5,443	9,167	24
Total pounds	2,414,347	604,909	648,103	145,287	143,893	58,780	20,326

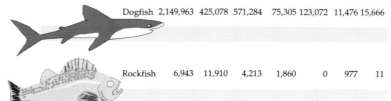

Source: Washington Department of Fisheries

The Economics of Fishing

Can a person make a living fishing in Puget Sound and Hood Canal? Not if you owe money on your boat, say those familiar with the commercial fishery. And even if you're free and clear, it's still a marginal proposition.

A typical purse seiner has about 25 days to fish Puget Sound waters, which include Hood Canal and the water around the San Juans, according to Robert Zuanich of the Purse Seine Vessel Owners Association.

"It takes about $15,000 for insurance and maintenance to start the season if the boat is paid for," Zuanich said. "The typical boat might earn $65,000 from the Fraser River sockeye run, about $30,000 from the Hood Canal chum run, and between $15,000 and $20,000 in the south sound fishing coho and chum. Out of that, you have to pay for your crew of three or four."

What's left, in a typical year, would be $35,000-$40,000 for the boat and skipper, from which must come that $15,000 needed to start the next season.

With a $150,000 investment in boat and gear, most purse seiners are forced to seek additional earnings from fisheries outside Puget Sound.

Even for gillnetters, with a much smaller investment, the economics are not favorable.

Larry Charrier fishes exclusively in the Puget Sound region and says he earns a "modest" living. But he said he could not pay for his boat and gear on his earnings.

Gillnetters tend to do better in other parts of the sound than in Hood Canal, where the terminal type of fishery seems to favor the purse seine method. In addition, Charrier said, the canal's large seal population can raid fish from a gill net much easier than from a purse seine.

By Jeff Brody

Four years ago, the non-Indian commercial season for Fraser River sockeye was 117 hours; this year the season was 28 hours. That puts more presure on the Hood Canal fishery.

---

production in Hood Canal. The chum run was enhanced significantly."

State statistics show a general improvement in the non-Indian commercial catch on Hood Canal since the Boldt decision. The average annual Hood Canal non-Indian commercial catch in the first four years after Boldt was 876,750 pounds; the average annual catch was 2.5 million pounds from 1986-1989.

Despite that, Zuanich said, "I don't think you'd find any commercial fisherman who would say that the fishery is better because of Boldt."

There are more fishermen going after those salmon, and there are fewer fish available elsewhere in Washington waters.

State licensed commercial fishermen once had a right to half the 12 million-15 million Fraser River sockeye that run through the Strait of Juan de Fuca every year. But the most recent U.S.-Canada agreement limited U.S. fishermen to 7 million sockeye from that run during 1989-1992.

American fishermen were allocated only 2.2 million of the record 21 million run of sockeye this year, and that was split 50-50 between the white and the tribal fishermen under the terms of the Boldt decision.

Jerkovich questions the basic finding of the Boldt decision and believes original treaty language should be interpreted to give the tribes equal opportunity to catch, not a guarantee of 50 percent of the fish.

But the Boldt decision is history now, and the real question is about the future. The economic problems of commercial fishing in Puget Sound existed before the decision, and still exist today.

"I think Hood Canal is probably one of the best places for enhancement," Jerkovich said. "I would say there are more fish now in the canal than before. We're barely fishing now and we're making money; we used to fish for days and get less. But the fishery doesn't have stability. Enhancement should be the No. 1 priority. We can raise enough fish for sportsmen and Indians and the commercials," Jerkovich said.

"I would like to see it where every sportsman could go out and catch a fish or two every week, and I see no reason why that can't happen, and still have a commercial fishery."

Boosting hatchery production can't

solve all the problems, however.

Charrier sees sportsmen fail to land hatchery raised chinook even when they are present in the canal.

"Hatchery fish don't feed when they get down toward the rivers. Kings (chinook) from the natural runs do," he said. Commercials may catch them in nets, but fish that aren't feeding won't take a sports fisherman's bait or lure.

"I fished in the canal when I was 8," said Charrier, who was born in Shelton and now lives near Port Townsend. "I understand why the sportsmen are concerned. Sports fishing has really declined in the canal. But, in general, it is difficult to understand why there's so much conflict between sports and commercial fishermen. We have the same enhancement goals. I still think that sport and commercial fishermen have more in common than they have at odds. It is important that we work together on enhancement."

• • • • • • • • •

"They could split the money they spend on Department of Fisheries among the commercial fishermen and we'd earn as much without going out in the boat."
—Nick Jerkovich, Gig Harbor seiner

Bait Business a Family Affair

If you've eaten salmon caught in Puget Sound by a sport fisherman, quite likely you've got Bert Nelson and his family to thank for helping bring the meal to your table.

The Nelsons catch and package the herring many local salmon fishermen use for bait. They've owned and operated Kitsap Bait Sales for more than 25 years.

Nelson, 68, a Bremerton native and 1940 graduate of Bremerton High School, has been fishing in Puget Sound since 1936. He switched from salmon to herring in the late 1950s, when "politics squeezed the little guy out — that was me."

Nelson's bait business began in the early 1960s after cutting a deal with his daughter, Janet, who was in high school, and sons Malcom, Marvin and Orrin, in junior high.

"I told them that if they wanted to pack our own herring, I'd pay them a dollar an hour. But, I said I'd give them only 10 cents, that I'd keep the other 90 cents to save for their schooling. They agreed, we tried it and it worked."

The herring packing operation that began as a family business still involves most of the family. Janet lives with her husband and still works sorting and packing herring. Marvin, 40, spends most of his time between April and October on the family's herring boat. His wife, Marie, supervises crews at the bait packing table. Orrin, 35, manages the whole operation which also includes the 26-slip Kitsap Marina and a boat and equipment sales operation. His wife, Kristine, handles the firm's books.

About half of Nelson's bait fish are "toughened up" in net pens at Squamish Harbor, across Hood Canal from Lofall. Summer herring caught by Nelson's son Marvin with the family boat in Skunk Bay on the north end of the Kitsap Peninsula or Mutiny Bay on the west side of Whidbey Island tend to be fat and "soft." But after spending a few weeks in the holding pens losing their fat, the herring are more suitable for salmon bait.

Nelson said fishing is good in Hood Canal, if you're looking for perch or squid, "but there's no demand, no price, no money in those kinds of fish."

He feels the biggest threat to Hood Canal is not overfishing: "It's pollution. I'm in favor of getting rid of all those (Department of) Fisheries biologists and hiring more (enforcement) patrol officers. We don't need to study it more. They need to patrol it more."

By Gene Yoachum

Sports fishermen angle for chinook in the waters of the Skokomish River.

T he salmon runs in Hood Canal are the stuff of legend. An old S'Klallam woman recalls the days in the 1920s when the fish were so thick "you could walk from shore to shore on their backs without getting your feet wet."

Families caught so many they got sick of smoking them.

But man's intrusion on nature has taken its toll. The salmon fishing isn't what it used to be. Some blame the commercial fishermen. Others blame nature. Others blame man.

"There was a time when this was a paradise for salmon anglers, too," says Bob Mottram, a Tacoma newspaper columnist and author of one of the Northwest's most popular fishing guidebooks, "Saltwater Salmon Angling." "But the canal started

falling on hard times in the late 1970s, when sport catches dropped off dramatically."

The decline has been attributed to a variety of factors, from an exploding population of fish-eating marine mammals, to the destruction of stream habitat, to driftnet fishing on the high seas and increased competition from Indian and non-Indian commercial fishermen in Washington waters.

Local fishermen don't think the reasons are all that complex. Leroy Trammell of Belfair fished in Hood Canal for 45 years until he gave it up in disappointment and frustration a couple of years ago.

"When they brought the commercial fishermen in, within two years, you couldn't buy a bite out there," he says gruffly. "In the '50s, '60s and early '70s, I could go out any day of the week before the kids went to school and be back by breakfast with a limit of three steelhead.

"The fisheries people want to talk about the Boldt decision, but the Boldt decision didn't come in until after the fish were gone."

The Boldt decision, named after the judge who rendered it, guarantees Indian fishermen half the salmon and steelhead in Northwestern waters.

Trammell blames the administration of former Gov. Dan Evans in the early 1970s for allowing commercial fishing to start up again. Commercial fishing had been banned in the canal since the passage of Initiative 77 by the voters in 1934.

But here is where the complexities that Mottram talks about come into play. The number of fish in the canal has actually increased during the last few years, according to Fisheries Department figures. The fish are there; people just aren't catching them.

More salmon are in Hood Canal than at any time since the 1970s, asserts a report released last January by the Washington Department of Fisheries.

"Unfortunately, recreational catches have been declining despite increasing runs of chinook and coho," admit the authors of "Hood Canal Salmon — A Contemporary Management Issue in Puget Sound."

"Fishery managers at the (department) sought an explanation for this paradox of increasing run sizes and declining sport harvests," the report says. "For chinook salmon, the case seems to involve discontinuance of the spring chinook program at Hoodsport Hatchery in the 1980s and low survival of chinook released from Hood Canal hatcheries."

Local fishermen have another theory. After commercial fishing began depleting natural stocks in 1970s, Indian tribes and the state began dumping millions of hatchery-raised fish into the canal.

Hatchery chinook and coho compete with the natural fish for food in the canal but

Skokomish River

Intensive harvesting of fish coming back to the George Adams Hatchery at Purdy Creek has depleted natural salmon runs on the Skokomish.

seem to have a poorer survival rate at sea. In contrast, hatchery-raised chum salmon, which don't take bait, seem to survive very well.

Trammel and others say the hatchery fish have supplanted the natural salmon runs. And they say hatchery fish don't go after fishermen's lures the way the natural stock does.

Fish biologists tend to pooh-pooh such theories and claim that Hood Canal is one of the best all-around fishing spots in the Northwest. It is one of the few areas where fishermen can catch something nearly any time of the year. And fishermen can use just about any method there is, from wading in the river to trolling from a boat to spin-casting from shore.

But Jim Talbot, who runs the Seabeck Marina when owner Dennis McBreen is out campaigning for improving the sport catch, said 1990 fishing in the canal was "way off."

"There's just no harvest out there," Talbot said. "The problem is the purse seiners come in here and there's nothing left for the sportsmen."

Why not ban commercial fishing altogether? State Sen. Brad Owen, D-Shelton, whose big orange and black campaign sign adorns the side of a building on McBreen's dock, has been unable to win passage of a bill that would do just that.

The fisheries department has an ambitious plan to improve sport fishing in the canal, but results won't begin showing up for several years.

A progress report issued in 1990 showed that several key parts of the plan had been delayed for at least a year. The report says the department has made "significant progress," however, in changing the production schedule for hatchery raised chinook salmon that could increase fish catches in 1991.

The department has opposed an outright ban on commercial fishing in the canal.

Fisheries officials say they can't

Hooking Big Chinook on Light Tackle

The crystal waters of the Skokomish River swirl around Cleo Grigsby's hips as he flicks a big No. 1 hook and a ball of orange fluff across 40 feet of open water.

With pinpoint accuracy, the hook plops just at the edge of a deep pool and a sinker pulls it out of sight into the depths where king salmon like to rest on their way upstream.

Grigsby lets the hook ride down the current then gives it a yank, swearing under his breath. Snag. He wraps the 15-pound-test line around his fist, turns his back and walks away until the line snaps. He ties another hook and ball of colored fuzz to his line and goes back to casting.

It is noon on a warm, late-summer day. Grigsby and half a dozen other fishermen have contributed a dozen hooks to the unseen hazards of the deep hole across the river during the past two hours. And not a fish among them to show for it.

"Been fishing this hole for 20 years," grouses one of Grigsby's companions, sitting on a rusted old lawn chair. "Never been this bad. It's those damn nets."

He points downriver where just around the bend is a row of white foam balls supporting an Indian gillnet.

Earlier that morning on our way to this fishing spot from Hoodsport, we passed an Indian fisherman on the highway, his pickup loaded with freshly caught king salmon. A fish broker had just bought the lot for $2 a pound.

"The Indians have to take the nets down this evening. This weekend, fishermen will be out here shoulder-to-shoulder," one of Grigsby's friends observes.

The men who fish the Skokomish wear ancient coveralls with tatters and patches but their fishing gear is spotless and expensive. Grigsby, a retired military man, says he paid $125 for the slender carbon fiber pole and another $75 for the new reel that adorns it. The other men have similar rigs.

Pat Kelly has come all the way from Aberdeen to fish in the Skokomish this day, passing up other good salmon streams closer to home because he heard the kings are running on the canal.

In 1989, Kelly said, he hooked and captured a 42-pounder using the same light fishing gear as the others. He hasn't caught another fish since, but the memory of that epic battle keeps him coming back every weekend he can get away.

By Jack Swanson

• • • • • • • • • •

"I've been fishing the Hood Canal probably 45 years. When they brought back the commercial fishermen, within two years, you couldn't buy a bite out there."
—Leroy Trammell

prevent Indians from fishing commercially anyway. And because the salmon population is so large, sports fishermen couldn't possibly catch all of the fish that would otherwise spawn and die if they weren't caught.

The department has set up meetings with sports fishing groups to try to get their cooperation and involvement in fish management programs, but the fishermen remain skeptical.

"Frankly, I think they're just going around in circles," said Duane Linkmeyer, president of the Kitsap Poggie Club. "For months one group from the department has been going around to groups showing off a new device that is supposed to help increase the salmon hatch in local streams. Now another part of the department is telling us they don't want us to fool around with the streams because it might have an adverse effect on wild salmon in the stream.

"Our response was, 'What wild salmon?'"

Like many old-timers, Linkmeyer said he has given up fishing in Hood Canal.

"It's a waste of time and money," he said. "I'm not going to go out there and chase my shadow."

He, too, blames the commercial fishermen for the drop in salmon available to sport fishermen.

"You turn loose 400 gillnetters and 260 purse seiners for two weeks and everything is gone. Everything. The rockfish, baitfish. They tear up the kelp beds and the eel grass. Even the shellfish are affected. Also, the seal population has grown. Andy Rogers, an old-timer around here, thinks the seals do more damage than the commercial fishermen."

Linkmeyer and Trammell say they feel the Fisheries Department favors the interests of commercial fishermen over sport fishermen.

"They can say what they want, but they're 100 percent commercial," Trammell says angrily. "They're not doing a damn thing for the sportsmen."

Criticism of fisheries isn't limited to those who fish in Hood Canal.

Sport fishermen throughout the state claim the state earns far more from them than it does from commercial fishermen. Anglers pay more than $30 million annually in taxes, licenses and boat fees, while commercial fishermen only pay the state around $5 million, asserts the Pacific Salmon Sport Fishing Council.

The council also claims taxpayers pay as much as $15 to produce a 7-pound coho salmon that a gillnetter sells for $1.50 per pound.

Fisheries department officials heatedly deny any bias against sportsmen and say recent changes in fish hatchery releases will enhance sport fishing in Hood Canal. Eventually, the state says its enhancement program will double the number of angler trips to the canal each year to 40,000, and double the angler success to nearly one-half fish per trip.

Linkmeyer and others snicker at such predictions because they've heard them before. And they are tired of going to meetings where they hear the same old thing.

"I told them the first meeting we had: we're not going to be able to do anything about improving fishing in the canal until we do something about commercial fishing," Linkmeyer said. "And we won't be able to do anything about that until the commercial fishermen and the Indians are sitting here with us."

• • • • • • • • •

"It has been established that commercial overfishing is the primary cause of declining sport fisheries in this country."
—Keith Herrell, president, Pacific Salmon Sportfishing Council

Finding Tranquility with Rod and Reel

As he does just about every night after work, Al Bower squints against the setting sun and catapults the long silver spinner out into the water just north of the Hood Canal Bridge.

He pops the bale of the spinning reel back into place and reels line in rapidly, tugging occasionally to give the spinner more action in the water.

Three casts. Four casts.

He picks his way carefully among the boulders near the boat ramp at Hicks County Park, finds solid footing and addresses the swift-running currents of the full tide once again.

Half a dozen casts and he is moving, working the length of the shoreline. I have been watching Bower perform his evening ballet several days a week for two years now. The point is one of my favorite writing spots. I have never seen him get a bite. Other fishermen come and go. They seldom speak.

"Ever caught one?" I ventured one night as he moved past my makeshift table.

"Yup. Right ... here."

The silver spoon flumps dutifully into the waves about 30 yards from shore. Pull, reel. Pull, reel.

"A 35-pounder. Felt like a whale. Took me an hour to bring him in."

Does the lack of fish bother him?

He chews on the question a minute, working the line by long habit.

"No. I do it mainly for the exercise."

By Jack Swanson

Wildlife biologist Ron Egan of the state Department of Fisheries is counting fewer and fewer wild salmon in the streams that empty into Hood Canal.

Ron Hirschi, a local biologist and author of delightful children's books, likes to visit local schools. He looks into the smiling faces of young people and informs them that they are the hope of the future, that their generation is called upon to save the environment.

Privately, Hirschi tells adults that the natural wonders of Hood Canal — particularly the magnificent wild salmon — might not survive that long.

Hirschi grew up around Hood Canal, fishing many of the streams in his youth. He watched careless loggers and ruthless developers destroy natural runs of salmon and trout.

"I wish I could be more positive," he said, "but the rules aren't strong enough; they aren't enforced; and people are basically uncaring, I guess."

Fishermen are taking too many salmon, from the ocean to the inland waterways, says Hirschi. Hatchery-produced fish — introduced to help fishermen increase their catch — only compound the problems facing the wild salmon.

Hirschi's assessment is echoed by other biologists, but his voice is filled with emotion as he goes beyond the cold calculations of his fellow scientists.

Consider Laudine DeCoteau Creek, a small stream that flows into Port Gamble.

"When I was a kid, I went there," said Hirschi. "It was the first stream I saw fish spawning in."

To get to the stream, he would walk through tall, aging stands of douglas fir and cedar. Gravelly stream beds were darkened from the sun as vine maples and heavy logs cast their shadows upon the cool water.

Hirschi observed sea-run cutthroat trout making their way up and down the stream — that is until logging changed everything five years ago.

"Clearcutting totally altered the character of that stream," said Hirschi. "Then 2,4-D (herbicide) was sprayed on the maples

• • • • • • • • • •

SECTION 5

CAN THE WILD SALMON SURVIVE?

By Christopher Dunagan

adjacent to the creek. In the wetlands that form the headwaters, wood waste and sludge from septic systems was dumped."

Dirt, eroding out of the clearcut area, covered spawning gravel with a layer of silt. Watercress plants took root in the muddy bottom, forming dense vegetation that made passage of salmon and trout more difficult.

"The end result," said Hirschi, "was that we couldn't find any more cutthroat trout. It will take a long time for that stream to recover."

Similar assaults on wild salmon have been under way for years throughout Hood Canal, said Hirschi, who left a job as a habitat biologist for the S'Klallam Tribe in 1990 to work fulltime writing children's books.

To be sure, Hood Canal remains in much better shape than most areas of Puget Sound — not to mention Southern California or the East Coast. Many Hood Canal streams still contain considerable spawning grounds, but they are disappearing.

As people become increasingly concerned about the environment, state and local regulations call for safer practices, said Hirschi. But, more often than not, the end result is still less than adequate.

In the early 1800s, the state of Maine contained nearly 31,000 square miles of majestic pine forests. Atlantic salmon were plentiful in bubbling streams known by French and Indian names.

Laws, some adopted as early as 1741, presumed to protect the mighty salmon. Between 1820 and 1880, 400 additional fishery laws were passed. But enforcement was uneven.

In California, commercial fishing for wild chinook, coho and steelhead began with the gold rush of 1849 and peaked with a catch of 12 million pounds of fish in 1882. Logging, mining, road construction, gravel extraction, grazing practices, pollution and dams destroyed spawning areas. Of the original 6,000 miles of spawning grounds in the mighty Sacramento-San Joaquin watershed, only 510 miles remained in 1929.

Between 1926 and 1943, the commercial catch in California never reached 7 million pounds.

Recently, and at great expense, California residents have launched programs to bring back the salmon. Efforts include artificially replacing lost spawning gravel,

• • • • • • • • • •
"The Pacific Northwest is simply this: wherever the salmon can get to. Rivers without salmon have lost the life source of the area."
—Tim Egan,
The Good Rain

but it is not easy.

The same story repeats itself throughout Europe, Asia and the United States — everywhere man has disturbed the fragile stream habitat so vital to the roving salmon.

"Isn't it funny that you don't get any action until the habitat is so degraded that people finally say something has to be done," said Mike Reed, Hirschi's successor for the S'Klallam Tribe.

When the insult to a stream is temporary and the salmon are not killed or their passage blocked, the natural runs tend to restore themselves. But man is often in a hurry, and there's a tendency to depend on man-made hatcheries that pump out thousands of fish, all fed by hand.

It is a doubtful expenditure of funds in the long run, claims Jim Lichatowich, habitat biologist for the Jamestown Klallams and former assistant fisheries director for the state of Oregon.

"With all the money we're putting into hatcheries," he said, "we are just keeping up with the wild populations disappearing because of the habitat we are losing."

Hirschi pulled on his wading boots and led the way down into the dry stream bed of Seabeck Creek. In winter, water flows over the wide expanse of gravel, but in August the stream's dirt is dry.

Walking toward Hood Canal, but still a mile or so away, Hirschi suddenly stopped. Last year at this time, he said, water was flowing at this point in the stream bed.

"People can't get used to the fact that they really need to look at the same stream again and again to understand it," he said.

Though dry at the surface, water may be moving underground here, since upstream portions of the 3 1/2-mile stream remain flowing year-round. The creek is still a fair producer of chum and coho salmon.

A little farther downstream, Hirschi stopped in front of a tiny pool, the first sign of water. Using a machine to shock organisms in the water, Hirschi spotted a baby coho, which he examined and then let go.

"This stream," he said, "is right on the edge of destruction. It could go either way."

He points toward a nearby hillside. See that scar. Imagine this area filled with old-growth timber. Now, take everything off it. There goes the sediment."

The young forest today doesn't have the water-holding abilities it had before

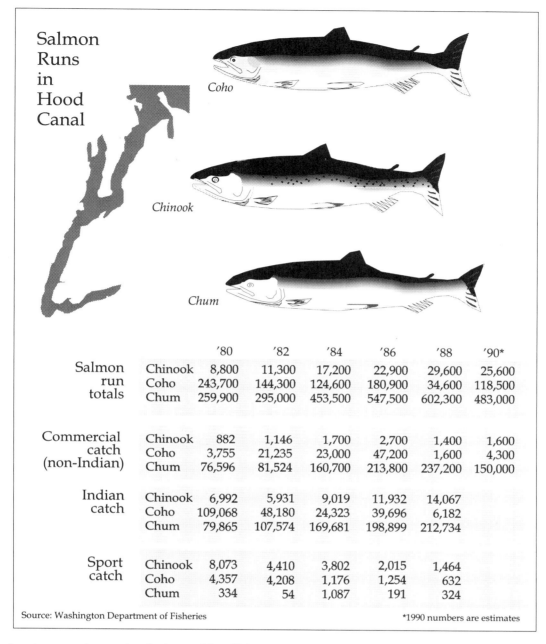

Salmon
Runs
in
Hood
Canal

		'80	'82	'84	'86	'88	'90*
Salmon run totals	Chinook	8,800	11,300	17,200	22,900	29,600	25,600
	Coho	243,700	144,300	124,600	180,900	34,600	118,500
	Chum	259,900	295,000	453,500	547,500	602,300	483,000
Commercial catch (non-Indian)	Chinook	882	1,146	1,700	2,700	1,400	1,600
	Coho	3,755	21,235	23,000	47,200	1,600	4,300
	Chum	76,596	81,524	160,700	213,800	237,200	150,000
Indian catch	Chinook	6,992	5,931	9,019	11,932	14,067	
	Coho	109,068	48,180	24,323	39,696	6,182	
	Chum	79,865	107,574	169,681	198,899	212,734	
Sport catch	Chinook	8,073	4,410	3,802	2,015	1,464	
	Coho	4,357	4,208	1,176	1,254	632	
	Chum	334	54	1,087	191	324	

Source: Washington Department of Fisheries   *1990 numbers are estimates

Hatchery raised chum are very productive. But hatchery coho and chinook have high mortality rates.

logging, so winter rains drain quickly off the land. The stream goes dry in the summer.

An old railroad grade, once used to haul big timber down to Hood Canal, was constructed through the middle of the creek in places. A big earthen berm today, it provides an ongoing supply of deadly sediment to the stream.

Sediment fills the spaces between spawning gravel, making it impossible for salmon to dig a nest in the stream bed. It also destroys the microscopic habitat for stoneflies, mayflies and caddisflies — all important food for growing salmon and trout.

Despite these problems, Seabeck Creek remains a good salmon producer compared to many streams. Clear Creek, for example, is clogged with silt as it flows through the expanding urban area of Silverdale. The Seabeck area is not yet severely affected by housing or commercial development, though that may be its greatest threat today.

As a tribal biologist, Hirschi has dealt with landowners who have lied to his face, he said. One developer listened as Hirschi explained about the value of trees along a stream.

The developer seemed to understand and promised to preserve a wide greenbelt, said Hirschi, but a short time later the man stood and watched his loggers cut to the edge of the stream.

"Landowners are saying, 'It's not our responsibility to pay for the mistakes of the past,' " said Hirschi.

He says individuals should visit streams, observe them closely and teach their children to protect them.

"I think," he added, "that everyone should take a kid to see a stream at least once a year."

• • • • • • • • • •

Every stream in Hood Canal is unique. Some are swift with great waterfalls. Some are slow. But for every stream in Hood Canal, there exists — or once existed — a unique race of salmon adapted to that stream.

Habitat biologists — those who wade around in streams and complain about logging and development — are a different breed from harvest managers — who count fish, divide them up between various fishermen and hope enough adult fish make it home to spawn.

One problem for Hood Canal is that productive streams are so numerous that managers find it virtually impossible to keep track of all the wild runs that come back at various times of the year.

Consequently, Hood Canal runs are managed on a regional or "aggregate" basis. Commercial fishing seasons are designed to protect wild runs, while assuring fishermen the greatest amount of fish from year to year, said Dennis Austin, assistant director for salmon with the state Department of Fisheries.

But in net fishing, wild fish are caught along with hatchery fish — whether they're in the ocean or the entrance to Hood Canal.

Whether enough wild salmon are getting through to their home streams is a subject of considerable debate, but there's little doubt that miscalculations can impact wild salmon populations, especially if a run is barely surviving.

"In most situations, the natural runs are better off now than they were 15 years ago," said Nick Lampsakis, senior biologist for the Point No Point Treaty area. "But one has to be cognizant of all the pressures that exist."

Managers must take a balanced approach to the resource, he said.

"The extreme harvest perspective says, 'Let's forget about these wild stocks. People are going to be building houses and putting up roads anyway,' " he explained. "The extreme environmentalist will say, 'Don't touch any of those fish.' The best answer is somewhere in between."

Hirschi argues that one problem for Hood Canal is that the harvest managers rarely, if ever, see the streams. Salmon, to them, are simply numbers on a computer screen, he says.

"Harvest managers believe in their system," he said. "It gives them good statistics that they believe tells them where each of the stocks are coming from. Obviously, it is not working or there would be more fish coming back ..."

If salmon were caught closer to their streams of origin, he said, managers could be certain sufficient fish could get through. But as long as there is stiff competition in the ocean, the Strait of Juan de Fuca and northern Hood Canal, it just won't happen.

"In ancient times, the natural production was 100 percent of the total production," said Hirschi. "If you can believe just one of those old pictures that showed the salmon that were here, you would know we are living in an area that could truly be the salmon capitol of the world."

• • • • • • • • • •

SECTION 6

PRESERVING
THE NATURAL
SALMON
RUNS

*By Christopher
Dunagan*

E very stream in Hood Canal is unique. Some are swift with great waterfalls. Some are slow, with no noticeable flow in summer months. Some streams contain beaver dams. Some are inhabited by unusual strains of bacteria.

But for every stream in Hood Canal, there exists — or once existed — a unique race of salmon adapted to that stream.

From a genetic standpoint, the "wild" salmon of Hood Canal have the ability to overcome just about any obstacle put forth by nature. Protecting that "genetic diversity" is a great challenge for fisheries biologists; for state, local and tribal governments; and for society as a whole.

"The genetic material contains all the information needed to solve the problems of that particular population," said Jim Lichatowich, habitat biologist for the Jamestown Klallam Tribe and a leading expert on wild salmon.

As humans produce changes in the natural world, survival of the species may well depend on having the right combination of genes, he said.

"You can't hire an engineer to design a new fish able to cope with the greenhouse effect or acid rain," said Lichatowich.

While it would be theoretically possible to eliminate the natural runs and grow all of Hood Canal's fish in hatcheries, biologists agree it would be a stupid mistake.

Wild fish are not only free in an economic sense, said Lichatowich, they provide the only gene bank available for hatchery fish. In-breeding in hatcheries tends to reduce diversity and increase the salmon's susceptibility to disease, he said.

Scientists have learned a lot about hatchery operations, and they're better

managed today than ever before. But there's still a lot nobody understands about the interaction of hatchery fish with natural salmon, about their competition in the wild, and about the ultimate effects of in-breeding.

"In the plant community, the United States is spending a lot of money protecting wild and domestic varieties of seeds," said Lichatowich.

Horticultural scientists know that if they rely on only a few varieties of corn, beans or potatoes, that unknown diseases could impact the world's food supply.

With salmon, he said, "you can't put the stuff in an envelope, store it in the laboratory and grow it out every few years. Wild fish are important."

Beyond the scientific arguments on behalf of wild salmon are those that appeal to a deeper sense of understanding man's place in the environment — what Lichatowich calls "esthetics."

"Man, in this area, has had a relationship with salmon for 9,000 years," he said. "The last 150 years has seen a shift from a natural economy to an industrial economy."

If Hood Canal's wild salmon become extinct, it doesn't say much for our sense of values, he said.

Concerned about declining runs of wild coho salmon in Hood Canal, the Skokomish Indian Tribe in 1991 filed documents in federal court protesting "unilateral" action by Washington state officials in setting fishing seasons that would not allow the minimum number of natural coho to return to spawning streams in the canal watershed. Under the Boldt decision, the tribes and state had agreed to a management plan that calls for a return of 19,100 coho salmon each year to Hood Canal. Both the state and tribes conceded that the goal

Hood Canal spawning grounds

KEY

P = Pink
K = Chinook
C = Chum
S = Coho
T = Steelhead and sea-run cutthroat

Quilcene River: In the Big Quilcene, coho and chinook runs are dominated by hatchery releases. Chum spawn downstream. Both the Big and Little Quilcene salmon production have been damaged by logging, road construction and agricultural practices.

Little Quilcene River
K,S,T

C,S,T   C,S,T

Big Quilcene River
P,K,C,S,T

Gamble Creek
C,S,T

Gamble Creek:
The largest producer of coho in the North Kitsap area.

Dosewallips River: Despite steepness, chinook, coho and pinks manage to spawn 12 miles upstream. Chum spawn in the lower 4.5 miles.

C,S,T

Big Beef Creek: The 10-mile stream is the largest draining from the Central Kitsap area. Still an excellent salmon producer, though development is beginning to degrade the stream. The construction of Lake Symington destroyed coho rearing habitat, and the lake's elevated temperatures reduce the capacity for downstream coho rearing.

Dosewallips River
P,K,C,S,T

Duckabush River
P,K,C,S,T

Little Anderson Creek
C,S,T

Little Anderson Creek:
Excellent coho stream for one only two miles long. Produces chum and steelhead. Impacts are from residential development.

Duckabush River: Despite much pristine habitat, the potential of this river is handicapped by past logging practices.

Big Beef Creek
C,S,T

Hamma Hamma River C,S,T

Stavis Creek
S,T

Stavis Creek: Watershed is largely undeveloped, good habitat for coho and chum. In 1989 pinks were found in the system.

Hamma Hamma River
P,K,C,S,T

C,S,T

Union River
K,S,T

DeWatto River: This 30-mile river is one of the most pristine salmon habitat left in the state, Planners face a major challenge here as Central Kitsap becomes developed.

Hamma Hamma River:
A series of falls restricts salmon migration on the main stem, but the first two miles, plus two miles of John Creek support chum and pinks.

C,S,T

De Watto River
C,S, T

Tahuya River: The largest river draining the Great Peninsula, it has been affected by the incursion of residential development. It remains a fine salmon stream; like the DeWatto, it produces a triple-run chum.

C,S,T

Tahuya River
K,C,S,T

Union River: Coho migration to the upper areas is prevented by Bremerton's Casad Dam and McKenna Falls. Habitat has been degraded by logging, residential development and farming.

Skokomish River: The North and South forks and major tributaries comprise 200 miles of riverbed. Much of the South Fork has been heavily logged, causing problems throughout the system. Intensive harvesting of salmon runs has depleted natural stock. The North Fork contains two dams and Lake Cushman, all of which damage the salmon habitat.

Skokomish River
P,K,C,S,T

Source: U.S. Department of the Interior: Fish and Wildlife Service

could not reasonably be reached in 1991, but the parties could not settle on an interim goal.

State officials went ahead and set fishing seasons expected to allow 16,000 coho to return. The Skokomish sought a return of 17,000. But to get that extra 1,000 coho into Hood Canal would have required reducing the number of fish caught off the Washington coast by 120,000 — something state officials found unacceptable.

Randy Harder, executive director of the Point No Point Treaty Council said the court filing called attention to the state's action, which Northwest tribes maintain will result in overfishing the coho stock, but did not attempt to overturn the established fishing season. He said the state's decision to ignore earlier agreements appears to be based solely on economic considerations at the expense of the fragile resource.

"This court action serves as a warning of the tribes' resolve to rebuild the Hood Canal's wild coho salmon and to insure that the state will honor the spirit of co-management in the future," said Harder. "It is clear that the state has acted without regard for the law or needs of the resource this year."

Joseph Pavel, president of the Skokomish Tribe's General Council and chairman of the Point No Point Treaty Council, said tribal fishermen have been willing to make sacrifices to allow more salmon to survive. The tribes canceled their directed commercial coho fisheries in Hood Canal, Admiralty Inlet, the Strait of Juan de Fuca and the San Juan Islands.

The state, on the other hand, adopted plans that reserve for itself more than twice the number of wild fish than what the tribes will harvest, said Pavel. The state's regulations will lead to a sport fishery catch in the Strait of Juan de Fuca and Admiralty Inlet of more than 150,000 coho salmon and 336,000 to be caught in the ocean north of Cape Falcon, Ore.

"No group of fishermen will take the brunt of conserving the depleted wild coho salmon stock more severely than the Hood Canal tribal fishers who rely on these fish for their livelihoods," Pavel said. "But tribal fishers do not want to be a co-conspirator in perpetuating the problem of devastated coho returns. That is why the tribe cannot accept the state package, which will result in less fish than the established escapement goal."

The number of wild Hood Canal coho returning to spawn has generally declined for the past several years. In 1989 and 1990, when the tribes and state managed for the full escapement of 19,100 wild coho, just 15,300 and 6,800 wild coho, respectively, returned.

Scott Brewer, fisheries manager for the Skokomish Tribe, said the tribe is committed to rebuilding the wild coho runs.

"Despite claims by the state to the contrary," he said, "we anticipate the situation we are witnessing this year will continue or be more severe over the next several years. How will the state respond in 1992, 1993 and especially in 1994 when the offspring of this year's spawning fish return?

"They have demonstrated their willingness to gratify the immediate needs of their fishing constituents," he continued. "It remains to be seen whether they have an equal concern for the long-term needs of the resource."

Salmon are much more than an economic commodity, argues Tom Jay of the group Wild Olympic Salmon. "In a way, salmon are the crown jewels of the ecosystem. They are a very important symbol about what this place is all about."

In ancient times, salmon survived in sufficient quantities to feed the human population, plus a multitude of animals from eagles to bears. As an essential link in the nutrient cycle, salmon also carried trace minerals from the sea into the highest elevations of the forest, replacing micronutrients leached out of the soil by Northwest rains.

"A curious thing," said Jay, "is that East Coast salmon don't die (after they spawn). It may be a little romantic to think so, but maybe salmon here die because the forest needs them to."

To restore natural salmon runs to a semblance of what they once were would be the greatest contribution humans could make to Hood Canal, said Jay. The health of the salmon runs are a measure of the health of the watershed.

Fish hatcheries, on the other hand, are a measure of man's desperation in the complex issue of fishery management, he said.

"In the '30s and '40s, economic interests had trashed so much habitat that the state stepped in and said, 'We have to do something.' But when you look at the investment, dollars spent on habitat protec-

Hood Canal remains in much better shape than most areas of Puget Sound. Many Hood Canal streams still contain considerable spawning grounds, but they are disappearing.

tion and restoration would go a lot further than dollars spent on hatcheries," said Jay.

"There are millions of dollars on the table here, and people aren't necessarily going to tell the truth. They're going to fight for their own interests," he continued.

"But think about the long-term values.

The gravel in those streams is probably worth more than all the lumber and all the development you could possibly get from (the area). When you're talking about true community resources, the gravel in those streams is probably worth its weight in gold."

A Sport Fishing Preserve

Washington state Sen. Brad Owen, D-Shelton, is convinced that Hood Canal would become the sport fishing capital of the nation if the waterway were to be turned into a fishing preserve.

Owen, who continues to push the idea in the Legislature, says the proposal would not affect Indian fishermen, but it would phase out non-Indian commercial fishing south of the Hood Canal Bridge.

Recreational fishing groups have eagerly endorsed Owen's proposal, which they say would expand the number of fish to be caught with rod and reel as well as restoring natural runs of wild salmon.

But the state Department of Fisheries opposes the plan, saying Owen's fish preserve idea isn't necessary to improve sport fishing in Hood Canal. Furthermore, tribal officials fear it will disrupt the carefully balanced management regime they have worked out with the state.

On a sunny day in 1990, Owen invited Jerry Pavletich, West Coast representative for Trout Unlimited, to join him on his boat to catch coho salmon in Hood Canal. Shortly after noon, Owen threaded a piece of herring on his hook and cast his line over the side.

"Hood Canal," he said, "is a very defined body of water. It is easy to get to and so easy to 'fish out' with nets."

Rays of light glistened on the water. The sun was hot, but the fishing was poor. In fact, signs of salmon — such as birds flocking over the water or schools of herring — were practically nonexistent.

"No birds, no herring balls," lamented Pavletich. "They've finally raped and plundered Hood Canal until there's nothing left but dogfish."

Like many rod-and-reel fishermen testing their luck on Hood Canal these days, Owen and Pavletich pulled in half a dozen little dogfish sharks, but not much

else for their day of fishing.

"We're not affecting the Indians (with the proposed legislation). We're just trying to get a fair share of the non-Indian allocation," said Owen, speaking for sport fishermen. "And I want to emphasize this isn't an issue of commercials versus recreationists either. The objective is to restore the levels of the (salmon) runs to what they used to be."

Dennis Austin of the Department of Fisheries calls Owen's plan "overkill and unnecessary," though he admits Hood Canal is in trouble.

"The state needs to look at our fisheries," he said. "This one area has collapsed. It's stinko. There's no question about that."

But a simpler answer, he said, is to increase the number of "resident" chinook and coho in Hood Canal, to give sportsmen more fish to catch. That's exactly what the state is doing with its delayed release program, which it hopes will show results in 1991.

Nick Lampsakis of the Point No Point Treaty Council calls Owen's bill "a giant step backward."

Commercial fishing is carefully managed to protect the long-term viability of the runs, he argued. Seasons are opened and closed as the runs demand.

"There is no way to close a recreational fishery the way you can open and close a commercial fishery at a moment's notice," he said.

Owen's Hood Canal preserve proposal won Senate approval in 1990 and 1991, but never made it out of a House committee that listens more closely to commercial interests and the wishes of the Department of Fisheries.

But he plans to keep up the effort. "It took me three years to get drag fishing (bottom trolling) out of Hood Canal," he noted.

By Christopher Dunagan

SECTION 1

TO PROTECT
THE
CANAL...AND
OYSTERS

*By Christopher
Dunagan*

*A Hood Canal oyster
starts the trip to
market.*

L ouis Martin's left hand gripped the oyster firmly, holding it against the stainless steel table. His right hand quickly slipped the razor-sharp knife between the two shells.

"You have to be careful you don't cut the oyster," said Martin, 70, of Brinnon, "and you have to make sure you don't cut your hands to pieces."

Martin quickly sliced the oyster muscles close to the shell, first one side, then the other. He plopped the naked oyster into a bucket.

Martin has worked for a lot of people. He's been an elementary school teacher, a logger, an equipment manufacturer. In 1980, at the age of 60, he took a job with Hood Canal Seafood, joining the ranks of more than 2,000 people employed in Washington's shellfish trade.

"I needed something to do," Martin explained. "I would go crazy doing nothing."

Oysters make for a crazy business. Age-old techniques of knife-in-hand shucking form a partnership with ultra-modern procedures, such as genetic engineering.

Statewide, it's a $25-million-a-year business, but oyster growers ally themselves not with industry, not with timber companies and certainly not with real estate firms. If anything, they're anti-growth.

Oyster farmers, in fact, have been called Washington's first environmentalists, advocating clean-water laws since the turn of the century.

Outside the building where Martin and two other shuckers were opening their oysters, cold November rains ceased for the time being. Martin's boss, Kirk Lakeness, prepared to transport a load of oysters to a restaurant in Port Townsend.

"We sell to San Francisco — all over," said Lakeness, whose father started Hood Canal Seafood on the shores of Dabob Bay in 1958.

By most standards, the company is a small operation. Three shuckers together open an average of 20 gallons of oysters each day.

At that rate, noted Lakeness, it would take his company 15 years to equal a single month's production by Coast Oyster Company, which manages oyster beds in Hood Canal, Puget Sound and Willapa Bay on the Pacific Coast.

In terms of nationwide oyster production, Washington state recently moved up to second place behind Louisiana, due mainly to declines on the East Coast, principally Chesapeake Bay, and the Gulf Coast. In both cases, the biggest problems are pollution.

In the best years, Hood Canal contributes little more than 10 percent of the statewide production of oysters, but it is famous for its sweet-tasting Quilcene variety.

Even more important are the microscopic baby oysters produced naturally in Quilcene Bay and shipped to oyster growers throughout the United States. In addition to natural production, the bay is home to the world's largest oyster hatchery.

An estimated 75 certified oyster farmers are located throughout Hood Canal if you include all the small growers. Many are centered on the natural spawning grounds of Quilcene and Dabob bays.

● ● ● ● ● ● ● ● ● ●

More than 2,000 people are employed in Washington's shellfish trade. It's a $25-million-a-year business.

In 1988, Pacific Oyster Growers Association hired a contract lobbyist — a "hired gun" in the slang of political power brokers. Tim Smith had worked for insurance companies, local governments and real estate brokers.

"I didn't know the (oyster) industry at all when I came down from Alaska two years ago," said Smith. "I thought my job would be in marketing. I took a month and studied the industry. It became pretty evident to me right away that the problem was not in selling oysters. We can't supply everyone as it is. The challenges are in keeping the growing areas open."

By 1984, when pollution struck Hood Canal for the first time, a dozen important shellfish growing areas had already been restricted in other parts of Puget Sound due to extreme levels of bacteria. Then came the 1984 closure of a portion of Quilcene Bay, followed three years later by closures in Lynch Cove near Belfair and Dosewallips State Park. In 1988, tidelands near the Duckabush River also were closed.

Statewide, the Department of Ecology estimates dollar losses in excess of $3 million a year due to the closures.

Smith had never before worked for a seafood business or an environmental organization. Now, he says, he heads a group that is both.

"That's the main issue, protecting water quality."

Oyster Harvests for Washington State and Hood Canal

| | In pounds | | % of |
Year	State	Canal	harvest
1979	6.1 million	309,000	5.1
1980	5.5 million	163,000	3.0
1981	5.6 million	186,000	3.3
1982	6.0 million	305,000	5.1
1983	6.1 million	419,000	6.9
1984	7.1 million	758,000	10.7
1985	5.9 million	770,000	13.1
1986	8.7 million	360,000	4.1
1987	9.4 million	448,000	4.8
1989	8.8 million	267,000	3.0
1990	7.8 million	402,000	5.2

Although Hood Canal harvest rarely exceeds 10 percent of the state total, the canal does produce half the commercial oyster seed for the entire nation. Hood Canal seed also is used extensively in Puget Sound and Willapa Bay, the state's major oyster growing regions.

An ancient pile of shells found buried at Seal Rock Campground north of Brinnon offers testimony that Native Americans gathered oysters from Hood Canal beaches before white people arrived.

Early settlers to the Puget Sound region found an abundance of Washington's native oyster, the Olympia. It wasn't long before a commercial trade developed, starting with the California gold rush in 1849.

When the burgeoning trade depleted the natural stocks, a few pioneers began culturing Olympia oysters in Southern Puget Sound, using a system of dikes. The dikes kept the sensitive oysters submerged and at a more constant temperature during freezing winters and hot summers. But expansion of the industry was stymied because oyster growers didn't own the land, and they couldn't be assured of control over their expensive dikes.

In 1890, one of the first acts of the Washington Legislature altered the future of the state's shorelines. Those first legislators agreed to sell state-owned tidelands to oyster growers as long as they would continue cultivation.

Thus the state lost ownership of many valuable shorelines, but it also created a powerful advocate for clean water, said Smith. The complexion of the industry changed immediately and became different from that of many East Coast states, where oyster harvesters continue to compete with one another for the same shellfish.

"In the wild harvest fishery, when pollution has degraded the water quality in an area, the fishermen all pack up, and it's a race to the next fishing area," he said. "You lose that built-in environmental protection — that of the grower out defending his livelihood."

Despite those early efforts, the native Olympia oyster has all but disappeared today. The little oyster with excellent flavor turned out to be sensitive to environmental changes and too small to compete on the market with larger oyster species.

Beginning in 1905, Japanese oysters were shipped across the ocean as small adults. They could be fattened for market in Puget Sound, but natural reproduction was not very successful.

In 1919, a curious thing happened that altered the course of oyster production. A shipment of adult oysters died, yet the baby oysters attached to their shells were able to survive.

In time, shipping cases of shells with these pinhead-sized "seed" oysters attached became the standard method of transport. By 1935, annual shipments from Japan to the West Coast exceeded 71,000 two-bushel cases of shells. The oyster was named the Pacific oyster.

About that time, growers discovered that consistent natural reproduction could be expected in Quilcene and Dabob bays, though the oysters grew more slowly there.

Normally, an adult female releases up to 10 million eggs a year into the water. A male can release 1,000 times that many sperm. When fertilized, the eggs becomes free-swimming larvae, moving with the currents.

After several weeks, the oyster larvae will attach to rocks, shells and other solid objects.

In Quilcene and Dabob bays, this "set" is successful about seven out of 10 years, compared to just less than once in 20 years for many areas of Puget Sound, said Al Scholz, a biologist with the Point Whitney Shellfish Laboratory on the canal at Brinnon.

An oyster set is considered successful when at least 10 baby oysters attach to an average shell placed in the water. Not all survive, however. The summer of 1990 proved to be one of the most successful years in history on the canal, with more than 1,000 oysters per shell. Warm, stable temperatures along with clean, calm waters are important factors, said Scholz.

The only other natural spawning areas on the West Coast are Pendrell Sound in British Columbia and Willapa Bay on Washington's coast.

Natural production from Quilcene Bay began to spread Pacific oysters throughout Hood Canal beginning in 1935. And when World War II broke out and Japanese imports were cut off, local production became crucial.

In the 1950s, Pacific Coast Oyster Growers Association became a major force in reducing the poisons pouring out of pulp mills around Puget Sound. Beginning in 1954, the organization orchestrated a statewide educational campaign involving sports and fishing groups, local granges, resort owners and parent-teacher associations.

Groups such as Citizens for Clean Water allied themselves with the oyster growers, while the paper industry fought back with its own public relations effort. But by 1960, when the state's Pollution Commission had begun tightening controls on industrial effluent, it was already too late for many areas.

Sources of pollution today are becoming more difficult to identify, let alone eliminate. In Hood Canal, pollution seems to come from all directions — houses, farms, timberlands, even pleasure boats — thus the name "non-point pollution."

"A lot of us have moved into what were vacation homes and summer homes and fishing homes," said Teresa Barron, water quality planner for Jefferson County. "Our grandads built these homes, and septic standards weren't what they are today."

Geological conditions only make the problem worse, since people built their homes and farms in valleys, where the ground is flat and close to Hood Canal.

Washington State ranks second in the nation in oyster production, behind Louisiana. Pollution in Chesapeake Bay has closed many oyster producing areas.

Hood Canal contributes little more than 10 percent of the statewide production of oysters. But Quilcene Bay is home to the world's largest oyster hatchery.

In Quilcene Bay, studies have shown that septic pollution and poor animal-keeping practices are major contributors to bacterial pollution.

Allowing cattle and horses to drink directly from streams makes it possible for their waste to get into the water and create pollution problems miles away, she said.

Another serious problem is sediment unleashed during logging activities. High levels of sediment can smother baby oysters, a problem sometimes noted in Quilcene Bay.

At Dosewallips, bacterial pollution seems to come from another source altogether. Near the Dosewallips Delta, where human activities are minimal, seals seem to be leaving a trail of waste that has contaminated the oysters and clams.

Nobody knows if waste from seals can actually make humans sick, as is the case with human and livestock waste, said Gretchen Steiger, a biologist with Cascadia Research Cooperative. But the state's certification procedure demands closure anytime fecal bacteria counts are high.

Oyster growers are increasingly worried about the effect of seals on their Hood Canal beaches, since seal populations may be growing quickly, according to research by Cascadia Research.

As commercial fishing and timber industries go into a decline in Hood Canal, the shellfish industry seems to be coming alive.

Shellfish production ranks high in employment in both Mason and Jefferson counties. The demand for clams and oysters — especially from restaurants — is growing, and the future seems limited only by clean water.

"Here on the Olympic Peninsula, we have so few industries to sustain our economy," said Barron, the water quality planner. "As we use up our natural resources, people tend to look around to expand their economic base."

What kind of industry comes to the region will determine whether Hood Canal's clean water can survive, she added.

"Aquaculture is a clean industry, and you'd think it would be welcomed with open arms."

While there isn't much controversy about oysters growing scattered on a beach, waterfront property owners have begun to raise protests against more intensive shellfish culture, such as stringing shells on lines suspended from floats.

In August 1990, the Kitsap County commissioners turned down a mussel-farming proposal off Misery Point near Seabeck. Neighbors said their main objection was that the operation would spoil their view of the Olympic Mountains.

The commissioners also imposed a moratorium on all aquaculture, pending approval of the county's updated shorelines management plan.

If waterfront property owners worry about the impacts of shellfish growers, shellfish growers are even more concerned about the arrival of more property owners.

"One of the factors that degrades the water quality is shoreline development," said Smith. "Also, as more people move in, we're going to hear more about aesthetics. Those issues are going to impact the industry's future."

Gordon Hayes of Coast Oyster Company says new housing developments around Hood Canal should attempt to avoid pollution, and old developments must begin to clean up problems.

"All of us in the industry see what happens with population expansion," said Hayes. "Our industry is the canary in the coal mine, but we're not just a prophet. We actually make our living from this resource.

"If we were not here," he added, "the water would become more polluted before an alarm is sounded."

Homely Bivalve Becomes a Restaurant Favorite

Head thrown back, mouth open, a diner at Ray's Boathouse on Seattle's Shilshole Bay slurps a raw oyster directly from its shell.

To an oyster lover, there's nothing quite like the fresh taste of the bivalve in the raw. It's as if you're ingesting a bit of life's primal matter, tasting the ocean itself.

Wayne Ludvigsen, executive chef at Ray's, says raw oysters have grown in popularity over the past five years. He now sells 200-250 dozen oysters each week. Fanciers gladly pay $5.95 or more for a plate of six of these briny gems.

Ray's serves the tiny, distinctive Olympia oysters as well as Pacifics from three different parts of the state — Hamma Hamma on Hood Canal, Shoalwater Bay on the Southwest Coast and Race Lagoon off Whidbey Island.

Like wine grapes, oysters take on the qualities of their growing conditions, as Fred Brack and Tina Bell point out in their book, "The Tastes of Washington." Selecting them, particularly for eating raw, is as much an individual preference as choosing a wine.

The Hood Canal bivalves are "your classic oyster," says Ludvigsen. "They're not necessarily very sweet, and they don't have a beautiful shell. But they're a good, solid, healthy oyster with a strong oyster flavor."

Hood Canal oysters come back from the summer off-season earlier than the other types, he adds.

Although he'll pan fry oysters and make the occasional oyster stew, Ludvigsen says he's a real proponent of eating them raw. "We're purists," he says.

Tim Smith, executive director of the Pacific Coast Oyster Growers Association, says half-shell consumption is on the increase across the country.

"Oyster bars are popping up everywhere," he says. "We've seen a dramatic decrease in liquor consumption over the past few years, and my own theory is that bars and restaurants are out looking for a high-margin item to compensate for lost liquor revenues."

Kim Baxter, manager of the Hamma Hamma Oyster Co., says he can't keep up with the demand for oysters. He supplies several posh Seattle restaurants in addition to Ray's — Fullers in the Sheraton Hotel, Le Tastevin and Anthony's Homeports.

"Our oysters are prized for their clean, crisp flavor," he says. "They're slow-growing in clear water, so they never have a muddy taste."

By Ann Strosnider

• • • • • • • • • •

The demand for clams and oysters — especially from restaurants — is growing, and the future seems limited only by clean water.

Coast Oyster Co. has made a science of raising young oysters. They feed on algae grown in these jars.

• • • • • • • • • •

Section 2

Where
Genetics
and Luck
Meet

*By Christopher
Dunagan*

Row upon row of gleaming white tanks, each containing 5,000 gallons of greenish algae, might make one wonder what this strange laboratory near Quilcene has to do with raising oysters.

After all, tough-skinned oyster farmers have been putting shells out on their beaches for centuries. Nobody's ever needed halogen lights or giant flasks of strange-looking liquid with air bubbling through them.

But times have changed, and this is where the modern world of genetics blends with the old-fashioned, keep-your-fingers-crossed world of oyster growing.

Coast Oyster Co., which owns this hatchery on the shores of Quilcene Bay, leads the world in the production of oyster seed. The company ships 20 billion baby oysters to growers throughout the nation in the form of free-swimming larvae.

"In fact," says president Gordon Hayes, "the second biggest hatchery is in Oregon, and it produces just 10-20 percent of ours."

The key to the operation is the carefully guarded brood stock, which produce the sperm and eggs for the big Pacific oysters, the tasty Kumomoto variety and the succulent Belon or European flat oyster.

The oysters eat an incredible amount of algae, which is grown under bright lights in tanks, some of which are 10 feet tall.

Temperatures in tanks containing the brood stock are maintained to simulate ideal spawning conditions. When the time is right, free-swimming oyster larvae are filtered out, packed and quickly shipped out, or else they're allowed to set on oyster shells.

The oyster seed can be grown on just about any beach where the tides won't carry the shells away.

Maintaining excellent brood stock is one thing, but a true scientific breakthrough came five years ago when Coast Oyster, in conjunction with University of Washington scientists, developed a sexless oyster — the seedless grape of the oyster world.

Unlike most oysters, which become puny and watery as they use their energy to create sperm and eggs, the trademark "Four-Season Oyster" skips the spawning season altogether.

Forget the old saying about not eating oysters during months that lack an "R" in their name. These oysters are firm at all times of the year, which gives the company a foot up on the summer market, previously dominated by frozen oysters.

The idea for a neutered oyster came from Hayes' father, the late Vern Hayes, who got the idea from a magazine article about a neutered salmon that grows faster but never returns home to spawn.

Hayes was a dominant force in the oyster industry beginning in 1947 when he started Coast Oyster. In 1974, he built a hatchery at Willapa Bay, then moved the operation to Quilcene in 1978.

To get a neutered oyster, the egg is "shocked" with a special chemical. Shocking prevents the egg from dividing just before the genetic material from the sperm combines with the genetic material from the egg. As a result, two sets of chromosomes from the female and one from the male result in a sterile "triploid" oyster, normal in all other ways.

Quilcene Bay

Although closed because of bacterial pollution at the north end, Quilcene Bay is the center of Hood Canal's oyster industry, including Coast Oyster Company's oyster hatchery.

Kenneth Chew, a shellfish biologist at the University of Washington, says the triploid oyster has found a specific market niche, but the growing demand for oysters on both East and West coasts creates an even bigger challenge for the industry.

"We have to look at new and innovative methods of growing them," he says.

According to Chew, at least 90 percent of the oysters today are grown right on the beach, as they have been for the past 100 years. But oysters also can be grown on stakes or on racks when wave action or a muddy bottom would threaten the oysters' survival.

A more intensive method is to grow oysters on strings hanging from racks or rafts.

These are not actually new methods, noted Chew, because they have been used in Japan for decades, but researchers are attempting to develop even more advanced techniques to grow more oysters with limited space. As more areas are closed because of pollution, oyster growers are likely to invest more and more money in these alternative methods.

Meanwhile, researchers are attempting to grow strains of oysters that are resistant to temperature changes, that grow faster and are more uniformly shaped and that have good color, flavor and appearance. Hybrid oysters, which combine the characteristics of two or more varieties, also are on the drawing boards.

Since hatchery success depends so much on what oysters are fed in the tanks, researchers are studying oyster nutrition and developing new strains of algae as well.

And growers seem willing to meet the challenge of a growing market. Despite tried-and-true methods of oyster farming, a 1984 survey of the state's oyster growers revealed that 40 percent would try new techniques such as as artificial setting tanks, more intensive rearing methods and use of hybrid strains.

• • • • • • • • • •

"Here on the Olympic Peninsula, we have so few industries to sustain our economy. Aquaculture is a clean industry, and you'd think it would be welcomed with open arms."
— Teresa Barron

George Usnick, who lives on Misery Point near Seabeck, is a strong spokesman for the rights of private waterfront owners.

• • • • • • • • • •

SECTION 3

TIDELANDS TUG'O'WAR

By Jim Rothgeb

Charlie Trevathan stands over his set net just off the sandy beach north of Boston Spit and hunches his shoulders against the wind blowing off Port Gamble Bay.

It's a cold wind, signaling the approaching winter and the end of another fishing season. On this day he hopes his nets will snag coho and chum but he knows the fish he catches now are mostly scraggly. The salmon harvest is nearly done.

It's time to think about securing his boat and gathering his nets to prepare himself for the traditional shellfish season. Winter tides on Hood Canal are more suited for shellfish digging, and for most young men in the S'Klallam Tribe of Little Boston and Port Gamble Bay, shellfishing is a family tradition.

"My mom used to dig a lot," said Trevathan. "I always knew it was one of those resources where a guy could go out and make money. I remember digging from when I was a kid, and when I came back here about eight years ago, I started doing it again."

He's lived in Tennessee and California, but Trevathan's roots are with the S'Klallams. He and his wife, Mary, both harvest shellfish, selling them to wholesale buyers, to help provide for care of the nine people living in their home.

"I think it's fun," said Trevathan. "You

can go out and spend three to four hours digging and be tired the next day. But you can make enough for grocery money and you eat well."

On Hood Canal, two tribes do the majority of shellfish harvesting. The Skokomish mostly harvest oysters in the southern extremes of the canal while the S'Klallams gather clams on the north end.

Much of the time, they work in the pitch black of nighttime low tides, sometimes to the backdrop of car headlights left shining across the sand. They dress in waders and carry buckets, shell sacks, and digging forks. It's no wonder their backs often ache after days of digging.

"That's the hardest part," said Mary Trevathan. "You bend over at all hours of the day and you've got to pack what you dig. Our longest pack is probably a half-mile, and we pack anywhere from 80- to 100-pound packs. It's a lot easier if you've got a boat, but on a lot of beaches we can't get a boat."

The Trevathans both say that shellfishing has become easier in the '90s because state-owned tidelands have been opened to the tribes. But their access obviously is nothing compared to what Western Washington Indians had on tidelands more than 100 years ago.

While the Trevathans scratch the sands for harvestable shellfish, the fate of their tribal tradition and a source of livelihood may soon be affected at a negotiating table, or in a federal courtroom — far from the surf that laps against the sandy beaches of Hood Canal.

On a map of Hood Canal, the land forming Misery Point juts into the water like the head of an eagle.

Located between Seabeck and Scenic Beach State Park, this lush, tree-covered point is far from a source of misery for George Usnick, a retired engineer who moved here from Pittsburgh, Pa., in 1985. A friend back East jokes that it's more like Happiness Point.

From his home, Usnick sees a breathtaking panorama, bounded by The Brothers to the south and the Toandos Peninsula to the north.

His beachfront home is perched on a wooded cliff overlooking the canal. From his patio, he can see fishing boats dotting the blue water with a backdrop of Pleasant Harbor State Park and the Olympic Mountains.

"There is no place like this I've ever seen in my whole life," said Usnick, who traveled the world as part of his job with the Continental Oil Company. "That's why I like it here so much."

His property includes about 200 feet of beachfront, and he and Delores often take leisurely walks along the sand.

Like flowers from a garden, occasionally the Usnicks will pick oysters from their beach. Usnick says he's always been a lover of shellfish, and his wife has developed a taste for them since they moved to Misery Point.

Several hundred feet south of the Usnicks' property is a public boat launch, which attracts mostly pleasure boaters and recreational fishers. Until a few years ago, when waterfront neighbors got together and posted "No Shellfishing" signs, Usnick says trespassing was a big problem along the point.

"When we first came here, there were a lot of people who decided to come up and pick oysters," said Usnick. "I kept arguing with the state that they had to do something, put a sign up to stop them. We did that and now I'd say 99 percent of the problem has gone away."

Like many private landowners on Hood Canal, Usnick prefers to keep his beach closed — to anyone. He has genuine concerns about garbage spilling onto the shore and firmly believes in his constitutional right to privacy.

"People walk on the beach, but I would rather they don't," Usnick said. "That really doesn't bother me. It's just when they come with five-gallon buckets and they're only supposed to take 18 oysters. That's what really gets me upset.

"They'll get five gallons of shucked oysters. Or they'll fill five-gallon buckets and throw them in their truck. They break the laws left and right. But all that's simmered down now (with the placement of the signs)."

Because he's so fiercely protective of his property, Usnick feels threatened by a lawsuit filed by 16 Western Washington Indian tribes in May of 1989. To his knowledge, he's never seen Native Americans collecting oysters on his beach. But if the

Tribal shellfishing has become easier because state-owned tidelands have been opened to Indians, but the access is nothing compared to opportunities Western Washington Indians had more than 100 years ago.

courts rule in the Indians' favor, or if negotiations give the tribes certain entitlements to private beaches, that will all change.

The two men, Charlie Trevathan and George Usnick, have never met. But because of a two-paragraph article scribbled on a piece of parchment 135 years ago, they've become unknowing opponents.

In 1855, Isaac Stevens was the territorial governor of Washington, and in negotiating with the Indians over land rights and settlement of reservations, he granted the Indians permission to specific customs. The 1855 Point No Point treaty with the Western Washington tribes states the following:

"The right of taking fish at usual and accustomed grounds and stations is further secured to said Indians, in common with all citizens of the United States; and of erecting temporary houses for the purpose of curing; together with the privilege of hunting and gathering roots and berries on open and unclaimed lands. Provided, however, that they shall not take shell-fish from any beds staked or cultivated by citizens."

The Boldt decision in 1974 recognized the Point No Point Treaty as the final law in matters regarding the territorial rights of Native Americans, but U.S. District Judge George Boldt didn't carry the lawsuit beyond salmon and steelhead harvests and rule on the taking of shellfish.

A lawsuit filed by the tribes in 1989 pursues a continuation of the entitlement issue. And unless it's negotiated outside the courtroom, this one could be quite a fight, possibly more costly, drawn out and emotionally charged than the fight over the salmon.

The federal government represents the Indians while the state currently represents the rights of private landowners and commercial interests who own tideland property.

The Indians contend that under the provisions of the treaty, all beaches, either public or private, should be open for shellfishing. They add that private access to those beaches should be open to all tribal harvesters.

"The treaty language is real clear," said Tony Forsman, fisheries director for the Suquamish Tribe. "When the treaties were made, there was no State of Washington and there was no concept of private ownership of tidelands, except for some commercial development of shellfish that was provided for in the treaty."

From 1859 to 1970, the Indians claim that 80 percent of all Western Washington tideland was sold to private landowners who were not told of the Indian shellfishing rights. Thus, there currently is a standoff.

Landowners say they are protected by their fundamental right to privacy and plan to argue over the legal definitions of cultivated tidelands.

In a letter to the Justice Department last February, Washington Attorney General Ken Eikenberry wrote: "The shellfish claim is therefore a much greater direct challenge to the traditional ownership prerogatives of thousands of individuals than was the earlier Phase I (original Boldt decision) allocation of the free swimming fish in public waters."

For Mary Trevathan, legal squabbling over shellfish rights seems pretty far removed from her day-to-day world. But she is aware that animosity exists between tribal and non-tribal interests. She also knows of a group, the United Property Owners of Washington, that's consolidating the efforts of the landowners.

"They don't really know what's going on," said Mary Trevathan. "They think that we're out there to just dig every clam we can get. They're scared of what they call 'raping the beaches.'

"But we're taking just the harvestable clams, which have to be 1 1/2 inches or bigger. We can't take the smaller ones. We're taking the bigger ones but leaving the little ones to grow. They don't realize that. They just think we're taking everything."

Certain federal and state politicians would prefer that this case never goes to court. They're pushing for a cooperative settlement and the Indians say they want to comply.

But the tribes also argue they are not getting the necessary cooperation from landowners to reach that settlement. United Property Owners of Washington officials say publicly that they would rather litigate the issue than possibly give away their rights in a negotiated deal.

They are spurred by thoughts from people like George Usnick, who says a settlement is not acceptable.

"I'm protective of my beach," said Usnick. "Number one, because it's mine. I paid for it and I pay property taxes here. I just don't want people on my property.

Would you walk up on somebody's yard? Of course not."

Meanwhile, the environmental clock is ticking. The state has apportioned certain lands — state parks and property controlled by the Department of Natural Resources — to be open to all shellfish harvesters. Of the approximate 2,000 miles of beach in Western Washington, roughly 21 miles are open to tribal and non-tribal harvesters.

Recent studies show that up to 40 percent of those public beaches are too polluted to collect shellfish. Many Hood Canal tidelands fall into that category.

"I think it's obvious that we are all rapidly running out of beaches to harvest shellfish," said Carson Boysen, spokesman for the Northwest Indian Fisheries Commission.

The tribes say that through enhancement, they want to expand the shellfish population. But far more cleaner beaches are needed to do it.

Private landowners say they, too, are environmentally conscious.

But before both sides can make a concerted effort to protect the shellfish, there is a huge legal hurdle to cross.

• • • • • • • • • •

• • • • • • • • • •

SECTION 4

TOWARD CLEANER BEACHES

By Christopher Dunagan

Waterfront owners can have this kind of bounty because of Hood Canal's excellent oyster growing opportunities.

I f every waterfront property owner would grow his own oysters, the rate at which beaches are being ruined by pollution would decline, according to Jon and Loanna Day, who moved to Misery Point near Seabeck to take advantage of the fine oyster-growing conditions there.

"When I'm down on the beach and tending my oysters, I feel like I have it all," said Day, a marine biology teacher at Olympic High School.

Day sells a few oysters on the side, so the state Department of Health keeps a regular watch on the bacterial levels at his beachfront property.

"One of the nightmares always nagging at the back of my mind," he said, "is whether I'll be recertified. You hear of hot spots where coliforms (bacteria) are increasing, such as the area near Seabeck Store and where Big Beef enters (Hood Canal)."

If everybody would grow oysters, Day says, maybe the word would spread about the importance of caring for septic systems, reducing lawn pesticides and cleaning up after pets and livestock.

Growing your own oysters is not particularly difficult, he maintains.

Added Mrs. Day, "You hear people say, 'We used to have oysters here.' To me, that's like saying, 'Gosh, we used to have carrots in our garden.' "

Many of Hood Canal's beaches are

Hood Canal's Treasured Oysters

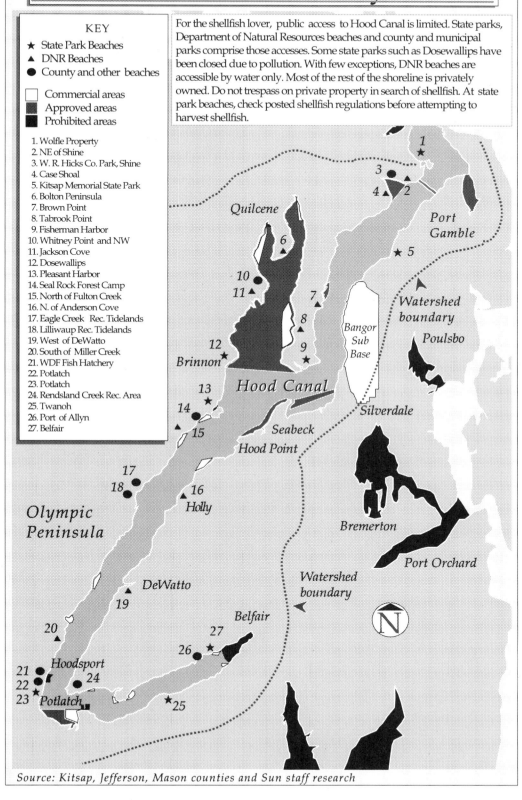

KEY

★ State Park Beaches
▲ DNR Beaches
● County and other beaches

□ Commercial areas
▦ Approved areas
■ Prohibited areas

1. Wolfle Property
2. NE of Shine
3. W. R. Hicks Co. Park, Shine
4. Case Shoal
5. Kitsap Memorial State Park
6. Bolton Peninsula
7. Brown Point
8. Tabrook Point
9. Fisherman Harbor
10. Whitney Point and NW
11. Jackson Cove
12. Dosewallips
13. Pleasant Harbor
14. Seal Rock Forest Camp
15. North of Fulton Creek
16. N. of Anderson Cove
17. Eagle Creek Rec. Tidelands
18. Lilliwaup Rec. Tidelands
19. West of DeWatto
20. South of Miller Creek
21. WDF Fish Hatchery
22. Potlatch
23. Potlatch
24. Rendsland Creek Rec. Area
25. Twanoh
26. Port of Allyn
27. Belfair

For the shellfish lover, public access to Hood Canal is limited. State parks, Department of Natural Resources beaches and county and municipal parks comprise those accesses. Some state parks such as Dosewallips have been closed due to pollution. With few exceptions, DNR beaches are accessible by water only. Most of the rest of the shoreline is privately owned. Do not trespass on private property in search of shellfish. At state park beaches, check posted shellfish regulations before attempting to harvest shellfish.

If everybody would grow oysters, Jon Day says, maybe the word would spread about the importance of caring for septic systems, reducing lawn pesticides and cleaning up after pets and livestock.

Source: Kitsap, Jefferson, Mason counties and Sun staff research

seeded naturally, thanks in large part to the tremendous amount of oyster larvae produced in Quilcene and Dabob bays. Larvae that survive drift for two or three weeks before setting on rocks or old oyster shell.

One can enhance the amount of oyster "set" by moving shell from the upper beach to the lower beach. Do not, however, move uncertified shell from just anyone's beach, warns Day. It is illegal, and uncertified shell carries the threat of spreading a dangerous parasite, the Japanese oyster drill, a snail which was introduced with early shipments of oyster seed.

One can also lay bags or strings of shell out on the beach to catch swimming larvae. The shell can be purchased from certified oyster growers, and the state Department of Fisheries keeps track of water conditions and announces the best time to put them out.

Where oysters don't set naturally, one can buy bags of oyster seed, or spat, which are tiny oysters that have already been captured and grown for several months on shell.

• • • • • • • • • •

"You hear people say, 'We used to have oysters here.' To me, that's like saying, 'Gosh, we used to have carrots in our garden.'"
— Loanna Day

Oysters grown in Dyes and Sinclair inlets cannot be certified for sale due to pollution problems, but Day intends to have his high school class plant some oyster seed there anyway.

"We can see how fast the oysters grow, and it may be a good way of monitoring pollution levels," he said.

Day says he is disappointed that some waterfront property owners object to any kind of commercial oyster or mussel farming near their homes. More than anything, he argues, such operations prove that the waters are still clean.

"You will never see a mussel farm in Commencement Bay," he added.

Day worries about the upcoming decision over whether tribes have a right to take shellfish from private beaches. But his concern doesn't slow him down.

"This entire shoreline is a very rich resource," he noted. "I hope that people are not so afraid that they stop cultivating seafood or stop trying to protect the water quality."

Increasing levels of nutrients in Hood Canal from human waste and fertilizer runoff may help feed plankton blooms that cause red tide.

In June 1991, the first major red tide outbreak in the history of Hood Canal alarmed Puget Sound researchers, who were the first to admit they don't know exactly why it happened.

But one researcher, Jack Rensel of the University of Washington Fisheries Department, says further plankton blooms in central Hood Canal could doom the southern part of the waterway, where conditions appear to be more favorable to the one-celled organisms.

The closure came after state health officials noted that high levels of paralytic shellfish poison had been found in mussels from Seabeck Bay. The resulting closure affected all of Hood Canal from Seabeck north to Hood Canal Bridge, on both Kitsap and Jefferson county sides.

"Things are happening in that area," said Kenneth Chew, a UW Fisheries profes-

sor and longtime shellfish biologist. "Before 1978, I used to say that if you eat shellfish south of a line drawn even with Port Townsend, you never have to worry."

Since then, he noted, red tide blooms have moved south into lower Puget Sound and now are threatening Hood Canal.

The cause is unknown, said Chew, but he personally believes that plankton may be following the growth of human population.

"The more people living in these areas, we see an increase in phosphates and nitrates," said Chew. "That's what the organism desires.

"We are holding our breath on this," he said. "A massive outbreak in 1978 spared Hood Canal, but I've always been wondering when it might poke through there."

Rensel, a graduate student who is doing extensive studies on plankton, has proposed a theory about why Hood Canal

● ● ● ● ● ● ● ● ●

Section 5

An Invisible Threat

By Christopher Dunagan

• • • • • • • • • •
*Since 1978,
University of
Washington
shellfish
biologist
Kenneth Chew
has seen red
tide blooms
move south
into lower
Puget Sound,
to the point
that they now
threaten Hood
Canal.*

has avoided red tides so far.

Every spring, Hood Canal undergoes blooms involving one-celled plankton called diatoms, he says. Stable weather, sunlight and high water temperatures are all factors.

After the spring bloom, central Hood Canal, which is fed by the clear waters flowing out of the Olympics, becomes depleted of inorganic nitrogen, said Rensel.

Dinoflagellates, free-swimming plankton, are unable to move past the clear layers of water in central Hood Canal and die, according to Rensel's theory. *Gonyaulax catanella*, the red tide organism, is one of the dinoflagellates.

So far, the clear waters of central Hood Canal have saved lower Hood Canal from serious red tide problems, he said. But conditions in lower Hood Canal may be more favorable to the red tide organism due to the high level of nutrients that have been measured there.

During winter months, most plankton drift to the bottom as cysts and lie dormant.

"Once you get the cysts in the sediment," said Rensel, "there is the possibility that it may be there from now on. The only thing keeping it out of South Hood Canal may be that it hasn't been there in such numbers before."

Don Miles of the Bremerton-Kitsap County Health Department said he has heard unconfirmed reports of a major red tide bloom during the 1940s, but he is not sure of conditions present at that time. Old-timers recall a reddish bloom of plankton, but the color may be due to another species of plankton unrelated to the red tide organism.

Rensel has proposed a study of Hood Canal that would measure the dangerous

Red tide closing

Hood Canal suffered its first-ever closure to red tide in 1991. Now that the plankton is present in the canal, shellfish growers are concerned the blooms could become more frequent and widespread.

plankton and conditions affecting it.

The amount of toxin that led to the closure was 226 micrograms of toxin per 100 grams of shellfish tissue. The level for closing the beaches is 80.

Normally, plankton blooms "take two or three weeks to develop, then can disappear almost overnight," said Louisa Nishitani, who studied red tide for 20 years until her retirement as a University of Washington researcher in 1985.

The plankton weren't known in large numbers in southern Puget Sound until 1978, when a major bloom occurred up north. After that, the organism has been gradually moving into southern waters.

"We knew it was in the main basin of Puget Sound for years before 1978," she said, "but the conditions weren't right for it to bloom before that — or it could have bloomed in isolated spots but just wasn't picked up."

The same could be said of Hood Canal today, she said.

Hood Canal beaches in the affected area were reopened two weeks after closure. During that period, Jon Day of Seabeck was the only grower waiting to harvest oysters from his beach.

But the threat of red tide extends to oyster growers throughout central and southern Hood Canal, especially when one realizes that cysts of the organism can remain dormant, waiting like tiny time bombs for the right conditions to return.

Increased population in the Hood Canal watershed may heighten the risk of poisonous plankton blooms and add to the threat already posed by growing pollution.

*USS Florida returns from a shakedown cruise
in the depths of Dabob Bay on Hood Canal.*

A bout midway along the meandering eastern flank of Hood Canal, the rocky beach is blocked by a fence that extends from the wooded bank all the way down into the waters of the tidal zone.

On the fence is a prominently displayed sign. "Warning. Restricted area. Keep Out. Authorized Personnel Only."

This is where wild and natural Hood Canal meets the orderly structure of the Navy.

What lies beyond the fence on the shoreline is one of the most extraordinary military installations in America — the Naval Submarine Base at Bangor.

It houses a support complex for a weapon system so incredibly powerful that it could, in the space of less than an hour, turn the sprawling mass of the Soviet Union into a cratered, smoldering hulk.

It has never been used for this purpose. And it won't be as long as the Soviet Union doesn't attack America first, say those who run the program. Its purpose is to deter warfare, not cause it, they say.

The base does this by keeping the eight

SECTION 1

HOOD CANAL
BECOMES THE
NAVY'S
CHOICE

By Lloyd Pritchett

nuclear missile submarines based there ready and rotating constantly out to sea.

But the 7,100-acre installation on Hood Canal is more than just the physical base for a weapons program. It is part nature preserve, small city, industrial facility and Navy home port — all contained within a setting of breathtaking grandeur.

••••••••••

Almost as soon as they leave Hood Canal, Trident submarines based at Bangor can reach most of their Soviet targets with their nuclear-tipped missiles.

Where is the ideal home for a fleet of eight Trident nuclear missile-firing submarines?

Back in the early '70s, when the Trident system was ready to move from the drawing boards to reality, the Navy asked itself that question.

The answer it came up with then, after much searching, was a site along a vast, natural fjord sandwiched between the snow-laced Olympic Mountains and the undulating evergreen hills of Kitsap Peninsula in Western Washington.

We, of course, know the waterway as Hood Canal.

Now, 20 years later, there is wide consensus among the submarine community at Bangor that the choice not only was correct but also a stroke of genius.

But how can that be? How could a remote waterway surrounded by vast brooding forests, far from any industrial support facilities, be considered an ideal place for a strategic submarine missile base and the 10,000 sailors and workers who run it?

The reasons may be unclear to a landlubber, but to most submariners they are obvious.

"It's a deep body of water without a lot of navigational hazards," said Capt. Malcolm Wright, commodore of the Trident fleet, which first became operational in 1982.

That means the giant subs based on Hood Canal can submerge almost as soon as they pull away from their pier. It also means that very little dredging was required to build the base's waterfront facilities.

Another plus — the 7,100-acre site chosen for the Trident support base already was owned by the Navy.

Bangor had been a sleepy ammunition depot established in the final years of World War II and named after a nearby tiny community on the shore of Hood Canal.

The area's relative remoteness from urbanized industrial areas is a plus, too — to the submarine Navy.

Said Wright: "If you have to make a choice between, say, Elliott Bay or a remote area — especially one that you already own — then you pick the less populated area."

Not only does that increase the margin of safety, but it means less marine vessel traffic to interfere with and observe submarine movements.

There are the characteristics of Hood Canal itself.

One of the deepest inlets in Western Washington, Dabob Bay, is 35 minutes from the Trident base as the submarine goes — offering a perfect test site for the giant subs before they leave on an operational patrol.

"Having Dabob Bay so near is great," said Cmdr. Keith Arterburn, the base's public affairs officer. "We can come back to the pier and fix any problems that are discovered."

"It (the bay) serves the Navy a great purpose," added Cmdr. Henry Gonzales, executive officer aboard one of the Trident subs. "It saves us a lot of hours. In a little less than an hour (from home base), we can dive."

Then there are the less tangible, but no less important factors.

Hood Canal country is a scenic, friendly place to live for the submariners and their families.

"Look at how many people stay here. (Navy) people do all they can not to leave here," said Wright. "Why is that? It's the quality of life. The people are friendly. The crime rate is low. This is America at its best."

The Navy's top submariner, Vice Adm. Roger F. Bacon, and his wife Joan may live in Washington, D.C., but they own property on Hood Canal.

They're not the only ones.

"I asked specifically to come to Bangor, and I got what I wanted," said Lt. Cmdr. Jay Perkins, training officer for Trident Submarine Group 9. "I plan to die here."

Chris Mygatt, wife of a Trident sailor aboard USS Florida, added: "People here are very warm and welcoming. I've never lived in a community that had so much support for the Navy."

Despite all that, Hood Canal does have its drawbacks.

For one, it's a long way — 155 miles — from the Bangor base to the open ocean. Submarines on patrol spend most of their first and last days traversing that distance on the surface at slow speeds.

Another disadvantage is that the Hood Canal area's distance from urban areas can be trying for young single sailors stationed there.

But these are minor problems when compared with the tremendous advantages, including what may be the ultimate advantage. That is, Hood Canal's strategic geographic location within the Trident missiles' 4,500-mile striking range of the Soviet Union.

Said Capt. Wright: "I think the real reason (the Hood Canal area) was picked — and this is just Malcolm Wright talking — is its geographical location. If you wanted to hold at risk all the targets in the Soviet Union, (they are) very close to being in range as soon as you get out of the Strait of Juan de Fuca."

"I think one reason for having the base here is its proximity to the most dangerous scene of a conflict."

He said it may not be possible to hit all potential targets in the Soviet Union from just off the Washington state coast — "but your steaming time is much shorter (to reaching those targets)" — especially if missiles are fired over the polar region.

"It complicates (the Soviets') efforts to locate us in the ocean (and gives us) more pre-launch survivability," said Wright.

And, he added: "Yes, we could hit some targets from right inside Hood Canal."

Petty officer Mike Schriver remembers well the first time he rode a submarine, USS Barb, into the crystalline waters of Hood Canal.

As the nuclear-powered sub docked at its berth in the Naval Submarine Base at Bangor, Schriver looked down and was astonished to see the submarine's black shape under the water, in detail, as if he were peering at it through glass.

"The water was so clear, you could see

Dabob Bay

The deep waters of Dabob Bay offer a convenient place to "shake down" a Trident sub after refit at the Bangor base across the canal.

the curvature of the sub's hull all the way down as far as it went," he said.

In no other port in the world had he ever seen what the sub looked like below the water's murky surface.

Then, looking up, he took in the vast forests and mountains surrounding Hood Canal and he knew he had entered a special place.

It is a feeling shared by many of the sailors and officers stationed at the sprawling base, the only industrial facility anywhere on the canal's 242-mile shoreline. It catches by surprise many of those who are stationed there for the first time. It is like no other military compound in the world.

Envious sailors based at other local facilities refer to the Bangor Navy base as "that national park."

"You can go right down to the Service Pier on base and go crabbing or clamming," says sailor Shawn Steele of USS Alabama.

The park-like beauty of the area has led Navy officials to exercise more than usual care in protecting the environment at Bangor.

The base's huge Delta Pier was specially constructed away from the shoreline to keep from disrupting salmon runs. The pilings supporting it are wrapped in a protective, nonpolluting plastic.

A number of systems also are in place to prevent oil, hazardous waste or radioactive material from spilling into the waterway. Spills of hazardous materials still occur sometimes, but are quickly cleaned up.

So far, though, the Navy's painstaking and thorough precautions have prevented a devastating accident from destroying the canal and its ecosystem.

The sailors and civilians stationed at Bangor love Hood Canal as much as, perhaps more than, the rest of us. Their activities pollute the fjord and its watershed less than many of Hood Canal's less imposing neighbors.

• • • • • • • • • •
"Our interest today is to preserve our way of life without being unduly threatening."
— Capt. Malcolm Wright, Submarine Squadron 17

• • • • • • • • • •

SECTION 2

THE CANAL'S
LARGEST
COMMUNITY

By Lloyd Pritchett

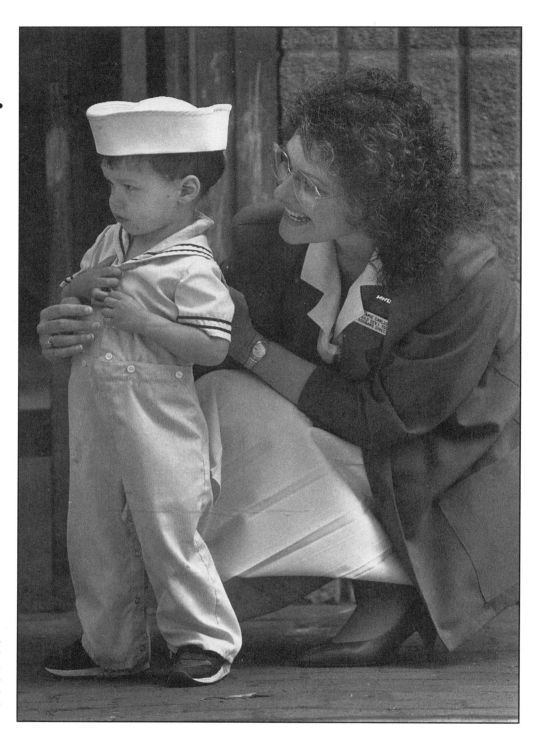

*Camie Carlson, director
of Bangor's Child
Development Center, is
just one of the people
who make the nuclear
submarine base a true
community.*

When a wicked wind and ice storm came screaming out of the night, shutting down civilization in Western Washington for days in December, 1990, everything fell apart for the young Navy wife living in rural western Kitsap County.

Her power went out, her driveway piled with snow, her car would not start, she was low on groceries, her two preschoolers were hungry.

And her husband was hundreds of miles out to sea, aboard a Trident submarine, somewhere in the North Pacific. He would not be returning for weeks.

Fortunately, her phone still worked. So she made a call.

"Hello," said a familiar voice on the other end of the line.

"I need some help," said the Navy wife.

Within a short time, another wife whose husband was aboard the same submarine drove up in a four-wheel-drive vehicle with three bags of groceries.

The second wife helped out until the first could get reorganized and back on her feet.

This is the kind of drama that Chris Mygatt — the familiar voice on the end of the line — is trained to deal with.

She is the "ombudsman" for the Blue Crew of the Trident submarine USS Florida, based on Hood Canal at the Naval Submarine Base at Bangor.

One of her jobs during the sub's patrols is to find USS Florida wives who can help out others in need.

For wives and family members of Florida crewmen, many of them new to the area, she is the one person they can count on 24 hours a day when the crew is at sea for 2 1/2 months at a stretch.

She knows all 114 wives with a husband on the Blue Crew (which alternates patrols with the sub's Gold Crew).

"It's like a big family," she said. "I feel like I have 114 sisters."

Although extreme winter storms don't come along every day, other types of problems crop up constantly while the Florida is out at sea.

Mygatt is there when there's an illness in a USS Florida family, she's there when someone has a question, she's there when someone needs a sympathetic shoulder to cry on.

She knows about every pregnancy that is likely to terminate while the crew is away. And she makes sure a plan is worked out in advance — with volunteers ready to escort the mothers-to-be to the hospital and take care of their homes during the husbands' absence.

She's also there to help in more serious cases — when a wife is assaulted or when there is a death in a family.

"I'm the captain's representative to the families," said Mygatt. "Last patrol I took over 700 phone calls from family members. I'm on call 24 hours a day for the entire deployment."

She is the only civilian adviser on the captain's small personal staff.

She said her role is to "help sailors keep their minds on their mission when they are at sea for 75 days and make them confident there's somebody back home to take care of their families."

Every crew of every Trident submarine at Bangor has an ombudsman like Mygatt who serves as a link to the families of crewmen.

Mygatt says she understands what the families go through because her husband, Cliff, has been in the Navy for 13 years and aboard the Florida for two years. They have gone through 10 patrols aboard different subs. They have a daughter, Heather, 6 1/2, who she says is "very proud of her father."

The base is the equivalent of a small city. It has its own housing, supermarket, department store, child care center, restaurants, clubs, library, movie theater, recycling center, swimming pool, bowling alley, gym, archery range, sports center, fishing lakes ... The list is endless.

It is a community of 10,000 people, the largest on the canal.

Mygatt and the other submarine ombudsmen are just part of a network of people in place at Bangor to support the families and crewmen who maintain their constant vigil out in the lonely depths of the ocean. Navy people, and the self-contained community at Bangor, call the concept "taking care of our own."

"The submarine force does it better than anybody else in the Navy," said base spokesman Cmdr. Keith Arterburn.

New Navy families arriving at Bangor first make contact with the extensive support system through the base's Family Service Center, which offers a packet of information about the area — and that's just for starters.

The center, headed by Cmdr. Marie McElligott, also offers financial and personal counseling, hosts 100 workshops and classes in everything from first aid to stress management and serves as a link between the Navy community and local school systems.

It helps Bangor families when they arrive and when they have to leave, and the entire time between.

Here, too, is where the subs' ombudsmen get their training.

And the center recently put together a new program called "junior ambassadors" — in which youngsters who live at the base

The base is a community of 10,000 people, the largest on the canal. It has its own housing, supermarket, department store, child care center, restaurants, clubs, library, movie theater, recycling center, swimming pool ... the list is endless.

volunteer to befriend new Navy kids arriving in the area and show them the ropes.

The center offers such an array of services that "there's really nothing like it in the civilian world," said Arterburn.

Besides the Family Service Center, the Trident base offers a child care center (open Monday through Saturday), housing referral offices, Navy Relief Society and chapel.

Altogether, these support services are given high marks by sailors when they are surveyed to find out why they decide to stay in the Navy.

The support activities not only help the families, but they help each submariner at sea keep his mind on his job, secure in the knowledge that there is a network of people there to help his own family while he's gone on patrol.

Nevertheless, despite the extensive support services, there come those times when each submariner, his spouse and family must learn to rely on themselves.

"You have to be tough-skinned and independent (to be a submariner's wife)," said McElligott. "You have to have confidence in yourself."

While the husband is away on patrol, the wife plays the role of mother and father. The kids, meanwhile, learn to get by with the attention of one parent.

Loneliness can be a big factor during a patrol, too, McElligott said. "If you're a wife, you see your children doing new things and he (the husband) is not there to watch."

To help bridge the communication gap between families and seafaring submariners, the Navy allows each wife to send eight short upbeat messages called "family-grams" to her husband during each Trident patrol.

But there is no cure for some of the feelings that plague wives and families when a submarine is on patrol.

"There's a point with every wife, there's always that inkling of fear in the back of your mind (that the sub might not return)," said Mygatt. "You have to remember that the men ... are highly trained, experts in what they do. ... They can do their jobs in their sleep."

"All these men are professionals, from the seamen recruits to the captain," she added.

With so much of their time taken up with meeting the demands of the submarine service, the wonder is that the Trident community at Bangor also has the time to extend a helping hand to the civilian community.

But it does.

Trident sailors volunteer at local schools through the Personal Excellence through Cooperative Education (PECE) program.

The Trident Training Facility operates a community action program, called "Helping Hands," that helps out civilian organizations and individuals with projects on Saturday mornings.

And the base recently "adopted" a two-mile stretch of State Highway 3 near Bangor, which it keeps clean through regular litter-gathering patrols.

If all this creates the image that the base is a good citizen made up of regular Americans, well — it's no image, but the truth, say the officials who run the place.

"These are everyday American citizens aboard these ships," said Capt. Malcolm Wright, commodore of the Trident squadron on Hood Canal.

• • • • • • • • • •

"You can go right down to the Service Pier on base and go crabbing or clamming."
— Shawn Steele, USS Alabama

A Canal Portfolio

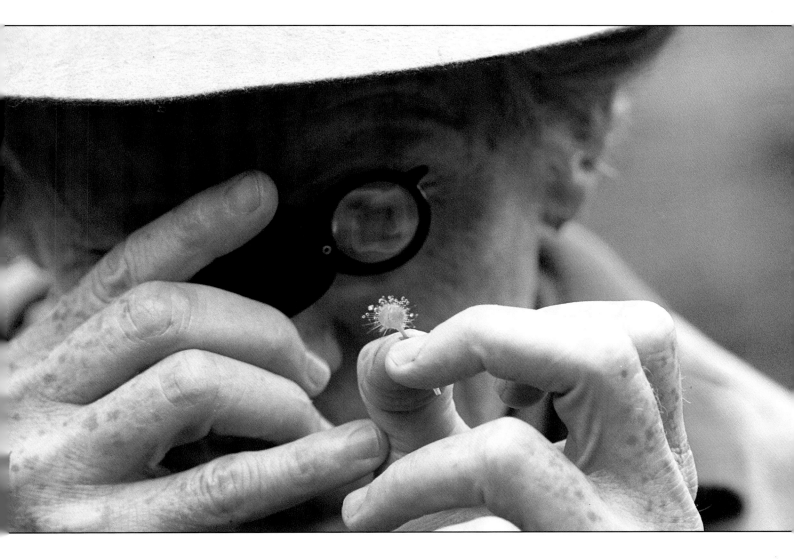

Botanist Jerry Gorsline inspects a tiny sundew plant, which catches insects with sticky secretions. Gorsline has studied much of the Hood Canal watershed in detail, and he's found a few areas, like Devil's Lake, that have withstood the encroachment of foreign plant species. Gorsline has called for state protection of such ecosystems.

John and Iriss Blaine (right) escaped a hectic urban setting to pursue their art on the shores of Hood Canal. Brad Kauzlaric (below), a Seabeck artist, worked for months on a painting that represented his perception of the waterway.

Elders, like Joseph Andrews Sr. of the Skokomish (top), still remember when the bounty of the canal was the source of their sustenance. The culture of the Northwest Coastal Salish people, who originally inhabited the Hood Canal watershed, was systematically attacked by the whites who settled there. Only recently has there been an attempt to revive the old ways. Port Gamble S'Klallam Jake Jones (left) learns to make a bentwood box in the way of his ancestors.

The canal's beauty is appreciated by many people in many different ways. But the canal may be loved too much. People flock to the waterway, its beaches, and to developments nearby, placing

demands on the canal that its natural systems cannot meet. Only careful use of this marvelous resource can preserve it for future generations.

The rich and the poor stake claim to the Hood Canal watershed. Chuck and JoAnne Haselwood (facing page) play on the golf course they built on the grounds of their home near Olympic View. Farmer John Davis (below) found it increasingly difficult to scratch out a living from the soil around Belfair, so he moved his family to Wisconsin in 1991. Alvin Ackerman (left) moved to Quilcene from Montana as a teenager in the late 1930s and found that the canal provided a "quiet life" for his wife and four children.

The waters of Hood Canal still offer a bounty, but the waterway's ability to provide is being challenged by pollution and sedimentation from human development, logging and agricultural uses. Harvesting oysters (right) is possible only because most of the canal's waters remain clear. Tribal fishermen on the Skokomish River (below) see fewer and fewer returning salmon, a result of overfishing on the oceans and the destruction of spawning habitat upstream by dams and development.

Petty Officer 2nd Class John Mosley at the helm of USS Florida beneath the surface of Hood Canal.

In the control room of the Trident submarine USS Florida, Petty Officer 2nd Class John Mosley munches rhythmically on a tasteless scrap of gum and nudges the small oval steering wheel before him to the right.

"Right 15 degrees rudder, steady course two-seven-eight," he says in a calm voice from the swivel chair where he sits.

Mosley, considered the best helmsman with the Florida's blue crew, can't see where he is going.

Instead, he eyeballs a panel clustered with gauges and instruments and responds to course headings ordered by the ship's officer of the deck.

For the moment, the 18,700-ton sub is cruising along the surface of Hood Canal. The officer of the deck, known as the "OOD," is perched at the top of the submarine's towering black sail, out in a brisk spring wind. He communicates to the control room below via intercom.

Also atop the sail is the Florida's commanding officer, Capt. Paul Sullivan. He watches wordlessly and stoically over the OOD's shoulder.

Today the crew is taking the billion-dollar strategic sub from its berth at the Bangor naval base to 600-foot-deep Dabob Bay in Jefferson County for a test spin. It's a short 35-minute cruise across Hood Canal.

The idea is to put the submarine through its paces one last time before it heads out on another 75-day patrol under the unforgiving ocean after nearly a month in port.

"If the ship gets out (on a patrol) and something doesn't work ... it can create a real domino effect," said Cmdr. Henry Gonzales, the Florida's executive officer. "One reason that doesn't happen much is because we have Dabob Bay here to use for testing."

The crew also needs to know if all

• • • • • • • • • •

SECTION 3

400 FEET
BELOW THE
CANAL

By Lloyd Pritchett

systems are working noiselessly, since a sub that makes noise is a sub that gets found. And Trident subs aren't in the business of being found.

Any noises detected by sensitive sound detectors planted on Dabob Bay's bottom must be tracked down and silenced by repair crews before the sub can head out to sea.

As the sub enters the bay, it begins a long, looping racetrack circuit. It is nearly time to dive.

The personnel on the sail — the OOD, the junior OOD, the captain and two lookouts — clamber down a long metal ladder through two hatches into the control room below. The last one down closes and seals the hatches.

Now the officer of the deck will guide the ship by periscope.

A command passes over the ship's speaker system: "Watchstanders, man your phones in preparation for submerging the ship."

At the helm, Mosley chews his gum faster as the moment for diving approaches. His right leg moves up and down rapidly in a nervous rhythm.

Also at the ready is the ship's planesman, to Mosley's left, who controls the sub's angle of descent, and the chief of the watch, who mans a panel showing which valves, hatches and openings on the ship's hull have been closed.

Before the sub can submerge, every opening must be shut.

"We don't want water getting into what we call the people locker," explains the submarine group's training officer, Lt. Cmdr. Jay Perkins.

The OOD orders more course changes and the helmsman answers.

"Right full rudder, aye," says the helmsman, just the slightest bit of tension entering his voice. "All ahead one-third, aye. ... Passing course one-eight-zero to the right, sir. ... Continue course two-zero-zero, helm aye. Officer of the deck, steady on course two-zero-zero, sir."

"Very well, helm," answers the OOD.

Then the planesman receives his orders: "Submerge the ship, make depth seven-eight feet."

And just as it has been portrayed in a thousand Hollywood movies, a voice crackles over the ship's speaker system:

"Dive! Dive!" A horn alarm sounds twice, and then the order is repeated: "Dive! Dive!"

"All vents open!" answers the chief of the watch, as he throws open switches. Thousands of gallons of Hood Canal water begin pouring noiselessly through valves into the sub's ballast tanks.

A rush of cool air passes through the control room.

Immediately, the red digits on the sub's keel depth gauge begin increasing as the sub starts on its way below Hood Canal's gray waves. The planesman calls out the increasing depths.

"Three-eight feet," he says. "Four-six. ... Four-eight. ... Five-zero feet. ... Five-two."

"Deck's awash," calls out the officer of the deck, signalling that the waves are now combing over the sub's outer deck.

When the keel depth reaches sixty-eight feet, the huge submarine is completely submerged.

Once it passes below 84 feet, it will be too deep to use the periscope.

"Order depth one-nine-one," intones the OOD.

Shortly after, he lowers the periscope.

The helmsman seems to relax. His leg stops moving up and down. But he still gives his gum a workout.

Now is the time when the ship's sonar room takes over.

"We're the eyes and ears of the boat when we're not at periscope depth," explains Sonar Technician 1st Class Michael Guinn.

What the sonar crew does is listen to sounds in the water — very carefully — using a multimillion-dollar hightech electronic system called the AN/BQQ6 that analyzes sounds on a screen.

The system is so sophisticated that, with a crackerjack operator, it can put together a three-dimensional acoustic "picture" of all sounds surrounding the ship, identify where they are coming from and what is causing them.

It can tell whether a nearby sound is caused by a whale, a supertanker, an ocean tug — or a Victor class Soviet submarine — and then allow the sub to avoid it.

"Just by listening, we can tell how many screws (propellers) a contact has, and how many blades are on each screw," said Guinn.

Today, in Dabob Bay, the sonar system picks up the tiny sounds of hundreds of snapping shrimp. The sound of a passing

"The average age of the crew is only 21 years old. A lot of times a new crew member senses the weight of the whole world is on his shoulders. But I remind him that it's really a team effort ... I call it 'Team Florida'."

— Capt. Paul Sullivan, USS Florida

patrol boat also leaves a thick acoustic wake down the sonar system's screen.

But out in front of the sub, all is clear.

Down below on the ship's lowest deck, in the Florida's torpedo room, another crew is getting ready for action.

Today the crew will test-launch a Mark 48 torpedo — a million-dollar weapon so smart that if it misses its target it is programmed to come back and try again.

The torpedo being shot today has no warhead on it. After launching, it will be retrieved and put back into service.

No tense, sweaty-faced officer barks "Fire one!" into his headset as a torpedo roars from its tube. Instead, there is a calm countdown, after which a technician pushes a button in the control room.

A loud hiss, lasting less than a second, is the only sign that the torpedo has been pushed from its tube by pressurized water.

After the launch, a burly torpedoman opens the tube to check it. Inside he sees the smashed remains of two Hood Canal shrimp sucked into the screens during the launch.

"It's the catch of the day," he says.

The Trident submarines based at Bangor spend more than twice as much time out on patrol as they do in port.

For 75 days at a time, 160 crewmen stand ready at a moment's notice to launch 24 missiles packing up to eight warheads apiece toward targets in the Soviet Union, if called on by the president to do so.

The chances of that call coming are almost incalculably remote. Nevertheless, the crew must be ready to act.

They live inside their enormous steel vault on manufactured air, surrounded by pipes, cables, computers, machinery — and missiles — never contacting the outside world, from an undersea world about as alien as any found on this planet.

A shakedown cruise in Dabob Bay is part of the preparation for a cruise that starts about three weeks before the sub actually leaves on patrol, a time called "refit."

"This is the most painful period in a submariner's life," said Senior Chief Machinist's Mate Greg Mercer of Bangor, who has served aboard Trident subs for years.

Refit period means 18-hour work days, hard work, no sleep, inspections, extra duty and very little time for anything else, including one's family. And it's all domi-nated by the certainty that it will be followed by about 75 days at sea.

It takes most of a day for a sub to get from Bangor to the sea. Once the Trident reaches the western end of the Strait of Juan de Fuca, "it's time to pull the plug," said Gonzales, executive officer of the Florida's blue crew.

After the sub dives, it needn't come back to the surface until the patrol is over. Air is manufactured, water is purified from the sea and tons of food are stashed aboard.

During all this time, one thing is more important than any other to the ship and its crew: silence.

Aboard a Trident sub, any sound can jeopardize national security if a listening Soviet sub is anywhere within miles. Therefore, silence is not just a virtue; it is a necessity, a habit, a way of living.

Machinists don't drop tools. Cooks don't bang pots and pans. Doors and hatches aren't slammed, they are closed with great, gentle care. Whenever possible, crew members climb into their bunks, or "racks," to avoid making noise. Toilet lids aren't even lifted for fear they will fall back down with a bang.

"Something like that can be heard miles through the water," said Senior Chief Mercer, who adds the crew goes "to any length to eliminate" noise.

Meanwhile, the work load hardly lets up.

"The average officer can easily work 18 hours a day," said Perkins.

Every crew member stands six-hour watches, which are followed by 12 hours of work, training and drills. The remaining six hours can be used for sleep if there are no more drills during that time.

It's easy to forget whether it's day or night, said Mercer, so most crew members orient themselves by which meal they are eating — breakfast, lunch, dinner or midnight rations.

Under this kind of regimen, the excitement of heading out to sea wears off after about the first two weeks of the patrol.

The sameness gets to some people. It's always the same shipmates, with the same mannerisms, telling the same sea stories in the same way.

And there are the worries of isolation. "I'm confident in my wife's abilities; she can handle anything," said Mercer. "But you still worry. You worry about your family. You worry about the unknown."

• • • • • • • • • • •

The sonar system picks up the tiny sounds of hundreds of snapping shrimp. After test firing a torpedo, a torpedoman removes the smashed remains of two Hood Canal shrimp sucked into the tube.

"If the ship gets out (on a patrol) and something doesn't work ... it can create a real domino effect. One reason that doesn't happen much is because we have Dabob Bay here to use for testing."
— Cmdr. Henry Gonzales, USS Florida

By the midway point of the patrol, the crew is ready for some diversion. So, by tradition, there is mid-patrol night — an evening of skits, auctions and other hilarity that crew members don't talk about to outsiders.

After that, the world begins to look brighter as crew members start counting off the time until the end of the deployment — four weeks, three weeks, two, one ...

And then comes that magic day when the submarine returns to the Strait of Juan de Fuca, rises up from the ocean depths and surfaces.

The hatch is opened and for the first time, the smells of the world above come pouring down into the filtered atmosphere aboard the submarine. So strong is it that some crew members with sensitive nostrils nearly swoon.

Hours later, the Trident berths at its Bangor pier and the crew files off, eyes blinking in the harsh, unfamiliar sunlight and straining to focus on distances farther away than the end of the missile deck.

Microbes in the air — absent in the submarine's manufactured atmosphere — give everyone in the crew a cold.

But the hardest thing to get used to is the excess of noise — horns honking, people jabbering, dogs barking, television, radios, car engines ...

It can all be overwhelming to a submariner not yet weaned from the culture of silence.

About three days later, the sub's alternate crew takes over and the just-returned sailors get some well-deserved time off.

The Florida's Blue Crew has all this to look forward to as they spend the rest of the morning and afternoon steering their huge sub around the underwater Dabob Bay course. They change depths, submerging as deep as 400 feet. They test equipment, they monitor everything. Then it is time for the final test.

"Emergency surface the ship!" orders the officer of the deck in the control room. The diving alarm sounds three times.

The chief of the watch reaches over and throws open the emergency blow actuators, forcing tons of water from the ship's tanks. The sub angles upward and the red digits of the keel depth gauge race from 400 to 350 to 300 to 250 ...

As the sub breaks the surface, there is a momentary surge of weightlessness. Then the sub goes level.

A sailor scrambles up the ladder to the top of the sail, opening the hatches on his way.

The outside air floods into the control room, bringing with it the scents of the outdoors that have been missing all day in the sub's sterile, manufactured atmosphere — the salt air, trees, flowers ....

The OOD orders a course heading back toward home at the Bangor base.

The helmsman tosses his gum into the trash.

The Concept of Deterrence

A long shadow is cast on the golden glitter of sunrise on Hood Canal by the tall sail of a Trident nuclear missile submarine pulling away from the enormous Navy pier complex at Bangor.

The giant billion-dollar submarine, the most fearsome weapons platform in the U.S. arsenal, is about to disappear beneath the sea for 2 1/2 months with its crew and 24 nuclear-tipped missiles.

The sub's mission while there is to act as a well-hidden persuader — to convince the Soviet Union that America is ready and able to respond with megatons of nuclear fury to a Soviet attack against it.

This is what the Navy calls "strategic deterrence."

At any given time, there are five or more of the huge Trident subs patrolling the waters of the Pacific off the Soviet Union.

But the subs can't carry out their mission without a home base to keep them supplied and working. And this is it — the 7,100-acre Naval Submarine Base in Kitsap County, with its high-tech facilities, equipment and thousands of skilled workers.

And the base can't operate without the Hood Canal itself. This is the subs' conduit to the sea, 155 miles away.

Together, the waterway, the subs and the base offer a very persuasive argument against starting a nuclear war with the United States. And that's the

The Trident submarines based at Bangor spend more than twice as much time out on patrol as they do in port. During all this time, one thing is more important than any other to the ship and its crews: silence.

whole idea.

"The worst thing you can have in deterrence is uncertainty," explained Capt. Malcolm Wright, commodore of the eight-submarine Trident fleet based on Hood Canal. "That lets (the enemy) think, 'Maybe we can get away with (a nuclear strike).' You don't want him thinking that."

In fact, everything at the Navy's Bangor base on Hood Canal is designed to keep the Soviets from thinking that.

First, there is the Strategic Weapons Facility Pacific, or SWFPAC (pronounced "swiffpack"). This is where the submarines' missiles and warheads are stored, maintained and serviced. It is guarded by a company of Marines authorized to use deadly force against intruders.

There is the Trident Refit Facility, in essence a small shipyard that keeps the submarines operating flawlessly and silently.

The base's Trident Training Facility, with simulators that replicate all the equipment on a Trident sub, is used for teaching and re-teaching crew members how to operate their ship before they ever go to sea.

On the waterfront is a huge offshore pier complex, complete with drydock, that can accommodate several submarines at once and provide support for the nuclear reactors that power them.

A covered explosives handling wharf, the tallest structure in Kitsap County, is where the ships' missiles are loaded and unloaded.

Using all these facilities, a Trident submarine returning from patrol can be repaired, loaded and readied for another patrol in 25 days. Then it's back out to sea for another 75 days with a new, refreshed crew.

"Deterrence is a funny concept," said Commodore Wright. "We have to have the ability to do something that nobody wants to do — and do it so well that we never have to do it."

To keep its edge, the crew constantly practices missile launches — going through the procedures without actually launching missiles or, less often, launching missiles armed with dummy warheads.

Eventually, the procedure becomes so ingrained in each crew member's mind that he can do it without thinking.

But could the average middle Americans who man the launcher and fire control consoles — guys raised on mom, baseball and apple pie — be able to fire weapons knowing they would destroy much of the world and the people in it?

"I don't think they (crew members) could do it. I *know* they could," Capt. Paul Sullivan, commanding officer of the Trident sub Florida, said. "The (nuclear) threat has to be a viable deterrent. I have no doubt that the crew could perform its mission."

By Lloyd Pritchett

● ● ● ● ● ● ● ● ● ●

SECTION 4

MISSION: KEEP IT CLEAN

By Lloyd Pritchett

Bangor is where Hood Canal nature coexists with the awesome firepower of the nuclear weapons age.

T he two Canada geese were winging northward, high over the treetops of Western Washington, when they spotted a small pond below in the midst of an enormous grassy field, near Hood Canal.

The pair descended and landed on the pond's glassy surface.

The large birds immediately liked what they found. No humans or dogs intruded on the pond's solitude. Plenty of wild food was available in the immediate vicinity. The waters of the pond were clean and ample.

So they stayed. And in the following months, they hatched and reared a brood of goslings there.

Little did the geese know or care that the little pond they had chosen for their nest was in the midst of the largest concentration of nuclear weapons in the region.

Surrounded by a double row of barbed-wire-topped chain link fence, the cleared grassy field with its small seasonal pond is home to the Strategic Weapons Facility Pacific, inside the Naval Submarine Base at Bangor.

Sitting at the top of a bluff overlooking Hood Canal, it is the storage and maintenance area for hundreds of nuclear missiles and warheads carried on undersea patrols by the giant Trident subs homeported at the base.

Any unauthorized humans who might

try to enter the area could be shot by Marine sentries constantly on guard. But the Canada geese were welcomed.

As the pair raised their young family there, they often took the goslings for walks between the earth-topped concrete bunkers where the weapons are stored, oblivious to the megatonnage around them.

The geese aren't the only creatures perfectly happy to live inside a military installation known more for its powerful weapons than for its plentiful wildlife.

Some 5,000 acres of the 7,100-acre submarine base are wooded, and it also is home to lakes, wetlands, fields, small estuaries, a dozen streams, and other habitats, including four miles of shoreline along Hood Canal.

All this diversity supports a teeming population of wildlife.

Here are great blue herons and great horned owls, osprey, kingfishers, mountain quail, ducks, widgeons, mergansers, coho salmon, rainbow and cutthroat trout, red fox, bobcats, river otter, beavers, coyotes, raccoons and more than 150 blacktail deer.

And Tom James, the base's fish and wildlife biologist, said even cougars have been sighted inside the compound, attracted by the deer.

The Bangor base goes to extraordinary lengths to prevent oil or waste from getting into Hood Canal. "I've never seen a military base where the water is so pristine," says Lt. Robert Rothwell, base operations officer.

Preserving the Environment

Here is a sampling of specific things the Naval Submarine Base at Bangor is doing to preserve and enhance the environment at the installation on Hood Canal:

• A coho salmon hatchery has been established and salmon runs restored on streams feeding Devil's Hole, a natural wetland on base. So far, 500,000 salmon have been released.

• Old hazardous waste sites on the Bangor base, created years ago before modern disposal methods were available, are being investigated for possible cleanup. Two are on the shore of Hood Canal. Crews tentatively are scheduled to begin an interim cleanup of the worst site, known as "Site F," in the near future.

• All waste discharges from the base are being pumped away from Hood Canal. Hazardous industrial wastes are trucked by licensed haulers to a federally approved site off-base. Waste oil is processed at a recycling plant. Sewage discharges are pumped off-base to the Brownsville treatment plant, operated by Kitsap County.

•The amount of hazardous waste generated by the base has been slashed in half in the past few years. The facility now is embarking on a program to cut the amount of ozone-depleting chemicals it uses.

• The base's forests are logged on a 100-year cycle, or about 30 to 40 acres per year, providing income to support the base's forestry program and some extra funding for area schools.

• Contract loggers hired to log on the base are required to leave 10 large trees per acre, leaving a diverse environment behind instead of a clearcut. "If you leave large trees, you attract hawks and eagles that eat the voles that might chew down little trees," said base forester Arthur K. Schick.

• Natural areas of the Trident base, including all wetlands and lakes, are off-limits to construction and development.

• Cattail Lake, at the base's north end, is stocked with rainbow trout. Cutthroat spawn naturally in the lake, and an 11-pounder was recently caught.

• Submarine pier facilities on Hood Canal were built far off-shore to allow room for migrating salmon to pass.

• The base is cooperating with researchers to find white pine trees on base that are resistant to blister rust — a killer disease that is wiping out whole stands of the tree across the West.

• Each winter, the local chapter of the Audubon Society is admitted to the base to conduct a bird species count.

• Wildlife is monitored across the base, leading to interesting discoveries about habits of different species. A recent study found that each blacktail deer on the base ranges over an area of only about one-third square mile.

By Lloyd Pritchett

On the shoreline, there are mussels, geoducks, butter clams, oysters and crabs in abundance.

And, of course, everywhere there are hundreds of smaller animals — from voles to salamanders to several species of frogs.

As the rest of Kitsap County has become increasingly urbanized, the Bangor base, protected behind its fence, has become a *de facto* nature preserve — with wild animals sometimes spilling into the human-occupied areas of the compound.

"I couldn't get into my parking place the other day because a deer was blocking the way," the base's operations officer, Lt.

Robert Rothwell, recently said in a mock-serious complaint.

The miracle is that the habitat remains so pristine despite the base's industrial mission — which includes repairing and maintaining eight Trident missile submarines based there and the nuclear weapons they carry.

The presence of 15,000 people who live and work on the base also has not frightened away the wildlife or tainted the waters of Hood Canal.

But Marvin Frye, the base's environ-

• • • • • • • • • •

A policy of environmental protection along with a strict, centralized authority over operations means the submarine base, with 10,000 residents, pollutes the canal watershed less than many communities with just a handful of homes.

A Legacy of Toxic Dumping

Like other military bases around the nation, the Naval Submarine Base at Bangor faces serious environmental problems related to historical disposal and spills of hazardous waste on the base.

The Bangor base, formerly an ammunition depot, includes 22 scattered sites, ranging from places where explosive materials were burned or buried to places used for general waste and chemical disposal.

The cost of cleaning up all the sites has been estimated at $24 million by Navy officials, but authorities at the federal Environmental Protection Agency say costs could run considerably higher. At most of the sites, studies are under way to determine the best method of dealing with the pollution.

The following is a summary of the sites listed on the federal "Superfund" list of hazardous waste sites:

• Operable Unit 1 — Site A: The first Bangor site placed on the Superfund list was used from 1962 to 1977 for ordnance (explosives) disposal. Ordnance included TNT, flares, fuses, primers, smokeless powder and black powder. The site is located at the north end of the base. Toxic soils, runoff and contaminated groundwater have been found, but no drinking wells are threatened so far.

• Operable Unit 2 — Site F: A wastewater lagoon in the south-central part of the base is now considered one of Bangor's most significant hazardous waste sites. The lagoon was used for dumping various military compounds from 1957 to 1972. Tests find toxics moving slowly through the water table toward homes a mile away.

• Operable Unit 3 — Site 24: A torpedo fuel incinerator was operated in the southeast corner of the base from 1973 to 1983 before removal. Tests uncovered heavy metals, ordnance and PCBs in the soil.

— Site 16: Adjacent to Site 24, the spot was the storage area for the torpedo fuel incinerator. Drums of wastewater and contaminated rags, along with waste solvents, were stored there. Small spills also were reported.

— Site 25 is made up of a number of stormwater drainage ponds which accepted runoff from industrial activities at Bangor.

• Operable Unit 4 — Site C West: Fill material was removed from this site located under Building 7700, an area used for the disposal of picric acid and torpedo fuel from 1946 until 1973. The material was moved from Site C East. An investigation will determine if all the material was removed.

• Operable Unit 5 — Site E: This was a dump area for electroplating wastes from 1960 until 1973. Tests found low levels of metals in groundwater.

— Site 5: A metallurgy test build-mental program director, says it's really no miracle. Rather, it's all the result of careful planning and follow-through, he says.

"We operate a full-scope integrated environmental management program. We take a holistic approach, if you will ... a balanced approach," said Frye, who has run the program since its beginnings in the 1970s, when the Navy compound was converted from an ammunition depot to a submarine base.

The environmental program "emphasizes man and nature living together in harmony," he added.

Its three "overriding goals" are to preserve and enhance the environment, to comply with all environmental laws — including state and local laws — and to cooperate with all environmental regulatory officials, Frye said.

It's a big order, considering the environmental damage the base could do. It is, after all, an industrial facility larger than most private businesses.

Even more important, the base handles some of the deadliest materials known to man.

Take nearly 200 nuclear warheads

Some 5,000 acres of the 7,100-acre submarine base are wooded, and it also is home to lakes, wetlands, fields, small estuaries, a dozen streams, and other habitats, including four miles of shoreline along Hood Canal.

ing located here was torn down about 1973. Experts suspect the site may be contaminated with mercury.

— Site 11: Close to Site E, this area was used for the disposal of barrels and cans of pesticides. Consultants have begun removal of the material.

• Operable Unit 6 — Site C East: From 1946 to 1973, unknown amounts of torpedo fuel wastewater, explosive material and solvents were disposed of in a gravel pit.

— Site D: Explosive compounds were burned on the ground here from 1946 to 1965.

• Operable Unit 7 — Site 26: Discharges from various industrial and disposal operations may have contaminated sediments along the shore.

— Site B: Floral Point at the north end of the base was a testing area for pyrotechnics from 1950 until the early 1960s and became a burn/disposal area for garbage, explosives waste and scrap metal until 1972.

— Site 2: A dump site along Nautilus Avenue, across from the Fleet Deployed Parking Lot, contains scrap metal and inert explosive material.

— Site 4: Carlson Spit may have been used to dispose of ignition devices. Further site inspections are planned.

— Site 7: One-gallon paint cans and 55-gallon drums were dumped over a hillside near a creek feeding into Cattail Lake. The material was removed in 1981.

— Site 10: Buildings 1676 and 1677 in the southeast corner of the base were used for herbicide storage from the late 1950s to 1979. Some containers apparently leaked through wooden floors. The two buildings were demolished in 1983 and a new building was constructed with a paved parking lot.

— Site 18: Between 5 and 10 gallons of PCB fluid were spilled at Building 1016 in the southeast corner of the base. The area has since been covered with asphalt.

— Site 27: A pit in the southeast corner of the base was used to steam-clean locomotives. When the pit was full, the grease and residue were hauled away. The pit was filled during the 1970s.

— Site 28: A ditch adjacent to Building 1032 in the southeast corner of the base was used for paint waste and solvents.

— Site 29: Empty pesticide/herbicide tanks were rinsed with water that flowed onto the ground in the main garage and public works area in the southeast corner of the base.

— Site 30: From 1977 to 1985, neutralized pesticide and herbicide rinse water was disposed of on the ground near a stretch of railroad tracks near the Fleet Deployed Parking Lot.

By Christopher Dunagan

packing 2.3 megatons of explosive power, stack them on 24 rockets filled with 25 tons of high-explosive propellant apiece, then line them up inside a steel submarine housing a fueled-up 90,000-horsepower nuclear reactor.

What do you get? An extreme case of safety-consciousness, say personnel at the base who work with this high-power techno-wizardry every day.

They say the Navy goes to such lengths to minimize the hazards of its nuclear submarine operations on Hood Canal that there is really nothing for people in the vicinity to worry about.

With the pervasive culture of safety in the submarine service, the risk level is reduced to as near zero as possible, they say.

"To the Trident sailor, safety is paramount. We breathe safety, we train safety and we live safety," said Lt. Cmdr. Jay Perkins, training officer for the Trident submarine group at Bangor.

"The emphasis on safety really precludes any major catastrophes."

Officials won't discuss the specifics of their safety precautions, but they are willing to discuss them generally.

Nuclear warheads are designed with multiple safety features, then are subjected to rigorous analyses and testing to ensure weapon integrity even in the event of a handling accident, said Cmdr. Keith Arterburn, spokesman for the base. That means a weapon won't explode unless it is activated, prepped and launched thousands of miles away during an actual nuclear war.

The missiles that propel the warheads on their way are touchier. Loaded with tons of solid rocket fuel, they are listed as a "Class A" explosive — the most sensitive type.

To prevent an accidental ignition of the fuel by lightning, buildings where the missiles are maintained are outfitted with enormous 50-foot lightning rods.

To keep the fuel from degrading, it is kept at a constant temperature and humidity. Safety procedures guard it against being bumped or jolted during handling.

When missiles are loaded aboard submarines at the base, they are moved inside containers carried aboard special vehicles that transport them at extremely slow speeds.

A half-hour before the missiles are transported from their bunkers to the base's explosive handling wharf, the entire road surface and roadbed is inspected visually, electronically and with guard dogs.

During the loading procedure, blast shields are in place.

In case the worst happens and a missile accidentally ignites, they are only stored or moved in areas of the base away from community facilities, public highways and private property that could be damaged.

The subs' nuclear reactors are built to exacting standards. All radioactive fission products are contained within high-integrity fuel modules that can withstand battle shock.

No radioactivity is released to the environment, and tests are conducted annually in the air and water at Bangor to confirm this.

A few environmental problems have cropped up from time to time — including chemical and oil spills.

But Frye said all spills are immediately cleaned up, no matter how minor.

Old hazardous waste sites on the base, created back when it was an ammunition depot, also are being readied for cleanup, he said.

And all waste from the base is pumped away from Hood Canal, he explained, to prevent contamination of the water. Small residential areas outside the installation put more pollution into Hood Canal, through their septic systems, than the entire Bangor base.

The fact that so many wild creatures are thriving and that the waters of Hood Canal remain unpolluted is a signal that environmental programs and safeguards established by the base are working.

"Hood Canal is a tremendous asset to the United States Navy and to national security and we're doing all we can to make our presence as neutral environmentally as we can," said Capt. Malcolm Wright, commodore of the Trident submarine squadron.

Added Capt. Lawrence J. Kramer, commanding officer of the submarine base: "It really is a beautiful place. I hope it will always be that way."

• • • • • • • • • •

The miracle is that the habitat remains so pristine despite the base's industrial mission. Marvin Frye, the base's environmental program director, says it's the result of careful planning and follow-through.

SECTION 1

WHEN
BEACHES HOST
MILLIONS

By Seabury Blair Jr.

A state parks ranger patrols the crowded beach at Twanoh State Park. Nearly half a million people visit the park near Union each year.

T he sun tints the beach as it rises red from an August haze at Twanoh State Park. A lone man and his leashed dog leave tracks in the rough gravel just below the high tide line. Soon, others amble down to the beach to stretch and watch the midweek morning paint pockets of snow pink on the Olympic Mountains to the west. Most people visiting Twanoh's beach at this hour come from the park's tiny campground across Highway 106.

Forty-seven camp spots are available at Twanoh, Hood Canal's finest public beach. It is a rare August day that the campground isn't full, even if it rains.

But campers won't erase the early tracks from the beach. By day's end, as many as 4,000 people will visit Twanoh to splash or swim or sunburn. Their tracks will obliterate those of the dawn visitors.

A city larger than Seattle settles on the public beaches around Hood Canal every year. In July 1990 alone, more than 130,000 people enjoyed Twanoh's beach. Only about one in every 36 of those people camps at the park.

Visitors to the seven state parks around the canal bring their boats and fishing poles, their water skis and water wings. They bring vacation cheer and the emerald water works its magic upon them.

When many of these nearly two million people go home at the end of the summer, they may think they leave Hood Canal just as they found it. Their tons of trash have been properly disposed, their sewage treated. They are conscientious visitors, for the most part.

But heavy recreational use takes its toll on these glorious waters. Some bays in the canal record huge increases in bacterial contamination during weeks of heavy recreational use.

• • • • • • • • • •

It is a rare August day that the 47 camp spots available at Twanoh State Park, Hood Canal's finest public beach, aren't full, even if it rains.

Nobody is certain how many more people can enjoy the canal without killing it. What is certain: those who enjoy the canal today are eager to preserve it for their children tomorrow.

"I'm not an ecology nut, but I do believe in keeping things for future generations. I believe we need to take the steps necessary now to keep this place for the people who follow," says Chuck Stuart, a 72-year-old Bremerton resident who has been visiting Twanoh for more than a half century.

Stuart and his wife, Marie, sat by their campfire at Twanoh as three generations of the family stopped to talk. The afternoon sun burned through clouds and began warming the beach across the road. Children's shouts drifted from the beach to the quieter campground.

"I think it's the old-timers who want to see this place preserved," said Marie Stuart.

Stuart's sons, Jim and John, and daughter, Beth Schmidt, recall visiting Twanoh every year when they were growing up in Bremerton. Now they gather every August for a family camp-out. They stay in the same spot every year.

"If there's somebody here," jokes Jim Stuart, "we throw 'em out."

The Stuarts agree that public beaches like Twanoh are vital to building a consensus of canal savers. They fall in love with the place; they want to keep it lovely.

"This is our only shot," says Jim Stuart, indicating the green campground with its whispering creek. "People like us will never be able to afford waterfront along the canal."

"That's why we have to preserve this," says his father.

Families like the Stuarts can be found camping every year at all of the canal's state parks: Shine Tidelands, Dosewallips, Potlatch, Belfair, Scenic Beach and Kitsap Memorial. Children grow up there and bring their children to grow up there.

Al Giersch, who served 10 years as

Twanoh State Park

There are times in the sunny summer months when Twanoh State Park beach is wall-to-wall people and the campground is filled Wednesday for the next weekend.

manager at Dosewallips State Park and now works at Fort Flagler State Park, says most campers at Dosewallips came there to stay.

"We had to be one of the busiest campgrounds in the state. Senior citizens would come to stay in the winter and we had massive attendance around May, when people came to shrimp."

Jerry Rice, manager at Kitsap Memorial State Park, says most of the campers who stop there are probably on their way to the Olympic Peninsula. "But we're becoming more of a destination camp," he said.

At Twanoh, however, what is happening across the road from the campground may be more important to the canal's future. The beach draws scores of canal savers.

Last year, 1.98 million people visited state parks on the canal, according to the Washington State Parks and Recreation Commission's annual report. Only 135,236 stayed overnight.

Perhaps 100 sunbathers are on the beach by 2 p.m. as Twanoh Park Ranger Larry Otto makes a sweep through the main parking lot. Compared to a weekend crowd, he says, the park is empty.

"I've seen good years and bad years, as far as crowds go," says Otto, a Bremerton native. "I know that the last three weekends, the whole park has been close to total gridlock."

He posted "LOT FULL" signs at all three entrances, and cars lined up along the highway. As soon as one day visitor pulled out, it seemed, three cars pulled in.

The incoming tide warms itself on the gravel, so that by 5 p.m., perhaps 400 swimmers at Twanoh splash in the warmest water of the day. On the weekend, Otto says, easily 10 times that number might enjoy the day-use area.

Nearly a half-million people — 469,431 — stayed a day at Twanoh in 1989. Almost all visited between April 15 and Sept. 30. The 180-acre park sustains greater day use than any other public area on Hood Canal.

Almost 20,000 more visitors stopped at Twanoh than at Potlatch, the second most popular of the canal parks for day visitors.

In fact, Twanoh ranked 20th among the state's 144 parks in daytime attendance in 1989. Otto is pleased that his park's big crowds don't bring big problems.

"When I first came here (12 years ago), we seemed to have a lot of younger kids, and they created some problems. But we are a family-oriented park, and we don't have a lot of problems. There just isn't much vandalism at all.

"We had a couple of professors from California last week. They came specifically to this park so they could play on their sailboards on Hood Canal. They've come here for years and years," he said.

"To me, that says something. You see the same people every year. It's like getting to be a family. And they take this park on as their own personal area, and they don't want to mess it up."

Sunset is as spectacular as sunrise at Twanoh. The Olympics turn purple while the sky burns. The day area closes at dusk, so campers are often the only witnesses to nature's finest fireworks.

The camper and his dog return for an evening walk. The dawn tide will erase their tracks, but visitors will make more tomorrow.

• • • • • • • • • •

A city larger than Seattle settles on the public beaches around Hood Canal every year. In July 1990 alone, more than 130,000 people enjoyed Twanoh's beach.

A Community of Familiar Faces

George and Maryjane Becker started camping at Twanoh State Park in a tent 40 years ago. Today Becker is Twanoh's volunteer "campground host."

He registers campers and helps the ranger and manager around the campground.

Becker says Twanoh has changed since he first visited. "When I first camped in here, there were stumps everywhere. And the road was dirt. The roads weren't paved until '74 or '75. Of course, it's gotten a whole lot more crowded, too."

"It seems like most campers here come from Seattle, Tacoma or Olympia," he says of the people who come to this unique fjord to play. "We get groups from Oregon and Idaho who come over in the spring for shrimp season."

Families choose Twanoh as a destination, says Becker. They aren't campers who stop there on the way to the Olympic Peninsula.

"The kids are well-entertained here. There's a lot for them to do. That's why families come here. It's pretty safe here, normally."

Not unlike the salmon that annually return to spawn in Twanoh's tiny creek, families annually return to the park to camp. "You meet a lot of people and some of them get to be good friends," says the campground host.

While weekends are still busiest, Becker says the pace of the campground is picking up during the week.

"A lot of times, it can be raining, and I'll still have campers coming in. It's crowded all the time, but pretty near every weekend, you're going to have to turn people away. There's always some that don't believe the 'Campground Full' sign."

When the campground is full, Becker says he sends campers to Belfair or Potlatch state parks, the closest public campground alternatives on Hood Canal.

"We'll try to send them to Manchester, but they don't want to leave the canal. They'll go there if it's the only place to go."

When the campground and most other activities at Twanoh closes for winter, Becker moves to Belfair State Park on the other side of the canal to serve as the host there. But he tries to find time in the winter to take the 12-mile drive from Belfair to Twanoh.

"We come out to watch the salmon run. That's all us old folks have to do in the winter."

By Seabury Blair Jr.

• • • • • • • • •

SECTION 2

A LONG
HISTORY
AS A
RECREATION
SPOT

By Seabury Blair Jr.

"Doc" Eddy's Rose Point Resort is gone from Hood Canal, but the spirit of the place lives on at motels and resorts from Quilcene to Belfair.

"It was mostly loggers and trappers," says Virginia Trammell, the late Doc Eddy's 65-year-old daughter. "They came out to have fun, and that's why people come out to the canal today."

Sixty years ago, Trammell moved out to the resort and 400 acres of prime Hood Canal real estate her father purchased for $25,000. Remnants of a once-grand lodge, above Lynch Cove three miles west of Belfair on the South Shore, is all that is left.

But in 1929, Rose Point Resort was a hot spot for residents from Bremerton, Seattle and Tacoma.

"In those early days," she said, "loggers from nearby camps on the canal would get down here any way they could to let off steam."

Timber that will never again grow as tall was falling everywhere along the canal. The men who were cutting and moving the trees to mills were a rugged breed.

"I remember stories Dad told that were told to him: There were wild and woolly fights and war-whooping on those week-ends. It was about the only outlet for the people who worked in the woods.

"I remember one year, a logger brought in a bear cub. Everybody fed it and it grew up pretty fast. It got out of its cage and here was this lady getting a bathing suit on in her room and in walks this young bear."

The bear was invited to leave shortly thereafter.

Early photos show a resort sign advertising "fine fishing, sandy bathing beach, cabins, tents, boats, catering to family picnics and outings."

"There were so few people out here then," says Trammell, who resides in Belfair but owns a lot at the resort site. The country was in the midst of the Great Depression; resort rent took different forms. Tents rented for 50 cents a night. But Dad would let a lot of the loggers and trappers pay with venison or ducks instead of rent."

The resort operated until 1941, when World War II brought gas rationing and the country was in no mood for recreation. In 1943, several feet of snow collapsed the roof of the lodge.

That was the beginning of the end for the Rose Point Resort. But now, as then, the myriad of recreational opportunities along the canal attract growing numbers of people. Trammell believes they will be either the salvation or the death of the spectacular fjord.

She is sorry to see Hood Canal so crowded, but happy so many can enjoy its beauty.

"When I grew up, the nearest neighbor was more than a mile away. Now the population is so wall-to-wall. My dad always used to say 25 years from now, it would be like this. Boy, was he right. It's changed. There are so many more people here, bless 'em. They love it and we do, too. But it really does affect everything."

She talks of a day in the not-too-distant future, a day when sewers will be necessary along the canal. She thinks people will be more than willing to pay for it.

"If we don't pay for it, it will kill the canal. If we don't look at the big picture, we'll just be down the tube. People who don't think about it aren't looking beyond today. We have to think about it. I hope to heaven it's not too late now."

"In those early days, loggers from nearby camps on the canal would get down here any way they could to let off steam."
—Virginia Trammell

- - - - - - - - - -

SECTION 3

BUSINESS
FOLLOWS THE
MERCURY

By Travis Baker

Small, independent retailers are the rule around Hood Canal, and many depend on the summer tourist season for the bulk of their annual sales.

For Bob and Anne Hart at the Hoodsport Grocery, septic tanks are good omen. "Whenever you see a septic tank go by and up that hill," said Hart, "that's new business."

Up that hill is Lake Cushman, a 3,000-lot recreational development that is the lifeblood of the Hoodsport business community in Mr. Hart's view. He estimates that two-thirds of his increased business in the summer is from summer residents. The rest is from tourists passing through.

And a septic tank bound for Cushman means another lot owner has decided to invest money in a residence there — and probably time and shopping dollars in the future.

Like nearly everyone on the canal, the Harts see business swell in the summer, tripling that of winter. "It's not unusual to do as much on a three-day weekend as the whole month of January," he said.

The end of the hot selling season varies from business to business, but for Hart, it's Labor Day. "It chops in half the day after and goes downhill from there."

In this statistics-laden society, there is remarkably little hard data on the economic impact of tourism and recreation along Hood Canal.

There is a widespread assumption that population along the canal triples during the summer, but proof of that figure is hard to come by. Public Utility District No. 1 in Mason County, which provides electricity from near Alderbrook Inn at Union to the Jefferson County line, provides as firm an indication of the impact of summer residents on the area's population as exists.

Debbie Knipshield, manager of the PUD, said 41 percent of its 3,864 customers are seasonal or recreational, denoting residence there 180 days or less per year. The PUD gets about four new customers a month in the winter, twice that in the summer, she said. Alderbrook Inn is its biggest customer.

Pat McGary with PUD No. 3, whose coverage area includes Lake Cushman and the canal's South Shore from near Alderbrook to Belfair, said about 30 percent of its customers are sent bills at addresses away from Hood Canal. A greater percentage used to be seasonal, he said.

The Mason County Tourist Center near Shelton keeps careful track of where the tourists and information seekers who stop there have come from. June's total of 1,982 was five times January's number of stops, which totaled 390.

The state's traffic counts at the Hood Canal floating bridge and where Highway 101 intersects Highway 20 near Discovery Bay provide an indication of what tourism and summer residents mean on the roads. Traffic at both places doubles in warm weather.

Ron Bergt of the state Department of Transportation says there were 7,505 crossings of the bridge in January 1989 compared to 14,148 in August. The counter at Discovery Bay recorded 5,522 vehicles in January, and 11,564 in August.

When the motor-homing tourists and backcountry campers —hundreds of thousands in the Olympic Peninsula and Hood Canal area each year — return home, people like the Jay and Dick Johnsons of Glen Ayr RV Park, Bob Koeppen at Snooze Junction on the North Shore, Bill Campbell at Rest-A-While north of Lilliwaup and John and Dee Wilcoxen at the Trails End Tavern at South Point depend on the camping clubs to generate business.

Those clubs have helped make a success of the Johnsons' decision to go year-round when they bought a fishing camp named Glen Ayr north of Hoodsport five years ago.

Closing in the winter was the norm on the canal then, Jay Johnson said, and "we bucked big odds" in challenging that trend.

But "the clubs come out in the winter, from all over within two hours of Hood Canal — Eagles, Elks, Moose lodges, the VFW, they all seem to have large travel clubs and they like to get together."

Campbell at Rest-A-While, north of Hoodsport, said they often have two clubs per weekend helping fill their 97 RV spaces in the winter.

The Wilcoxens do a fairly good business at their tavern, considering it lies at the dead end of a rural road, on the tarmac of a defunct ferry landing. But that tarmac has become a sub rosa campground for RVers, and when a camping club rolls in, such as the Port Angeles Eagles on Memorial Day, things are really hopping at Trails End, said fill-in bartender Dawnie Davis.

Hoodsport

Home of the Hoodsport Winery and gateway to Lake Cushman and Staircase in Olympic National Park.

• • • • • • • • • •

"It's not unusual to do as much on a three-day weekend as the whole month of January."
— Bob Hart

Chris Gunter learned a lesson when shrimp season opened in 1990. It was the first shrimp season since he bought the Sunset Beach Grocery in 1989 and he had the wrong cat food on his shelves.

"Shrimpers use only one kind of cat food," said Gunter, who lives in Seabeck and commutes each day to the South Shore store. "Puss'n Boots Supreme Seafood Platter." Once his distributor straightened him out, he sold cases of the stuff.

Gunter figures his business quintuples in the summer over the off-season, when he keeps his store open but closes the hamburger stand next to it.

Labor Day was his high point last year, he said, with $570 in burger sales in one day, and 28 people waiting for burgers at one time.

His merchandise includes the $40-to-$400 wildlife paintings he does, on canvas and on fungus "conks" he takes off trees when deer-hunting in the fall. "People tend to buy that stuff out here," he said of his artwork.

As one goes north along Highway 101 up the west side of Hood Canal, there is a subtle shift in the tourist draws. Scott Hatch, working behind the counter at the rebuilt Eldon Store owned by his brother, Craig, said campers in the Olympic National Forest contribute greatly to the store's fair weather business.

Backpackers and campers arriving and leaving, or getting provisions if they outstay the supplies they brought with them, are good customers. But weather is crucial, said Hatch, remembering one rainy July 4th when no one stopped in the store.

Overnighters at campgrounds operated by and in the Olympic National Forest brought 265,000 people into the forest in 1989, said Ken Eldredge, assistant recreation staff officer for the forest. But they are just the tip of a very large iceberg.

Day use, mostly one-day car tours, is the largest part of what forest officials calculate to have been 4.6 million visitors to the forest last year. Another 3.5 million were counted within Olympic National Park, though most of those went to attractions reached from the western side of the park.

"We have wilderness, hunting, fishing, auto touring. A lot of people just like to drive the backroads," said Eldredge. "That's one of our biggest uses."

He figures 60-65 percent of those people use facilities in the part of the forest bordering Hood Canal "simply because it's close; it's a tank of gas from Seattle and the metropolitan areas." And he figures only 5 percent of the forest's visitors come in the winter.

Mike's Beach Resort north of Lilliwaup was named after Bob and Trudy Schultz's son Mike shortly after his birth 39 years ago and has been run by the family ever since.

"That's the way of the canal, family-owned," said Trudy, who has run the resort with her son since her husband passed away. "The season's so short you can't afford an employee."

And, in fact, there is scant corporate or out-of-county ownership along the canal. Minerva Beach RV park at Hoodsport, owned by a Seattle limited partnership, is a

There is a widespread assumption that population along the canal triples during the summer, but proof of that figure is hard to come by.

She Finds "Pushing" the Canal an Easy Job

When a group of Shelton business people formed the Mason County Tourism Council in 1989, they chose 75-year-old Mary Helen Anderson to run it. A fourth-generation Mason County resident, she decided to end 10 years of retirement to begin her fourth career.

"I think we live in the most beautiful part of the United States, and I like to push it."

In her younger years, she did leave the area and wound up in Washington, D.C., a single girl during World War II, helping print money with the Bureau of Engraving and Printing. But she returned here in 1944. The war was winding down "and I was homesick," she said.

She married George "Andy" Anderson, a Montanan, in Seattle, and she brought him to Hood Canal country.

While he worked at Simpson Timber, she ran the Holiday House floral shop in Shelton, then was a nursery manager.

She retired in 1979 and stayed retired (but did a lot of volunteer work) until agreeing to head up the tourist center.

The center handled inquiries from nearly 6,000 travelers in the first six months of 1990, she said.

Mary Helen was born in Aberdeen on Christmas Day, as her parents were returning from visiting family in Hoquiam.

"My dad was a captain on a four-master schooner sailing out of Port Townsend, Port Ludlow and Port Gamble," she said, "back in the days when they sailed out of those places instead of Tacoma and Seattle. My family on weekends would go on little trips" along Hood Canal, she recalled, establishing her love for the area that remains to this day.

By Travis Baker

rare exception. There are few businesses of any size. Alderbrook Inn has no rival along the length of the canal.

The 100-unit inn, Hood Canal's most sumptuous hostelry, depends less on sunshine, tides, and drive-by traffic than most of the canal's tourist businesses. Alderbrook's Wes Johnson, who seems always to have the inn up for sale but somehow never sells it, has carved out a niche in the conference and meetings area.

Operations manager Beverly Scherer says Alderbrook does more and better business in the summer than the winter, but conferences are the heart of that business, whatever the season.

They regularly have no-vacancy nights, winter and summer, she said, and have had single conferences that fill the inn's 80 rooms and 20 cottage units. For some of the biggest, they've had to farm out the overflow to motels in Shelton and Belfair, or to some cabins nearby.

Though the inn gets individual customers from all over, it doesn't do much marketing out of state and overseas, she said. Despite such robust business, there is no talk of expanding.

As with just about everyone else catering to tourists and summer residents along the canal, shrimp season means business — non-conference business — for Alderbook Inn, said Mrs. Scherer. Shrimpers rent many of the rooms during the season. The inn's dock, where spaces are rented, is filled with boats at that time of year. Inn operators don't make any special effort to avoid conference business at that time of year. But shrimpers have their own means of making sure there's room. "Shrimping customers normally will book for the next year when they check out," she said.

Hunting season contributes little to the inn's business, but holidays do, even winter

Alderbrook Inn

Alderbrook Inn, the most complete resort on Hood Canal, defeats the seasonal doldrums by hosting conferences and meetings.

ones. "New Year's Eve we're always full," said Mrs. Scherer, though Christmas isn't that good.

When Johnson bought Alderbrook Inn 35 years ago (it's existed for 75 years), it was strictly a summer resort, said Mrs. Scherer, and all that was there were the cottages and a restaurant and lounge where the pool is now. Now there's a golf course and 36 motel units that were added around 1980.

Helen Nickels swept the sidewalk in front of the True Value Hardware she and her husband owned for the last time one sunny July morning in 1990. That afternoon, they were scheduled to sign papers selling the Hoodsport business they had for 20 years. They were retiring.

It took three months to sell the business, but only 14 days to sell their double-wide mobile home on the canal. "Everyone seems to want to get a house on the water all of a sudden," she said.

And where does one retire to after living in a tourist mecca like Hood Canal? Moses Lake, said Helen. "They have more fishing lakes there than anywhere else."

John Skelton, owner of the Hungry Bear restaurant in Eldon for seven years, says his business still is increasing but he wonders if everyone's is.

"The big drawing cards aren't here any more," he said. Fishing is a shadow of what it used to be; shrimping is limited to a couple of weeks in May before school is out; and clamming and oystering is shut down at the Dosewallips, because of seal feces.

"It seemed like before the parks were running full most of the summer months," he said. "Now you can get into most any of them most of the time.

"We're still increasing (at the Hungry Bear). There's still plenty of people coming through, but I don't think there's as many people staying here anymore," he said.

> • • • • • • • • • •
>
> *"If we don't pay for (sewers), it will kill the canal. People who don't think about it aren't looking beyond today. I hope to heaven it's not too late now."*
> — Virginia Trammell

The Port of Seattle regularly brings travel writers from Japan, Germany and Britain here to tour Washington state. One such tour, 11 journalists from Germany, made a rare stop along Hood Canal on the Kitsap side in June, gladdening hearts at the Visitors and Convention Bureau in Bremerton.

"They did a seven-day trip of the Olympic Peninsula, and Hood Canal was their favorite place of the whole trip," said Mim Heuss, head of the bureau. "We put them up in four different bed and breakfasts along the canal, and they will be going back to Germany fired up about telling people about the canal."

B.J. Stokey, tourism manager for the Port of Seattle, acknowledged that it was a rare stop along the canal for their media tours, and her staff who accompanied the Germans reported that they were highly impressed.

"We hope to do it more often," she said of the canal stops.

Heuss also tells of a California couple who, after seeing Hood Canal, asked "Why hasn't someone developed this for tourism?"

Some very likely will try, and soon, observes Jay Johnson of Glen Ayr.

Family-owned tourist and recreation business are "the usual thing at this time," he said. "But we see land values growing and it will force some big changes out here. These mom-and-pop operations may go by the wayside because of the value of the land. You may have to either get big or get out.

"On this side of the canal, there's nothing like Alderbrook Inn and it's close to demanding that kind of place. Once someone whacks out something like that, it will be a lot tougher for the smaller ones."

*By Christopher
Dunagan*

*Boaters enjoy Hood Canal waters and help
determine whether they stay clean.*

P leasant Harbor is a snug, teardrop-shaped bay along the western shore of Hood Canal. Evergreens grow to the water's edge, and eagles soar over the bright water. Even at the marina, where boaters pull in for food and gasoline, one can discern rocks and pebbles in water up to 10 feet deep.

Pleasant Harbor is the last place you would expect people to be dumping raw sewage from their toilets. Yet during the opening days of boating season in 1988, the harbor was suddenly hit by bacterial pollution, according to researchers taking samples there at the time.

In the quiet, undeveloped bay, boats were the only logical source of pollution on that busy Memorial Day weekend, said researchers from the state Department of Health. Two months before, bacteria were practically nonexistent, they noted.

"Shellfish tissue was clearly adversely affected by the presence of boats," the report states, "in that 91 percent of the samples from within the harbor exceeded the commercial shellfish meat standard."

That's not to say boats are the principal source of pollution for Hood Canal as a whole. Other studies point to failing septic systems, livestock and even harbor seals as main sources of bacterial contamination in other areas of Hood Canal.

But even occasional visitors can damage water quality, said John Heal, administrative director of the Hood Canal

Coordinating Council.

"Boaters like to say, 'It's not us' — like farmers and loggers and septic tank owners," said Heal. "But there's no question it's happening, and the impacts are noticeable in certain small embayments on busy weekends."

Such impacts are believed to be the result of pleasure boaters and commercial fishermen who pump their marine toilets overboard in violation of federal law. The increased pollution can be measured, especially in shellfish that concentrate organisms in their meat, and poses a threat to human health, officials say.

Jay Wilkens of Fresno, Calif., marveled at the clear waters of Pleasant Harbor, where he moored his boat "Good Times" while on a trip to Canada. "The delta at Antioch (near Stockton, Calif.) is like a sewer. You can catch fish, but they're not fit to eat. People there just dump the stuff overboard."

It's important, said Wilkens, that boaters understand what they have in Hood Canal and do whatever they can to protect it.

"When you can see the bottom in 8 or 10 feet of water, that is wonderful."

Boaters also may spill small quantities of oil and gasoline into the water, threatening the health of marine organisms, particularly at marinas. Oil forms a toxic layer on the water's surface, where many microscopic plants and animals spend a critical part of their lives.

Non-boaters also need to pay attention to their impacts on Hood Canal, officials say. For example, summer visitors may overtax inadequate septic systems along the waterfront, and litterbugs can turn the canal into a garbage can — with dangerous impacts on wildlife.

Some boaters become defensive when people talk about sewage. Certainly not all boaters are to blame, said Heal, but small bays are especially vulnerable.

"There are enough studies that I'm convinced bacterial contamination is a problem, and a good portion of it comes from boats," said Heal.

In a 1988 survey of more than 3,000 boaters around Puget Sound, nearly one out of five readily admitted their boats had a toilet with direct discharge into the water. Coast Guard regulations require that such boats have at least a holding tank to contain the wastes.

Of boaters whose vessels had a "Y-valve" — which directs the waste either to a holding tank or into the water — some 14 percent said they always leave the valve open to the outside waters. Another 38 percent said they discharge sewage only in the main channels of Puget Sound.

Federal law prohibits discharges within three miles of shore — that is, anywhere in Puget Sound or Hood Canal.

A shortage of shoreside facilities is the reason cited most often for illegal discharges. In Hood Canal the only pump-out station in operation in 1990 was at Port Ludlow Marina.

The state Department of Parks and Recreation and the Hood Canal Coordinating Council both launched programs to teach people about the impacts of boating, and boaters may be listening.

Lance Willmon, assistant manager at Port Ludlow, said the number of boaters using the marina's pump-out system have increased from just a few over the course of a year to as many as 20 on a typical weekend.

Pleasant Harbor Marina manager Wayne Harris said so few boaters used the marina's pump-out station that it was hardly worth the constant repairs.

"The pump itself was not designed for a saltwater environment," said Harris. "The pump froze up, and I ended up just throwing it away."

But more and more boaters started asking about the facilities.

"I've turned down tenfold the number of inquiries this year than we pumped out last year," said Harris in 1990. "People are becoming aware. I think the advertising is getting out to people."

Harris wanted to get the facility back in operation, but a replacement pump is costly, $3,000-$4,000. It was running again in 1991.

Under a new program funded by boat taxes, the state will pay for construction of pump-out stations if marina owners agree to maintain them and pay for electricity. One of the first pump-out stations under the new program was built at Twanoh State Park on the South Shore of Hood Canal and opened in 1991.

Holding tanks aren't the only approved method of handling sewage, according to Coast Guard officials.

Bob Cromes of Lilliwaup installed a $1,500 sewage treatment system that grinds and treats the sewage with chemicals. The treated effluent can be legally discharged,

> **"Boaters like to say, 'It's not us' — like farmers and loggers and septic tank owners. But there's no question it's happening, and the impacts are noticeable."**
>
> — John Heal, Hood Canal Coordinating Council

but the method isn't without controversy.

"We would never pump it out in a bay like this," said Cromes, sitting in the galley of his boat "Blue Chip", docked at Pleasant Harbor Marina. "We live on Hood Canal, so we're very protective of it."

Cromes and his wife often travel to Canada, where officials prefer that he discharge the sewage without chemicals, which contain formaldehyde.

"They'd rather have (waste) in the water than formaldehyde," said Cromes.

Formaldehyde can be toxic to marine organisms, as it is to bacteria, but the U.S. government puts the first priority on human health and won't allow discharge without chemical treatment.

"There is no question that people have gotten disease from waters that are infected," said Dr. Willa Fisher of the Bremerton-Kitsap County Health Department.

On the East Coast, contaminated water is associated with hepatitis and intestinal illness, she said. In the Gulf of Mexico, people have contracted cholera. Tuberculosis is another disease passed through raw sewage.

"The other thing you see," she added, "are eye infections and skin infections related to bacteria in the water."

The Coast Guard, charged with enforcing illegal discharges from boats, appears to be cracking down on violators.

"MSDs (marine sanitation devices) are regularly checked whenever we do any Coast Guard law-enforcement boarding," said Dennis Booth, chief of marine law enforcement for the Seattle District. "For the last two years now, we have really worked hard at enforcing the MSD regulations in Puget Sound."

In a 12-month period ending in June, 1990, 578 MSD violations were noted in Washington and Oregon, said Booth, and about half of those resulted in fines ranging from $150 to $350. The others were warnings.

Coast Guard officers regularly check to make sure that boats with an installed toilet have either a holding tank or a treatment system. The Y-valve must be "secured" in a closed position to prevent discharge overboard, said Booth. That means using a padlock, heavy tape or non-releasable tie. One can also remove the valve's handle, he said.

Boaters are allowed to use portable toilets, said Booth, but they can't dump them overboard.

Dennis McBreen, manager of Seabeck Marina, said he finds boaters often stop at the marina to use the dockside restrooms rather than disposing of their waste in Hood Canal. Some also are carrying portable toilets onto their boats — even if they have an installed toilet already, he added.

"People don't want to get their in-boat toilets dirty; that's a continual line we hear," said McBreen. But the use of shoreside facilities also means people are thinking about pollution, he said.

"In Hood Canal, the number of people who dump it overboard is quite small," added McBreen.

It is hard to compare the impacts of different types of pollution, according to Bill Cleland of the state Department of Health. But raw sewage dumped into the water creates a more hazardous problem than the same amount of effluent from a malfunctioning septic tank.

Unlike liquid effluent, which is diluted by saltwater, floating solids can harbor huge colonies of dangerous bacteria for long periods of time. When the solids finally break apart, they release bacteria that can ruin shellfish beds and swimming areas, he said.

Donna Simmons of Hoodsport, who grew up on Hood Canal and recently headed an education project aimed at area boaters, says people must be willing to change if Hood Canal is to survive.

"From the time I was a little girl until now," she said, "there has been a tremendous increase in the number of boaters."

Her Hood Canal Boater Task Force, sponsored by the Hood Canal Coordinating Council, drew together local people who concluded that education was the solution. The group produced a brochure/boating map and erected signs last summer at 15 marinas and boat launches.

"The signs basically ask that people properly dispose of sewage, trash and engine-maintenance products," she said. "They point out that Hood Canal is a very fragile body of water and is susceptible to that kind of pollution."

The message is getting through, she added, because it comes from the hearts of local people — including boaters who care about Hood Canal.

• • • • • • • • • •

In a 1988 survey of more than 3,000 boaters around Puget Sound nearly one out of five admitted their boats had a toilet with direct discharge into the water, in violation of Coast Guard regulations.

Wildlife Victim to Debris

Despite its natural beauty, Hood Canal is marred by the trash of many people.

Habitat, seemingly abundant for seabirds, includes killing traps made of abandoned fishing line and plastic six-pack rings. And natural food sources in the water and along the shore are tainted with tiny bits of plastic that birds pick up and eat, mistaking them for fish eggs and tiny creatures.

Hood Canal is actually cleaner than many areas around Puget Sound, observers say, and residents and visitors are generally good caretakers of the water. But the human record is far from spotless.

"People for the most part want the water to stay clean," said Donna Simmons, coordinator of a boater education program for Hood Canal, "but there are always those who do not make the connection between throwing a six-pack ring into the water and the idea that they might be destroying wildlife."

The answer is to keep plastics out of the water — but that's easier said than done, said Ken Pritchard of Adopt-A-Beach. While it is illegal to dump any waste off a boat — and boats over 26 feet must display a sign saying so — a surprising amount of the debris comes from the land, he said.

"The bulk of the debris in Puget Sound is land- and shore-based. A lot comes from roads, ditches and storm drains."

The most common type of marine debris is plastic foam used in drink cups as well as food and bait packages. It's also used as flotation in docks, and a tremendous amount breaks off into the water, said Pritchard.

Eventually the foam chunks break down into round "cells," small enough to be eaten by birds and fish. The solution, he said, is to sheath flotation material in vinyl, so the plastic foam can't get loose.

Pritchard says the problem will only be solved when enough people realize that every plastic cup they leave behind at a picnic, every plastic bag they fail to grab when the wind comes up, is part of Hood Canal's debris problem.

By Christopher Dunagan

Devil's Lake near Mount Walker has been isolated from encroachment of non-native plants but is vulnerable to even the most innocent human visits.

Visiting Devil's Lake is like stepping back in time, perhaps 200-300 years, to a period when civilization had not yet carried the seeds of foreign plants to the Pacific Northwest. At one end of the lake lies an enchanted world — a rare bog, where the sound of distant bubbles accompanies each footstep in the spongy moss.

Here, tiny sundew plants secrete a sticky residue to capture microscopic insects; wild cranberries cling to delicate vines; and spongy lichens grow in 3-foot-tall mounds called hummocks. Nearby, a "pygmy old-growth forest" grows ever so slowly in the wet peat.

Only a botanist could fully appreciate the precious values of this ancient lake, hugging the slopes of Mount Walker south of Quilcene. One botanist, Jerry Gorsline, is ecstatic.

Gorsline, a member of the Washington Native Plant Society, has identified five different types of wetlands and dozens of native plants within the lake's drainage, all

• • • • • • • • • •

SECTION 5

INNOCENT VISITS AND A PRISTINE LAKE

By Christopher Dunagan

on state land. To his delight, the lake has escaped invasion from alien plants that tend to drive out survivors from prehistoric times.

"I don't think we have any non-natives here," said Gorsline. "That's why we've got to protect this area."

Gorsline is worried about human activities that threaten the lake, activities that seem routine to fishermen who crowd the lake on summer weekends.

He's particularly concerned about a dirt road that winds its way to the edge of the water. Vehicles could easily carry the seeds of foreign plants to the water, where they could invade the delicate marsh. Boats could introduce other exotic plants, including prolific Eurasian milfoil.

Up the road a short distance lies an outpost of alien plants — early invaders so common that Northwest residents often claim them as their own. There's foxglove. ("That's everywhere but these pristine areas," said Gorsline.) There's the broad-leafed English plantain, nicknamed "white-man's footsteps" because it followed settlers across the continent.

There's also wall lettuce, a plant from Northern Europe that was first noticed in the San Juan Islands in the 1920s. It is unknown in most areas of the United States, but in the Northwest it has spread from the lowlands into the subalpine slopes of the Olympics.

Gorsline's greatest fear of all is a tall, wide-bladed and "extremely vigorous" grass called reed canarygrass. He spotted the plant along the rutted road to the lake, not more than 1 1/2 miles away.

Canarygrass is a "rhizomatous" plant that spreads rapidly through underground shoots as well as by seeds. It will grow in moist soil and even under a few inches of water. Once the plant takes hold, it is nearly impossible to eliminate, said Gorsline.

The Eurasian plant did not invade Washington state until the 1950s, but today canarygrass is stealing habitat from native plants everywhere. Lake Ozette on the

Visiting Devil's Lake is like stepping back in time, perhaps 200-300 years. The lake has escaped invasion from alien plants that tend to drive out survivors from prehistoric times.

Devil's Lake

The pristine lake, unspoiled by invasion from non-native plants, hugs the slopes of Mount Walker south of Quilcene.

western side of the Olympics has become plagued by it.

"The grass forms dense patches, and few plants can compete with it," said Nelsa Buckingham, often cited as the leading authority on native plants in the Olympics.

Less than 100 feet from Devil's Lake, the dirt road becomes so muddy, even in summer, that vehicles skid around in it as they pass through.

"That kind of disturbance," said Gorsline, "provides a perfect seedbed for canarygrass."

Though worried that publicity might bring even more people and more impacts, Gorsline said the lake is headed for ruin unless the public understands how precious and fragile it is.

"Only by attracting attention to this place is there hope of saving it," he said, adding that people can enjoy it for recreation — if they're careful.

The road to the lake is difficult, and Gorsline is not encouraging visitors. But those who do come should stop at the ramshackle A-frame building near the lake. Visitors should not trample through the marshy areas, he said.

The bog, he explained, "is very sensitive to compaction. I'd never suggest a trail to direct people into the bog."

What he would like to see is protection for the lake, located on land managed by the state Department of Natural Resources. The land borders Olympic National Forest.

In 1992, the DNR intends to auction off the trees around the lake. Included in the timber harvest would be a number of "residual old-growth" trees, survivors of a fire that raged through the Mount Walker area in 1864.

Some of the old trees, still showing charcoal-black "fire scars" from the Mount Walker fire, may date back to 1701, when an earlier fire destroyed most of the timber on the eastern edge of the Olympics.

Gorsline, employed by the Washington Environmental Council, uses his expertise to help arrange agreements about how timber will be harvested. The process is known as "TFW," for Timber-Fish-Wildlife. Gorsline has proposed keeping the logging back from the lake.

"As a TFW person," said Gorsline, "I have to respect the harvest goal, so I didn't go to (DNR) and say, 'I want no harvest at all.' "

But what Gorsline would really like is a trade of land between the DNR and the Forest Service that would bring Devil's Lake within the Olympic Forest boundary.

In doing so, he said, protection could be extended to the old-growth timber, the five wetlands, as well as a hillside that contains some rare and unusual "sapro-phytes" — plants that grow on decaying material.

Few undisturbed lakes are left any-where today, said Buckingham. Devil's Lake may be especially at risk. "Lakes are like people. You can compare them loosely, but every lake is different. I can't think of any other lake quite like it."

● ● ● ● ● ● ● ● ● ●

"Only by attracting attention to this place is there hope of saving it."
—Jerry Gorsline

● ● ● ● ● ● ● ● ● ●

PART

IV

THE PEOPLE OF
HOOD CANAL

CHAPTER

11
· · · · · · · · ·

DEVELOPMENT

SECTION 1

THE CANAL
PAYS
FOR OUR
LIFESTYLES

*By Christopher
Dunagan*

*There are few places
along Hood Canal where
new construction is not
evident from the water*

D ressed in a red flannel shirt and blue jeans and wearing a tool belt hitched up with wide suspenders, Keith Daniels took aim and pulled the trigger. "Wham! Wham! Wham!"

Shiny steel nails surged into smooth lumber as Daniels directed the powerful nail gun with little effort.

It had taken the 29-year-old carpenter, with the help of one or two others, 3 ¹/₂ weeks to create the basic structure of a 1,800-square-foot home.

Daniels smiled warmly as he stepped down off the 6-foot ladder. He was nearing the end of another honest day's labor. A few more days like this and he would be finished framing this house overlooking Hood Canal. Then he would move on to the next job.

Construction is everywhere in Hood Canal country, where new houses sprout like spring flowers.

Some builders carve out choice building sites on steep lots overlooking Seabeck, Union and Quilcene. Some squeeze expensive new structures onto the last remaining waterfront lots along the South Shore. Others transform older vacation homes into modern

• • • • • • • • • •

"What is the good of a house if you don't have a tolerable planet to put it on."
—Henry David Thoreau

waterfront wonders.

For nearly every new house going up, one can find a family-in-waiting, fostering dreams of moving into a new neighborhood, making new friends, enjoying the natural setting. Waiting for the house Daniels is erecting are Glen and June Forbes, who sold a house with a Puget Sound view to build their new home overlooking Hood Canal.

Every silver lining has a dark side, and the dark side to a new house is the unavoidable damage it brings to the Hood Canal ecosystem. For every human family moving into the forest, some wildlife must move out. For every family improving its quality of life, there is some effect on the quality of water.

The damage is dictated by the location of the homesite as well as the concern of the builder and future occupants of the building.

The damage at each lot may indeed be slight. But already, tens of thousands of human beings have become an integral part of the Hood Canal ecosystem — and planners tell us that real growth is just now coming to the region.

With the arrival of spring, Daniels has been working 10-hour days on this house in the Driftwood Key development near the tip of the Kitsap Peninsula. He feels good about the work.

Earlier in the day, a rare April hail storm pelted the unfinished roof with frozen iceballs. As Daniels talked, melting ice still dripped through the cracks.

"It's nice out here," said Daniels, glancing toward the cloud-covered water. "This is where I'm going to buy. We just rent now."

Like other areas once considered distant from civilization, Hansville doesn't seem so remote in today's real estate market. "People moved to Bellevue until they found that Bellevue wasn't so nice anymore, so they moved to Bainbridge," said Daniels. "Now they're moving here."

Trained by North Kitsap High School, Daniels says his job as a carpenter is "creative," better than the "menial" job he had for three years working in a lumber yard.

Construction is an important force in any economy. Statewide, more than 5 percent of the labor force is employed in construction trades. Housing construction in particular is going strong in the Hood Canal region.

Driftwood Key, developed in the mid-1960s, once had the appearance of a lazy resort community. Today, funny little houses with upside-down rowboats in their yards still capture timeless views of Hood Canal and the Olympic Mountains.

Disappearing, however, are the undeveloped lots. Modern new houses have gone up almost as fast as the price of lots still for sale. From almost any vantage point in Driftwood Key, one can spot two or three houses under construction.

People looking for a natural view and quiet setting are finding it throughout the Hood Canal region, one of the last unspoiled areas in the Lower 48 states.

The price of growth is very real, says Rick Kimball, environmental planner for the Kitsap County Department of Community Development, but it's not easy to see the environmental impact of a single home.

"I think we're dealing with these things better and better," he said, "but if you have 50 acres of forest land and you put 50 houses on that, you can't help but have an impact."

One of the first, and most noticeable, results of clearing land for a house can be seen after the first rainfall, said Dave Dickson, a drainage specialist with the Kitsap County Public Works Department.

In a forest, trees, vegetation and organic groundcover soak up moisture like a sponge, releasing it slowly into streams and into the ground itself. But human encroachment removes a portion of that natural sponge. The roof of a house, a driveway or a street prevent water from soaking back into the ground. Even a grassy lawn has only a fraction of the absorption qualities of a thick organic carpet on the forest floor.

"Everybody likes nice wide streets, paved sidewalks and driveways, but all those things cover the pervious surfaces we have left," said Dickson. "A well manicured lawn looks nice but ... there's not a lot of percolation through a lawn unless it is underlain by gravelly soils."

Seeking lower ground, water will drain off such hard surfaces, pick up speed across steep slopes and then carve out drainage channels that never existed before. Streams swell more rapidly due to the surge of water. Flows are higher than the last time it rained equally hard. But after the rains stop, there is less water released by the remaining vegetation. Streams decrease in size during dry periods.

This fundamental change in drainage affects fish habitat. Silt transported by water can smother salmon eggs buried within a stream's gravel. High water flows can rearrange the gravel, dislodging eggs from their nesting place.

It's the same boom-and-bust pattern of water flow caused by logging clearcuts, but the effects of development are even more pervasive. Clearcuts eventually grow back; developments are forever.

Daniels was hired to frame this new house by Dan Forbes, a contractor who has built numerous homes in the Hansville area. The owners are Dan's parents, Glen and June Forbes, the former owners of the resort in Hansville known as Forbes Landing.

"For 20 years, we had the same view," said Glen Forbes, 65. "Ships came in all the time, but after a while I didn't even notice the view."

Now, they have a view of Hood Canal with the Olympic Mountains standing tall on a clear day.

"Hood Canal is a beautiful piece of water," said Forbes. "I hope people recognize the value and try to protect it."

A growing list of building codes, health codes and energy codes — not to mention environmental regulations to protect wetlands and reduce stormwater runoff — keep raising the price of a basic house, says Dan Forbes. But he recognizes the need for most of the rules, he said.

"We're all working on a level playing field," he noted. "You figure you have to get so much money from each house to make a living for you and your family."

The extra cost is just passed along.

A major problem for younger families is that the price of even the cheapest homes may be out of reach. Daniels, married with a 7-year-old daughter, hopes to work out an arrangement whereby he can use his building skills to obtain his own home. Most young families don't have that option.

Driftwood Key

Built on the northeast bank of the canal, Driftwood Key, with building sites for 726 homes, relies solely on septic systems.

Larry Ward, owner of Olympic Homes in Poulsbo, argues that some of the new regulations represent a basic shift in the philosophy of who should pay for community services.

"When I was a kid, I went to public school," he said. "I lived on a city street with city sewer and water and paved sidewalks. The local government paid for them, because it was perceived that the whole community benefitted by the sidewalks we walked on and by the schools we went to.

"Now, government spends the money and sends the bill to our children. We have shifted the burden to the home buyer. We ask them to pay for schools and sewer systems."

Those against growth support the higher cost of housing, said Ward. But the strategy may backfire on Hood Canal because it forces new home buyers to move to more remote areas where land is cheaper, such as the forested lands of Kitsap County and even the foothills of the Olympic Mountains.

Within the entire Hood Canal drainage area, it is getting difficult to find an area unspoiled by human development, according to local planners and biologists.

Newcomers transplanted from cities — and even some people who have lived in the country all their lives — drag a host of urban-type problems into the woods with them.

In addition to causing increased stormwater runoff, the average family consumes 300 gallons of water a day, said Jerry Deeter of the Bremerton-Kitsap County Health Department. Families who water their lawns in the summer may use up to 1,000 gallons a day, he added.

In most areas, water is pumped out of the ground. So far, water is plentiful in most locations in the canal watershed, but increasing growth may reduce groundwater supplies and bring a day of reckoning.

An average family also generates nearly 100 pounds of garbage a week

Construction is everywhere in Hood Canal country, where new houses sprout like spring flowers.

throughout the year and recycles about 10 pounds, according to a new study in Kitsap County. In addition, laundry and cleaning chemicals are flushed down the drain, where they enter the septic tank and ultimately flow back into the groundwater.

With the exception of Alderbrook Inn at Union and Port Gamble, sewage treatment plants don't exist on Hood Canal. Sewage goes into septic tanks, some so old that nobody knows if they even work anymore.

When David and Carol Smith built their home near Union in 1984, they tore down an old structure that started out as nothing more than a sleeping platform, built by David's grandfather about 1912.

"A lot of the old buildings just sort of grew as people wanted more comfort," said Carol Smith. "They'd build a wall here, a kitchen here, a bathroom there."

When the Smiths tore down the old house, they were dismayed to find nothing more than an antique cesspool buried not far from the water's edge.

Health officials from all three Hood Canal counties continue to discover drainfields that no longer work, if they ever did. High bacterial counts have been measured in several places, spoiling prime shellfish beds — one of the canal's great resources.

If normal wastes aren't bad enough, you don't have to look far to find an isolated spot in the woods where somebody has dumped a pile of garbage. Often, the pile is near a stream, which means it is not so isolated after all. Then there are people who believe that disposing of motor oil means dumping it on the ground.

Vehicles themselves leave a trail of pollution, including oil and heavy metals such as lead, copper and zinc.

Even green space, that lovely grassy lawn, can create serious water quality problems. The owner of a quarter-acre lot, following manufacturers' recommendations, would apply as much as 40 pounds of nitrogen and 80 pounds of phosphorous each year to keep a yard nice and green.

Fertilizers and weed killers can migrate into natural areas, upsetting native plant communities. Washed into surface waters, they can generate algae blooms and decrease dissolved oxygen, even to the point of killing fish, as has been seen several times in lower Hood Canal.

Insecticides used on lawns create a variety of problems. In at least two places on the Kitsap Peninsula, Diazinon pellets killed flocks of ducks after the birds ingested the pellets, apparently mistaking them for food, said Greg Schirato, a biologist with the state Department of Wildlife.

Even when the insecticide does its job perfectly, it may not have desirable results. Birds may eat poisoned insects, thus poisoning themselves, or else the insects may disappear, eliminating an important food supply for both birds and fish.

In general, people are much too casual about their use of pesticides, says Cha Smith, director of groundwater protection for Washington Pesticide Coalition. "The way they (pesticides) are advertised and promoted really encourages their use and overuse."

As development spreads into remote areas, new houses crowd wildlife out of the forests, said Schirato. Dead or dying trees — ideal habitat for birds and small animals — are often removed to prevent their falling onto someone's house.

Rotting vegetation, including fallen logs, are cleaned up, destroying an important part of the food chain. Overhanging trees and vegetation may be chopped back from alongside streams, altering the water temperature, eliminating a source of fish food and causing stress to salmon and trout.

New home owners never realize the damage they cause.

"People don't think much about it because they don't see dead animals," said Schirato, "but the animals are gone. They either die or move someplace else, crowding other animals out."

Many families wouldn't think of moving to a new home without the family pet. But a dog or cat can do more damage to wildlife than the house and all the people in it, said Schirato. Dogs chase and kill deer. Cats go after birds and fish.

Some people think the woods are a perfect place to let their animals run loose, he noted, but nothing could be further from the truth.

People love rural areas for a variety of reasons, and some are very careful about their actions. Still, anyone who becomes a part of the Hood Canal ecosystem alters the balance that went before.

Every new house brings unavoidable damage to the Hood Canal ecosystem. The amount of damage is dictated by the location of the homesite as well as the concern of the builder and future occupants.

Timber management consultant Gary Hanson encourages land owners to consider options to clearcutting.

• • • • • • • • • • •

SECTION 2

CHOOSING PRUDENT DEVELOPMENT

By Christopher Dunagan

Many of the private lands that drain into Hood Canal have been carved up into building sites and appear headed for development.

But not every property owner has dollar signs in his eyes.

Consider David Smith, 62, a Seattle insurance agent who inherited 90 acres near Union and would like to pass on the land to his children.

"I was born and raised up there," said Smith. "I dearly love the area. I have seen my kids raised up there and now my grandkids are coming up."

Smith's land spans both sides of Highway 106 and includes a waterfront lot where his grandfather gradually constructed a house in the early decades of this century. In 1984, Smith replaced the old home with a modern house, which he visits on the weekends.

Smith's management of the remaining forest land is a lesson for property owners who are conservation-minded but have no desire to lock up their land strictly for fish and wildlife.

"We are thinking about keeping it in timberland," said Smith, "unless someone would agree to do a reasonable job of development."

Smith hired a forestry consulting firm, Washington Timberland Management of Union. Gary Hanson, owner of the company, worked out a plan to thin the timber, which provided Smith the cash he needed to subdivide the property into five-acre lots and put in a high-quality all-weather road.

If an excellent builder came along with the right price and a sensitive plan for development, Smith admits he might sell the lots. But his preferred plan is to divide them among his children.

Hanson, the consultant, said some loggers take advantage of landowners by offering deals that sound too good to pass up.

"We find," said Hanson, "that too many people don't know the value of their trees."

Smith's own father allowed a logger to clearcut the lower portion of the land for some quick income. But the logger failed to replant any trees. The bare land eventually grew alder trees, which were worth considerably less than the fir trees they replaced.

"My dad got taken," admitted Smith, who had the ground replanted with fir seedlings.

Hanson, who graduated from the University of Washington in 1967 with a degree in forestry, advises clearcutting only for specific purposes. For Smith's land, Hanson thinned out about a third of the trees, clearcut small patches where disease was evident and retained several trees strictly for their habitat value.

"We were able to thin this, rehabilitate the lower end, and put a substantial amount of money in his pocket," said Hanson.

Hanson planted grass seed along the new road where vegetation had been removed. In the areas that contained diseased fir, he planted white pine. State law requires reforestation within three years, but it is best to plant right away — before the brush takes over, said Hanson.

Hanson advises landowners to research forestry issues before signing a logging contract. That goes for anyone — even owners of a single acre. A consultant isn't required, he said, but an owner should certainly get an independent appraisal and advice on harvest and replanting.

Hanson also suggests that owners take bids from loggers on the basis of total weight or volume of timber, as opposed to a percent of gross value, because markets are always changing.

According to Hanson, the trees on Smith's property add value to the building sites, and homes can be worked in among the trees with less environmental damage than in a clearcut area.

Smith says the future of his land is uncertain, but he's not about to let the community down with shabby development. After all, his own home is at the bottom of the hill.

"If someone wants to pay me a lot of money, I might be swayed," he said, "but I don't think it is worth screwing up the area."

> *"I dearly love the area. We are thinking about keeping it in timberland, unless someone would agree to do a reasonable job of development."*
> — David Smith

Smith property

Dave Smith used careful timber management practices, including selective thinning, in logging the 90 acres he owns on both sides of Highway 106.

*Residents near Union scurry to fill sandbags in
an attempt to keep runoff from a golf course
development from damaging their homes.*

I t seems like only yesterday that Hood
Canal was a frontier kind of place.
Turn around, and there are highways.
Turn around, and there are developments. Turn around, and there are golf
courses, gravel pits and shopping
centers.

At an alarming rate, forest land is being
converted to housing and other uses in
Kitsap County, said Mike Reed, who reviews
forest practice applications for the Port
Gamble S'Klallam Indian Tribe.

"The conversion applications just pile
up every week," he said. "If we lost this
amount of timber in a blowdown in two
days, we would call it a national emergency.

But we are doing the same thing over
months."

In North Mason and some portions of
Jefferson County, trees are being removed
for development at nearly the same pace.

No single housing development,
grocery store, marina or golf course creates a
significant problem for Hood Canal, but the
combination of all them together does have
significant impact, experts say.

A typical golf course, for example, uses
at least 10 tons of fertilizer a year, said
Dwane Erich of Alderbrook Inn Resort near
Union. Alderbrook also uses 18 million
gallons of water a year to keep the grass
green.

• • • • • • • • • •

SECTION 3

LOSSES COME
SO EASILY

*By Christopher
Dunagan*

Nobody knows how much of the chemicals escape to Hood Canal, but Alderbrook is just one of four golf courses either operating or proposed in the Hood Canal watershed.

Despite the growth, Hood Canal remains in pretty good shape, experts say. Vast tracts of forest land remain undeveloped, and important fish and wildlife species still make their home in the watershed. Hood Canal offers Washington residents one last chance to preserve an area that has not yet been spoiled by growth.

"We are not yet at a point where we have lost so much habitat that wildlife can't migrate through the area," said Greg Schirato, regional biologist for the state Department of Wildlife.

While native salmon have declined drastically, only part of the problem can be attributed to stream damage, according to Dennis Austin of the state Department of Fisheries, which intends to study the habitat issue in the coming months.

All three Hood Canal counties — Kitsap, Mason and Jefferson — are struggling to deal with the growing number of people moving into Hood Canal.

Straining the Limits of Septic Systems

In most places, septic systems do an excellent job of treating household sewage, experts say. But aging systems along the southern shorelines of Hood Canal may be killing the canal's production of living things.

No longer can you take shellfish at Belfair State Park; commercial oyster-growing operations have been shut down; and fish kills the past few years have been attributed to low oxygen levels due to pollution.

"The whole canal is dying an inch at a time," said James Lockhart, a Port of Allyn commissioner who has pledged to bring sewers to the Belfair area.

The port commissioners have proposed a sewer project for most of Belfair and for homes along the North Shore of Hood Canal out to the edge of the district. But the project has been stymied while the state Department of Ecology considers the best location to dispose of the effluent.

Hood Canal should not be used for disposal because of its extremely low flushing rate, Ecology officials have said.

"The one thing that makes you frustrated," said Lockhart, "is that there's too much government bureaucracy. Nobody is coming up with answers, and you can't move but at a slow crawl."

After Ecology gives the go-ahead, it will take another two to three years of studies, design and financial planning before any work can be done, said Lockhart.

Nobody doubts the need for sewers, he says. An ongoing study by Mason County shows that some 50-60 percent of waterfront septic systems are already failing in nearby Allyn, which drains into Puget Sound.

"As far as septic tanks on Hood Canal," he added, "I'd say probably 60-75 percent drain right into Hood Canal. Some sit just 6 to 8 feet from a bulkhead."

Poor soils and high water tables mean that septic systems don't always function properly, even when there is adequate room for a drainfield, according to a report by Edmunds-Ludlow Associates, consultants for the port.

Alderbrook Inn near Union operates one of the few sewage treatment plants on Hood Canal. When the system failed to function properly in 1990, the Department of Ecology took over management. Today, the quality of effluent is much better, officials say.

All around Hood Canal and along the streams that drain into it, failing septic systems have been discovered by health officials from Kitsap, Mason and Jefferson counties.

In most cases, old drainfields can be replaced or new drainfields can be installed farther back from the canal. Jefferson County has even implemented a low-interest loan program to help with the cost.

But nowhere is the problem as severe as along the north and south shores of lower Hood Canal. Much more pollution in that area will mean increasing fish kills, said Herbert Curl, who studied the chemistry of the area for the National Oceanic and Atmospheric Administration.

Nutrients from sewage, as well as fertilizer, may be to blame for pockets of low-oxygen water that sometimes spread from lower Hood Canal into the main channel.

Sewers may be the only answer for Belfair's Lynch Cove and the shallow areas of Hood Canal out to the Great Bend near

• • • • • • • • • •

"If we lost this amount of timber in a blowdown in two days, we would call it a national emergency. But we are doing the same thing over months."
— Mike Reed, Port Gamble S'Klallam Tribe

Union and Tahuya, according to a growing number of residents.

"The people on the canal in the port district are all for it," said Lockhart. "We have had public meetings to find that out — and we'll have more as soon as we get a decision from the Department of Ecology."

Lockhart says he will continue to pour his energy into the dream of building a sewer system.

"That's the reason I ran for the port district. We need it bad. After that, I don't give a damn. I don't want the job."

Changing Nature's Buffer

Waterfront residents along Hood Canal often claimed their piece of paradise by filling a shoreline lot and building a bulkhead to protect the fill from the water.

In doing so, they unknowingly speeded the destruction of the canal's shorelines and beaches.

In many places in Hood Canal — notably from Union to Belfair and out to Tahuya — homes were built upon fill placed behind bulkheads, according to Sean Orr, a shorelines administrator in Mason County.

Ever since then, homeowners have clung to their valuable piece of waterfront property, replacing the bulkhead whenever necessary. Only recently has Mason County begun to question the need for every new bulkhead, said Orr.

"When we try to discourage bulkheads," he said, "people think we are crazy."

Orr, along with state Department of Fisheries officials, may force a property owner on the South Shore of Hood Canal to remove an expensive new bulkhead built 4 feet in front of an old one that was failing.

"There was a massive smelt spawning area below his failed bulkhead," said Orr, "and 250-300 square feet of spawning area was lost because he stuck that bulkhead out there."

Tom Terich, a geographer and regional planning expert, argues that bulkheads are "entirely unessential as far as serving any purpose for the common good... The miles and miles of walls and piles of rock simply serve to protect the private property of a few individuals who built too close to the shoreline to begin with."

Local government should do everything to encourage people to build their homes farther back from the water — and to leave the natural systems in place, he said.

The concrete bulkhead could well be a fitting monument to man's ongoing battle against nature.

There it stands at the edge of Hood Canal, solid, unyielding, absorbing the punishment of waves, day after day in all kinds of weather. Then it cracks and collapses.

The folly of bulkheads, argues Terich, a professor at Western Washington University, is that they attempt to hold back natural erosion, but end up altering the entire shoreline. "One of the major problems with bulkheading is that we are putting a very rigid material in a fluid, mobile environment."

Beaches are the result of natural erosion from sandy bluffs and upland areas, he said. In fact, beaches have been called "rivers of sand" due to the consistent movement of sand along a shoreline.

"The one thing I am most concerned about is if we keep putting up structures, we will prevent that sediment from getting down to the beach. We will start having a loss of beach."

During slide presentations to the public, Terich shows photographs of beaches that have been altered in a matter of years due to bulkheads, which also have destroyed wetlands and near-shore habitat for fish and shellfish.

The easy flow of fresh water into saltwater is disrupted by bulkheads, which create vertical walls at the edge of the water.

No bulkhead can be considered permanent due to the dynamics of upland erosion and lateral movement of sand, not to mention wave action, said Terich. Waves cause increased turbulence in front of a vertical bulkhead, undercutting the wall and causing failure.

Where bulkheads are necessary to protect property, Orr said, neighbors should work together to consider the entire system.

"Oftentimes, one property owner puts up a wall, which causes wave energy at the end of the wall, so the next property owner feels he has to do something to protect his property."

Researchers are studying new designs for bulkheads that minimize damage, he said.

One of the "softer approaches" to protecting beaches, said Terich, is to add the

• • • • • • • • • •

No single housing development, grocery store, marina or golf course creates a significant problem for Hood Canal, but the combination of all them together does have significant impact.

right type of beach material in a particular location and allow the waves to spread it out along the beach.

"You have to treat the whole beach as a unit."

• • • • • • • • • •

Despite the growth, Hood Canal remains in pretty good shape. Vast tracts of forest land remain undeveloped, and important fish and wildlife species still make their home in the watershed.

Ribbons of Development

Highway 101 along the western shore of Hood Canal offers travelers a beautiful introduction to the scenic waterway, but that road would never pass today's environmental rules, experts say.

The same goes for Highway 106 along the South Shore and Highway 300 along the North Shore.

"To fill the wetlands and in some cases the beach itself, to cross the rivers and creeks and cedar swamps and bogs would be an almost impossible job today," said Mike Leitch of the state Department of Transportation in Olympia.

Throughout the Hood Canal area, development would not exist were it not for all the roads and highways that carry people to and from their homes. These long ribbons of pavement break up wildlife habitat and cause drainage problems in every spot touched by concrete or asphalt.

Highway records are somewhat sketchy, but it is easy to imagine the huge cliffs that had to be excavated for portions of Highway 101 and 106. Rock and debris from the cuts no doubt were used to fill wetlands along the route.

The long stretches of uniform highway in place today once were smaller county roads. Since the 1920s, the state has upgraded various sections of the roads, officials say.

But few roadways in the state come as close to a sensitive body of water as those around Hood Canal — and runoff from roads can be a major source of water pollution.

"Any time you have an impervious surface, you have two things to worry about: water quantity and water quality," said Gary Kruger of the state Department of Ecology.

Major pollutants include petroleum products dripped from automobile engines and gas tanks, lead deposited from gasoline, and zinc and copper loosened during wear and tear on the engine. In addition, pesticides used to reduce roadside vegetation can be carried along with stormwater.

Ecology and the Transportation Department are working jointly on a $50 million program to redesign highway drainage systems throughout the state to reduce the amount of water pollution. Strategies include using existing right of way and buying new land for the installation of settling ponds and grassy swales, both of which reduce toxic chemicals.

Unfortunately, the major roads around Hood Canal were built at the edge of the water, sometimes next to a sheer cliff. Room enough for such pollution control measures may not exist, said Clay Wilcox, a DOT maintenance supervisor for the area.

Grass-lined ditches, proposed for some areas around Puget Sound, simply aren't practical there, he said.

"Along Hood Canal, we are lucky to have any ditch at all," he said. "There are areas where there is just barely enough ditch there to say there is a ditch."

To make matters worse, the ditches flow more or less directly into Hood Canal.

"Over by the marina on Highway 106 (at Union), there are cross culverts that wash directly onto the beach," he said.

The district has three areas that create a tremendous amount of sediment in the ditches due to sloughing from steep banks, said Wilcox. In addition to the marina area at Union, one is where the Skokomish River approaches Highway 106 and the other is near the Purdy Creek crossing of Highway 101.

It takes two or three days of work each year to clean the stretch of ditch called Purdy Canyon, he said, and about 1,600 yards of debris is removed in that time from that one ditch.

Nobody knows how much sediment along the highways fails to settle out in the ditches, thus washing into Hood Canal, said Wilcox, but it is no small amount. Cleaning out the ditches isn't considered pollution control, he said, but without that maintenance the ditches would fill up and all the contaminated sediments would wash into the canal.

Demand for Gravel Alters the Landscape

Al Hoover used to have a nice little duck pond in his front yard. Now, his yard is nothing but a pond. And the water is still rising.

Hoover's entire neighborhood along

Old Belfair Highway is affected by excess water.

"The ducks and geese love it," says Hoover. Not so the neighbors, however, who claim their problems began a decade ago when Anderman Sand and Gravel took over a surface mining operation on a hill behind their homes.

Gravel mining is needed to build roads and concrete foundations for all types of development. In fact, state law considers surface-mining programs as vital as timber and agriculture.

"We moved out here in 1980 because we liked the area," said Hoover, a quality assurance inspector at Puget Sound Naval Shipyard. "We purchased property across the street and lived there until 1987, when we moved here."

Until 1983, the gravel pit was owned by Service Fuel Co., which operated a small asphalt plant on the top of the hill. The operation went bankrupt a few years later when the quality of gravel declined. In 1986, the current operator arrived.

"When they came, the area had been logged," said Hoover, "but it was select logging. They cut the rest of the trees."

Among the trees cut down, he said, was a 50-foot buffer between his land and the gravel operation. Anderman also expanded the pit down the edge of the hill, he said.

Anderman officials choose not to comment, but during legal proceedings, they maintained that the operation has complied with all state and local rules.

Hoover climbed the bank behind his house and pointed out a natural swale on his land, where water accumulates during heavy rains. But silty water from the gravel pit has begun to fill in the swale, he says.

Despite an earthen dike between the two properties, Hoover's land still gets more water than it ever did, he says.

Hoover's neighbor, Richard Medeiros, also has a low-lying area on his property to the south. The area has turned into a swamp, filled with cattails and other wetland plants.

Joe Watson, who lives across the street with his backyard to the Union River, said surface and subsurface water has flooded his yard and even run into his well under pressure.

"Sometimes we used to get water in the yard," he said, "but it didn't stand like this."

Katie Littlefield, who lives next to the Watsons, sat at her kitchen table and glanced out the window at the gravel pit, which dominates her view.

"We have lived here about 18 years," she said. "It was really beautiful then."

The Department of Natural Resources, which has responsibility for surface mining operations, has attempted to reduce the flow of water from the pit by requiring a series of sedimentation ponds on the pit property. But one mitigation plan after another has failed to keep silty water from flowing onto the neighboring property.

One answer would be for the neighbors to grant easements to get the water swiftly to the Union River, but nobody wants to be part of a plan that directs dirty water into the already troubled river.

Besides, say the neighbors, that would only complicate the problem because environmental agencies such as the state Department of Fisheries and Department of Ecology would never allow the discharge.

"They've approached me to buy my land," said Medeiros, "but it's not for sale. My contention is if the state requires them to contain the water on site, then that's what they have to do. The only solution I see is to put the vegetation back to the original condition."

The Department of Natural Resources ordered that Anderman solve the drainage problem, but Anderman appealed the matter to a state hearing examiner. Christine Clishe ruled that the current system of drainage "removes that runoff to a safe outlet, namely the natural drainage pattern in the area, which includes the adjacent properties."

Furthermore, said Clishe, "Anderman is not by law and should not be required to correct the community water problem of the area. That long-standing problem has been created by nature and several property owners."

Needless to say, the neighbors weren't pleased with the ruling, and Hoover pledged an appeal to Superior Court.

The Results of Clearcuts Show Up Downhill

More than a few Mason County residents have grumbled the past few years that their county government was failing to control development. But, they say, a single event in November 1990 may

• • • • • • • • • •
Hood Canal offers Washington residents one last chance to preserve an area that has not yet been spoiled by growth.

have jarred the county to its senses.

The awesome power of stormwater runoff was demonstrated near Union during the heavy rains over the Thanksgiving weekend, when water gushed down a steep ravine, depositing tons and tons of soil and gravel across Highway 106 just above Hood Canal.

"The material was coming faster than we could get rid of it," said Clay Wilcox, a maintenance supervisor for the state Department of Transportation.

Despite the best efforts of both state and county crews using heavy equipment, they couldn't beat the onslaught of sand and gravel washing down the hill. They ended up closing the highway for a day.

Since then, Mason County has filed a $250,000 lawsuit against the property owner blamed for the mess, George Heidgerken, a Shelton developer building a 230-acre golf course and resort community on the hill overlooking Hood Canal.

The county claims that Heidgerken cleared the property of all trees and vegetation without proper drainage controls. He also failed to install a system ordered by county officials after they discovered the problem but before the flooding occurred.

The lawsuit was filed to recover the county's emergency costs as well the cost of hiring a consultant to work out drainage controls, said Mike Clift of the Mason County Prosecutor's Office.

"I think we can make a case that what they did led step-by-step to the damage up there," he said.

Heidgerken says he should not be held responsible for damage from natural runoff, and he blames most of the problem not on the clearcutting, but on the heavy rains.

It's an argument that most residents don't buy.

> • • • • • • • • • •
>
> *"I'd say probably 60-75 percent (of the septic systems) drain right into Hood Canal. Some sit just 6 to 8 feet from a bulkhead."*
>
> — James Lockhart, Port of Allyn commissioner

"That area handled every rain event for the past 30 years," said Bob Close, president of the Mason County Protective Association, which represents property owners in the area.

After the clearcut, water coming down the 50-acre ravine cut a path between two homes and flowed down a driveway to Highway 106.

"It was most fortunate that the driveway was there," said Close, "or one or two houses could have been in jeopardy."

Since then, culverts have been installed to bring the water off the hill, carry it across the road and release it into Hood Canal.

The county ordered the developer to prepare an environmental impact statement before any more work was allowed on the project, known as Black Bear Resort. The first priority was to stabilize the slope and prevent further damage.

Close and Clift agree that the incident has alerted Mason County officials to the potential problems of development. At the time, the county had no ordinances for dealing with the kind of clearing and grading taking place on the steep hill.

Since then, the county has adopted a grading ordinance, approved a North Mason water quality plan and is gaining speed on new requirements under the state's Growth Management Act.

"They are looking at things much differently," said Close.

The Growth Management Act requires counties to identify problem areas and take steps to protect them. Mason, along with Jefferson County, could have opted out of the requirements of the act based on their population, but the two Hood Canal counties agreed that planning for growth was in their best interests.

Local officials are searching for a way to manage the growth that's threatening to overwhelm the Hood Canal watershed.

State requirements for managing growth couldn't come at a better time to protect Hood Canal, says Larry Dennison, a Jefferson County commissioner.

But normal, everyday people hold the real key to the future, he added.

The Hood Canal counties — Kitsap, Mason and Jefferson — are rapidly moving toward new policies they hope will protect forest and agricultural lands from the onslaught of development.

State law also requires that they identify and protect:
• Fish and wildlife habitat.
• Wetlands.
• Groundwater recharge zones.
• Landslide areas.
• Areas prone to flooding.

Under the law, the public gets to help design land-use policies that protect the natural system — and that should mean more than government just going through the motions, argues Dennison, who chairs the three-county Hood Canal Coordinating Council.

"Policies are worthless unless you have the constituencies to support them," he said. "Until enough people value these kind of ideas, we will not be able to make them work."

Dennison wants the environmental movement to have personal meaning to all who live in the Hood Canal region. He wants to see "politics" at work — not the kind of backroom politics that has gained a bad reputation, but the original meaning of the word. "Politics is the process of creating public policy. The power has to be close enough to the people that they can feel it."

All three counties have begun planning at the grassroots level, but they eventually hope to coordinate their efforts for Hood Canal. It is a different process than one evolving in Oregon, where such policies are set at the state level.

Kitsap County Commissioner John Horsley said he believes people can understand the goal of protecting public resources.

"But I think we are going to get into some tremendous controversy when we go a step further and try to restrict what people can do with their land."

Horsley knows about planning for growth. As the county's first Trident coordinator and later as county commissioner, he helped prepare for the population boom that arrived with the giant Naval Submarine Base at Bangor.

As a result, Kitsap County is ahead of both Mason and Jefferson in growth-management planning. But with five times the population of Mason and 10 times the population of Jefferson, Kitsap also suffers the greatest environmental damage from development that's already occurred.

"We can handle the next 100,000 people who come in," said Horsley, "if we

• • • • • • • • •

SECTION 4

PLANNING FOR GROWTH

By Christopher Dunagan

Hood Canal Shores Under Pressure
Carving up what's left of a limited resource

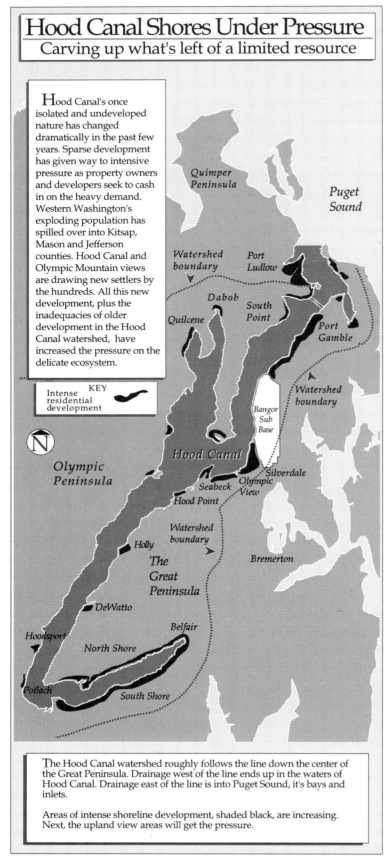

Hood Canal's once isolated and undeveloped nature has changed dramatically in the past few years. Sparse development has given way to intensive pressure as property owners and developers seek to cash in on the heavy demand. Western Washington's exploding population has spilled over into Kitsap, Mason and Jefferson counties. Hood Canal and Olympic Mountain views are drawing new settlers by the hundreds. All this new development, plus the inadequacies of older development in the Hood Canal watershed, have increased the pressure on the delicate ecosystem.

KEY
Intense residential development — Watershed boundary

Quimper Peninsula
Puget Sound
Watershed boundary
Port Ludlow
Dabob
South Point
Quilcene
Port Gamble
Watershed boundary
Bangor Sub Base
Hood Canal
Silverdale
Olympic Peninsula
Seabeck
Olympic View
Hood Point
Watershed boundary
Holly
The Great Peninsula
Bremerton
DeWatto
Belfair
Hoodsport
North Shore
Potlatch
South Shore

The Hood Canal watershed roughly follows the line down the center of the Great Peninsula. Drainage west of the line ends up in the waters of Hood Canal. Drainage east of the line is into Puget Sound, it's bays and inlets.

Areas of intense shoreline development, shaded black, are increasing. Next, the upland view areas will get the pressure.

Source: Kitsap, Jefferson, Mason counties and Sun staff research

develop a land-use pattern that concentrates people in our urban centers and protects the rural areas from overdevelopment."

None of the major urban centers proposed are within the Hood Canal watershed, though Port Gamble may become a much larger community than it is today, said Horsley.

"What we're trying to discourage is a checkerboard pattern of 2 1/2-acre tracts or 5-acre tracts without adequate road systems, water systems or open space," he noted.

Phyllis Myers, a habitat biologist for the Suquamish Indian Tribe, says she is weary of the growth battles taking place as rural areas are forced to make room for more people.

"I'm feeling sad these days," she said. "Someone said to me recently, 'We don't have growth management; we just have growth.'"

Myers helped put together a new water-quality plan for Dyes Inlet between Bremerton and Silverdale. The plan calls for new populations to move into areas already paved over by development.

"Development should take the form of redevelopment in the city of Bremerton," she said of the county's future.

Maintaining areas in forestry is a goal required by state law, though it may be easier to accomplish in the lesser-developed portions of Mason and Jefferson counties than in Kitsap.

Horsley said he hopes to be able to convince major forest land holders in Kitsap to retain their property in timber — perhaps by allowing them to build higher-density communities in more urban locations.

But he says he's "discouraged" about the declining runs of wild salmon and about management by the state Department of Fisheries.

The numbers of fish reaching their native streams are governed by two factors: 1) the success of their reproduction — which depends on the local water quality, and 2) the number caught on their way home.

In the spring of 1991, Fisheries announced a cutback in commercial and sport fishing to protect wild coho returning to Hood Canal. But Northwest Indian tribes say it is not enough.

It is sad to think that the magnificent fish may be on a permanent decline, said Horsley. He suggests that salmon may be a good yardstick for measuring the success or failure of local controls on development.

"They are like the canaries that went down into the mines as a test of when the air was bad," said Horsley.

Unfortunately, studies are lacking on just how severely the streams already have been degraded.

One section of the Growth Management Act which has gotten little attention calls for innovative techniques in managing growth.

"It is a very short, but I think powerful section," said Steve Wells of the state Department of Community Development. "Think of a tool kit in the hands of the counties and cities. They are right now deciding what tools are going to go into that kit."

They may choose a heavy hammer — the police authority of local government, including zoning controls and building restrictions. They may add a scalpel — the ability to purchase development rights precisely in areas that should be preserved.

In essence, the state has given the counties authority to decide.

Mike Reed, a biologist with the S'Klallam Tribe in Port Gamble, has urged Kitsap, Mason and Jefferson counties to adopt what he calls "urban thresholds," a concept originally proposed to protect resources from logging operations.

Thresholds are measurable values that reflect the amount of damage to an ecosystem, such as a watershed.

For example, biologists can measure the amount of sediment in a stream. One threshold level — perhaps a 10 percent ratio of sediment to gravel — would alert forest managers to an upcoming problem, and logging could be reduced. At a second level, perhaps 25 percent, drastic changes would be required to reduce the level of sediment — even if it meant stopping logging altogether.

Reed argues the same approach should be used "when you move down the watersheds into the urbanizing areas." Urban thresholds would put the burden on developers to prevent the kind of damage that has occurred in the past.

Only in this way, Reed says, will politicians be held accountable for commitments they make in the face of economic and political pressures.

Both Dennison and Horsley say they find the concept of urban thresholds appealing and would like to incorporate it into regional planning.

State and county agencies are getting better with environmental regulations. Not so many years ago, the Department of Fisheries failed to prevent, or apparently even notice, damage from development. Now, both Fisheries and Wildlife review the plans for new developments with an eye for potential impacts.

Fisheries can force developers to protect streams, and Wildlife can often protect habitat for migratory birds and other animals. Both are using their authority under state law to mandate stormwater controls to prevent excessive runoff.

Kitsap County, which has made some attempt to control the rate of runoff in the past, is now discussing strong new measures, including those that would reduce the amount of pollution, said David Dickson of the Kitsap County Department of Public Works.

Using a computer, engineers can now design a stormwater system that more closely matches the natural-flow conditions of a site. In addition, grass-lined ditches, known as biofiltration swales, can be used to absorb pollutants before the water leaves the property.

Already, the county has begun requiring such modern stormwater controls in new developments, though a full-blown ordinance and storm-drainage manual probably won't be ready until 1992, said Dickson.

Unmanaged growth has spoiled many areas of the country, including parts of Washington state. Some would argue that even Hood Canal has been damaged beyond recognition. But a majority of planners and biologists say Hood Canal still contains many natural wonders, despite the pressing growth.

"We may have let things get out of hand," said Reed. "We may have some dirty laundry that we need to clean up. I believe a lot of our actions are based on the remote idea that we will not be around to live with the consequences of what we do today."

That attitude, he argues, has got to change. And what better time than now?

• • • • • • • • • •

State law requires that counties identify and protect fish and wildlife habitat, wetlands, groundwater recharge zones, landslide areas and areas prone to flooding.

CHAPTER

12

· · · · · · · · ·

NATIVE
AMERICANS

SECTION 1

WHEN
INDIANS PLIED
ITS WATERS

By Gene Yoachum

*Skokomish elder
Joseph Andrews Sr.*

Hood Canal offered bountiful fishing amid cool waters and a picturesque aquatic highway to the three major Indian tribes living there in the decades prior to the 20th Century. The history of the canal was shaped by the Twana, Chemakum and S'Klallam tribes, but only remnants remain today: the Skokomish, the Suquamish and the S'Klallams.

Elders from the three tribes describe the canal as a much simpler, more pristine place in their youth, when it was a base for their subsistence.

Joseph A. Andrews Sr., 76, recalled the years just prior to 1920 as a time when he rarely wore clothes and when Hood Canal was a "beautiful place" to be while growing up. Early in the morning, he'd watch deer along the shores of the canal lick salt off rocks at low tide.

Andrews' eyes glistened as he talked

about how the autumn sky "just turned dark" as huge flocks of migrating geese flew overhead, issuing sounds "that were like a lullaby to my ears."

He remembered sitting in the bow of his grandfather's 24-foot shovel-nose canoe as a preschooler, "eating salmonberries that hung out over the canal. I wasn't a very good picker, but I could eat them pretty good.

"When I was a young boy, before I went to school, the Indians traveled the canal by canoes and rowboats equipped with sails," said Andrews, an elder among the Skokomish, whose reservation sits at the Great Bend of Hood Canal in Mason County.

"We had camps on both sides of the canal," he said. "There were plenty of fish and clams. There were trees along both sides; the logging camps were just getting started."

Andrews said he "didn't wear clothes until he was 8 years old. There was no need to because there was lots of privacy out there."

When he was about 13 years old, Andrews had an encounter with a couple of whales that he's not forgotten.

"About halfway across the canal, these two whales buzzed me," Andrews recalled. "They bumped the boat and made waves that bumped me, and the dogs barked, but they didn't tip me over."

When he told about being accosted by the whales, Andrews said his mother explained the huge beasts may have been trying to get to the dog and her puppies, noting that whales eat seals and other small animals.

Andrews' tribe shared use of the canal with two others, the Suquamish and the Port Gamble S'Klallams.

The Skokomish elder said his people had friends among the Suquamish Indians, although "they had a hostility among them. It seemed like they always had to have someone's permission to be in the area. We never worried about it, but they did."

Both sides of Hood Canal originally were inhabited by the Twana Indians, divided into three bands, the Du-hlelips, Skokomish and Kolsids, the Rev. Myron Eells wrote in *The Twana, Chemakum and Klallam Indians of Washington Territory,* published in 1887.

He said the word "Twana" was believed to mean a portage, coming "from the portage between Hood's Canal and the main waters of the Sound, where the Indian, by carrying his canoe three miles, avoids rowing around a peninsula 50 miles long."

Skokomish means "River People," derived from their settlement at the mouth of the large freshwater river that empties into the canal.

The Chemakums are believed to have originated from the Kwilleuts, who lived south of Cape Flattery on the Pacific Coast. Eells wrote that a portion of the Kwilleut tribe, according to the Kwilleut tradition, came inland from the coast following a very high and sudden tide long ago and settled near Port Townsend, calling themselves "Chemakums."

By 1887, Eells said the Chemakums were "virtually extinct," there being only 10 left who had not married whites or members of other tribes. Only one four-member family was included in the total. At one time, the Chemakums occupied lands from the mouth of Hood Canal to Port Discovery Bay.

The S'Klallam tribe derived their name from "Nusklaim," a word in their language which meant "strong people."

The S'Klallams had claimed territory from Port Discovery Bay to the Hoko River on the northern coast of Washington.

Shortly before the turn of the 20th Century, Eells noted many S'Klallams had moved to Little Boston, opposite Port Gamble; to Jamestown north of Sequim; and Port Townsend and Port Discovery Bay, where most were employed at sawmills.

Another band of S'Klallams made their home in Elwah, about eight miles west of Port Angeles, living largely on fish. (Although the Port Gamble clan changed the spelling of the tribal name to S'Klallam, the closest reflection to the correct pronunciation, the Jamestown and Lower Elwah clans still use Klallam in their names.)

The Suquamish and the Skokomish were the main users of Hood Canal during the latter years of the 19th Century, according to Lawrence Webster of Indianola.

At 91, Webster is the eldest of the Suquamish tribe, centered on the Port Madison Indian Reservation in North Kitsap.

"They used the west side, we used the east side" of the canal, he said. The Klallam Tribe, particularly those from Port Gamble, didn't begin to make substantial use of Hood

• • • • • • • • • •

The Northwest Coast tribes lost most of their creative traditions within a few decades of the treaties they signed with whites in the mid-19th Century. Indian culture was banished during the school year at boarding schools the children were sent to.

Canal until after Pope & Talbot built its lumber mill at Port Gamble in 1854, Webster added.

He recalled taking a cedar dugout canoe on a month-long fishing trip on the canal when he was about 4 years old.

"It was a family canoe, seven of us," he said. It was large enough for four adults, three children and the group's camping equipment.

They paddled the canoe northward from Miller Bay around the Kitsap Peninsula, into the mouth of Hood Canal and all the way to the south end of the saltwater channel.

The group had timed the journey to the canal to take advantage of the tides because without help from tidal currents, their canoe trip would have been much longer. Even with tides working in their favor, the trip required the better part of a day.

They spent the next month living in canvas tents pitched along the banks of the canal, sleeping on cattail mats, fishing each day and drying their catch over campfires to keep it through the winter.

After they'd caught and dried what they could take back in their canoe, they returned home. The trip back, however, took a full day's paddling and part of another, Webster recalled, because they had miscalculated the tides needed to make their journey easier.

When he was growing up, Webster said Anderson Hill Road in Central Kitsap and the Port Gamble-Suquamish Road in North Kitsap were not roads, but mere paths — routes used frequently by his people to get to and from Hood Canal. He said tribal members who were in fishing camps on the canal for extended periods often used the trails to tend to matters back home. The nine-mile trek could be made within a few hours.

Webster recalled the Suquamish didn't go over to the canal as much starting in about 1910. Older tribal members were less inclined to make the trip because of the effort

The S'Klallam Tribe derived its name from "Nu-sklaim," a word in their language that meant "strong people."

Hood Canal tribes

The Skokomish (1), the Port Gamble S'Klallam (2) and the Suquamish (3) all found sustenance in the bounty of the Hood Canal watershed.

it required. Younger Indians "began to get busy with other things."

Irene Purser, 90, an elder member of the Port Gamble S'Klallam Tribe at Little Boston, also remembers the canal as a major thoroughfare for early settlers.

She and two other S'Klallam tribal elders — her half-sister, Mildred Decoteau, 64, and Catherine Moran, 81 — recalled how game, fish and other forms of life were found alongside the canal. Then commercial ventures and increasing numbers of residences began to change the life they'd grown to enjoy.

"In those days, you could go where you wanted to dig clams or go fishing," Decoteau said. "It was an important part of daily life."

Purser said she could remember when there was "only one store on the canal — at Lofall. People went there to buy hardtack, flour and sugar."

She recalled her grandparents taking her to Puyallup with them to pick hops and going to Brinnon to catch and dry fish for the winter. She also remembered family members baking bread by burying loaves in hot sand and "eating fish on a stick every day and never getting tired of it."

Moran said her people would dig clams each winter and sell them for 50 cents a bushel.

Purser's family had a large canoe, large enough for a bed in the middle for the children in her family to sleep, with room on each end for adults to sit and paddle the craft.

In addition to paddling and using tidal currents to their advantage, the Indians also relied on the winds to power their canoes and flat-bottomed boats, Moran said. She recalled how sails were created by sewing flour sacks together.

"The canoe was how they got around," she said.

• • • • • • • • • •
SECTION 2

TRIBES
SEEK THEIR
SPIRIT SONG

*By Julie
McCormick*

*Skokomish spiritual
leader Bruce Miller
brought the old
cleansing ritual back to
his tribe.*

I t is mid-winter and pre-white man. The last of the yabu, the dog salmon people from the Skokomish and other rivers, have been hauled in and smoked. Food the Tuwa'duxq have gathered should last the season.

Now it's time for the 1,000 or more people of various bands scattered around the curled leg of water they call tuwa'duxqlsi'dakw — the Twana's saltwater — to congregate in their plank houses and devote their time to more spiritual matters.

Nine communities surround the Twana's saltwater, occupied by three or five bands, depending upon whose account constitutes history.

Edward S. Curtis, who photographed tribes throughout the West at the turn of the century, located the Duhle'lips at Union Creek, the S'kokomish at their river, the Soatlkobsh along both sides from what is now Hoodsport to the Dosewallips at what is now Brinnon.

Members of the S'Klallam tribe apparently camped at Brinnon, but farther to the northeast there were more Twanas — the Kolsids at what is now Quilcene, another version of their name, and the Slchoksbish on both sides beyond.

Farther were more S'Klallams at Little Boston and Port Gamble, Port Ludlow, Hadlock and Port Townsend.

The S'Klallams spread into the former Chemakum territory from their original camps along the Strait of Juan de Fuca as the Chemakums — depleted, it is said, by war and smallpox — declined first to a remnant of a people, then to a memory, then to a footnote.

By 1859, only a few years after the federal treaty had been signed with the three tribes, the S'Klallams were very much in evidence all along the passage to the canal.

Their chief, Chetzemoka, hosted a three-day ceremonial gathering of 400 S'Klallams in 1859 that a San Francisco newspaper correspondent described as an "invocation to their Tomanawos, or Great Spirit." Tomanawos was a Chinook word, the trading jargon spoken by Indian and white alike.

Once into the canal, the saltwater belonged to the Twanas. Before century's end, their five bands were all called Skokomish after the river where their 4,000-acre reservation was located, and where most of their depleted population eventually settled.

●●●●●●●●●●
Unlike the northern tribes, many of whose similar ceremonies were attended, described in detail, explained and analyzed by white scholars, most of the Coast Salish were — and still are — secret. And the artifacts of their rituals gone.

They had named 32 different places on the river, 146 on the canal, including some whirlpools and other special spots that were to be avoided lest the salmon people become offended and not return.

This intimate relationship with their natural surroundings, upon which they relied for their relatively abundant existence, was shared by all the Coast Salish and other tribes throughout the Northwest Pacific Coast.

Winter was the time when those relationships were most often displayed in song and dance. It is the time when tribal members may become "Indian sick," the term members of Xanxanitl, the Skokomish tribe's secret society, have given to a state of mind that requires certain prescribed spiritual steps.

"Indian sick is when you go through a sudden or maybe a gradual character change in your life," says Bruce Miller, a Skokomish spiritual leader.

Miller brought the old practices back to the tribe after his initiation in a Lummi ceremony in 1977. Indian sick is like a flu for which there is no detectable cause.

"That means that your spirit song is trying to be born," Miller explains. "We live in a society in which the majority of people are without a song, and from my observation they wander lost. They leave their own culture to find a culture that will give them a song."

Song — harmonies of human sound that precede and underlie formal language — was given by the Great Spirit to express basic human emotion.

It's the same old song — and dance — Miller notes with a slight smile. Spirit dance accompanies song in the longhouse or smokehouse where rituals known only to members resemble those of ancestors like Frank Allen, one of the last dancers.

Allen's death in the 1950s, at the same time as that of Miller's grandmother, also a dancer, was the end of spirit dancing for the Skokomish until Miller reintroduced the practice.

Song is a cure for Indian sickness, an expression of the power of the spirit whose name you have taken in a naming ceremony. In the old days, says Miller, a person without a song wasn't really alive.

The ceremonies described by the San Francisco newspaper correspondent in 1859 were full of color — although he was not allowed to witness much — but not grounded in meaning.

Four people went into extended trances and were revived by mask-wearing dancers. Spirits were called by the beating of rattles upon the roof of the lodge house.

People danced masked as bears, lizards, cranes. People blackened their faces and filled their hair with white feathers. One man appeared to swallow an arrow.

None of that should have been recorded, remarks Miller. The correspondent notes that Chetzemoka was admonished for permitting whites at an evening performance, where they disgraced him with laughter.

Unlike the northern tribes, many of whose similar ceremonies were attended, described in detail, explained and analyzed by white scholars, most of the Coast Salish were — and still are — secret. And the artifacts of their rituals gone.

"You could pass along the right to have a mask, but not the mask itself," explains Miller. "To have an uninitiated person observe vilified the ceremony."

Until the 1978 Native American Freedom of Religion Act, ceremonies were also technically illegal. Tribal members were sometimes jailed for participation.

At the Skokomish Reservation, only the Treaty Days ceremonies the last Saturday in January are open to the public. They are called Treaty Days because celebration of the Point-No-Point Treaty was the only justification government agents would allow for the forbidden practices.

Xanxanitl initiates must endure isolation and deprivation, based on the theory that it strengthens one for hardship that can come at any time. "That teaches kal, the utmost belief that the spirit will give you what you need to survive until you get better," says Miller.

The Salish and other Pacific coast people had wealth-based cultures. Status was achieved partly through the redistribution of wealth in the potlatch ceremony and the children of the wealthy particularly needed such training.

When an initiate ends his or her fast, each morsel must be shared, "because then you begin your new life by sharing ... in an atmosphere of thankfulness," says Miller. "They are forced to admire the beauty of the simplicity of their life."

Suquamish artisan Ed Carriere.

Ed Carriere's eyes gaze down at thick fingers tangled in their deliberate work. Lost in it, his voice is barely audible as he tells about the conviction that drove him to re-learn this painstaking task after so many years.

"My desire is to make baskets that aren't being made anymore," says the Suquamish Indian, arching and weaving stiff cedar strips of limb and root into warp and weft.

"I feel like it's a link, a connection, and I'm doing it exactly the way it was done hundreds of years ago."

Carriere is starting clam basket bottoms for his class of novices. They often get stuck on this difficult initial part of the process, so he is sparing them that frustration in their early work.

Although there are many basket makers among the coastal tribes, only Carriere regularly attempts the traditional open-weave clam basket. They are sturdier and less showy than the more tightly woven grass and cedar bark baskets used for storage, carrying and cooking.

Clam basket makers did not adorn their creations with meticulous fancywork like that of the other types. They would last only a season or two before breaking down from heavy use and saltwater decay, while the others lasted generations.

The Northwest Coast tribes lost most of their creative traditions within a few decades of the treaties they signed with whites in the mid-19th Century.

They were quick to adapt to new ways. Manufactured goods replaced many of the materials they had collected for centuries to

• • • • • • • • • •

SECTION 3

HE WEAVES
PAST AND
PRESENT
TOGETHER

*By Julie
McCormick*

carve, weave and decorate.

Denim and gingham replaced hide, beaten cedar and dog's wool clothing. Modern cooking in pots and pans replaced the tightly woven baskets used to make "stone soup," any water-based concoction into which hot rocks were dropped for heat.

People used pails to collect and wash clams. They lasted longer than the strong old baskets.

Only a few women retained the basket-weaving skill. One of them was Carriere's great-grandmother, Julie Jacob.

Once her fingers became too stiff for the work, the 15-year-old great-grandson she had raised was taught to help.

But when he was grown, Carriere, now in his late 50s, stopped making baskets, went to work at Puget Sound Naval Shipyard and raised a family.

"In '69 I started to work with it again and bring the art back," he said. "It took me about four years to make a fairly good, decent looking basket. I had to try to pull all that knowledge out and try to remember."

Carriere believes he owns close to every basket book ever written in English. Multiple examples from other basketry specialties have joined a broad assortment of Northwest native work on shelves in Carriere's living room.

For more than 20 years, his workbench has been the dining table in the house he built across from his great-grandmother's home. It is located on family land along the Indianola beachfront in North Kitsap.

But this year, Carriere is completing a workshop addition to house not only basketry but carving materials and tools.

He's taken up carving under the tutelage of S'Klallam Jake Jones and Duane Pasco, a white carver who has gained a worldwide reputation for meticulous work in the Northwest Indian tradition.

"Every artist needs something else," he says with a conviction born of experience. He has a log on his land all picked out for his next major project, a canoe carved in the traditional style.

Carriere sells every basket he makes, and he also likes to produce a bent cedar bark pouch of a type used to carry whaling tools in the bows of canoes.

People find him. He does not advertise, nor prepare work for galleries, nor take special orders, "because then it would be just like a job. I just do it when I have the time and I feel like doing it, because then I can make a better basket."

Completing the first of a long series of bottoms for the class he's teaching at the Port Gamble S'Klallam Art Center, Carriere muses aloud about his students and his work.

He says it takes 12 hours to make a medium-sized clam basket, not including gathering and preparing materials, which are stored in a freezer.

"It looks so easy, and then, when I start teaching class, no one can do it." He smiles into his hands. "My fingers get really worn and smooth if I'm weaving every day ... All the little fingerprints get worn off."

• • • • • • • • • •

The art of basket making waned from arrival of white society until the 1930s, when, ironically, government programs sought to teach basket making to impoverished Indians during the Depression.

Duane Pasco, a non-Indian who is an expert in traditional Northwest Coast tribal carving, teaches a class in bentwood box making.

"... *the construction of (these) boxes is somewhat peculiar. The sides and ends are made of one board; where the corner is to be, a small miter is cut, both on the inside and outside, partly through. Then the corners are steamed and bent at right angles, and the inside miter is cut so perfectly that it fits water-tight when the corners are bent.*" — Rev. Myron Eells, missionary and diarist, in *The Twana, Chemakum and Klallam Indians of Washington Territory*, 1887.

On the beach at Point Julia, Northwest carver Duane Pasco is tending a rock-filled fire and digging trenches in the sand. His students in the bent box class, several from the Port Gamble S'Klallam tribe, are putting finishing touches on their rectangular cedar boards, prepared at the reservation's new art building across from the tribal center.

The last bent boxes handed down within the tribe were reduced to ash several years ago in a fire that destroyed tribal chairman Jake Jones' home.

The tribe put up a building in 1989 to house a canoe carving project led by Pasco for the state's centennial. When that was done, the building became a classroom to help bring back the traditional arts.

Pasco, a non-Indian carver in the Northwest Coast tribal tradition, teaches design and box making to several older tribal members. They, in turn, will pass it on to the next generation, said Jones.

More modern steaming methods are available to soften the wood for bending, but the class also used the traditional method of burying it with hot rocks covered in sword ferns.

Bent box making methods were entirely lost, even among the more traditional northerly tribes, by the time Pasco first tried it 30 years ago. An account by pioneer anthropologist Franz Boas seemed complete until he tried it and failed, Pasco said.

The next step was to study examples collected in museums and — voila! — a key undercutting method could be discerned that allowed a scored piece of wood to fold

• • • • • • • • • •

SECTION 4

TEACHING THE TRIBES' LOST ART

By Julie McCormick

tightly in upon itself and form a watertight seal.

The bent boxes — unique to the world of the Northwest tribes — were often used for storage, and sometimes bound by woven strands of cedar bark for carrying and to bind them together inside canoes.

At the Skokomish Reservation, 40 miles south by canoe along Hood Canal, tribal member Bruce Miller has shared his basket making skills and experience with others, including children, since 1970.

Among the three Hood Canal area tribes, the Skokomish have been most successful at maintaining their traditional art.

"Actually, we have a budding community of artists," said Miller, known primarily for his twined and coiled baskets, but also as a carver and beadwork artist. There are 14 Skokomish basketmakers, who generally market their work to a steady clientele of collectors and galleries.

The work of carver Andy Wilbur, silversmith Pete Peterson and basket maker Richard Cultee has gained international recognition for beauty, Miller said.

Miller, 46, credits two key elders, Louisa Pulsifer and Emily Miller, for passing along before their deaths the traditionally female art of basket making to his generation.

Miller learned from Emily Miller, whose granddaughter Mary Hernandez recently decided to continue the family tradition into the fourth generation.

Baskets of all sizes and for all purposes continued to be made privately by tribal members, Miller said, because it was an enjoyable occupation and because it, unlike other arts associated with forbidden religious practices, was never banned.

Miller once found some "Louisa baskets" in New York shops and learned that one of his had reached a collection at the Museum of Folk Art in Berlin.

But the art waned from arrival of white society until the 1930s, when government programs sought to teach basket making to impoverished Indians during the Depression.

"We thought it was hilarious," said Miller. "It was like selling refrigerators to Eskimos."

The basket making is an integral part of the economic well being of the community because we're a poor people, basically," said Miller.

Miller and other basket makers in the tribe now often use modern dyes and materials, including raffia from Madagascar, rather than pursue the laborious process of gathering, treating and creating native dyes.

"The basket making itself comprises only about 5 percent of the whole process," he said.

But some entirely traditional baskets with trademark Skokomish dog, stacked-box and other designs are still made from beargrass, cattail rushes, shredded cedar bark and "sweet grasses."

Rit dye easily replaces and outlasts the "blue mud" of the marshes used to stain materials black, the roots of Oregon grape for yellow, the alder bark that once was chewed to a paste to obtain red. "Nowadays, we use a blender," Miller said, "but it's not the same red."

While such methods may not seem entirely authentic, Skokomish artists are quick to point out that the elders themselves were fond of innovative techniques that could save them time and trouble.

Hernandez laughs at the memory of her grandmother, who decided the best way to remove unwanted mucus from grass materials was to place it between plywood sheets and drive back and forth over it with a car.

"My grandmother didn't even know how to drive," she laughed, but it beat scraping off the stuff with dull knives.

It's not only troublesome, it's often hopeless to try to do things the old way.

Rediscovering the old methods is another matter. Miller said he learned most of what he knows about tribal traditions "by keeping my ears open. Some of this I've never seen, but was described time after time by my elders."

For several decades, renewed interest in the Northwest native arts has opened new markets and created a revival of interest among tribal members themselves, who can point to the work of their elders and ancestors with pride and appreciation.

The bent boxes — unique to the world of the Northwest tribes — were often used for storage, and sometimes bound by woven strands of cedar bark for carrying and to bind them together

Head Start students at the Port Gamble S'Klallam Tribal Center are introduced to the language of their ancestors.

A Cultural Appreciation

Many of their grandparents went to boarding schools, where much of the Indian culture was banished during the school year.

Today, the grandchildren attend Hood Canal School, where educators try to rekindle interest in Indian traditions.

Almost 100 Indian students attend the school, located at the Skokomish Reservation on the Great Bend of the canal. They represent about 40 percent of the K-7 student population.

Inside the school, students get reminders of the culture that existed long before white man's schools first came to the Skokomish in the 1870s. Interest in Indian heritage seems to rise during the fall when the curriculum includes a three-week session on Native American studies.

"Just that time of year everybody says "I am part Indian,' " said Pat Hawk, director of Indian Education at the school. Hawk, an 18-year Hood Canal employee, directs the session, where students learn cultural comparisons among the American tribes.

"They didn't all live in tepees; they didn't all wear feathers."

The session also includes visits by people in the tribal community who share skills in storytelling, puppetry, dancing and fishing lore.

She also directs a year-long art class for the older students, who worked on painting an Indian mural in the hallway.

"We want to keep the traditional arts alive," Hawk said.

The school's funding for Indian education is limited, said Superintendent

• • • • • • • • • •

SECTION 5

USING THE
CLASSROOM TO
REKINDLE
TRADITION

Robert Weir. State funds totaling $5,200, and federal Title V funds totaling $17,000 went to the school for Indian education in 1990.

"We have to squeeze salaries from that, as well as things for the kids," Weir said.

Tied to the money is the requirement that Indian people in the community stay involved with the school. An Indian Parent Education Committee meets monthly to discuss curriculum and classroom problems.

"We are a liaison between parents and the teachers and staff," said Laurie Byrd, parent and Head Start teacher.

If parents raise concerns, committee members act on their behalf.

"A lot of the parents are uncomfortable with the teachers," Byrd said.

Only two of the school's 22 teachers are Indian. The underlying cultural differences may have something to do with parental discomfort. Whatever the reason for any discomfort, Byrd believes the solution is getting people together to talk.

"We need to keep communication open," she said.

The Indian Parent Education Committee was successful in arranging tutoring for Indian students last year. The Skokomish Tribal Council foots the bill, paid for out of the council's fish tax. Many of the Skokomish are fishers.

The tutoring sessions include not just emphasis on any skill the students need to practice, but also about 15 minutes a session on native arts or crafts.

"We want to ensure that there is a multi-cultural concept in all the curriculum," said Sally Brownsfield, a fifth-grade teacher at the school and a parent member of the Indian Parent Education Committee. She is a member of the Squaxin Island tribe.

Brownsfield contends that Indian students have different learning styles from their Anglo classmates.

"It's been shown that Native American students learn better by doing. They pick up more from discovery than from books," Brownsfield said. With that knowledge, she plans her classes so the students can be interactive.

"I let them do the experiment first, then the reading, then the experiment again," she said. "With other classes, I might give the reading and instruction first."

By Jessie Milligan

• • • • • • • • • •

Native American students learn better by doing. They pick up more from discovery than from books.

Reviving the Language

N uts'oo ... chasa ... lleewh."
The guileless pre-schoolers in the Port Gamble S'Klallam Tribe's Head Start class wrap their throats around the clustered syllables of their ancient language as if born to it.

"...ngoos ... lhq'achsh ... t'xung."

They hold up each little finger and repeat with teacher Myrna Milholland from the Lower Elwha Klallams, who holds flashcards with pictures of familiar traditional objects.

Nuts'oo kw'ayungsun — one eagle. Two whales — chasa ch'whe'yu. They run out of fingers at 'oopun.

Milholland is out of numbers after nineteen, she admits to her adult class later in the morning. She had only a few words of nuwhstla'yum ootsun — the S'Klallam language — until, as a young woman, she began helping her mother, Nellie Sullivan, with the sometimes unruly mixed summer classes of adults and children.

Milholland recalls that children in the tribe had begun to mimic the language when her mother used it, poke fun at the old sounds, until she stopped speaking it.

She loved working with her mother and tries to keep up the work despite occasional feelings of inadequacy. "Some of the words are so hard, I'd almost have my face in her mouth trying to pronounce them," she smiles.

When her mother died a few years ago, only six elders in the Elwha tribe retained any use of the spoken tongue.

Now Milholland must use a tape recorder to preserve what is left of the language among her elders and hopes to get access to the University of Washington language tapes made decades ago and stored somewhere. A book of the language created by University of Hawaii researchers is flawed, based upon only one source who spoke two tribal languages and mixed them up. Her mother told her to ignore it.

Milholland's mother needed her help because she was educated to teach children and she knew how to keep them busy and deal with their short attention spans. Today, as with every Wednesday language class, the children are learning something new and adding it to the small store of basics.

Out come the animal puppets. You

remember sta'ching, the wolf, says Milholland.

He played a key role in the story of pretty Nakeeta, heard last week and related again today. Straying from her mother during a berry picking expedition, she became lost and was eaten. Her mother's grief was so strong that she was given Lake Sutherland as consolation.

Tsyas, hand. They trace the outlines of their ten fingers onto their book of coloring pictures. Later, they will take these books home and maybe their parents will take an interest.

It is with the children that the future of the traditional culture rests, tribal leaders say.

Most adults share a legacy of generations of white control that included bans on the language and customs, distrust and contempt for the "savage" ways of a Pacific Northwest Coast culture rich in personal industry, art and religious ceremony.

"I think we were one of the first people to give them up," S'Klallam chairman Jake Jones says of the old ways, mostly because of early and persistent contact with whites, he surmises.

Separate S'Klallam bands once ranged from Neah Bay at the far western tip of the Olympic Peninsula to Discovery Bay near Port Townsend; from Lower Hadlock, where artifacts at a beach called Tsetsibus indicate a meeting ground centuries old; and later to

Port Gamble, where tribal sources say the camp was displaced by the white community's graveyard after the mill town was established in 1853.

The ancients were known as excellent traders and fierce warriors. But by the time Jones' generation was born, there were no more canoe makers, no more spirit quests, no more "nuts'oo ... chasa ... lleewh."

The Port Gamble S'Klallams recently put the traditional "s" prefix back before their name. Like many of the words, it works best if you suck in on the prefix, breathe out on the next syllables, much like playing harmonica.

The tribe hired Milholland to help regain their culture, which as any linguist or poet knows, is embedded in the words.

Jones' sisters, Ginger and Geneva Ives, signed up for the adult language class and added to Milholland's vocabulary with memories of sounds buried since the death of their grandmother 47 years ago.

All three agree on the variable meaning of umit, which can be sit down or get up, depending on what you do with your hands.

But nu can't be the only way to say "no," says Geneva. "She always said 'aunu'," she muses about the large old lady she waited upon in old age. Maybe she meant "no more."

Myrna Milholland writes that down. Maybe her elders will know.

By Julie McCormick

• • • • • • • • • •
Most adult tribal members share a legacy of generations of white control that included distrust and contempt for a Pacific Northwest Coast culture rich in personal industry, art and religious ceremony.

CHAPTER

13

• • • • • • • • • •

LIFE ON THE
CANAL

Bill Bruns enjoys a cup of coffee at the Belfair Cafe.

SECTION 1

GROWING
PAINS IN
BELFAIR

By Jim Rothgeb

Bill Bruns wrapped his fingers around a cigarette, gulped a shot of black coffee and smiled from his seat at the counter of the Belfair Cafe.

"I consider myself very fortunate," said Bruns. "I've lived in the best of times for a sportsman like myself. For someone who likes to hunt and fish, I can't think of any more desirable time and place to be than right here."

For an innocent moment, Bruns, a 69-year-old retiree from Puget Sound Naval Shipyard, was Belfair's chief spokesman. The chamber of commerce couldn't have said it better.

Located at the eastern most point of Hood Canal, Belfair and its surrounding territory have become a haven for people in search of tranquility.

But Bruns also knows that if he were 20 years younger, he might not so willingly sing such praises of Belfair and its rural appeal. He knows there are signs that the parade of newcomers may be sapping Belfair of its small-town foundation.

"In 20 years, you probably won't even be able to recognize this town," said Bruns. "We'll see large residential areas developed because of the spillover from Kitsap County."

In the last two decades, Belfair's cup already has filled.

• There once were two mom-and-pop

grocery stores in town. Now there's a large supermarket, and rumors persist that another large supermarket chain will soon announce plans to build in Belfair.

• In 1965, there was only the Belfair Cafe. Now there are at least six family-style eateries along the strip on Highway 3.

• There were no senior housing facilities. Now there are two, each funded through the federal government.

• There were two churches serving mostly an interdenominational audience. Now there are six churches with 12 separate denominations.

• The most prosperous banks were once a hole in the backyard or a space under the mattress. Now Belfair has a bank, a savings and loan, and a credit union.

They're all signs of a spreading population and one wonders just how much longer Bill Bruns can call Belfair and this corner of Hood Canal an outdoor paradise.

It was in 1964 that Carol Wentlandt and her husband, Sanford, first moved to Belfair from their home in Seattle. He worked at Puget Sound Naval Shipyard and had grown weary of the daily commute to Bremerton. Land around Belfair was cheap in the 1960s and the Wentlandts were eager buyers. By today's standards, land values around Belfair are still on the downside.

Wentlandt says now she can relate her experience then to author Betty MacDonald in the Western Washington classic, *The Egg and I.*

"I was used to life in the fast lane and this place was so quiet," said Wentlandt, who lives along the south shore of Hood Canal. "It was hard to make the adjustment because this place seemed like we were moving to the end of the world."

Now Wentlandt manages the Mary E. Theler Community Center, carved from the estate of one of Belfair's most influential families and the closest thing the unincorporated town has to a full-time tourist information center and chamber of commerce.

"It used to be that people would just occasionally come in with questions about the area," said Wentlandt. "Now we're getting newcomers at about the rate of three times a week. People come in and say, 'I've just moved here, what is there to do?'

"What I tell them is that they really have to like the outdoors — camping, fishing, birdwatching. There's not many cultural things to do here so you have to like the rural atmosphere and appreciate the outdoors."

Just off the Old Belfair Highway, near the intersection of North Shore Road, sits a ramshackle house behind a row of trees.

The back half of an old Mercedes Benz hangs out the garage and immediately through the front door of the house a few feet away is the kitchen. Turn right and there's a bedroom so filled with smoke and heat from a wood-burning stove that it's uncomfortable to breathe.

This the modest home of Cecil Nance, an 82-year-old Belfair character who clings mostly to his memories. Nance often walks through town, stopping at the Belfair Cafe, the post office and Thriftway. He has very few teeth, but it doesn't stop him from bearing a wide grin, even for strangers.

"I lived here when the only time you'd see anybody, it was in a horse and buggy," said Nance. "I liked it here a lot better then."

Those were the days when Belfair was known as Clifton, a town of homesteaders who depended on Hood Canal for its fishing and the timber around it to eke out a living. The canal was too shallow to make Clifton much of a port town, so it depended mostly on a criss-cross of roads over which loggers towed their loads.

"This has always been a crossroads town," said Irene Davis, who's compiling a history of Belfair. "The center of the community was the intersection of the roads to North Bay (now Allyn) and Seabeck."

That center has changed through the decades, as Highway 3 eventually replaced the Old Belfair Highway as the town's most important artery. Later came the development on the roads lining the north and south shores of the canal, shaping Belfair into what it is today.

According to Nance and Davis, the old Clifton post office was closed in 1913. Nance says it was because the postmistress was too busy reading everyone's mail instead of distributing it. Two years later, the townspeople demanded the post office be reopened, and changed its name to Belfair.

"The name Belfair came from a novel, called *St. Elmo*," said Nance. "Lizzy Murray was reading the book at the time and they just decided on that name, for no special reason. My mother thought Belaire would

Located at the eastern most point of Hood Canal, Belfair and its surrounding territory have become a haven for people in search of tranquility.

have been a better name, but I wish it would have stayed Clifton."

"New Clifton" is still a crossroads town and a lot of people view that as a problem. Despite its constant flow of traffic, there is only one traffic light — flashing at a crosswalk.

"Traffic has always been tough around here, especially in the summer," said Neil Werner, owner of Neil's Lumber and Garden Center. "I can remember many years ago having to wait to cross the street, and I still have to wait."

Werner, like others, favors a new highway to eliminate the problem but it could hurt his own business.

"The solution is to put a bypass on the ridge around the town," said Werner. "That way you could eliminate a lot of the traffic that's just passing through."

The state highway department supposedly is studying it, but bureaucracy moves slowly — just like the horse and buggies that Nance remembers from his childhood.

• • • • • • • • • •

"In 20 years, you probably won't even be able to recognize this town. We'll see large residential areas developed because of the spillover from Kitsap County."
— Bill Bruns

Belfair

Belfair, the fastest growing community on the canal, is adjacent to some of the watershed's most fragile areas.

The key to Belfair's future may not rest with the people running over the top of the land as much as it does with the water running under it.

Sewers are a hot topic in this North Mason area, where, according to Werner, the population numbers about 10,000 in the winter but swells to more than 60,000 during the summer.

Because of the pressure that septic systems place on the delicate ecology of Belfair's wetlands, some people say there are very few bathrooms along the row of commercial businesses on Highway 3 that work properly.

"Belfair had better solve its septic problems, but there is a sharp division on this," said Jerry Walker, a retired midwesterner who moved here about five years ago. "The oldtimers say a well-managed septic tank is best, but the newcomers say sewers are the only answer."

But if Mason County government yields to the demand for sewers in Belfair and the surrounding area, it may open a land rush even more prominent than today.

And there goes the rural neighborhood.

A growing population does, however, have its benefits. The North Mason School District, growing at the rate of about 10 percent per year for the past decade, has prospered with the steady stream of 20th Century homesteaders.

In 1980, it was one of the poorest districts in the state, so bad it faced discontinued school bus service in an entirely rural district.

"The community was divided between the upper class on the shoreline and the lower class living inland," said Walker. "It was a stratified population, but the middle class was missing."

Since then, more and more baby boomers with school-aged children have moved into the district, and schools have prospered with the passage of each new levy that couldn't get passed 15 years ago.

That led to better times. North Mason is now one of 33 school districts in the state serving as a model for the state's 21st Century educational program.

"It was amazing to see this small, rural, economically undernourished school system become a model for the state," said Walker.

About 39 percent of the students in that school district come from families with incomes from the federal government. It's proof that much of North Mason has become a bedroom community catering to workers from PSNS and Bangor, and military families in general.

They're willing to trade 30 to 35 minutes commuting one-way to their jobs in exchange for reasonable housing prices and the promise of a quiet, rural life.

Bill Bruns, who likes the coffee at the Belfair Cafe, paid $18,000 for 10 acres of undeveloped land near the Tahuya River in

1973. He figures with his 9-year-old house, it's worth about $125,000 to $130,000 today. Those figures are mild compared to the soaring property values today in Kitsap, King and Pierce counties.

But with its preferred location and bargain prices, Belfair teeters on the verge of prosperity. It almost seems that everything good about it — land bargains, rural atmosphere, friendly people — is also bad — increased pollution and overcrowded roads.

The one constant that won't go away is an ever-increasing population.

"If Sea-Tac Airport eventually takes off and decides to build a satellite at Kitsap (Bremerton) Airport, this place will be another Mercer Island — a fast-growing metropolis out of control," Carol Wentlandt said. "That's why a sub-area plan is needed for this area. You can't stop progress, but you want to make sure people appreciate it and make sure that it grows properly."

And if the Bremerton Airport doesn't align with Sea-Tac?

"Belfair will still grow," she said, "only slower."

• • • • • • • • • •

Homes crowd the waterfront of the Bridgehaven development at South Point.

Bridgehaven is a posh community off South Point, near the spot where Hood Canal kisses Puget Sound. Perched on its miniature peninsula 10 feet above sea level, Bridgehaven forms a canal within the canal.

In some respects, it is a microcosm of the splendid fjord it faces: perhaps 30 Bridgehaven homes line the beach on both sides of the peninsula. About a football field wide, this man-enhanced sand bar — like the shores of Hood Canal — serves as the sole filter for the septic drainage from these homes.

Some residents of Bridgehaven sail past a marina at the north entrance of their micro-canal to moor their 40-foot sailboats at their homes. Some drive their Buicks and their Jeep Cherokees onto their treeless sandspit from the community of Trail's End.

They cross speed bumps and 10-miles-per-hour signs, and pass a sign that advises all who enter that Bridgehaven is a private residential community.

The folks who live above Bridgehaven at Trail's End look across the roofs of the Bridgehaven houses to the emerald stretch of Hood Canal.

The Trail's Enders don't often cross

paths with the Bridgehavenites. If they visit the spit, they dig clams or sun themselves on their community beach at the south end of the finger of sand that scratches the eastern tideline of Hood Canal.

Where the two groups are more likely to meet, however, is at South Point's only commercial establishment.

The Trail's End Tavern once rocked and bulged with people, when South Point was the eastern terminal for the barge that ferried cars across Hood Canal during a four-year span after the Hood Canal Bridge sunk on Feb. 13, 1979.

Dee Wilcoxen took over the tavern several months after the bridge was restored in the early 1980s. On the day the Beach Girl stopped running, the tavern's former manager closed the doors and never came back. It's been quiet ever since.

"Some days," says Wilcoxen, looking across the old parking lot to the canal, "I'm here by myself until 4 o'clock. It's pretty quiet around here these days."

On this day, Don "Rocky" Rockefeller, who lives in a motorhome across the parking lot, is counting pulltab tickets for Wilcoxen. Rockefeller ("They tell me I'm his ninth cousin."), 46, spent his teen years at South Point and relates how Trail's End got its name.

"Yeah, it used to be the end of the trail for the Pony Express. See, they made Port Angeles the official west end of the Pony Express, and this is where they would ride to."

The tavern and restaurant were built more than three decades ago, before the bridge was built and the new Highway 104 bypassed South Point by three miles. Hunters and fishermen still stop by the tavern, says Wilcoxen, but mostly it serves the folks of Trail's End.

"Not too many people from Bridgehaven come in here regular," she says. Wilcoxen sips from a glass of bottled water. The tavern's well, located across the parking lot within 100 feet of the canal, contains salt and iron and cannot be used for drinking.

Outside, a survey crew is attempting to find old property lines between the tavern's parking lot and Bridgehaven property. Most of the stakes are buried under the asphalt of the old ferry parking lot.

South Point

The Bridgehaven development at South Point has filled a narrow sand spit with up-scale houses.

The surveyors are harbingers of a new wave of growth that is about to slam into the shores of South Point. Wilcoxen and Rockefeller talk of the proposal to build a 60-acre shopping center just east of the intersection of the South Point Road and Highway 104.

"I don't think it'll get in there. Pope and Talbot won't let it happen," says Wilcoxen. The Port Gamble timber giant has its own plans for a shopping center closer to its burgeoning vacation-retirement community of Port Ludlow.

From his Trail's End vantage point above Bridgehaven, Bill Shipley watches a developer dig three septic percolation test holes in two remaining lots on the spit. Shipley, a Gorst resident, lives in a travel trailer parked permanently on his recreational vehicle lot.

He's fixed his trailer up, with a big deck facing the sunrise across the canal. A catwalk to a feeding station for squirrels and birds arches from his bank to the trunk of a big fir, perhaps 30 feet off the ground. It's an airy lookout, one Shipley says his wife doesn't like to visit.

The retired Puget Sound Naval Shipyard worker is proud of his getaway. He says he's camped up and down Hood Canal most of his adult life. He fishes — "I caught an 18-pound salmon right off the point last year" — and puts out his crab pots regularly.

Shipley says he hasn't noticed any decline of shellfish in the canal, and says, though there are fewer salmon, "you can still catch them if you know where to go." He says that when the salmon run, you can practically walk across the canal on the decks of commercial fishing boats off South Point.

He keeps a small boat at the marina, he says. He waves in the general direction of

• • • • • • • • • • •

John Barber of Bridgehaven is glad that most of the houses along the sandspit are built because it couldn't handle too many more.

Bridgehaven before continuing: "But if you want to see some boats, you ought to go down there in the summer. That's where the money is."

• • • • • • • • • •   Seventy-four-year-old John Barber was among the first Bridgehaven residents. Freshly retired out of Bellevue, Barber moved to Bridgehaven to watch it explode with houses after it was "discovered" by those seeing the vacant lots from the decks of the Beach Girl.

Barber says he helped establish a resident-controlled Public Utility District to get water piped down to the spit from wells up above. As he talks outside his beachfront home, he waves to a passing car, explaining that a neighbor is driving her husband to the Trail's End Tavern for an hour of socializing.

"She'll drop him off and then go back and pick him up later," he said.

Barber says he's glad that most of the houses along the sandspit are built because it couldn't handle too many more.

*The "Schafer Castle" on the canal's
South Shore, designed from a
European postcard in 1926, is one of
Hood Canal's plush properties.*

Hood Canal houses a number of the rich and reclusive along its shores, but there's no truth to the rumor that Clark Gable once lived in a turreted castle not far from Twanoh State Park.

"That's just a story," says Bob Close, who owns the landmark known as the Schafer Castle. "The ranger up at Twanoh likes to send cyclists down here to see 'Clark Gable's house.' "

About four miles west of Twanoh, the striking half-timbered house — with well-groomed topiary trees at its entrance — is a real head turner.

Close says his grandfather, Albert Schafer, had architect Elizabeth Ayer design it from a postcard he had received from friends in Europe.

"I think the postcard showed a place along the Rhine. He said, 'Here's the postcard, Elizabeth, now you design it.' "

Ayer, the first woman architect licensed in Washington state, took him up on the challenge. Working with Edward J. Ivey, she included many castle-like details: a huge fireplace with a little seat inside it; a romantic window seat facing out on the canal; a turret with a winding staircase; and a leaded arched window made with old bottle glass.

It was built as a summer place in 1926. Schafer and his two brothers were owners of Schafer Brothers Logging Co. in Grays Harbor.

Close, who manages industrial parks in Seattle, grew up in Aberdeen where his father practiced law. But he spent summers swimming and waterskiing at his grandparents' place on the canal.

"They'd open it up Memorial Day

• • • • • • • • • •

SECTION 3

PLUSH
PROPERTIES

By Ann Strosnider

weekend and close it on Labor Day weekend."

A perfect place for children, the house includes boys' and girls' bunkrooms, where a child could have as many as five friends stay overnight. The unusual purple fixtures in all the bathrooms are originals, says Close.

"I've noticed Kohler is introducing new colors, but I've never seen a color quite like this."

The inside of the house is lined throughout with clear Port Orford Oregon cedar. The sandstone around the big central fireplace came from Tenino, and the antelope, mountain goat and moose heads on the walls were supplied by his father, a big game hunter.

A visitor notices modern touches as well. An outdoor shower has been converted into a hot tub and spa, and the roof, originally made of cedar bark, has been replaced with slate.

Down the road — on the west side of Alderbrook Inn — is the compound owned by Bill Gates, the founder of Microsoft whose net worth was recently reported at $4 billion.

From the road, a thick stone wall keeps rubberneckers away; from the water you can see a group of low, tastefully designed modern houses. The Nordstrom family also owns two houses on the South Shore of Hood Canal, on the Belfair side of Alderbrook.

If you're in the market and a cool $1.2 million doesn't phase you, check out the Daviscourt estate, also on the South Shore. The 4,000-square-foot main house, hidden from the road by a discreet cedar hedge, includes a solarium, a family room with a pool table, 230 feet of waterfront and deep water moorage.

"You can bring your yacht," says listing agent Jim Avery of John L. Scott.

Bud Daviscourt of Bellevue had it built as a summer house 16 years ago. He also bought 10 acres on the other side of the road and built two additional houses there. It would make a perfect family compound, Avery observes, but it may be broken up into two parcels.

Bob Close may have a turret and the Daviscourts their own dock, but how many people have their own private golf course?

Chuck and JoAnne Haselwood do.

Their sculpted 10-acre course slopes down to their white Mediterranean-style stucco house and swimming pool. The Olympic View property — near Subase Bangor — overlooks Hood Canal and the Olympic Mountains.

Haselwood, owner of Haselwood Buick and West Hills Honda in Bremerton, says he's no golfing fanatic.

"I play once in awhile, but mostly, I like the atmosphere," he says.

Maintaining that atmosphere of palm trees and manicured greens keeps three workers busy full time. Equipment for course upkeep is stored in a building the size of some folks' houses.

The course was nearly three years in the making — last summer was the first time the Haselwoods and their friends got a chance to play on it.

The sloping ground had to be shaped and mounded to create three greens, two ponds and 11 tees. "You can play 18 holes if there's only one foursome," says Haselwood.

Designers from McCormick Woods built the course, and bonsai specialist Dan Robinson did the landscaping.

The Haselwoods moved to the canal 15 years ago from a house on Lansing Street in Navy Yard City. "A friend owned the property," recalls Haselwood. "When we came out here to look at it, the woods were pretty thick, and we had to paw our way through. When we saw the view, we said this is for us."

The scenery is always different because of the play of the sun and the clouds around the mountains, the Haselwoods say. Their 333 feet of waterfront is high bank — 85 feet high, in fact — but they're now in the process of installing a tram down to the beach.

Chuck Gilman, a local architect, designed the house. At the time, the Haselwoods still had four children living at home, so they had a four-bedroom, two-bathroom "kids' wing" built at one end of the house and their own master bedroom wing at the other.

Between them, they have seven children and 11 grandchildren, so the swimming pool and the extra bedrooms get plenty of use, especially during family gatherings in the summer.

It was Dan Robinson who suggested

Down the road — on the west side of Alderbrook Inn— is the compound owned by Bill Gates, the founder of Microsoft whose net worth was recently reported at $4 billion.

the palm trees. Mediterranean fan palms do just fine in the Northwest, Haselwood says. They've been thriving on his Hood Canal property for 13 years and can be seen on the road to West Hills Honda too.

Clark Gable may not have lived on the canal, but he would have felt right at home among the palms.

Find a Place to Visit

Clark Gable may never have owned the castle-like home on the South Shore of Hood Canal, despite persistent rumors, but he once stayed at the elegant Willcox House on the canal.

And those who can't afford to buy a place on Hood Canal can still experience the serene beauty of a night or a weekend on the water, as Gable did.

In recent years, a number of owners have opened bed and breakfast inns or single cottages to the public. Accommodations range from refurbished cabins to the Willcox House. Here's a listing of canal-side accommodations:

• Canal House, 29993 Hudson Ave. NE, Poulsbo 98370, 779-2758: A guest house right on the beach. Cook-your-own breakfast. $80 per night. Coburn Allen, owner.

• Clark's Seaside Cottages, E. 13990 Hwy 106, Belfair 98584, 275-2676: Three rooms in cottages across Highway 106 from the water with beach access and water views. $85-$115 per night. Jim and Judy Clark, owners.

• Right Smart Cove Cottage, 426 Wawa Point Rd., Brinnon, 796-4626: Cottage on private beach, sleeps 4. $65 per night/$350 per week. Sandy Spalding, owner.

• Seabreez Cottage, 16609 Olympic View Rd. NW, Silverdale 98383, 692-4648: Private house on the beach with hot tub and view of the Olympics. $99-$129 per night. Dennis Fulton, owner.

• Summer Song, Bed and Breakfast, P.O. Box 82, Seabeck 98380, 830-5089: One beach cottage, breakfast served on the beach when weather permits. $55/weekdays; $65/weekends. Sharon Barney, owner.

• Tides End Cottage, 10195 Manley Rd. NW, Seabeck 98380, 692-8109: One cottage on beach, full equipped. $60 per night/weekly rates. Gerry Taylor, owner.

• The Walton House, 12340 Seabeck Hwy. NW, 830-4498: Decorated with antiques. Two guestrooms with private baths, $63 and $72.50; vacation apartment, $75. Shirley and Ray Walton, owners.

• The Willcox House, 2390 Tekiu Rd., Bremerton 98312, 830-4492: Five rooms with views, $100-$155. Private beach and pier; guests may arrive by boat or seaplane.

Prices quoted were for 1990.

The scenery is always different because of the play of the sun and the clouds around the mountains.

Demand for waterfront homes on Hood Canal has outstripped supply.

Section 4

Waterfront Land Rush

By Travis Baker

The story of hordes of Californians washing over the landscape and driving up land prices around Hood Canal may be an urban myth.

They don't exist, unless they're stopping off in King County first.

Real estate people and canal residents seem to agree. The price pressure that has made canal property hard to find and harder to pay for is coming out of the Seattle area, not from the Golden State.

"We took a poll in the office," said Bonnie Davies, associate broker at Reid Realty in Belfair, "as to who was buying here, and it was mostly Seattlites getting ready to retire and thinking ahead and coming over and buying acreage."

"The demand comes from the Seattle market, the I-5 corridor, at least 80 percent of it," agreed Leonard Schmidt, broker at Realty 7 in Belfair.

Added Jerry Rogers of ERA Olympic Realty in Jefferson County, "The I-5 corridor is growing, and some of those folks want to get back to where they used to be but they're not anymore."

A lot of new residents and recreational owners have come to Dewatto Bay in the 15 or 20 years she has been spending the warm half of the year there, notes Lydia Wood, an Old Belfair Highway resident the rest of the year.

"Most of them are from Kent and Auburn," she said, "a few from Seattle. Most of the time a friend comes out and brings a friend, and then buys a little piece of property."

That pattern isn't universal, however.

Karen Ramsey of John L. Scott's Poulsbo office said Californians make up a good share of that office's clientele.

But Kitsap County statistics compiled by the Digest of Real Estate Sales and Loans, a Port Angeles publication, said that of 5,338 sales throughout this county in the first seven months of 1990, 250 buyers came from California and 1,185 were from the Seattle area.

Whoever is buying Hood Canal

property, there's a lot less to buy than there was just three years ago, said the real estate people. A buying spurt in 1988 and 1989 cleaned out a backlog of unsold properties, and new listings have not been plentiful enough to replace them.

But once again, the answer changes somewhat as one moves north. Jerry Rogers, a sales associate at ERA Olympic Real Estate, located alongside Highway 104 a couple miles north of the Hood Canal Bridge, said there is a lot of undeveloped waterfront property that changes hands from time to time. And Jack Westerman, Jefferson County assessor, said "We have a large number of bare-land waterfront sales."

But land with homes on it is as scarce as to the south, said Rogers.

"People just don't want to sell their homes."

What sells does so for increasingly higher prices.

Westerman said his staff is reappraising the Chimacum School District this year and he expects land values there to double from the previous appraisals four years earlier. Rogers said prices of canal waterfront had been going up 10 percent a month until the middle of last summer, "but it was way behind everybody else to start with.

"People came and bought the Seattle area waterfront, then the (San Juan) Islands, then suddenly they discovered Jefferson County wasn't very far away and prices went up."

But they're still lower than in Seattle, he noted, and Frank Leach, associate broker at John L. Scott in Silverdale agreed. "Values here are miniscule compared to King and Snohomish county," he said. One hundred and thirty feet of waterfront on Hood Canal that might bring $130,000 here could go for 10 times that at Maidenbauer in Bellevue, he said.

Darryl Cleveland, assessor in Mason County, said property valuation increases on Hood Canal waterfront have moderated. His staff reappraised that end of the county for this year's taxes and found only 13 to 20 percent growth over the previous four years.

The land is the thing on the waterfront.

"Improvements are the lowest part of the assessment," noted Mac McKenzie of All Points Properties and past president of the Kitsap County Association of Realtors. Davies with Reid Realty in Belfair agreed.

"It makes it hard to do a market analysis for a client," she said. "We have such a diverse kind of house out here. We can have a $200,000 house with what looks like a $50,000 house next door, but it will cost you $150,000" because the land is so valuable.

Waterfront buyers are a breed apart when it comes to financing, too, said Schmidt at Realty 7. VA purchasers are becoming more plentiful with interest rates at 9 percent, he said. But they're the upland buyers.

"Waterfront buyers (often) put down 50 percent cash," he said.

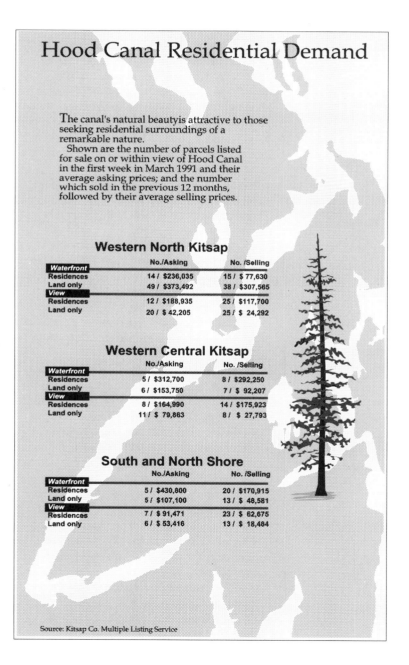

Bev Horning, who sold the Happy Hollow convenience store to the Templeton's chain early in 1990, said her six years in the business saw the South Shore of the canal become more permanently populated. She knew of a lawyer and a father and son in the contracting business who flew to work from their homes on the canal.

"You also have a lot of young business people who are more affluent than others. They have beautiful homes on the canal and spend four days on the canal and work three in Seattle. Others commute from Tacoma and Olympia.

But the area remains essentially "a giant retirement community, but one of extremely vivacious people. They might be 55 or 85 years old, jogging down the road."

Many were not full-time residents. "We'd see the influx of people on Thursdays. And it became a very consistent business for me at Happy Hollow whenever there were storms or high tides as people came to check their homes."

Buyers on the canal want summer homes, a place to retire and, occasionally, a place to live now. Retirees and those planning their retirement make up a huge proportion of canal real estate prospects.

Not all retire there.

"Many people buy with a dream of a chalet on an acre," said Leach in Silverdale, "But they don't — for medical reasons or being closer to shopping."

No matter. They buy the land, often paying top price and creating the impression that newcomers are resented by the longtime residents.

If that's true, it appears to exist more in the abstract than in connection with specific individuals. And it tends to erupt around the time the county assessor sends out notices of revaluation. The tax statements themselves are easier to take, said Westerman.

State law cushions the property owner from the full impact of his escalating value, so that taxes increase substantially less than the land value.

"We've seen that if we look in other areas," said Westerman. "There was an unbelievable reaction to value increases in King County last year, but not a fraction of the same concern now that the tax statements have been mailed."

But some, like Ester Starcevich of King's Spit south of the Bangor submarine

base, have a much longer view than one year. Ester says the progression of higher and higher taxes, however moderated by cushions in the laws, worries her.

But she holds no animosity for the individual moving here.

"The Californians we've known have been very nice," she said. "I don't blame them for getting out of there, do you?"

Buyers, Dig Deep

Is $1.2 million more than your pocket book can stand? Can you go $219,000, or $209,500, or $159,500?

Those are the prices of four of the ever smaller array of Hood Canal waterfront homes on the market earlier this month.

The $1.2 million place is the 10-acre-plus Daviscourt complex on low-bank South Shore Road in Mason County.

The $219,000 was the asking price for a two-bedroom home with 1,400 square feet on 1.25 acres with 100 feet of low bank waterfront in Jefferson County. It's on the remote Coyle Peninsula, halfway down the west side of the canal.

For $209,500, you could get a brand new 1,200-square-foot rambler with three bedrooms and two baths on a 70-by-300-foot medium-bank lot in Kitsap County near Hood Canal Bridge.

And if you can scrape together $159,500, it would buy you a double-wide mobile home at Bald Point, 18 miles out North Shore Road from Belfair at the Great Bend in the canal. You'd get a 50-by-100-foot lot with no-bank, bulkheaded water frontage.

That, it would appear, is rock bottom for buying a home on the canal.

A reliable inventory of available real estate all around the canal isn't easily available. But the Computer Multiple Listing Service in Silverdale can give a good picture of prices between Union in Mason County and the northern extreme of the canal in Kitsap County, providing the land is listed with a CMLS-member Realtor.

A CMLS printout in March 1991

The price pressure that has made canal property hard to find and harder to pay for is coming out of the Seattle area, not from the Golden State.

listed 24 waterfront homes for sale by its members between Union and Foulweather Bluff. There had been 43 waterfront homes sold between the two points in the 12 months prior to that week.

Comparable figures for homes with a canal view (27 available, 62 sold), raw land on the water (60 available, 58 sold) and raw land with a canal view (37 available, 46 sold) suggested there are properties to look at.

As with all waterfront, undeveloped Hood Canal frontage is sold by the front foot. Darryl Cleveland, assessor in Mason County, said North Shore waterfront is worth between $1,200 to $1,250 per foot just now, with South Shore going for up to $1,400. A hundred feet of shoreline in those areas, therefore, could set you back $120,000 to $140,000.

That's for land with good depth, and room for a home and septic tank. Beachfront property on which a home would have to be built across the road drops to about $400 per front foot, he said. Construction on such lots can be difficult due to the steepness of the terrain lining the canal.

High-bank waterfront in the difficult-to-reach Dewatto area goes for $200 to $300 per foot, he added.

The economics of lots with a view of the canal, but no frontage, can be peculiar, he said. In some places, it doesn't matter how big the lot is — within reason. The view is what's being purchased, and the price is the same to be looking out from a third-of-an-acre lot as a half-acre, he said. Twenty thousand dollars is a likely price for those lots, if unimproved.

Jeff Chapman, chief appraiser for Assessor Jack Westerman in Jefferson County, says the mostly high-bank canal frontage in his county ranges from $500 per foot on the Coyle Peninsula to about $1,000 near Port Ludlow. Just south of the Hood Canal Bridge, $600 to $700 is a common per-foot price, he said.

Elmer Harding, a salesman with ERA Olympic Real Estate alongside Highway 104 in Jefferson County, said his firm had only one canal home listed, the one on the Coyle Peninsula.

But for $145,000 a person could claim 10 acres with 371 feet of unimproved lowbank waterfront and extensive tidelands. That's only $390 per foot, but it's located on remote Tarboo Bay in Jefferson County.

Two-and-a-half acres of high bank waterfront on the Coyle Peninsula sounds like a bargain at $39,500, Harding said. But add another $15,000-$20,000 if you want electricity, which would have to be run to the lot.

Asking prices near Hood Canal Bridge vary. There was 7-10ths of an acre with 76 feet of high bank for $102,000. For $155,000, there was a whole six acres just four miles away. And $130,000 would buy five acres with 284 feet of high bank in the same area.

There were other homes available on the North and South shores in Mason County, said Bonnie Davies of Reid Realty in Belfair. For $175,000, you could get an old fixer house suitable as a summer cabin on a good-sized 75-by-235-foot lot. That's $2,333 per front foot and the house may subtract value rather than add it.

South Shore also offered homes on the water from $205,000 and $350,000. The latter one has a dock.

Frank Leach, associate broker at John L. Scott Real Estate in Silverdale, said canal waterfront in Kitsap County can run from $600 per front foot for "really lousy waterfront" — high bank and mostly unusable beach — to $3,000 for low bank and some high bank with good depth.

Mid-range prices for Hood Canal waterfront homes is $450,000, he said, but a 110-by-325 waterfront lot on Stavis Bay Road with a 1,500-square-foot home in average condition could be had for $175,000, according to CMLS data.

By Travis Baker

SECTION 5

MORE THAN
THE SUM
OF ITS
HUMAN
PARTS

John Davis

A Farmer Is Displaced

As a young boy growing up near Belfair 35 years ago, John Davis has some fond memories.

On most weekends, he and his brothers and sisters would pile into the family wagon on the family farm and head to town, where they sold fresh produce between the gasoline pumps at Pope's Grocery Store.

Beans and pumpkins sold for a nickel, and an average take for each of the Davis children was about 25 to 30 cents a day.

"We used to sell out of all our vegetables and then go home," Davis remembers. "But today? People wouldn't dare send a kid to do that today."

What happened then and what's happening now weighs heavily on Davis. He's probably one of the most traditional farmers in Western Washington and yet he feels that tradition has been squeezed from its place, even in once-sleepy Belfair.

Now, the 45-year-old Davis says, "I'm outa here." And he means it literally.

Davis and his wife Judy left the family farm north of Belfair and Hood Canal in 1991 to make a new home on an 80-acre spread near Ladysmith, Wis.

And in Belfair, losing Davis is big news. He is one of its most well-known and recognizable citizens and certainly one of its most ardent farmers.

The streets of town have been wiped clean of Davis and his favorite mode of travel — an old-fashioned horse and buggy.

Davis' reasons for leaving seem to reflect a few facts of life in Belfair. He said the last straw happened about a year ago when he was hired to plow a lot on Treasure Island, in Puget Sound, about seven miles south of Belfair, and, in turn, the islanders complained about the way Davis crossed their one-lane bridge with his wagon team and the droppings his horses left behind.

"I told them that since they drive an automobile and use gas and oil, they are more a part of pollution than I am," said Davis, who refused to clean up after his animals.

Davis says he can remember when Treasure Island had only a handful of houses, and now it's covered with permanent homes and summer cottages. In essence, that's what has turned him off to the area of Hood Canal closest to the population centers of Bremerton, Tacoma and Seattle. "This is suburbia now. It's gone."

Dressed in overalls and a workshirt, the dark-bearded Davis talked about life in general a few weeks before his move.

Davis is strongly opposed to the urban sprawl he believes has come to Belfair. He's watched it since he first located here in 1952. "Instead of adjusting to the city and suburban life, these people have come out here and destroyed this," Davis said. "Loggers have been driven out of the lowlands, and the price of farming has become so expensive around here it's impossible to even consider it. So I am going where there is no urban sprawl."

Sand Hill Road was once a dirt strip, at best, and now it's a major asphalt artery linking Tiger Lake with North Shore Road. Just a few years ago, a new elementary school was built about a mile from Davis' farm — another sign of a growing population.

Many of those newcomers to Belfair are people who work on federal military installations in Kitsap County and commute to Bremerton and Silverdale. Like the first homesteaders who settled this territory nearly a century ago, they're looking for low-priced land in a natural setting. And they are willing to commute more than a half-hour to work in order to live there.

"If they want to work a 40-hour-a-week job, they should live where they work and try to make that community a better place to live," said Davis. "It's just not necessary for everybody to have five acres of land and have to commute such long distances to work."

The car has caused much of the problem, he adds. And that's one reason he prefers to get around with a team of horses and a wagon instead of an automobile. His wife still drives a car, but Davis likes horse-power, both on the road and on his farm.

Davis sold his dairy cattle several years ago when the wholesale market dried up. He has raised corn, potatoes, oats, and timothy.

"Farming is more than just a job," he said. "It's a place you want to be 24 hours a day. It's a place you hope your children will take over some day and you want that farm in a place your children would be willing to accept.

"But there is no way I could stay on this farm and expect to turn it over to my children. If I stayed, I'd be giving them a third generation farm — and I'd be giving them nothing."

By Jim Rothgeb

Love of the Outdoors Drew Them to the Canal

Teresa and Mark Barron of Quilcene know why they live on Hood Canal. "Our love of the outdoors drew us together," she said. "Our courtship was in kayaks."

They celebrated their first wedding anniversary on June 21, 1990.

From their residential vantage point on Thorndyke Bay along the deep, cold canal, the Barrons enjoy "just watching animals and seeing what they do," she said.

Barron is a native of the region and his wife came to this area 12 years ago from Los Angeles.

He is an artist, crafting pottery mostly

• • • • • • • • • •
"But there is no way I could stay on this farm and expect to turn it over to my children. If I stayed, I'd be giving them a third generation farm — and I'd be giving them nothing."
— John Davis

and firing it in an ancient-style Japanese kiln he built himself. He is also a self-employed carpenter.

She is employed by the Jefferson County Planning Department, and formerly worked with the Makah Tribe near Forks, the Olympic National Forest, Olympic National Park and with fisheries in Alaska. She has a master's degree in resource management planning and also raises miniature horses on their Hood Canal acreage.

Forests of the nearby Coyle Peninsula burned around the turn of the century and now is in various stages of second growth, including some "remnant monster" trees that have survived.

The 70-year-old second growth creates a "canopy of green" for the Barrons and the wildlife living along the canal.

"We've got deer, osprey, owls, pileated woodpeckers, just to name a few animals," she said. "Having this privacy and rapport with nature ... makes us feel protective of our environment and puts pressures on us to keep the extraordinary quality of life we have, to keep it as nice as it is now."

The area is experiencing "lots of spillover from Kitsap and King counties," she said, as folks burned out on urban life seek a different lifestyle.

"The world is coming to us now. It's at our threshold, although we really don't want the world to settle here. Everyone who lives here feels especially privileged to be here. Besides New Zealand and Alaska, I've never seen a more beautiful, undisturbed place," she said.

By Gene Yoachum

Afraid That the Best Is Gone

Growing up, quite literally, on and in Hood Canal had an effect on Ron Hirschi, a former fish and wildlife biologist and author of children's books.

The 43-year-old Hirschi and his wife, Brenda, have lived on Miller Bay near Suquamish for the past three years. Prior to that, they lived at Vinland, north of Bangor.

He worked several years as a fish and wildlife biologist, most recently with the Port Gamble S'Klallam Tribe at Little Boston. This year, Hirschi decided to devote his energies to writing full-time.

"My inspiration for doing what I do

• • • • • • • • • •
"My inspiration for doing what I do came from having grown up on Hood Canal and getting to know and love the wild places I knew as a kid."
— Ron Hirschi

came from having grown up on Hood Canal and getting to know and love the wild places I knew as a kid," he said.

Much of the historical perspective Hirschi has about the canal came from his grandmother, who told him about her grandfather settling at Seabeck in the 1850s. Later, Hirschi's great-great-grandfather bought the Brinnon homestead at the mouth of the Duckabush River.

"My grandma always told stories about big elk herds at the mouth of the Dosewallips River, of cougars, of signs of elk in Kitsap County when she was small," Hirschi said. "Then, I started seeing changes in my own lifetime, and I became worried about losing what we have on Hood Canal and wanted to pass on what I knew about the natural world to kids."

That inspired him to write his books.

"The canal has been my roots, my home," Hirschi said. "I grew up in Port Gamble. My father worked in the mill, my grandfather and great-grandfather. I never worked a day at the mill, but I spent a lot of time following my dad around and fishing from the docks."

The decline of fishing in the canal is something Hirschi has viewed with sadness.

"In Kitsap and Jefferson counties, the streams are really being neglected," he said. "Maybe it's because we tend to think that it's the bigger streams where all the fish come from, but it's all the small creeks where they really come from."

As a 12-year-old, Hirschi and his friends, had an informal agreement relating to a small, unnamed stream where an alder sawmill was located.

"This was the first place I ever saw fish spawning and even as kids, we had an agreement that you couldn't keep fish you caught in that stream," he said.

But a few years ago a local logging company clear-cut along the banks, sprayed 2-4D on maple trees along the banks and then piled wood chips in the headwaters.

"The combination of all that means there are no more fish in there now," Hirschi said. "A very valuable run of cutthroat trout was wiped out."

The gradual destruction of the natural habitat of Hood Canal by increasing numbers of people has been disheartening, Hirschi said. It's prompted him to make a "painful decision," to leave Hood Canal and Puget Sound for a life in Montana. The

Hirschis planned to leave the area sometime during 1991.

By Gene Yoachum

Enjoying the Lush Greenery

Moving to Hood Canal from Montana more than 50 years ago "was the best move we ever made," according to Alvin Ackerman, now 66, of Quilcene.

The hot, dusty, grasshopper-infested wheat fields of Wolf Point, Mont., were no match for the lush greenery and mild climate of Puget Sound and Hood Canal, Ackerman said, recalling when his parents and 10 of the family's eventual 13 children came to Washington.

"We couldn't imagine all these green trees and winter; it was so warm," he said. "There were all these fruit trees and such. We'd never seen apple trees before, and we got out of the car and climbed up and picked some of those apples."

Ackerman's wife, LaVerle, 63, also came to Washington from elsewhere. She was 5 years old when her parents "got tired of Wisconsin and came here to dig clams and find a job," she said.

The two went through Quilcene schools together and then Ackerman went into the Army during World War II and was awarded a Purple Heart after being wounded in Germany.

After his return to civilian life, her husband-to-be came to her house one day on the pretext of "looking for some timber," she said. "My folks, they always laughed about that."

The couple has been married 42 years and had four children, three of whom live in Quilcene.

Quilcene has offered the Ackermans a quiet life, "well, at least it used to be quiet," she said, adding that even as the pace in their community has picked up some, "at least we're not like Silverdale."

By Gene Yoachum

He Fights for the Canal

The water of Hood Canal nearly laps at his doorstep, but he cannot eat its bounty.

The oysters and clams in front of his home are tainted by septic runoff.

The contrast between natural beauty and pollution is evident to Ralph Lartz, 60, of Belfair.

"We can shoot for the moon, but we can't even take care of the earth," Lartz said, shaking his head.

Lartz, however, is willing to do his part.

He recently led a citizen group that developed North Mason's first water quality protection plan.

The plan, adopted in October1990, represents the first time in 20 years that Mason County has amended its comprehensive plan, the document that sets policies for development.

The water quality plan also represents the first time Mason County has developed a "sub-area" plan that looks at just one of the corners of the county instead of the county as a whole.

Past countywide changes to the comprehensive plan were shot down by people with their own neighborhood interests in mind, Lartz said. The solution was to allow large "neighborhoods" to develop their own plans.

"He's really done a tremendous job up there," said Eric Fairchild, Mason County planning director. "That subarea plan paves the way for other areas of the county to follow."

Lartz and a group of North Mason representatives spent three years pulling together factions to hammer out the water quality plan. Essentially, it limits development on environmentally sensitive lands.

"Citizens have to take the opportunity and do the work themselves if they want it to get done," Lartz said. He already is putting time in on his home computer to write drafts of ordinances to enforce the goals in the plan. He's working on a drainage and grading ordinance now.

Lartz isn't a professional land-use planner. But he has coupled his problem-solving skills with a concern for the environment.

Lartz retired 10 years ago from AT&T, where he set up a regional computer maintenance division that guided the Northwest AT&T region toward awards for more "up time" than anywhere else in the nation.

He and his wife bought property along the canal in 1983. He joined the Christ Lutheran congregation, and no sooner did he join than an opening occurred for the job of retreat manager at the Christ Lutheran center

• • • • • • • • • •

"Citizens have to take the opportunity and do the work themselves if they want it to get done."
— Ralph Lartz

on Hood Canal.

He joined the North Mason Kiwanis and North Mason Chamber of Commerce. Both have proved to be outlets for his environmental concerns.

Last year the Kiwanis Club sought a project to commemorate its 75th anniversary. The club wanted to see one-stop recycling in Belfair. Lartz organized a group of Kiwanians and Lions. The group secured a site at the North Mason School District complex. Now it's monitoring Mason County Garbage efforts to receive a hauling permit.

A year ago he set up a recycling center at the Christ Lutheran Retreat. It's used by the community as well as the congregation.

His involvement with the chamber eventually led him to its presidency, and to lead the committee that developed the water quality plan.

Lartz was intrigued by the grant-funded process of assessing community knowledge of water quality. He helped survey his neighbors, then helped work on a community education slide show.

"The really surprising thing of it all is how little we know about our own earth."

The water quality plan probably won't be the last of his efforts to understand.

By Jessie Milligan

*Sculptor Ken Lundemo was raised on Hood Canal,
and he returned to pursue his art full time.*

Inspiration from the Canal

For artists, Hood Canal is more than a pretty place. It's an inspiration, a refuge, an obsession, and sometimes a struggle.

Like everyone else, they watch sunsets paint the water pink and follow fog curtains up and down the mountains.

Unlike everyone else, they can turn a ridge of snowy mountains into an ice-blue painting. Or convert a circling seal and yellow trees into poetry.

Artists are not immune to the beauty of the fjord. But their connection is more complicated.

For John and Iriss Blaine it's been a sanctuary for the past four years.

The couple traded their big-bucks life in Chicago for a low-income, low-stress life in Union.

In their version of the popular American success story, they owned a 3,600-square-foot house and an acre of land in the suburbs. Their incomes added up to six figures. They both worked 60 hours a week in commercial art — he was an art director at an ad agency and she was advertising manager for a 46-store chain. Their lives yo-yoed around deadlines and other people's agendas. There was never time to paint.

"We were burnt out from creativity on command," said John. "And all we felt like doing was turning on the TV," added Iriss.

Though they wanted to get off the high-pressure treadmill, the Blaines didn't know what their alternative was.

To help them crystalize what they did want, they enlisted a therapist-friend to ask questions. High on both wish lists were closeness to nature, time to develop creative energies, and making a living at what they liked.

• • • • • • • • •

SECTION 6

A HAVEN FOR
ARTISTS

*By Deborah
Woolston*

● ● ● ● ● ● ● ● ● ●

"The canal changes so rapidly. It's so diverse and primal. Sometimes I think I'll get jaded after living here four years, but I still get a rush every time I see it. I don't care which way you turn, it's unbelievable scenery."

— John Blaine

The Blaines sold the house, squeezed what they could into a 29-foot trailer, closed the savings account, and headed west to a caretaker job they'd lined up outside Shelton.

The first two years were tough. Their old car sucked up their savings and the Blaines couldn't find work they had assumed would be available. Every minimum wage job, such as cutting Christmas trees, attracted dozens of contenders.

If money problems weren't enough, the couple got cabin fever in their little trailer home. The promised studio wasn't ready and they missed their friends, family, and the cultural attractions of the big city.

"But I'd go outside and take a deep breath and say 'Thank you,' " recalled Iriss. "Even with the financial difficulties, it was worth it."

"And never for one second did I think I'd made a mistake," said John.

By then, he'd developed moral objections to advertising.

What pulled the couple out of their financial quagmire was John's hobby of gardening. What he used to do for weekend relaxation in Prospect Heights paid the bills in Mason County.

Four years ago, he found the ideal job. In return for taking care of a 1.5-acre waterfront estate for a couple in their 70s, the Blaines get a paycheck, flexible work schedule, and a little cabin with a wide-angle canal view and studio for two.

They make a fraction of their Chicago income. Though they can only afford overnight trips if they camp out, they earn enough between John's gardening and handyman jobs and Iriss' housekeeping and free-lance commercial art work to survive.

Nirvana is how John described their new life in Union. They work at what they like to do, they set their own schedules, and there's lots of time for art.

In the beginning, John's imagination was a little rusty after years of catering to other people's creative agendas. To discover his own artistic style, he did a lot of spontaneous black-and-white sketching.

To his surprise, he'd changed from a photo-realist to an impressionist. The canal and the climate could have triggered the switch.

"What intrigues me are what artists call atmospherics," John said. "That's how the atmosphere affects the colors and the depth of field. On a gray day or late in the day, for example, the mountains look like they're cut out of cardboard.

"The subject matter is everywhere. If I have a problem here, it's that there's too much. I could spend the rest of my life painting the same view, and yet it's impossible to get in a picture. It's a challenge. But it's intimidating too."

Then Iriss rushed upstairs to announce a spectacular sunset in progress outside. The Blaines dashed outside to the edge of the canal and gawked. To the west, bands of pink and green sky glowed above the sawtoothed mountain ridge stretching north, while distant lights and stars winked on in the darkness of the north and east. Before them, circling ducks cut curves in the glassy pink water and quacked in the stillness.

"The canal changes so rapidly," John said. "It's so diverse and primal. Sometimes I think I'll get jaded after living here four years, but I still get a rush every time I see it. I don't care which way you turn, it's unbelievable scenery."

"Won Over" by the Canal

The poet and the violinist came for jobs. The sculptor came for marriage. Both the jobs and the marriage ended.

The three artists stayed, and now they wouldn't live away from Hood Canal. For them, it's the perfect mix of peace, scenic beauty, and urban availability.

"This is the best combination of solitude and accessibility to the city," said Katherine Michaels, the sculptor.

Though she deliberately left the city when she moved to 11 acres overlooking Paradise Bay 15 years ago, she still needs the city. Someone who makes a living from art can't ignore Puget Sound's artistic nerve center.

"What I like is that I can come to the woods, which is quite inspirational, and then can take the ferry to Seattle to do business and see people," she explained.

The other two artists agree. When they came to Seattle for jobs at the University of Washington, it seemed like cultural Siberia from their East Coast perspectives. After several decades, it's their cultural home.

"I thought it was exile," admitted William Matchett, whose two-year stint in the UW English Department stretched into 35 years. Four years ago, he retired and moved full time to the sprawling waterfront house in Nellita.

But Matchett and his wife, Judy, keep an apartment in Seattle. They almost qualify as commuters they take the ferry so often to go to the theater, music, and dance events, not to mention social occasions.

Seattle is for cultural fun, but Hood Canal is home. That's where Matchett writes poetry.

Alan Iglitzin, on the other hand, spends his summers on Hood Canal and lives in Seattle the rest of the year when the Philadelphia String Quartet is not on tour. Since it was cut from the UW's economic apron strings in 1982, the quartet has gone through a lot of changes.

But Iglitzin, the only original member left, continues his mission of demystifying classical music and performers. The derelict dairy farm he restored to house the Olympic Music Festival and Chamber Music Institute plays a big part.

"When we started, we had a very clear idea of what would be an ideal atmosphere for teaching young people and a having a music festival — relaxation and the beauty of nature," said Iglitzen.

During the 10-weekend festival, the musicians play in jeans and sweatshirts in the renovated dairy barn to an audience sitting inside on benches and hay bales and outside on the grass. The resident burros often bray in the background.

"We wanted to be more approachable by people who are put off by musicians who have the aura: I'm a great artist and I don't rake leaves. That's absurd.

"Besides, the country life gives you a reality which is different from winter planes and trains," he went on. "You hear the animals, play with them, and watch them grow. It puts you on another plane as a human being. I want to be a normal individual as well as be an artist — one thing doesn't preclude the other."

The concept of chamber music concerts in the country, a first in the Pacific Northwest, has been a hit with audiences. In fact, the festival is probably Hood Canal's biggest cultural event and attracts visitors from the throughout the Pacific Northwest as well as from the East Coast.

The flip side of Hood Canal's appeal

for artists is the solitude. It's a necessary part of the creative process.

"It's a beautiful place in which to create," said Michaels, the sculptor. "I like the solitude and peace and harmony.

"I work better when there's harmony — and I need a lot of different kinds of environments that make me think and feel."

In addition to a nurturing, creative climate, the canal also suggests subjects for her sculpture. Michaels, who used to teach environmental education, is drawn to natural themes such as her current series of oversized seapods.

Matchett also mines his Hood Canal life for ideas and images. The canal isn't richer than other places, though it's a lot more beautiful.

"Wherever I am, I write about it later," he explains. "I don't go and stare at the scenery, I sit in this room and think."

This room is a comfortable book-lined fireplace-equipped study, and what he thinks about are the patterns that emerge from his daily journal.

"This is where I live, so it has an impact. My poems tend to start as a response to a place and move to a quiet affirmation.

"But actually, I'm more involved in saving the canal than writing about it," Matchett said. Like several other canal artists, he's politically active, in his words, "to protect this place."

Making Time for their Art

On the wall of Ken Lundemo's huge, crowded Seabeck studio hangs a scarred white hardhat marked with a faded yellow-and-blue Bell Telephone logo.

It's a souvenir of the double life he led until his retirement from the phone company in 1983 after 28 years. The responsible breadwinner side of him stayed in a uninspiring job to support his family. The artist side of him longed to chuck the financial burden to become a full-time sculptor.

This conflict between family and art is a common one.

Virginia Hawkins experienced it from the domestic side. She postponed painting until her household responsibilities had eased. At the age of 43, she got a high school diploma in order to get into Olympic College to study art. Once Hawkins finally followed her dream, she's never looked back.

"It's a beautiful place in which to create. I like the solitude and peace and harmony."
— Katherine Michaels

"When I first moved into the woods, I did greens, the colors were overpowering. But I'm not good at green and I don't like it."

— Virginia Hawkins

Both artists are well-known in local art circles. Lundemo's sculptures in metal, clay and wood include a seagulls piece outside Edgewater East Apartments in Bremerton and the upended Viking ship at Poulsbo Middle School. Hawkins' paintings have been shown throughout Puget Sound, and her students number in the hundreds.

Their stories tell a lot about becoming an artist in the Hood Canal orbit. Not only do they experience opposite sides of the art-versus-family dilemma, they have different responses to the pull of this place.

Lundemo is a native who started a lifelong love affair with the canal when he was growing up in Seabeck. Over the years, he's boated, fished and scuba-dived in the water, and camped and gathered shellfish on the beaches.

Art trickled into his life slowly, first in high school and then in classes at Olympic College. After he met and married his wife, he bowed to economic reality at Puget Sound Naval Shipyard for a year, with the U.S. Navy for four years, and finally with the phone company.

"That had nothing to do with art," said Lundemo. "I just wanted to be a sculptor, a full-time artist doing what I wanted."

He tried. For eight years, he spent most of his free time in OC art courses and rarely saw his family. Though his sculptures sold, he had to fight for time to make them.

"You can't be an artist and a phone man," said Lundemo. "But maybe I should have been tough and gone fulltime. An artist is like any other profession — you have to be completely selfish and forget your family.

"But there's a problem of waiting until the time is right and time can pass you by — I may have waited too long."

By contrast, Virginia Hawkins has no regrets — except at first, when she moved very grudgingly to the Olympic View neighborhood from Long Beach, Calif., when her husband retired from the Navy 30 years ago.

"I liked city living," said the Brooklyn native, who didn't want to move to the boondocks.

But the family did, and Hawkins fell in love with the beautiful boondocks on the east side of the canal.

Her journey from busy homemaker to artist and art teacher started when she decided to go back to school after years of being a Navy wife.

"I used to draw," Hawkins said. "But when I got married and I made my choice — art or marriage. When we put roots down here and the kids were on their own, I did what I had wanted to do for a long time."

She took art classes at OC and painted in a dark basement in-between the household chores.

"I couldn't believe the changes in me," recalled Hawkins. "It opened doors, and I learned such confidence. At first I didn't believe I could be a good artist until I started winning awards and selling."

But it took a while for the canal to sink into her imagination and for Hawkins to find her style. The first paintings were traditional, realistic cityscapes of her native New York streets and the George Washington Bridge. Then came a wave of green landscapes that reflected the surrounding scenery of her new home.

"When I first moved into the woods, I did greens, the colors were overpowering," she said. "But I'm not good at green and I don't like it."

In recent years, Hawkins has specialized in impressionistic vistas of the mountains, which have filled her windows for years. A mix of acrylic paint over canvas and rice paper fragments, they have blurred outlines, steep angles, and soft blue-and-white tones.

"I've been exposed to this for so long," she said, nodding at snow-covered Olympics wedged between fir trees, "that I have mental images of the rocks and mountains."

Lately, stark images and colors of the Southwest and the Middle East, picked up during recent trips, have crept into her paintings.

"Now I'm going through a red period," Hawkins explained. "An artist paints what's available. To grow as an artist, you need to do different things.

"I don't paint just to sell," said Hawkins. "I paint to satisfy the creative urge. And sometimes I get so excited, I want to yell and celebrate."

Lundemo gets excited too, but one old temptation still lures him away from the studio. Three feet away from the faded telephone hardhat hanging beside the door, a short fishing pole leans against a workbench. It belongs to his young grandson, who is learning how to fish from a veteran.

"Fishing is a disease," says Lundemo. "Art is more of a blessing."

Once a Thriving Artist Colony

All that's left of the days when artists flocked to Hood Canal are some memories and a few pictures.

The glory days were after World War I, when passenger boats linked canal settlements with Seattle.

Union-bound artists made the 10-hour trip for all the reasons artists have fled cities for centuries. The little town on the southern crook of the canal had stunning scenery, peace and unhurried pace as well as local color in the form of loggers, fishermen and Indians.

After 70 years, the details are a little fuzzy. But Fritz Dalby, now 79, remembers. He ticked off members of the art crowd that included sculptors, painters, a piano-playing postmistress, musicians and writers. Of all the names, Ore Nobles and Waldo Chase are the most famous.

The story goes that Ore taught art at Ballard High School, traveled to the Far East, and hosted lots of studio parties.

Maybe he built the odd little cabins at Olympus Manor, the summer resort that became Hood Canal's art headquarters during the 1920s and 1930s. The pint-sized mansions had a Disneyland woodsy theme, according to Joe Morosco, who settled in Union 20 years ago and helped demolish the last one 10 years ago.

Waldo Chase, the other name that cropped up a lot, was one of the earliest Olympus Manor residents. Known as a woodblock artist and free-spirited bohemian, he moved into a tepee in 1929, recalled Dalby.

In 1935, Chase became front-page news the day after his pagan wedding to a vegetarian bride. Dalby, who was 22 at the time, remembered how this peculiar ceremony brought the townies, the loggers and the artists together on a hill above town.

"His bride was a natural-food faddist who could graze a hillside like burro," he said. "They were standing side by side in an old Indian robe, talking gibberish, and partaking of parched corn. A famous photographer from Seattle took a picture of that dumb dame running out of the brush and into the tepee. It made the magazine section of the Post-Intelligencer and went nationwide."

Dalby and Chase became good friends until Chase died in 1988. By then, most of the artists were gone from the canal. The cabins and studio were torn down in the late '70s to make way for the Blue Heron Time Share Condominiums.

It's the latest twist in the canal's fortunes. Dalby, who lives in Shelton, isn't very optimistic about its future.

"Before the developers moved in, Hood Canal was a beautiful place," he said. "They haven't ruined the mountains yet, but I figure they'll bulldoze the mountains and fill in the canal pretty soon. But I won't be alive to see it."

By Deborah Woolston

*Retired trapper Andy Rogers has
observed many changes during his
lifetime on Hood Canal.*

His white hair flowing in the breeze, Andy Rogers sat upon a driftwood log, watching the waves break upon the shore at Stavis Bay, a serene inlet 1 1/2 miles south of Seabeck.

Time has not changed the unceasing pattern of wind upon water — not since Rogers played in this same spot as a child, not since the first white explorers discovered Hood Canal, not since the original natives learned to hunt and fish here thousands of years ago.

Most everything else has changed, however, and Rogers has no room for regrets.

"I've worked as a logger and a trapper, and I've always been a conservationist," he said. "I never trapped to get the last animals. I trapped the dumb ones and let the rest remain free."

Rogers, 73, is independent, opinionated and even obstinate sometimes. He admits that he likes to argue. In fact, he's never happier than when jousting verbally with some high-minded environmental type.

"It's funny how well we've gotten along without dinosaurs," he told one young woman. "Was it clearcutting or logging that caused the problem?"

But when it comes to nature, few people can match Rogers' love for this Hood

SECTION 1

MEMORIES
OF THE
CANAL

*By Christopher
Dunagan*

Canal country, which is being altered day by day, week by week, year by year.

"Every time anybody moves here," he said, "it gets worse — and that includes me. You can't do anything about it. People have rights. It seems our rights are going to kill us in this country."

Others less independent-minded than Rogers, who have been here a shorter time, say it is not too late. But there is no agreement about how much government interference can be tolerated to protect public resources or how much taxpayers can afford to spend on keeping an ecosystem intact.

There is no doubt that the spread of human population continues to degrade the water quality and to drive away many species of wildlife (although a few animals, such as racoons and coyotes, have adapted quite well).

Rogers is old enough to remember the rise and fall of many trees. Much of the land was logged before he was born. Much has been logged again, and some even a third time.

"The '20s was the greatest era of logging," he said. "They were logging both sides of Hood Canal."

As for wildlife, most animals come back after a logging operation — some right away, some after the trees grow to a certain size. On the other hand, wild creatures have less tolerance for human habitation, which brings high-speed automobiles plus dogs and cats running wild through the woods.

In the early days, people were more direct. They'd shoot wild animals on sight, especially predatory beasts. Bears, cougars and wolves were considered a threat to people and livestock. Eagles and seals were a threat to salmon.

"All the things man killed as a matter of survival have become man's best friend," said Rogers with just a trace of scorn, though he agrees that Hood Canal becomes a lesser place when a species disappears forever.

The last cougar in the Stavis Bay area was killed in 1936, according to Rogers. A

couple others disappeared from the Big Beef area to the north in the 1940s.

Today, says Dave Brittell, a cat specialist with the Washington Department of Wildlife, the Kitsap Peninsula has been disturbed to the point that it cannot support an ongoing population of cougars.

On the other side of the Hood Canal watershed, in Mason and Jefferson counties, a curtailment in cougar hunting has allowed the population to stabilize at around 30 animals.

Cougars, said Brittell, tend to follow the migratory patterns of their prey — deer and elk — which move into the private lowlands in winter and onto higher federal lands in summer.

Putting even a single home in this migratory pathway could create additional problems for the animals, he added.

"If we have to have houses in those areas, we should concentrate the impact and not allow the scattering of houses up and down the valley," he said.

Ultimately, cougar populations are limited by their own density within the available habitat. Like other creatures at the top of the food chain, they have evolved a complex social system, including defined territories, said Brittell. Each male may command 50-60 square miles, likewise for females.

Younger cats have to seek out their own territories, which leads to conflicts with people living on the outskirts of civilization.

With the way things are going, says Rogers, there may come a day when there won't be room for cougars or even bears on private land.

Bobcats, being smaller and controlling less territory, remain plentiful in undeveloped parts of Hood Canal country. They may continue to co-exist with people to some degree.

"Bears could too if people would tolerate them," Rogers said. "But they can't because they are so dangerous."

According to Rogers, human beings have some major decisions to make about

Stavis Bay

Andy Rogers is old enough to remember the rise and fall of many trees along this Kitsap County inlet of Hood Canal.

the wildlife of Hood Canal.

"Man's the only one of the species who can control how many there are going to be."

Rogers, who had been rotating his time-worn hat in his hands, paused a moment, then plopped the soft object squarely upon his head.

"I remember my dad writing the governor and county commissioners, wanting to get a road out here," he said. "Then they wanted fire protection and utilities."

In those days, when people were few and far between, new residents helped improve the quality of life, at least in the minds of adults.

For a young boy playing in and around Stavis Bay in the 1920s, the world was the forests and the streams.

"When I was 10 or 11 years old," said Rogers, "I saw a sign that said, 'No trespassing.' I went and asked my mother what that was, because I had never seen that before. People went where they wanted to go."

Life seemed slower and more simple then, he said.

"There wasn't any ballgames to go to," said Rogers. "I spent my time going up and down the streams looking at fish."

Salmon were plentiful then, and you could depend on their migrations like clockwork.

"I knew the salmon would start up the creek about the 20th of August," said Rogers. "Pert' near all these streams were full of salmon by Labor Day."

Now almost all the salmon are gone, the result of too much fishing and too many seals, in the view of Rogers. For most of the streams, siltation from logging operations and man-made culverts have been only minor problems, says the old trapper, taking a somewhat contrary view to modern biologists.

When salmon are coming back in great numbers, they tend to clean the streams of silt as they dig into the gravel during spawning, he said.

As he talks, Rogers reaches down, picks up a broken clam shell and turns it over and over in his hand. He kicks at the sand with his tan, high-topped boots.

"Nature repairs itself awful fast when given the chance," he said.

Then he suggests something that seems out of character to this man who has made his livelihood from natural resources: If salmon fishing could be stopped for just four years (the life cycle of most salmon), natural production could recover to levels that would provide a wealth for future fishermen, he says.

Salmon numbers would rebound quickly, he continued. Bottomfish — some of which live to 40 years of age — would take longer to recover.

More than other species, the salmon is the symbol of Hood Canal and the entire Great Northwest. The magnificent fish expresses freedom by traveling thousands of miles through the ocean. It expresses an inborn responsibility by returning to its place of birth to begin a new generation of its kind.

"Salmon are keystone species," said Chris Frissell, a biologist at Oregon State University's Oak Creek Laboratory. "They are very critical for the food chain of the entire ecosystem. They provide food for dozens of species like eagles and otters and bears and ospreys, literally hundreds of species."

Because salmon are uniquely adapted to the stream of their birth, losing even one native run of wild salmon is losing something that cannot be replaced, says Frissell.

Frissell wrote a paper about the protection of salmon runs and entire ecosystems. He titled it "All the King's Horses and All the King's Men."

"An ecosystem is like an egg," he said. "It's not like a watch, which you can take apart and put back together."

The danger is that man does not understand what he is doing to the salmon resource, he said. Hatchery-bred fish from a distant river system are released in local waters, where they breed and compete with natural runs. It is not easy to measure the result.

Another example: Ocean fishing tends to catch the larger salmon because of the mesh size of the nets. This unnatural selection increases the proportion of smaller adults returning to spawn.

But it seems likely that in streams silted in by logging and development that the larger fish will be more successful at reproduction because they can dig deeper nests, called redds.

"Fishing is selecting for younger,

"Pert' near all these streams were full of salmon by Labor Day."
— Andy Rogers

smaller fish," said Frissell, "while a degraded stream habitat is selecting for older, bigger fish."

A decline of wild salmon in Hood Canal, particularly the coho, has intensified the debate over managing the salmon resource. The Skokomish Tribe, for example, has demanded that the Department of Fisheries reduce its commercial ocean harvest to allow more native coho to get back to their streams of origin.

"From our perspective," said Randy Harder of the Point No Point Treaty Council, "the department responds to public pressure. Right now, they are responding to the economic concerns of the fishing industry. They should be responding as well to public pressure to increase the escapement and rebuild the wild runs."

Harder objects to the "shortsightedness" of the Department of Fisheries, which advises people that Hood Canal will be all right within a few years.

"We are trying to educate the public that there may be restrictions on their fishing opportunities," he said. "The Skokomish Tribe has already accepted that they are not going to have a coho fishery on those stocks for some time. It is going to take awhile to get out of this hole."

Both the state and the tribes agree that more information is needed about the condition of stream habitat. They are

● ● ● ● ● ● ● ● ● ●

"An ecosystem is like an egg. It's not like a watch, which you can take apart and put back together."
— Chris Frissell, Oregon State University

negotiating toward a memorandum of understanding about how joint studies should be done and who will pay for them.

Rogers can remember steelhead in Stavis Creek. They had evolved there for thousands of years. But now they're gone.

"All these streams had steelhead," he said. "There was an old outlaw who had a bootleg market for them, and he'd put his nets out in front of the stream.

"After he died, they (steelhead) were so rare that our parents would show them to us whenever they would come in."

Rogers pushed himself up off the old driftwood log and began a short hike back to the road near his home. He had bought his 75 acres of land in 1952 for $10 an acre. Similar land had gone for $1 an acre during the Depression years, when few people had any money to spend.

Rogers supports the idea of using tax incentives to protect forest land and open space. He wants the county to offer incentives to developers who cluster their houses together.

"But you cannot shut the door and keep people out," he emphasizes, then glances again toward Stavis Bay.

"I'd sure like to stick around and see what this place is like in 50 years."

• • • • • • • • • •

SECTION 2

PRESERVATION
THROUGH
ACTION

*By Christopher
Dunagan*

In May 1991, The Sun asked five people who care a lot about Hood Canal to sit down together to discuss their concerns and ideas for the future.

They were:

Ron Hirschi is a former fisheries biologist for the Port Gamble S'Klallam Tribe. He now travels to schools around the country to teach children about the environment. He also writes books for children about ecology. He grew up in Port Gamble, but moved to Montana in 1991.

Marjorie Redman has been a member of the Puget Sound Water Quality Authority since its inception in 1985. A former member of the Kitsap County Planning Commission, she lives in a waterfront home on Hood Canal in North Kitsap.

Donna Simmons is a former president of Hood Canal Environmental Council and worked as education coordinator for the Hood Canal Coordinating Council. She is vice-chairwoman of the Washington State Ecological Commission and is a supervisor for a conservation district in Mason County. She lives in Hoodsport on Hood Canal.

Dennis McBreen owns and operates Seabeck Marina on Hood Canal. He is president of Hood Canal Salmon Enhancement Group and is active in Save Our

Salmon, Kitsap Poggie Club and Manchester Sports Club. He lives in Port Orchard.

State Sen. **Brad Owen**, D-Shelton, is a legislator from the 35th District, which includes a major portion of Hood Canal as well as the timber town of Shelton. Owen has served in the Legislature for 15 years. For the past three sessions, he has sponsored legislation that would make Hood Canal a sport fishing preserve.

Several others were invited but were unable to attend.

As the discussion opened, the atmosphere was lively, yet cordial. Like a group of friends who had gathered to talk about something important, they seemed to feel the freedom to disagree and even raise their voices at times.

One area of agreement was about what individual people can do. It all starts on a small scale, by working on a single stream, by improving small watersheds, they agreed. (Watersheds are areas of land that drain into a given body of water.)

What follows are excerpts from the two-hour discussion.

Hirschi: If we restore each of those streams, we may heal our community. When non-Indian people first came here, like my

"The question here is whether we now have the political will, whether environmental awareness has built up to the point where we're going to see citizen pressure put on decision makers..."

— Donna Simmons, Hoodsport

great-great-grandfather, they were here just to take, and we're still in that kind of mode. We're consuming and not giving back.

Redman: Working on smaller watersheds is a good way to get people involved. If you live on the stream, you are going to be concerned about what happens to it.

Driving around the southern part of Hood Canal, I must say that I don't know where the drainfields are. I see house, driveway, house, driveway, house, driveway — with no room for septic tanks.

For a small monthly fee — a lot smaller than what sewer districts charge — you could make sure that septic tanks are maintained. They are perfectly good ways of handling sewage, but they must be built right in the first place, and they have to be maintained.

Simmons: The big question here is whether we now have the political will, whether environmental awareness has built up to the point where we're going to see citizen pressure put on decision makers to put together some plans or regulations that will stick and start turning things around.

As for growth, it's not the level of growth so much as the kind of growth. Take a whole day and drive around the Hood Canal watershed and you will see this piecemeal chopping up of land, which I think is the greatest danger we face right now, and we don't have the controls in place.

I heard a friend of mine say the other day, in fact a developer, "We're five-acreing ourselves to death," and there's a lot of truth to that.

McBreen: I have three big concerns: that commercial development be done right. I'm also concerned about the marine life. And the third thing is that we have developed a rash of regulations that are no longer rational.

Owen: I believe we need to try to identify and set aside the canal as a marine fish preservation area and a natural area as much as possible for the nation and the world, because I believe the canal is a unique place.

We need to purchase sensitive lands along the canal ... We, as a state, need to find those lands that are still available and get those for the public, so it is not driveways all along (the shore). It's not going to get any cheaper.

Redman: The lack of opportunity for people to dig clams...is real sad.

Hirschi: Port Gamble Bay ... is right on the threshold of being decertified (for shellfish harvesting). Essentially the entire west side of Port Gamble Bay is undeveloped... Failing septic systems have something to do with the problem. A couple of small streams ... have something to do with the problem, because there are cows and horses still using the streams.

A frustration for me is in seeing the response of (public) agencies in not taking existing regulations, existing authority and existing money and doing something about those streams.

Destruction of watersheds by forestry practices has completely devastated the chinook (salmon) population. The wild chinooks are gone in the Dosewallips (in Jefferson County).

McBreen: The wild chinooks are gone in the entire canal. But that is not because of the streams not being able to take care of them.

Hirschi: Well, it's a big factor. Trust me. All that rock that has moved downstream in any number of the small tributaries from logging, and that has been a big factor in the Dosewallips.

Why not get a corridor of national park along one of these streams so we have management for ancient forest conditions? The Duckabush would be another good one. It's a beautiful stream, but 10 years from now you won't know it.

McBreen: The streams are there, and historically the salmon went up the streams and had things to feed on ... We took an artificial system that was developed by the Department of Fisheries because they wanted to have an inland chum fishery ... and we started producing thousands and thousands and millions and millions of chums in the hatcheries...

We now release these chums and we send them back out, OK? The Department of Fisheries has raised these 18 trillion chum. Now they send in 18 trillion purse seiners to take them, and where are they going to take them? They are going to take them right where they concentrate, right in front of the streams where they sit.

We don't allow anything to go up the streams. We fish the mouth of each stream so hard that there is no brood stock going up.

It's just a crazy thing.

Redman: What about the bottom fish...?

Hirschi: There may be some things as sport fishermen we've done, too. I was raised a Catholic and grew up in Port Gamble. It was my responsibility to bring home mostly rock fish for Friday dinners.

Owen: What you are saying is that there's too many Catholics?

(Everyone laughed.)

Hirschi: As a true sport fisherman, it was my duty to go out and catch as many fish as I could. I had enough rock fish in our freezer, as a 13-year-old, to last for two years.

We do over-harvest as sport fishermen, too, and I think it is important to take some personal looks at what we've done and maybe even forego some opportunities.

Owen: The draggers (commercial bottom fishermen) also contributed to that. (Draggers have since been eliminated from Hood Canal as a result of a bill by Owen.)

And I think a major contributor to the decline of bottom fish...is that the Department (of Fisheries) is behind the eight ball. They will wait until there is a problem. I think they need to think about managing it conservatively.

McBreen: One of the nicest things we saw during shrimp season was the fact ... that the kelp beds are starting to come back (following removal of drag fishing). For the first time, you'd pull up a pot and find big kelp. Three years ago we knew there was nothing there.

Simmons: I see two really big needs in this whole issue. If we're really serious about turning this around in the Hood Canal watershed, it requires — along the more technical lines — a change in the way we do things. Possibly that means regulations and enforcement, tax incentives, all kinds of ways we can change the way we do things.

But there's also a need for a change ... in the way we think.

Sometimes I get furious when I hear people go on and on about their rights, the right to buy view property and put a big house on it ... But that is not a right. That is a privilege to have an unobstructed view of the water.

If he (a property owner) carries his perception of rights to the point where he helps to eliminate another legitimate use of the water (such as shellfish growing), then that, in my opinion, is carrying things way too far.

Hirschi: Another perception that we have to change is we have to recognize the base of what we have to start with before we can even think for a minute that we can take something from it.

We have been taking so much from the canal since we first got here that we've exhausted a lot of the resources. I think there should be a moratorium on a certain number of harvest activities before we even think about more enhancement. We keep dumping salmon out into the canal without knowing what the carrying capacity is for juvenile salmonids.

Why don't we try to determine what the natural carrying capacities of each of the streams of Hood Canal are and manage for those carrying capacities, allowing them to produce what they can produce, then harvest the excess.

What I am saying gets into the uplands and puts a moratorium on growth as well ... We're almost driving a herd of elk to extinction ... We've lost 50 percent of the winter elk habitat on the Dosewallips and yet we continue to allow both housing increases in the watershed and fairly extensive logging ...

There's an awful lot of people in resource agencies ... who know biologically what is going on. We aren't listening to them. We are listening to political statements by management people in agencies who are only acting like any other political animal will act. They will make decisions to keep their jobs, and it's usually counter to what the land is telling them.

McBreen: Everybody is talking about putting more rules and regulations on things. We build one set of regulations for this group and another for that group, and they're not working. Part of the educational process is pointing to the good side of things. If we could educate people to understand that if we do it right, we will have jobs for people down the line.

Simmons: I have been an educator, and I agree. But I have also been around the block enough times to know that you simply cannot limit your range of alternatives or your tools.

I work with the (Mason County) Conservation District, and our first and foremost tool is education. We offer money.

"A frustration for me is in seeing the response of agencies in not taking existing regulations, existing authority and existing money and doing something about those streams."
— Ron Hirschi, Kitsap County biologist

We are not regulators; we don't have badges.

If we work with a farmer and maybe two years go by ... and he still has cows in the stream and he still has water running through a manure pile into the stream, we feel we have to be backed up with regulations.

I am lucky enough to have worked on environmental issues from a more radical beginning ... and I, like a lot of environmentalists, thought the solutions were regulatory. But I've also had the chance to work for government now, and I can see the problems for government and politicians.

I will agree that environmentalists may have made some mistakes by only pushing for regulations ... If you keep imposing restrictions, one after another, and sometimes regulations that are not even consistent ... pretty soon you have that farmer so frustrated that he will do exactly the kind of thing you are trying to prevent. He will sell that farm to the nearest developer, who will chop it up into 5-acre tracts.

Hirschi: I'm not sure that is what's driving people. I think a lot of times it's used by the forest products industry as an excuse.

We are losing our forest industry in Kitsap County, which I also see as very sad. That's one of the things I would put up near the top of the list of things that are special about the canal.

The forest industry sustained a group of people for a couple thousand years. It only took us 150 years to completely devastate it ... Education is taking place very slowly within fisheries agencies and slowly trickling down to enhancement groups. We all want to do good. We all want to go out and plant a tree or plant a fish. But we don't want to take the more difficult task of fixing what we have been destroying.

We have blocked run after run after run (of wild salmon), and this includes the canal. There are culverts everywhere ... there are miles of devastated stream banks.

The regulations are not strong enough.

Owen: I think logging practices have improved dramatically over the years, but they are not to the point the environmental community would like to see them. They would like to see a real, real diminishing of logging in the state of Washington, which they are succeeding in getting.

We have seen the pendulum, which swung too far to the loggers at one time, when they would literally shut off a stream with a dam to back up the water to run the logs down. Now (it is) overkill on the other side.

The logger has a place because this society has depended on paper products and housing.

McBreen: There has got to be a certain amount of development to put our kids to work. There has to be logging some places to take care of building houses. We have to drill oil wells to keep the cars running.

We can't let one teeny minority control what is good for the whole population. The canal is good for the people of Kitsap County. It is a place to go, a recreational area. It is a source of food for a lot of people. It is a potential commercial asset. It is a place to live and have jobs. It is a beautiful area.

I am an environmentalist. I work real hard to keep my marina clean. Let's not stop everything because it is not the way it was 20,000 years ago.

Owen: There are people out there who want you to think that nothing is working, that everything is getting worse, that logging practices aren't working, that education isn't working.

I think that is baloney. I can see in the 15 years that I have been in the Legislature my own self that the public's attitude on environmental issues has taken a tremendous turnaround. So it's bogus to say we are getting worse. We are getting better, but it's not to the point it can be yet. The issue is, how do we make it better ... without taking an industry like the logging industry, and totally wiping it out.

As far as the canal, I think it is worse today in some instances, but the attitude and movement is in the right direction.

"We fish the mouth of each stream so hard that there is no brood stock going up. It's just a crazy thing."
— Dennis McBreen, Seabeck Marina owner

To a New Environmental Ethic

Who in his right mind, some people ask, would destroy an entire industry of hard-working loggers and their families for the sake of an owl that isn't much good for anything?

Who in his right mind, other people ask, would belong to an industry that has destroyed 90 percent of the unique old-growth ecosystem and now wants to take the rest?

What we are seeing in this country may be more than a debate over protecting the northern spotted owl from extinction. We may be experiencing a powerful collision of moral values related to man's place in the natural world.

The same morality clash is reflected in issues related to timber management, fishing, development and recreation, according to philosopher J. Baird Callicott. And what may be emerging out of the conflict, he says, is a new environmental ethic for the 21st Century.

Callicott, a professor at the University of Wisconsin at Stevens Point, became interested in what he calls the "big picture" in the early 1970s, as Americans renewed their interest in protecting the environment.

Callicott, who formulated one of the first university courses in environmental ethics, says today's battles are part of an evolution in thinking, which actually began before the first lumbermen came to the Hood Canal region.

In the mid-1800s, Ralph Waldo Emerson and Henry David Thoreau expressed a love of nature "with a spiritual twist," said Callicott.

Emerson wrote that nature can be a temple in which to commune with God as well as a quarry from which to mine the ore of industry.

Natural history became an important part of Thoreau's writing, but both he and Emerson relied more on the experience of nature — its ability to spark creativity and imagination in man — than on natural science.

"The romantics," said Callicott, "were into experience — Thoreau, with his eyes narrowly focused on the things around him, and Emerson with his head in the clouds."

It took naturalist John Muir to turn this romantic-transcendental philosophy into a national moral campaign to appreciate and preserve wilderness.

Muir was not opposed to material things in a puritan way, said Callicott. But he despised the lumber barons, mineral kings and captains of industry who seemed "hell-bent upon little else than worshipping at the shrine of the almighty dollar."

John Muir, who was read by Theodore Roosevelt, had profound influence on the creation of many natural areas, including federal lands in and around the Olympic Mountains.

About the turn of the century, a new environmental ethic began emerging, says Callicott. Gifford Pinchot, a younger contemporary of John Muir, is credited with formulating the ethic. It is based upon science and the utilitarian view that human happiness should be the primary goal of government.

The values of "nature" in the romantic views that went before were reduced to "natural resources" by Pinchot, who became the first chief of the U.S. Forest Service.

"Natural resources," wrote Pinchot, "must be developed and preserved for the benefit of the many and not merely the few."

He also declared that "conservation means the greatest good for the greatest number of people for the longest time."

Said Callicott, "The higher uses celebrated by Emerson, Thoreau and Muir had to compete on all fours with industrial, agricultural and other utilitarian uses."

Economics became an integral part of the ethic. One could preserve the Yosemite Valley or the wild Olympics, said Callicott, but only if society was willing to place a price on the wilderness experience.

World War II brought the issue of patriotism into the equation.

"Mechanized technology was

● ● ● ● ● ● ● ● ●

I can see in the 15 years that I have been in the Legislature my own self that the public's attitude on environmental issues has taken a tremendous turnaround."
— State Sen. Brad Owen, D-Shelton

developed for war purposes and unleashed on the domestic scene," he said. "The whole industrialization of nature ratcheted up a quantum leap."

Protesting the exploitation of natural resources became unpatriotic. Science and technology became the driving force, and people pledged their faith to the experts.

Attempts to increase the production of natural resources led to the science of forestry and methods of growing uniform stands of trees. The same thinking led to faster-growing fish, which could be mass-produced in fish hatcheries.

Thus developed the legendary battle of the Preservationists, represented by Muir, against the Conservationists, represented by Pinchot.

Muir's public campaign to preserve wilderness had been based primarily on the higher spiritual values of preserving nature, says Callicott. In that sense, both Muir and Pinchot argued from anthropocentric positions — that humans possess the only legitimate interests, that natural entities are only a means to man's ends.

But privately, said Callicott, Muir was already thinking in terms that would become the driving force for a new generation: that people are just a part of nature, that all creatures are valued equally by God.

According to Callicott, the conservation ethic depended so much on science that scientific advancement proved to be its major downfall. Scientists learned that nature is more than a collection of useful, useless and noxious species, all arrayed upon a landscape of soils and waters.

"It is a vast, tightly organized system, less like a vast mechanism and more like a vast organism," he said.

It fell to Aldo Leopold, who began his career as a Pinchot conservationist, to articulate this new ethic, based on the science of ecology — the interrelationship of all living things.

Human beings, wrote Leopold in 1949, "are members of a biotic team ... plain members and citizens of one humming biotic community."

"In relationship to these other views," Callicott said, "it is very different because it suggests that other forms of life have rights too."

That is not to place humans on a lower level or to say that people should not actively manage natural systems, he said.

Quoting Leopold: "A thing is right when it tends to preserve the integrity, stability and beauty of the biotic community. It is wrong when it tends otherwise."

Sometimes it takes active management to meet this goal, especially in light of economic and political interests.

The trouble is that changes in one part of the natural system may lead to unexpected, sometimes profound, changes in another part, Callicott said.

Leopold discovered this for himself during his years as a game manager in the Southwest. Destruction of predators caused the deer population to increase, which led to destruction of forage plants, which increased soil erosion, which had continuing impacts on the entire ecosystem.

Leopold's ethic — though it has now been around for about 50 years — still has not become ingrained in our thinking, says Callicott.

"From the public point of view, it is still pretty far out to think that nature has rights," he said.

Eventually, most Americans will shift to this new way of thinking, predicts Callicott, who sees no further ethical changes on the horizon.

The challenge for the 21st Century, he maintains, will be not merely to conserve our natural resources but to maintain and restore ecological integrity.

By Christopher Dunagan

The future uncertainty about Hood Canal can be put in human terms: Will Girl Scouts 50 years from now be able to enjoy the waterfront at Robinswold?

W hat Hood Canal will look like 10, 20, 50 years from now will be the cumulative result of many decisions, some big ones and many small ones, experts agree.

A small decision: How much fertilizer should a homeowner use on his lawn each year?

A big one: How much private timberland will local governments try to keep out of the hands of developers?

Hood Canal is not a clean slate by any means. Civilization has been here more than a century, and marks upon the landscape are not easily erased.

But the handwriting is not yet on the wall. For its size and resources, Hood Canal remains one of the most unspoiled areas left in the United States.

Decisions made today about land use and resource protection will echo down through history, says Nancy McKay, executive director of the Puget Sound Water Quality Authority.

"In some ways, the problems are so simple," she said, "more people creating more pollution. But when you try to solve these problems, it gets more and more complex."

• • • • • • • • • •

SECTION 3

AN
UNCERTAIN
FUTURE

By Christopher Dunagan

Growth management, now a major political force in Washington state, must try to reach for the more complete answers, she said.

"To me, one of the challenges is for each of us to take ownership, not necessary of the problem itself, but of our responsibility to be part of the solution," said McKay.

Cars, green lawns, boats, horses, septic tanks, bulldozers, garbage, house construction, dogs, cats, driveways... The list of potential problems goes on and on.

"Part of the challenge is to see that maybe one thing a person does may not matter so much," said McKay, "but when you take it all together, our presence on Hood Canal makes a real impact."

Donna Simmons, a resident of Hoodsport and vice-chairwoman of the Washington State Ecological Commission, scribbled a note to herself one night and taped it on her refrigerator. The note says, "Uncontrolled growth is suicide; controlled growth is controlled suicide."

"It came to me after one of the Mason County Planning (Commission) meetings," she said. "But I want to add that it doesn't have to be. In my more optimistic moments I realize that there are some good things happening."

The advance of environmental science and the intensity of new thinking is a positive force for the entire Northwest, says Chris Frissell, an ecologist at Oregon State University in Corvallis.

"We're in the throws of a revolution when you realize what is going on to protect things like endangered species and wetlands," he said.

We're also running out of time.

"For a long time, we could implement laws and still have wiggle room in terms of a surplus of natural resources," he said. "Now we are coming to the end of the surplus."

The use of the land itself is the greatest issue facing Hood Canal, says Frissell.

"In the lower 48 states, it is unique as an ecosystem," he said.

Land used for forestry or agriculture leaves future options open, at least to some degree, he said. With urban development, there is no turning back.

Alarms are sounding for western

Kitsap County, a critical part of the Hood Canal watershed, says Mike Reed, a biologist with the Port Gamble S'Klallam Indian Tribe. Development pressures there are growing intense, but people don't seem to realize it.

"I went over to the Stavis (Bay) area," said Reed. "There used to be lots of forest lands there. Now it's sold and will all be developed."

Unfortunately, urbanization of an area begins as an invisible transformation. Often, not a single tree is cut down when the land is taken out of forestry use.

Sometimes the change takes place with a handshake, when an agreeable buyer meets an agreeable seller. Sometimes, it takes place in the mind of the landowner, when he decides the time is ripe for development.

Over time, properties that have been removed from the timber base seem to get divided into smaller and smaller tracts, all ready for one or more homes. There is no particular pattern.

Clyde Stricklin, long-range planner for Kitsap County, says the county is studying ways to encourage developers to put smaller parcels back together. The county remains committed to a policy of clustering homes in an effort to save some open space.

The county is offering developers the opportunity to develop more homesites on their property in exchange for dedicating a portion to open space in its natural condition.

While the population of western Kitsap is growing, said Stricklin, the land base remains primarily forest.

"We have been doing a fairly good job with new developments," he said. "We know we have to continue to do that job and to do the job even better."

The job is much bigger for county officials today than it was even a year or two ago, says Bob Crowley of Port Townsend, executive director of the Olympic Environmental Council.

"County officials have traditionally been in the permitting business," he said. "They have not been in the resource-protection business."

The state's Growth Management Act has handed the counties major responsibilities to identify and protect forest lands, wetlands, wildlife habitats, areas prone to

"Kitsap County is quickly getting to be what a lot of other communities are, a bedroom community wihout a recollection of its history or wildlife values."
— Mike Reed, biologist for Port Gamble S'Klallam Tribe

erosion, areas prone to flooding and areas important for groundwater supplies.

How well the counties will handle that responsibility is yet to be seen, said Crowley.

"You've got to realize that county planning departments are staffed largely by urban planners," he said. "More than 90 percent of all the planners in the country are trained in urban planning. This new function of resource protection may take them some time."

Crowley would like to see the counties apply some new planning techniques, including an approach that has been given the fancy name "landscape ecology."

Landscape ecology might be called the art/science of finding a place for human habitation in the natural world. Its goal is to minimize impacts of development through an ecological approach to the landscape.

For wildlife, it goes beyond the idea of preserving scattered pieces of open space with the hope that animals can find and make use of the remnants of development.

Landscape ecology calls for preserving areas that are the most important as well as protecting natural connections from one area to the next.

It is no coincidence that a couple of the most important habitats have already been given special protections under the law. Wetlands, for example, offer a tremendous diversity of habitat for many species. Stream corridors — when they include a band of native vegetation — can be wonderful thoroughfares for wildlife.

The next challenge of landscape ecology, says Frissell, is to preserve as many natural connections between these areas as possible, while providing for the equally important needs of human beings.

"When you fly in a plane over the Northwest, there is a lot of space not occupied by human development," he said. "But the character of the land is the key. It so happens that the lower, flatter country — the coastal lands — are virtually gone. There are critters there that can't just pick up and move to the mountains."

Humans have managed to build highways to get from one community to the next, Frissell noted. In doing so, we have disrupted the natural pathways of some wildlife.

"In terms of effects on wildlife, roads are vastly underestimated," said Frissell. "Highways affect everything from elk to amphibians. Our road corridors need to be looked at in a landscape context."

It may sound farfetched, but overpasses can be built to channel wildlife from one side of a highway to another. On Interstate 90, highway engineers unintentionally designed an ideal passage for wildlife under the high Denny Creek Bridge near Snoqualmie Pass. But less expensive structures may also work well.

At the same time, says Frissell, we humans need to think about enlarging our existing communities rather than building brand new ones.

"We need to make sure our cities are livable," he said, "but I think we are probably going to have a hard time reversing the trend of people moving into the rural areas."

Traveling north on Highway 101 along the western shore of Hood Canal, one is suddenly presented with a long stretch of unspoiled forestland 15 miles beyond Hoodsport.

An immense wooden sign along the highway points out a Girl Scout camp known as "Robinswold."

Walking through the area, Jim Messmer, site manager for the camp, pointed out the dozens of activities available to the girls — from observing marine life on the shore to hiking among the 400 acres of forestland owned by the regional Girl Scout Council.

The gentle silence was pierced by a screeching noise coming from above. Messmer pointed to the top of a towering tree, where the ruffled head of an osprey peered down over the edge of a nest. The nest was nearly straight up from one of the cabins.

"This whole area was clearcut, starting about 1890," said Messmer. "Now we have 100-year-old second growth timber."

Messmer, who has a college degree in botany, says timber from upland portions of the camp and oysters from waterfront areas provide income for the Girl Scouts. Some areas are left alone for the wilderness experience.

"We are in an enviable position of not being market-driven by timber or oysters or whatever," said Messmer, who has managed the site for 13 years.

"This anti-logging movement is accelerating the movement of land from forestry and agriculture into urban and industrial development."
— Robert Lee, University of Washington sociologist

Adjacent to the scout camp is a much larger piece of property owned by the Robins family. Helena Robins was the one who donated the 430 acres to the scouts in 1928.

Now her grandson, Dave Robins, manages his family's timberlands and shellfish beds as income-producing property.

Surprisingly, however, management techniques on the Robins property are not so much different from those at the scout camp. It is simply good management, said Robins.

"There is nothing incompatible, in my view, about good forest practices, water quality and wildlife habitat," he said.

Selective thinning and even careful clearcutting are part of the plan, said Robins, who each year clearcuts about 40 acres — roughly 1.5 percent of the property — for sustained yield.

The last thing he wants to see is damage to water quality from logging operations, said Robins, "because the oyster business is a good part of our income."

Both Robins and Messmer say they plant a variety of tree species, not just the douglas fir that is in demand from lumber mills. Roads are constructed about two years before logging to allow settling and to reduce erosion. Clearcuts are planned to produce less impact to wildlife habitat.

It doesn't take a lot of acreage to provide for both income and the environment, said Gary Hanson, a timber consultant for the Girl Scout Council.

"Unfortunately," he said, "most property owners don't know how to manage their timberland."

If saving Hood Canal demands a softer approach to logging and development, it also requires a stronger commitment from state and county officials, says Reed of the S'Klallam Tribe.

"Until recently," he said, "all the counties were doing was ensuring that their areas were being degraded, but in an orderly manner."

Kitsap County is beginning to take on the appearance of a bedroom community for

metropolitan Seattle, he said. It is losing its identity as a rural community with a sense of history and valuable resources.

Controlling urban sprawl sometimes means saying "no" to a lot of landowners and would-be developers, said Reed.

Unlike some areas of Puget Sound, it is not too late for Hood Canal, but it requires political leadership in Kitsap, Mason and Jefferson counties, Reed argues. It also requires vocal commitment from the people who elect them.

"If a county commissioner were brave enough to speak out, I think he would be surprised at the support he would get," he said.

The Kitsap County Board of Commissioners recently made a major dedication of real estate taxes for the purchase and preservation of open space. The move has been widely applauded.

Land trusts, such as the Kitsap Land Trust, Jefferson County Land Trust and Hood Canal Land Trust, also stand ready to accept donations of valuable resource lands or conservation easements, both of which offer tax benefits to the donor.

"We found a lot of pent-up desire for landowners to preserve their property in some way," said Gary Parrot, founder of the Hood Canal Land Trust.

A conservation easement lowers the value of the land and thus the property tax — by setting limits on development, said Parrot. The reduction in value can become a deduction on the owner's income tax.

The landowner retains title to the property, which he can then sell or pass on to his children. But the easement puts the brakes on development, offering enduring protections for wildlife and other natural values.

"The greatest threat to Hood Canal," said Simmons of the Ecological Commission, "is continued uncontrolled growth.

"None of us should fool ourselves that things are going to remain the way they are," she added. "A certain amount of growth is inevitable. The best we can do is channel the growth to protect those things we find valuable."

• • • • • • • • •

"Economic growth and environmental preservation are interdependent, not mutually exclusive interests."
— Washington Environment 2010, a statewide task force

Making the University of Washington an Ally

Biologists today would call it a wetlands. But in the early days of Hood Canal, herds of cattle grazed on the vast meadows at the mouth of Big Beef Creek in Central Kitsap.

Just upstream from the meadows, the creek meanders through a semi-developed property covered by trees and containing scattered buildings, a rusty trailer and modern scientific equipment used for fisheries research.

This 300-acre area, where beef cattle once roamed freely, is owned by the University of Washington and is called Big Beef Research Station.

The site was almost forgotten the past several years when a shortage of funds forced the university to lease the site to a private salmon-farming operation. But now the facility is coming back to life as the university resumes control and pumps a quarter million dollars into reconstruction.

The university's presence on Hood Canal adds another voice in favor of preserving the natural values of the area, officials say.

The man in charge here, at least for the time being, is Dick Kocan, a professor in the UW's Fisheries Department.

"We had to make a decision whether we were going to lease it as a commercial operation or run it ourselves," said Kocan. "People in the various departments convinced the dean (of the fisheries department) and others that this place was simply irreplaceable."

Kocan finds himself fielding requests from a variety of university scientists who see the outdoor laboratory as an ideal place to conduct environmental studies that cannot be performed in a building in Seattle.

Walking through the site, Kocan points out a number of projects already under way.

One UW researcher, Tom Quinn, is studying how different types of stream habitat affect salmon. The creek flows through a series of pens, each containing different amounts of natural debris.

Researchers place coho salmon within the pens and measure their growth and survival.

In another part of the site, Mike Kellett of National Marine Fisheries Service tests a new machine that automatically decodes a tiny electronic fish tag as fish swim through the machine. The standard method requires killing the fish and removing tags by hand.

The state Department of Fisheries uses Big Beef Creek as an "index stream" for measuring the natural return of salmon to Hood Canal. For years now, juvenile salmon have been trapped and tagged on their way to the sea, while adult salmon are counted on their way back up the stream.

Kocan says he is being bombarded by requests from fisheries experts who want to use the stream for studies. And he has begun to receive requests from other researchers, such as those in zoology, who want to use upland areas.

Kocan's greatest task is to coordinate all the requests so that work on one project doesn't affect the results of another, he said.

"If somebody is doing a project at the mouth (of the creek), can you approve something upstream at the same time?" he asked. "This whole question has made me look at alternatives or safeguards when I approve a project."

The site was acquired by the UW in 1964, and by 1968 a few serious research projects were under way. Then in the 1970s, as the university was drawing up major expansion plans, state funding was cut.

Uncertain about the future of the research station, many university scientists chose not to commit to long-term projects at Big Beef, said Kocan.

As money dwindled, the university was forced to choose between selling the property and leasing it to a private party. It chose to lease the site to Scan Am Fish Farms, which ran the place until its lease ran out.

When Kocan took over, much of the

● ● ● ● ● ● ● ● ● ●

Hood Canal is not a clean slate. Civilization has left its mark on the landscape. But for its size and resources, Hood Canal remains one of the most unspoiled areas left in the United States.

area had become overrun with brush. The roads were in disrepair. Trash was strewn about.

Now, the university is cleaning up the site, rebuilding the roads and clearing out unused equipment, including an old trailer. Remodeling of a former laboratory building is planned to create living quarters where researchers can stay. A deep well, which provides pure water, is being improved.

Kocan says it is not unreasonable to believe that, in time, Big Beef Research Station could build a national reputation like that of the university's marine research lab at Friday Harbor in the San Juan Islands.

Gordon George, the resident caretaker at Big Beef, has lived in the Seabeck area most of his life. He even worked at the university site in the early 1970s while he was in high school. George worries about the future of Hood Canal and believes the university's renewed presence could become an important force in protecting the canal.

Kocan said he and other university officials are interested in protecting the water quality in Big Beef Creek, even though development and logging activities may already have increased the amount of silt in the stream.

Big Beef Creek begins in a marshy area near the tiny community of Crosby. It flows past Camp Union and into Lake Symington, where it spills over a dam, then makes a wide bend to the north before entering university property.

"Places like this are getting harder and harder to find," Kocan said. "For this place to have been retained by the university and saved for the future shows great insight, I think."

By Christopher Dunagan

You could scour Hood Canal from the bridge to Belfair, and you wouldn't find a soul in favor of defacing its beauty, of poisoning its life, of chaining its magnificent wildness. Not if you put it that way. Not one soul.

But nature puts it another way. Nature turns to each of us and asks what we will do to protect the canal. If we who live here do not answer, it will not be done — and in time, even the questions will scud away like clouds running before a cold mountain wind, and be forgotten.

We have examined Hood Canal in every season. We have explored from beneath its waters to the heights of its watershed, from its wild places to its logging camps, its cities and its submarine base.

Now it is time for us to recommend solutions to the many problems and challenges we have found. These are not the only solutions. We are journalists, not sages. Nor are they easy solutions. We aren't magicians, either — just people who live near Hood Canal and who, like you, are among its custodians.

What follows are seven approaches to protecting Hood Canal from the threats it faces. Only state government can accomplish some of them. Only you can accomplish others.

We do not claim to be the last word in setting an agenda for Hood Canal. But, with utter certainty, we do know this:

To do nothing is to lose Hood Canal.

The Watershed: Protection Starts Here

Across Hood Canal from Seabeck and down a bit from Dabob Bay, a logger is clearcutting a modest tract. A stream runs through the tract, on its way toward Hood Canal.

The logger is among the last of the small, independent breed, scrapping to be his own boss in a business gone global and tough. Time is more than money for the logger; it is survival. He must fell trees quickly, or he loses the economic race.

The logger is under state orders to leave a 25-foot buffer around the stream, but his hasty march through the forest carries him right to the bank in spots. Nobody notices.

Rain falls a few days later, and slowly, softly, dirt washes into the stream and works into the gravel along its bed. It is an old story for the stream. Already, it is silted almost to the threshold beyond which salmon eggs may not survive.

This time, silt builds past the threshold, and another salmon run passes into lore.

Such stories are told every day in the Hood Canal watershed. They are told by the waters and the winds, by the fish and the animals. They are stories of death drop by drop, of strangulation one microscopic squeeze at a time.

Such stories, such problems, cannot be countered by one grand scheme. Instead, they must be met in scores of small ways. If the Hood Canal watershed is to be preserved, it will be done the way the logger silted the stream: drop by drop.

Septic systems: Most of us aren't loggers. But most of us have indoor plumbing. And if we live within the Hood Canal watershed, that means our plumbing ends in a septic system.

Septic system failure is common. In a sensitive watershed like Hood Canal's, septic systems should be inspected frequently.

We recommend that a three-county utility district be formed throughout the watershed. It would charge homeowners a small annual fee and subject every septic system in the watershed to regular inspections. It would have the authority to order repairs or upgrades, with enforcement being handled by the county of residence.

Sewers: Some might argue that all homes around the canal should be sewered. We think better maintenance of septic systems would be far cheaper and just as effective in most areas.

But in a few high-density spots, sewers not only make sense, they are essential. An effort to sewer the north and south shores of Hood Canal outside Belfair is moving slowly — far too slowly — through the halls of government in Mason County.

Forestry review: When permission is sought to log a tract of land, the state's primary consideration today is to assure replanting within three years. The Hood Canal watershed would be well served if applicants also were required to leave individually calculated buffer strips around streams, lakes or wetlands, and if the applicant were further required to observe individually calculated sedimentation limits (called "thresholds") for streams.

Inspections — now a rarity — should be mandatory in the watershed, and penalties for not meeting the regulations should extend not just to the logger, but to the owner of the land.

Construction review: In the Hood Canal watershed, there's a good case to be made for extending building inspections to include stream and wetland protection. New buildings should be set back from wetlands and streams — especially salmon streams.

And construction methods should include temporary dams or filtered sedimentation ponds to keep dirt or sand from washing into streams. Portable toilets should be required for crews working near streams, and they should be properly serviced.

Runoff: Cover too much of the land with a hard surface, and a path to the canal has been paved for all of man's chemicals.

It makes sense to offer incentives — tax breaks, perhaps — to watershed property owners who drive on dirt or gravel, who favor natural vegetation over lawns, who collect roof runoff and ease it gently into the ground.

Bulkheads: Beaches are breeding grounds for many marine life forms. They filter runoff, and they give Hood Canal places to cast off its debris.

When people install bulkheads, beaches disappear. No further bulkheading should be allowed along Hood Canal's shores, and as old bulkheads fail, they should not be replaced.

Other methods of combatting erosion exist, and state and local agencies should help property owners learn about them. They also should require that new construction be set far enough back from the bank to let natural, beach-building erosion take place without threatening the structure.

Hazardous waste: The same public utility that provides septic inspections in the watershed should also provide frequent and convenient opportunities to safely dispose of hazardous household waste.

Garbage collection: Garbage pickup isn't available to all watershed residents. It should be more than available; it should be universal.

Mandatory garbage pickup would reduce illegal dumping throughout the watershed. It would be an added expense for many property owners. But the privilege of living so near the canal cannot be had without cost.

Off-road vehicles: Splashing through a creek in a fourwheeler can be great fun, but it rips up the stream bed and creates rutted channels that help silt find the stream.

Off-road vehicle recreation has its place. Some trails already are available in less sensitive areas, and more could be provided — away from salmon streams and wetlands.

Walk the last mile: Consider your auto or truck in a different light for a moment: It's a rolling tank of hazardous material. It picks up greasy road films wherever it goes and sheds them whenever it rains. It leaks.

Your vehicle is hardly Hood Canal's best friend. If every road to the water stopped a mile short, if a nice, well-maintained footpath continued from there, Hood Canal would gain breathing space from autos and the toxicity that comes with them.

Streams and livestock: Livestock and clean streams don't mix. But farmers do have water rights, and animals do need to drink. Streams and livestock can't be kept apart inflexibly, but land-use regulations in the watershed should limit livestock access to streams as much as possible. And livestock should be kept out of wetlands altogether.

Farmers, homeowners and chemicals: Financial incentives for farmers who voluntarily limit their use of agricultural chemicals would be a good investment in Hood Canal's future. And a program of chemical education and advice for all who live within the watershed would give them all the tools they need to make at least one contribution to a cleaner, healthier Hood Canal.

Marine Sanctuary: Give Hood Canal Special Status

Until two decades ago, Hood Canal was the mother of salmon by the millions, of cod and crab, of oyster and clam. From her fertile womb, life flowed into the great Pacific.

Today she is all but barren. She produces salmon through the artificial insemination of hatcheries. She breeds crab fitfully and is empty of cod. She is at risk, even, of losing her shellfish as her gentle tidal flush falls behind pollution's march.

Before Hood Canal can be such a source of life again, she must be made safe for life — a sanctuary.

Making Hood Canal a national marine sanctuary would require federal action. It also would require agencies to give up turf, commercial interests to give up a revenue source, anglers to give up haunts, tideland owners to give up a measure of control.

But it would give them — and all of us — life in return.

Sanctuary status would provide a strong impetus for a non-tribal commercial fishing ban in Hood Canal.

The commercials play a valuable role in feeding the world, but their shore-to-shore seines have filtered the canal's life. Their drag nets have scraped the bottom clean of habitat.

Hood Canal is not just another part of Puget Sound, not just another inlet to be dealt on the table of commercial fishing allocations. It is more fragile than the sound, almost enclosed, flushing so slowly over its shallow sills that much of its water is replaced just once a year.

It must be set aside.

But even such peace at home will not mean peace abroad for Hood Canal.

The canal's salmon fan out toward all points of the Pacific Rim and heavy fishing pressure threatens the canal's ability to renew wild strains. Be they pirates from Taiwan or legal commercials from Canada, the fishing fleets of other nations can be persuaded only through negotiation. Our State Department, prodded by our congressmen, will have a stronger case to make about Hood Canal salmon if the canal is a national marine sanctuary.

The first step toward creating a Hood Canal National Marine Sanctuary is to get the area on a site evaluation list. The Hood Canal Coordinating Council should draft a resolution in favor of the sanctuary, and the three county commissions should pass it — documenting local support.

Meanwhile, our congressional delegation will need to introduce and lobby for legislation establishing the site evaluation study.

The Harvest: Take the Canal's Bounty with Greater Care

Until Sen. Brad Owen stopped them in 1988, commercial fishermen seeking cod, halibut and other bottom feeders dragged heavy nets across the floor of the canal and scraped it clean of the kelp beds that breed fish and shrimp.

When a combination of fishing pressure and degraded spawning streams drastically reduced the canal's wild salmon, state officials responded with massive releases of hatchery salmon — and set fishing limits too high to assure natural spawning.

State officials have allowed sea cucumber to be harvested so intensively that divers are killing themselves seeking these exotic delicacies at ever-deeper depths.

And they have proposed that geoduck colonies, which regenerate themselves in 25-year cycles, be harvested 10 years after the last harvest, using methods that blast a series of craters along the bottom, up to 600 yards from shore.

And every time Sen. Owen and other Hood Canal defenders try to move commercial salmon fishing boats out of the canal, they run into a wall of hostility whose bricks are commercial interests and whose mortar is the state bureaucracy.

If Hood Canal were a marine sanctuary, and if its managers were devoted to the canal first and foremost, these changes could be made:

Top priority for wild salmon: Wild salmon provide the genetic material for hatchery salmon, and without them, no matter how successful our hatcheries, we face a future of genetic inflexibility — unable to respond to unknown diseases or to climatic changes we can't anticipate today.

Rather than respond to a diminishing supply of wild salmon by putting large chunks of our resources into hatcheries, we should respond by investing our resources in restoring streams, in research and in fishing enforcement to better protect the wild salmon.

Manage salmon in smaller units: For the computer modelers who determine what will be caught every year, a Hood Canal salmon is a Hood Canal salmon. But a Dewatto River coho is not a Big Beef Creek coho. Failure to manage Hood Canal salmon in smaller chunks means we'll miss opportunities to intervene through fisheries management when a particular run is at critically low levels.

Encourage shellfish farming: As new residents line the shore of Hood Canal, they increasingly complain about shellfish farming operations off their beaches.

Their objections primarily are aesthetic. However, they might think the sight as beautiful as the sun behind the mountains if they pondered more on the critical role shellfish play in protecting Hood Canal.

Shellfish are the first fruits of the sea to suffer when water quality deteriorates. They are succulent morsels, and when their harvest is forbidden because of pollution, people are quick to notice and to react.

Of all forms of aquaculture, shellfish farming is the least likely to disturb the landscape and should be considered as natural a sight on water as barns and pastures on land.

Severely limit other harvests pending study: We've come to associate geoduck and sea cucumber harvesting with trouble but it need not be so.

These marine resources also should be harvested in Hood Canal, but not until more is known about their cycles of renewal, and not until the methods involved can be less dangerous or disruptive of marine habitat.

Governance: Special Powers to Protect a Special Place

Neither watershed protection, nor a marine sanctuary nor marine harvest regulation can happen for Hood Canal under existing governmental bodies.

In all the agencies, all the layers, all the halls of government, nobody's first priority is looking out for Hood Canal. This special body of water needs a special protector.

A good approach would be to simply expand the role of the Hood Canal Coordinating Council, which presently is a discussion group of representatives from county governments and Indian tribes around the canal. With the help of the Legislature, the membership and duties of the coordinating council could be expanded, and it could become an effective protector for Hood Canal.

Makeup of the council: Besides the three counties and the tribes, the state departments of Natural Resources, Ecology, Fisheries and Wildlife, and the U.S. Forest Service and the National Park Service should have representatives on the council.

In addition, it would be helpful if a few citizens from the three counties who represent forestry, environmental and economic development interests were appointed by the three county commissions.

Regulatory oversight: One of the most important functions the expanded council could provide would be assuring that a wide variety of governmental regulatory functions take Hood Canal's welfare into account.

Within the watershed, various governmental entities regulate logging, construction, fishing, land use and zoning, public health, road construction, wells, sewers, septic systems and waste disposal.

In cases where county commissions hear regulatory appeals — such as zoning appeals from local planning commissions — it might be useful if, in watershed cases, the coordinating council heard the appeal instead.

In other cases where appeals are heard at a higher level or in the courts, the coordinating council should have standing to make arguments for or against appeals and to lodge appeals of its own.

Model legislation: Hood Canal's new bodyguard also should be charged with recommending legislation to the Legislature or ordinances to the three counties that set up watershed programs like septic system inspections or special logging standards.

Research: The coordinating council also should have central responsibility for environmental research in the watershed.

Available state and local research funds should be channeled to the coordinating council for distribution and the council should have funds from state and local sources to hire a technical staff that could advise local and other governments about matters ranging from stream flows to soils to wildlife populations in the watershed.

No taxing authority: Hood Canal needs a friend, not a tax collector, and there is no need for this body to have taxing powers.

The modest funds needed for staffing should be diverted from other agencies or should be shared by counties who each need, for instance, part of a biologist but can't afford one full-time. Several state agencies are active in the Hood Canal region, and some of their manpower could be shifted to the coordinating council staff. An excellent place to look would be in the Fisheries office that makes computer models for the Puget Sound fishing industry.

Research: Where Ignorance Wounds, Here Is Healing

People who are worried about Hood Canal's future often use a familiar word in a new way: "threshold." They're talking about the point where trouble begins, the place where a Hood Canal angel dare not tread.

There are — in theory, anyway —

thresholds for forestry and construction: the point beyond which those activities, depending on how they are carried out, can do irreparable harm.

There is an ultimate threshold for Hood Canal. We all know there's room here for the canal and for people. But how many people? The answer to that question depends on how we address the smaller thresholds. Address them well, and there's room for many more people without harming the canal. Address them poorly, and we already have too many.

Every threshold needs a definition — a definition thoughtfully created after careful research and thorough, public discussion. But we don't know enough about the canal and its watershed to effectively regulate human activity in a way that fairly balances economic and environmental needs.

Soon, urgently soon, we must develop a much larger body of knowledge about the watershed, particularly in these areas:

• Salmon breeding conditions, stream by stream and type by type.

• Sensitive land areas that are high-priority candidates for preservation.

• Stream flow conditions and needs, stream by stream.

• Stream siltation conditions, stream by stream.

• Stream by stream and wetland by wetland, tailored strategies to accommodate construction, agriculture or forestry while protecting the environment.

• Water supply, throughout our complex, glacier-tumbled geology.

In knowledge, there will be the power to make intelligent decisions. Money spent on gaining knowledge would, in the long run, be far more beneficial than money spent on hatcheries or on computer models of fishing seasons.

The Public: Improve Access and Knowledge

Hood Canal is one of our great public treasures, but it is walled off from the public by a ring of private property. So the public can appreciate, understand and support this natural treasure, more windows should be cut in that wall.

This is by far the most expensive of our recommendations for Hood Canal. But we think of the expense as an investment of extraordinary value.

Now, before waterfront land is only for the rich; now, when public support for and understanding of Hood Canal are so important; now is the time to open those windows.

Public beaches must be acquired, trails must be built, boat launches must be provided.

In the end, only whole-hearted public awareness and support will preserve Hood Canal, and it isn't reasonable to expect such support when access is so limited.

With access should come education.

Let the marvelous interpretive centers run by the National Park Service inspire us. Such a center in Belfair and at other crossroads around the canal could educate the public about wetlands, Indian cultures, forestry and marine life. The centers could expose hundreds of thousands of residents and vacationers to Hood Canal and do more to protect the watershed than any amount of legislation.

A special effort should be made to educate young people about Hood Canal. This generation of adults might manage to construct a sound framework of preservation for the canal, but coming generations will have to build the rest. Give them a head start of knowledge that most of us lacked.

And last, a modest proposal to raise public awareness of, and respect for, the Hood Canal watershed: On every road or footpath that crosses into the watershed, place a small sign marking the watershed boundary. Let none of use enter the watershed without being reminded that we have taken on a special responsibility just by being there.

To Save the Canal, Improve Our Cities

Everywhere you go in this region, you'll find a great sense of urgency to do something about growth around Hood Canal before growth does something beyond repair to the canal.

Urgency you'll find, but action — regionally coordinated, state-supported and adequately funded — is in short supply.

The sheer physical presence of people inside the Hood Canal watershed is a central issue that can best be resolved by making newcomers welcome in urban areas outside the watershed, by making those areas attractive, livable and stimulating.

Bremerton, for example, could be home

to tens of thousands more people who would not compete with the canal's salmon for water and who would not challenge the watershed's ability to filter pollution. Yet for every one of those new residents, the canal and its riches would be a short drive or bicycle ride away.

As Bremerton improves its housing, rebuilds its commercial core, cleans up its streets and, in scores of other ways, makes itself more attractive to newcomers, Bremerton helps not only itself, but Hood Canal.

Other urban areas are right on the shores of the canal, and they offer special challenges.

In the fast-growing Belfair area, for instance, a sewer system is urgently needed to protect wetlands at the tip of the canal, but action has been held up by an avalanche of red tape.

Almost at the other end of the canal, in Port Gamble, Pope Resources wants to build a good-sized town.

Kitsap County officials believe the idea has merit if Pope commits most of its other holdings, many acres in the watershed, to forestry.

How well Mason County meets the Belfair sewer challenge, and how high a standard Pope Resources sets for its Port Gamble project might well set a pattern for success or failure as growth continues around Hood Canal.

Whatever we do to manage that growth, we must do as a region — as a three-county community of environmentalists and developers, foresters and factory workers who accept our common responsibility.

Together, we can preserve a magnificent natural legacy.

Apart, we will allow growth to destroy it.

The Cost: A Clean, Healthy Canal Won't Be Free

In growth management strategies now being developed can be found Hood Canal's most positive hope. What will it cost to protect Hood Canal?

Not nearly so much hard cash as you might think.

The bigger cost of our agenda might be reducing governmental cash flow here and there in return for landowner concessions.

Here are some possible financial

impacts of a vigorous program of preserving Hood Canal and its watershed:

• Give tax breaks or transferrable development rights to watershed property owners who write conservation easements into their deeds.

• Offer tax breaks and free technical advice to farmers who use agricultural practices that might be less efficient but are friendlier to the watershed.

• Offer tax breaks or waive inspection fees or construction permit fees for homeowners who use good runoff practices like gravel driveways instead of concrete.

• Waive inspection, permit or licensing fees for builders who use watershed-friendly techniques.

• Set up a permitting fast track for builders who agree to a set of watershed construction standards that exceed the law. A successful program like this in Florida saves money and valuable time for the most conscientious builders.

• Make similar incentives available to loggers.

• With local and state contributions, fund a 5- to 10-member technical staff for an expanded Hood Canal Coordinating Council. Let this staff of biologists, geologists and public health experts provide the research and technical advice about the watershed needed by governments and the public. The cost would be $200,000 to $400,000 per year,

and some of that could be covered by moving a position or two out of related state agencies.

• Capital investments in interpretive centers and educational trails could come from a combination of state and local sources. Interpretive centers like one planned in Belfair would cost in the neighborhood of $3-5 million each. A well-designed interpretive center requires low maintenance, just a few staffers to conduct programs, and can take great advantage of volunteer docents and guides.

• Money to increase public facilities around Hood Canal would be the greatest expense of preservation. It probably would not be difficult to spend $40 million or so in the three counties setting aside waterfront land. Local bonding would be the most likely source of funds.

But the largest contribution would come from the thousands of watershed residents, who must be asked to approach their lifestyles a little differently, to pay septic inspection and garbage pickup fees and, most important, to accept their special responsibility as Hood Canal caretakers.

On that contribution, no price tag can be placed.

(This section is culled from a series of editorials written by Sun Editor Mike Phillips and published Aug. 12-17, 1991.)

It will be individual action, as much as action by government, that keeps the Hood Canal watershed healthy.

The protection, and in some cases, restoration of an ecosystem like that of Hood Canal's is not just up to governmental leaders or bureaucrats. They can pass laws, make regulations and enforce rules, but the fragile environment of the canal watershed would still continue to decline.

Chapter 11 explored the impact of a single home being built in the forest. The individual designer, home builder and home buyer have more influence on the ultimate health of the Hood Canal ecosystem than the nine commissioners of the three counties that border the canal. Landowners themselves have more to say about protecting fish and wildlife than any of the state agencies. If people who live in the ecosystem and visit it for business or pleasure choose a more benign path, the canal will be the beneficiary.

Here are some things each of us can do to choose that more benign path:

Become a citizen watchdog:

• Know state and county rules. Report improper clearing, grading, filling, logging and dumping. Also report failing septic tanks, damage to wildlife habitat and trespassing onto private property. (Start with county planning and zoning officials and go from there.)

• Get involved in growth management planning. The result may determine not only the future of Hood Canal but of Western Washington. Start with county planning offices.

• Take an active role as city and county agencies develop new wetlands regulations over the coming months.

• Be aware of nearby wetlands and make sure any planned development protects the wetland.

• Join a land trust or conservation group working to acquire deeds or development rights to important wetlands.

Get interested in protecting fish and wildlife:

• Learn about the ecological connections between plants and animals. Books and articles abound.

• Join the Audubon Society's Adopt-A-Forest program, which seeks to protect habitat in national forests.

• Investigate plans for state and private timberlands. Know the landowners near your home. Understand their intentions. Recognize what state rules allow.

• Obtain a copy of the forest practices application from the Department of Natural Resources when logging is proposed. Make sure streams, wetlands and critical habitat are listed — and protected. Work cooperatively with the DNR forester and biologists. When necessary, file an appeal.

• Know the hunting seasons and report poachers to a wildlife agent. They can be reached through the Washington State Patrol, 478-4646.

Conserve water and electricity drawn from the watershed:

• Know where your water comes from and how well the system is managed. Be aware of whether demands are increasing, and ask about conservation measures by the operator.

• Check the results of recent water quality tests for your water system to see that they meet all state and federal requirements.

• Learn to read your water meter if you have one. Keep track of daily water useage and how your consumption relates to activities such as watering your lawn.

• Conserve water outside your home by using native plants or special grasses that use less water. You can make an average lawn more drought tolerant by gradually extending the time between waterings. Also, remove thatch and aerate compacted soil to improve watering efficiency.

• Conserve water inside your home by repairing leaking faucets and toilets. Toilet leaks can be checked by placing a drop of food coloring in the tank and watching to see if it shows up in the bowl without flushing. Reduce daily consumption in showers, dishwashing and laundry.

• Get involved in water planning for your county. Kitsap County Public Utility District is in charge of developing a groundwater management program for the county.

• Conserve electricity by insulating your home adequately, turning off lights and appliances when not in use and reducing the use of hot water. A reduction in Northwest power demand eases the pressure to build new dams.

If you own timberland in the watershed:

• Keep your land as natural as possible, whatever your future intent.

• Consider thinning trees instead of clearcutting.

• For assistance, consult a state forester (1-800-527-3305), join a landowner association or hire a professional consultant.

• Keep a portion of your property in trees for birds and wildlife. The area need not contain the most valuable timber.

• Manage your land so you have trees in a variety of ages, sizes and types.

• Save standing dead trees unless they're a safety hazard. They provide homes for birds and small animals.

• Leave decaying debris on the ground whenever possible. It can provide food and/or shelter to many creatures.

• Protect trees and vegetation along a stream. Fence the stream to keep out pets and livestock.

• Avoid the use of pesticides. They can destroy important segments of the food chain.

If your property includes wetlands:

- Protect your property from pollution and disruption. Leave it natural. Consider a conservation easement to save it forever.
- Maintain buffers at the edge of your wetlands; 50 to 300 feet is recommended, depending on conditions.
- Keep pets and livestock out of fragile areas. Local conservation districts can propose alternative watering plans for cattle.
- Consider planting native species and avoid placing non-native plants in your lawn and garden that could invade nearby wetlands.
- Find alternatives to fertilizers and pesticides near wetlands.
- Be sure your septic tank is functioning properly and have it pumped every three to five years.
- If a wetland is already damaged, enhancement may be possible. Seek professional advice.

If your property includes streams or waterfront:

- Leave natural vegetation alone. Trees and shrubs shade the stream and keep water temperatures cool. Insects fall off the vegetation and provide food for fish.
- Plant vegetation to stabilize stream banks. Blackberry bushes, alder trees and willows provide good root systems to reduce erosion.
- Preserve natural debris. Fallen trees and boulders are part of the stream habitat and should be removed only if they block passage of fish.
- Be careful when building near streams. Heavy equipment can destroy spawning gravel, remove important vegetation and cause siltation.
- Keep pets and livestock away. Livestock can destroy vegetation and spawning gravel. Dogs may chase spawning fish and stir up mud in the stream.
- Use garden and lawn chemicals sparingly. Some are toxic. Others can encourage the growth of weeds and algae.
- Keep the beaches clean.
- Consider growing clams or oysters if your beach is safe.
- Never use the water for disposal of anything.
- Avoid bulkheads if possible, or at least coordinate construction with shoreline neighbors. (For information, contact Sea Grant through your local office of WSU Cooperative Extension Service.)
- Maintain your septic tank. Health officials recommend pumping every five years, but it should be checked more often.
- Be informed. Tell others about the importance of streams and how to protect them. If you see someone damaging a stream, contact the Department of Fisheries, 895-4756.

If you are developing your property:

- Learn about ecology and use the lightest touch in developing.
- Take pains to preserve fish and wildlife habitat, then take credit for your accomplishments.
- Design building sites with the least impact to vegetation, especially on slopes.
- Control runoff during construction.
- Avoid changing natural conditions near shorelines, streams and wetlands.

If you live in a home in the watershed:

- When making home improvements, reduce the amount of hard surfaces. Use paving stones instead of concrete, ground cover instead of grass lawns.
- Find alternatives to chemical fertilizers and pesticides or use them sparingly, and only at the right time of year.
- Recycle used motor oil. Never dump it. (In Kitsap County, call 895-3931 for recycling locations.)
- Dispose of garbage properly.
- Reduce use of toxic household chemicals, including cleaners and phosphate detergents. Most chemicals pass straight through municipal treatment plants and septic systems. (For information on alternatives to toxic chemicals, call the state Hazardous Substances Information Office, 1-800-633-7585.)
- Cut back on water use.

If you are a boater:

- Maintain your boat's sewage system. If it has an installed toilet, it must have an approved marine sanitation device (MSD), either holding or treating the sewage.
- Make sure there is no direct dis-

charge from your marine toilet. Pump out your toilet at an approved pump-out facility.

• To locate area pump-out stations, call Washington State Parks, 586-8592, or write 7150 Cleanwater Lane, Mail Stop KY-11, Olympia 98504. On the canal, Twanoh State Park, Pleasant Harbor Marina and Port Ludlow Marina have pump-out stations.

• Avoid pumping treated sewage in shallow areas or near shellfish beds.

• Use shoreside restrooms when possible.

• Keep track of your fuel level. Avoid "topping off" the tank, and wipe up spills on decks and docks.

• Use an absorbent sponge to soak up chemicals in the bilge.

• Check fuel lines for leaks.

• Recycle used motor oil.

• Report small spills to the marina operator. Report larger spills to the Department of Emergency Management (1-800-262-5990), Department of Ecology (753-2353) or Coast Guard (1-800-424-8802).

• Keep a secured trash container on board and use it. Don't throw any garbage or sewage overboard.

• Avoid throwing any debris overboard. It is illegal.

• Pick up floating debris and beached plastics, including tangled fishing line that can be especially hazardous to marine life.

• When maintaining your boat, use sanders with vacuum attachments. Catch paint scrapings and drippings with a drop cloth, then dispose of them in the trash.

• Clean up with non-phosphate detergents rather than toxic deck cleaners.

• Avoid paints that contain tributyltin (TBT), which has been banned on all but aluminum boats in Washington state.

• Dispose of chemicals during hazardous waste cleanup days.

If you like to drive around the canal:

• Keep the car tuned and patch any leaks that may drip oil on the ground.

Anderson, Helen McReavy, *How, When and Where on Hood Canal*, Puget Press, Everett, Wash., 1960.

Angell, T. and K.C. Balcomb, *Marine Birds and Mammals of Puget Sound*, Washington Sea Grant Program, Seattle, 1982.

Brown, Bruce, *Mountain in the Clouds: A Search for the Wild Salmon*, Simon and Schuster, New York, N.Y., 1982.

Buchanan, Iva Luella, *An Economic History of Kitsap County*, unpublished thesis, University of Washington, 1930.

Bunton, Donna, and Robert Sluss, *An Introduction to the Natural History of the Theler Wetlands*, for Hood Canal Wetlands Project, Belfair, Wash., 1991.

Burns, Robert, *The Shape and Form of Puget Sound*, Washington Sea Grant Program, Seattle, Wash., 1985.

Cheney, Daniel P. and Thomas F. Mumford Jr., *Shellfish and Seaweed Harvests of Puget Sound*, Washington Sea Grant Program, Seattle, Wash., 1986.

Clayson, Edward, *Historical Narratives of Puget Sound, Hood's Canal, 1865-1885*, Ye Galleon Press, Fairfield, Wash., 1969.

Downing, John, *The Coast of Puget Sound: Its Processes and Development*, University of Washington Press, Seattle, Wash., 1983.

Gilmore Research Group, *The 1988 Puget Sound Recreational Boaters Survey*, Washington Public Ports Association, 1989.

Hood Canal Advisory Commission, *Hood Canal Handbook*, Kitsap County Department of Community Planning, Port Orchard, 1977.

Hood Canal Advisory Commission, *Report to the County Commissioners*, 1979.

Hood Canal Coordinating Council, *Boating in Hood Canal: Boaters' Guide and Resource Map*, Silverdale, Wash.

Hood Canal Coordinating Council, *Educational Services Project Final Report*, Kitsap County Department of Community Development, Port Orchard, Wash., 1988.

Hood Canal Coordinating Council, *Hood Canal Regional Planning Policy*, Silverdale, Wash., 1986.

Hood Canal Coordinating Council, *Hood Canal Water Quality Policies Analysis & Element*, Port Orchard, Wash., 1987.

Jefferson County Historical Society, *With Pride In Heritage: A History of Jefferson County*, Port Townsend, Wash. 1966.

Jones & Stokes Associates, *Priority Wetlands Threat Assessment*, for U.S. Environmental Protection Agency, Seattle, Wash., 1988.

Kitsap County, Department of Community Development and Public Utility District No. 1, *Preliminary Assessment of Water Resource and Public Water Services Issues in Kitsap County*, 1986.

Kitsap County Ground Water Advisory Committee, *Kitsap County Ground Water Management Plan*, Kitsap County Public Utility District, Poulsbo, 1989.

Kitsap County Historical Society, *Kitsap County History: A Story of Kitsap County and its Pioneers*, 1977.

Magoon, C., and R. Vining, *Introduction to Shellfish Aquaculture in the Puget Sound Region*, Washington State Department of Natural Resources, Olympia, Wash., 1981.

Meany, Edmond S., *Vancouver's Discovery of Puget Sound*, Bindfords and Mort, Portland, Ore., 1935.

Nehlsen, Willa, Jack E. Williams and James A. Lichatowich, "Pacific Salmon at the Crossroads: Stocks at Risk from California, Oregon, Idaho and Washington," Fisheries, Vol. 16, No. 2, March-April 1991.

North Mason Sub-Area Planning Committee, *North Mason Sub-Area Plan*, Shelton, Wash., 1990.

Northwest Environmental Consultants Inc., *Theler Memorial Recreation Park Comprehensive Plan*, for Mason Regional Planning Council, 1979.

Puget Sound Water Quality Authority, *Puget Sound Water Quality Management Plan* (biennial) plus issue papers on numerous topics, Seattle and Olympia, Wash.

Simmons, Donna M., *Directory of Environmental Education Resources for the Hood Canal Region*, Hood Canal Coordinating Council, Silverdale, Wash., 1987.

Strickland, Richard M., *The Fertile Fjord: Plankton in Puget Sound*, Washington Sea Grant Program, Seattle, Wash., 1983.

Terich, Thomas, *Living with the Shore of Puget Sound and the Georgia Strait*, Duke University Press, Durham, N.C., 1987.

Washington State, Department of Ecology, *Coastal Zone Atlas of Washington*, Olympia, Wash., 1980.

Washington State, Department of Ecology, *Instream Resources Protection Program*, Including Administrative Rules, (multiple volumes by area), Olympia, Wash.

Washington State, Department of Fisheries, Fisheries Statistic Reports, Olympia, Wash., annual.

Welch, Janet L., and Bill Banks, *The Quilcene/Dabob Bays Water Quality Project*, Washington State Department of Ecology, Olympia, Wash., 1987.

Williams, Walter R., Richard M. Laramie and James J. Ames, *A Catalog of Washington Streams and Salmon Utilization*, Washington State Department of Fisheries, Olympia, Wash., 1975.

Yoshinaka, Marvin S., and Nancy J. Ellifrit, *Hood Canal: Priorities for Tomorrow*, U.S. Department of Interior, Fish and Wildlife Service, 1974.

APPENDIX

B

. . . .

THE SERIES

Much of the material in this book was originally published over the span of a year in The Sun, a newspaper in Bremerton, Wash., that circulates in the Hood Canal watershed.

The stories in the series were re-edited and updated for inclusion in the book. In some cases, whole new pieces were added; in other cases, articles were significantly shortened.

What follows, for researchers or readers who want to refer to the original material, is a listing of the dates of original publication.

Part I: Introduction

July 9, 1990: A waterway of national significance.
July 10, 1990: The canal's watershed
July 11, 1990: Native Americans in the canal's history.
July 12, 1990: Early logging and white settlement.
July 13, 1990: The people of Hood Canal.
July 14, 1990: Driving tour of the canal.

Part II: Recreation and Tourism.

Aug. 20, 1990: Recreational uses of Hood Canal.
Aug. 21, 1990: Economics of the growing tourist trade.
Aug. 22, 1990: Impacts of recreation.

Part III: Fishing

Sept. 24, 1990: The Boldt decision and tribal fishing.
Sept. 25, 1990: Commercial fishing on Hood Canal.
Sept. 26, 1990: Sports fishing.
Sept. 27, 1990: Habitat loss and its threat to salmon.

Part IV: Logging

Nov. 12, 1990: A Log's Long Journey.
Nov. 13, 1990: Logging's Delicate Economics.
Nov. 14, 1990: Profile of a logger.
Nov. 15, 1990: The spotted owl controversy.

Nov. 16, 1990: For Timber or the Environment.

Part V: The Oyster

Nov. 22, 1990: The oyster industry.
Nov. 23, 1990: Tribal claims to shellfish.

Part VI: The Culture of Hood Canal

Jan. 2, 1991: Northwest Indian culture.
Jan. 3, 1991: Creating art on Hood Canal.
Jan. 4, 1991: Artists of the canal.

Part VII: Wetlands

Feb. 18, 1991: Miracles of the Marsh.
Feb. 19, 1991: A Puddle of Life.
Feb. 20, 1991: A Regulatory Patchwork.

Part VIII: Life on Hood Canal

March 18, 1991: Growing Pains: A look at Belfair.
March 19, 1991: New Homes Jam South Point.
March 20, 1991: Plush Properties.
March 21, 1991: Waterfront Land Rush.

Part IX: Development

April 29, 1991: Houses Everywhere.
April 30, 1991: Turn Around, and It's Gone.
May 1, 1991: Planning for Growth.

Part X: Water Resources

June 10, 1991: A Precious Commodity.
June 11, 1991: Jockeying for the Resource.
June 12, 1991: Water Demand Grows.

Part XI: Bangor

July 2, 1991: A Setting for Awesome Firepower.
July 3, 1991: 400 Feet Below the Canal.
July 4, 1991: Mission: Keep it Clean.
July 5, 1991: Hood Canal's Largest Community.

Part XII: Conclusion

July 29, 1991: Memories of the Canal.
July 30, 1991: Preservation Through Action.
July 31, 1991: An Uncertain Future.